A HISTORY OF THE NET

Second Edition

A HISTORY OF THE NETHERLANDS

FROM THE SIXTEENTH CENTURY TO THE PRESENT DAY

Second Edition

Friso Wielenga

BLOOMSBURY ACADEMIC

LONDON • NEW YORK • OXFORD • NEW DELHI • SYDNEY

BLOOMSBURY ACADEMIC
Bloomsbury Publishing Plc
50 Bedford Square, London, WC1B 3DP, UK
1385 Broadway, New York, NY 10018, USA

BLOOMSBURY, BLOOMSBURY ACADEMIC and the Diana logo are trademarks of
Bloomsbury Publishing Plc

First published in Great Britain 2020

Copyright © Friso Wielenga, 2020

Cover design: Tjaša Krivec
Cover image: Light on the Canal (© Ellen Davidzon / www.ellendavidzon.nl)

A catalogue record for this book is available from the British Library.

A catalog record for this book is available from the Library of Congress.

ISBN: PB: 978-1-3500-8730-9
       HB: 978-1-3500-8731-6
       ePDF: 978-1-3500-8732-3
       eBook: 978-1-3500-8733-0

Typeset by RefineCatch Limited, Bungay, Suffolk
Printed and bound in India

To find out more about our authors and books visit www.bloomsbury.com
and sign up for our newsletters.

CONTENTS

Contents

FIGURES

Figures

MAPS

ILLUSTRATIONS

ABBREVIATIONS

AJC	Workers' Youth Movement (*Arbeiders Jeugd Centrale*)
AKU	General Synthetic Silk Union (*Algemene Kunstzijde Unie*)
ANWV	General Dutch Workers' Association (*Algemeen Nederlands Werklieden Verbond*)
AOW	General Old Age Pensions Act (*Algemene Ouderdomswet*)
ARP	Anti-Revolutionary Party (*Anti-Revolutionaire Partij*)
CDA	Christian Democratic Appeal (*Christen-Democratisch Appèl*)
CHU	Christian Historical Union (*Christelijk Historische Unie*)
CNV	National Federation of Christian Trade Unions in the Netherlands (*Christelijk Nationaal Vakverbond*)
CPB	Netherlands Bureau for Economic Policy Analysis (*Centraal Planbureau*)
CPN	Communist Party of the Netherlands (*Communistische Partij van Nederland*)
CU	Christian Union (*ChristenUnie*)
D66	Democrats 66 (*Democraten 1966*)
DS'70	Democratic Socialists 1970 (*Democratisch Socialisten 1970*)
DSM	Dutch State Mines
ECSC	European Coal and Steel Community (*Europese Gemeenschap voor Kolen en Staal*)
EDC	European Defence Community (*Europese Defensie Gemeenschap*)
EDD	Dutch Movement for Unity through Democracy (*Nederlandsche Beweging voor Eenheid door Democratie*)
EEC	European Economic Community (*Europese Economische Gemeenschap*)
EU	European Union (*Europese Unie*)
EVC	United Trade Union (*Eenheids Vakcentrale*)
FNV	Dutch Trade Union Confederation (*Federatie Nederlandse Vakbeweging*)
GDP	Gross domestic product
KLM	Royal Dutch Airlines (*Koninklijke Luchtvaartmaatschappij*)

Abbreviations

KNIL	Royal Netherlands East Indies Army (*Koninklijk Nederlands Indisch Leger*)
KNP	Catholic National Party (*Katholieke Nationale Partij*)
KRO	Catholic Radio Broadcasting System (*Katholieke Radio Omroep*)
KVP	Catholic People's Party (*Katholieke Volkspartij*)
LPF	Pim Fortuyn List (*Lijst Pim Fortuyn*)
MVM	Man-Woman-Society (*Man-Vrouw-Maatschappij*)
NASB	Dutch Workers' Sports Association (*Nederlandsche Arbeiders Sport Bond*)
NATO	North Atlantic Treaty Organization (*Noord-Atlantische Verdragsorganisatie*)
NCRV	Dutch Christian Radio Association (*Nederlandse Christelijke Radio Vereniging*)
NHM	Netherlands Trading Society (*Nederlandsche Handel-Maatschappij*)
NIOD	NIOD Institute for War, Holocaust and Genocide Studies (*Nederlands Instituut voor Oorlogsdocumentatie*)
NSB	National Socialist Movement (*Nationaal-Socialistische Beweging*)
NSDAP	National Socialist German Workers' Party (*Nationalsozialistische Deutsche Arbeiterpartei*)
NVB	Dutch People's Movement (*Nederlandse Volksbeweging*)
NVV	Dutch Association of Trade Unions (*Nederlands Verbond van Vakverenigingen*)
OEEC	Organisation for European Economic Co-operation (*Organisatie voor Europese Economische Samenwerking*)
OSCE	Organization for Security and Co-operation in Europe
P&C	Peek and Cloppenburg
PPR	Political Party of Radicals (*Politieke Partij Radicalen*)
PTT	Post Office (*Post Telegraaf Telefoon*)
PVDA	Labour Party (*Partij van de Arbeid*)
PVV	Party for Freedom (*Partij voor de Vrijheid*)
RKSP	Roman Catholic State Party (*Rooms-Katholieke Staatspartij*)
RMS	Republic of South Maluku
SCP	Netherlands Institute for Social Research (*Sociaal en Cultureel Planbureau*)
SDAP	Social Democratic Workers' Party (*Sociaal-Democratische Arbeiderspartij*)

SDB	Social Democratic League (*Sociaal-Democratische Bond*)
SER	Social and Economic Council (*Sociaal Economische Raad*)
SP	Socialist Party (*Socialistische Partij*)
SPD	Socialdemocratic Party of Germany (*Sozialdemokratische Partei Deutschlands*)
SS	Protection Squad (*Schutzstaffel*)
STAR	Labour Foundation (*Stichting van de Arbeid*)
TON	Proud of the Netherlands (*Trots op Nederland*)
UNPROFOR	United Nations Protection Force
VARA	Workers' Association of Radio Amateurs (*Vereniging van Arbeiders Radio Amateurs*)
VDB	Free-thinking Democratic League (*Vrijzinnig Democratische Bond*)
VNO	Association of Dutch Enterprises (*Verbond van Nederlandse Ondernemingen*)
VOC	Dutch East India Company (*Verenigde Oost-Indische Compagnie*)
VVD	People's Party for Freedom and Democracy (*Volkspartij voor Vrijheid en Democratie*)
WIC	Dutch West India Company (*West-Indische Compagnie*)

PREFACE

Every country's history is informed by its geographical position and its interaction with the world beyond its borders. There is no doubt that this applies to the Netherlands more than many other nations. Situated on a major hub between continental Europe and other parts of the world, the Dutch have a centuries-old trading tradition. During its Golden Age in the seventeenth century, this small country on the North Sea was a leading economic, political, cultural and scientific power, and reverberations from this past – as well as some from later centuries – still resonate all over the world to this day. Today's foreign tourists get an impression of this flourishing era when they visit Amsterdam or admire the art treasures in the many Dutch museums.

Foreigners who have dealings with the Netherlands soon become familiar with such historical images, yet questions about how this small federal republic could possibly have reached such heights usually remain unanswered. So, too, do questions about the Netherlands after the seventeenth century, when it had to find a place for itself as a small country surrounded by major powers. What international position has the Netherlands sought since its decline in the eighteenth century, and what role has it played since then in Europe and beyond? And when it comes to political culture, many people think of the Netherlands as a country where tolerance and democracy gradually developed over the centuries into today's permissive society. But is that really true? Or was this history more turbulent and difficult than it appears at first sight?

This book has been written for those seeking answers to such questions. The reception enjoyed by the earlier German, Dutch and English editions indicates there is broad interest in a concise history like this. It is used for courses on the history of the Netherlands in German and Dutch universities as well as for university courses in the English-speaking world. It has also attracted the interest of many members of the general public. The hope for this current edition is that it will be able to contribute to greater knowledge about this small land on the North Sea with its many international contacts.

Friso Wielenga
Münster, Summer 2019

CHAPTER 1
INTRODUCTION

The question as to when a country's history began is often answered by a reference to the outbreak of a revolt, the proclamation of sovereignty or the moment of international recognition. Such responses do not help, though, in the case of Dutch history, and it is striking that there is no national public holiday on which to celebrate the founding of the nation. Dutch national bank holidays date from the late nineteenth century (initially Princess's Day, later Queen's Day and now King's Day) or from the middle of the twentieth century (liberation from Nazi German occupation in 1945). No single heroic or symbolic moment during the Eighty Years' War (1568–1648), during which the Netherlands took shape, has been commemorated through such a day.

This is understandable. At the beginning of the Revolt against Spain in the second half of the 1560s, the overriding issue was not the independence of a particular area but the retention of aristocratic privileges in an empire that was centralizing, against a backdrop of Protestant resistance to Catholic repression. Even when it became clear in about 1580 that the secession of a few Dutch provinces from Philip II's Spanish Empire was inevitable and a division of the Netherlands into a northern and southern part was taking place (roughly the present Netherlands and Belgium), it was still not about the independence of a well-defined territory. It is striking, for instance, that during the 1580s the rebellious provinces twice offered their sovereignty to foreign royals. The northern provinces did not take charge of their own sovereignty until 1588, after these attempts had failed, and a federal republic was organized with independent provinces, towns and cities. Although it was dubbed the Republic of the United Netherlands, this name was never officially adopted.[1]

There was still no clarity about the ultimate borders of this loose alliance in 1588. They did not firm up until the 1590s, when the territory of the current Netherlands acquired an outline as a result of the military successes against Spain. This area consolidated in 1609, and around 1630, the current North Brabant and South Limburg were added. The war with Spain finally ended in 1648 with the Peace of Münster (an element of the Peace of Westphalia), and the Republic received definitive international recognition as an independent country.

The end result had little in common with the Revolt's objectives dating from the second half of the sixteenth century. In fact at that time the word Revolt was never used. Recollections of contemporaries and the first history publications talked about 'wars', 'troubles', 'riots' and 'wretchedness'. The concept was not coined until the eighteenth century, and its description as the Revolt evolved during the next century. It was not until then that a single story emerged from the chain of events, covering many decades and, according to Ernst H. Kossmann, that era was given 'coherence, purpose, unity'.[2] Historians now agree it was completely unforeseen and unintended that the struggle of the Dutch provinces against Spanish rule would create two different political units in the Netherlands, and that during the Revolt the concerns in the separate provinces, towns and cities were often about something else, with some for and some against the Spanish crown and others that changed sides. According to Anton van der Lem, the Revolt was 'a long succession of coincidental and unpredictable events, of political, military and economic chain reactions'.[3] It is consequently not surprising that the nature of the memories about it is primarily local and that to this day, commemorations remain geographically limited.

As late as the twentieth century, Protestants interpreted the Revolt as a deliberate national struggle for independence and for freedom to practise their religion. As we shall see in the following chapter, this simplified mythical picture departed from historical reality. Fables also developed about William of Orange (1533–84). He was said to have been the 'Father of his Country' and to have always pursued 'national' independence and consistently fought for it. There is no doubt that he took over leadership of the Revolt, which he paid for with his life in 1584, but for many years Orange did not want a split with Spain and certainly not a division between the north and the south of the Netherlands.[4]

Images of the Revolt such as these are part of nationalistic nineteenth-century historical writings and were dismissed long ago as incorrect. A number of insurgents advocated making Calvinism the only permitted faith, while others wanted religious tolerance and the principle – which was new at that time – of having multiple religions cheek by jowl in one governmental zone. If one contends that the religious issue was at the core, there is good reason for calling the conflict in the Low Countries a civil war, just as there were religious hostilities during this era in other European regions. Should we consider freedom to have been the key issue, however, a distinction needs to be made between those who initially wanted to retain their own – in many cases aristocratic – privileges, primarily old traditional liberties, which in this period of centralization, professionalization and bureaucratization were being jeopardized, and those who were fighting to be free from 'Spanish tyranny'.[5] In addition, during the decades of this struggle, the motives and objectives of the many players overlapped and shifted time and again.

In other words, the outcome of the Revolt was very different from its initial aspirations and goals, but looking back, it was without doubt the central factor in the creation of the Dutch state. At its end there was an internationally recognized Dutch Republic with more or less the same borders as the present-day Netherlands. Starting in the late sixteenth century, the Republic developed into a wealthy global trading power with outposts in every continent. It also took the international lead in culture and technology. The worldwide Dutch trading network that was built up during the Revolt has left traces that are visible to this day.

The Republic had a complex political decision-making process involving a great many people. The fundamental principle during the Republic was to seek agreement, not force decisions. The culture of compromise and negotiation that developed at that time is still part of the political scene in the Netherlands. This is not to say that consultation and consensus building have dominated Dutch political history – there are far too many examples of bitterly fought political struggles for that claim. Some will be discussed at length later in this book. What matters here is that Dutch political culture in later eras had many of its roots in the years of the Revolt and the early Republic, when 'freedom' and 'tolerance' became key Dutch concepts.[6]

The history of the creation of the state of the Netherlands, then, is closely associated with the Revolt, but this does not answer the question as to when Dutch history 'began', particularly since it is difficult to identify an exact date for the start of the Revolt. Histories of the Netherlands have long identified 1568 as the beginning, in reference to the failed military advance on three fronts in Dutch territory organized by William of Orange. It would now seem that this year was chosen primarily so that – working back from 1648 – one can talk about an 'Eighty Years' War' (from which, in any case, twelve years have to be subtracted for the truce between 1609 and 1621).

From a different perspective, 1566 could be taken as the start, because it was in that year that the minor aristocracy submitted a petition to the Governor, Margaret, Duchess of Parma, asking her to suspend the anti-heresy edicts and convene the States General. Later that year there was an outbreak of iconoclasm, primarily in the provinces of Flanders and Brabant – Catholic churches were stripped of statues and paintings, and church buildings were commandeered for Calvinists to use. This unarguably made 1566 a year in which opposition to Spanish rule increased dramatically. One of the leading authorities on this period, A. T. van Deursen, writes that the Revolt became 'a reality' in that year.[7]

The exact date that the Revolt began, however, is not actually that important in the search for a 'starting point' for the history of the Netherlands. Many historians who have written about the Revolt begin in 1555, when Charles V abdicated as Holy Roman Emperor and his son, Philip II, became Lord of the Netherlands. In his major standard work on the Republic, *The Dutch Republic: Its Rise, Greatness and Fall, 1477–1806*, the British historian Jonathan Israel takes a longer run-up. He starts with the death of Charles the Bold, Duke of Burgundy, ruler of the Netherlands, and the succession of his daughter, Mary of Burgundy, who married Habsburg Maximilian of Austria in the same year. Charles the Bold's death meant not just the end of the Burgundian Netherlands and the beginning of Habsburg rule, it also, importantly, gave the Low Countries the opportunity to reverse some of the centralization measures he had initiated. The effect was short-lived. During the first half of the sixteenth century, under Charles V, unification and centralization were pursued consistently, successfully and more forcefully than ever before. Jonathan Israel describes in detail this period prior to the Revolt – an obvious place to begin a comprehensive work that presents with animation and conviction the entire history of the Dutch Republic up to 1806. Horst Lademacher does not start his broadly based, wide-ranging *Die Niederlande: Politische Kultur zwischen Individualität und Anpassung* with a particular year, although his approach corresponds to Israel's. He, too, begins with the late medieval unification policy of the Burgundies, which was continued by the Habsburg dynasty after Mary of Burgundy's death in 1482.[8]

Against this backdrop, it is justifiable to start this overview of Dutch history in 1555, with a brief overture that began in the late fifteenth century.[9] The literature on the country's past since the sixteenth century is well-nigh inexhaustible and it would be going too far to produce a synopsis here. One is struck, though, by the modest number of publications that cover an extended period. The writings of Israel and Lademacher referred to above do span a number of centuries, but their bulk means they are not handy overviews. Besides, Israel stops at 1806 and addresses the late eighteenth century only very briefly, while Lademacher falls short when dealing with the years after 1945. Information about the period starting in the late seventeenth century is to be found in Kossmann's *The Low Countries 1780–1940*. Piet de Rooy wrote about the Netherlands since 1800 in both *Republiek van rivaliteiten* and *Ons stipje op de waereldkaart*.[10] Another important source is the publication by Maarten Prak and Jan Luiten van Zanden, *Nederland en het poldermodel*, which addresses the development of political institutions, government structure and the economy from the Middle Ages to today.[11] The entire period from prehistory to the present is presented clearly but in summary form in *Een kennismaking met de Nederlandse Geschiedenis* by István Bejczy.[12] Christophe de Voogd's *Geschiedenis van Nederland*, originally written for publication in France and consequently with very much the character of an introduction for non-Dutch readers, is more broadly based.[13] Han van der Horst's successful but chunky *Nederland. De vaderlandse geschiedenis van de prehistorie tot nu* is more comprehensive and primarily based on narrative.[14] James Kennedy recently published *A Concise History of the Netherlands*, starting in prehistory and ending in the present day.[15] Overviews by foreign authors include Paul Arblaster's *A History of the Low Countries*, Paul State's *A Brief History of the Netherlands* and Michael North's *Geschichte der Niederlande*, which are all readable and clear but concise.[16] The history of Belgium, the Netherlands and Luxembourg is described by German historian Michael Erbe in *Geschichte des niederländischen Raumes*. His writing about the early modern period is convincing, but disappointing and too perfunctory when addressing the nineteenth and twentieth centuries.[17] These, then, are the most important studies of Dutch history that cover a span of some centuries.

Of course there are also reference works and series with contributions from several authors. The fifteen-volume *Algemene Geschiedenis der Nederlanden* wins the prize for size but is now outdated.[18] The handy three-volume Delta series *Nederlands verleden in vogelvlucht*, covering the period from the Middle Ages to the late twentieth century is more accessible.[19] *Geschiedenis van de Nederlanden* edited by J. C. H. Blom and E. Lamberts serves as a very good companion. In common with a few other historical outlines, it describes the history of both the Netherlands and Belgium.[20] Finally, mention should be made of *Verleden van Nederland*, part of a multimedia project of the same name, which has been written for a general readership.[21]

Summing up all these works, there is scope for a history of the Netherlands from the Revolt to the present day that concentrates on political developments and their socioeconomic context. This is the gap that the present guide seeks to fill. It is an overview of manageable size that covers the nation's past from the period in which the Netherlands took geographical, administrative and political shape. The primary focus is on domestic and foreign policy, interwoven with the main themes of economic history. The visual arts, literature, architecture and science are not considered, except during the Golden Age.

The breakdown of history since the sixteenth century into chapters corresponds largely with that in other outlines. The Revolt and the creation of the Dutch Republic were followed by growth that made the country an economic, political, military, cultural and scientific world power in the seventeenth century (Chapters 2 and 3). How could a small federal state with a relatively loose-knit executive structure develop into a global force and maintain that position for over a century? What political and economic circumstances enabled it? What role was played by the bourgeois culture, with its comparatively generous religious tolerance, which was so characteristic of the Republic? These questions cannot be answered without examining the international political and economic contexts, so these are also discussed extensively in this book.

The Golden Age is addressed in relatively greater depth because of its huge significance in the nation's past. Another key element is the role of the Orange-Nassau stadholders, starting with William of Orange mentioned earlier, and ending with William III, who was stadholder in the most important Dutch provinces (1672–1702) and also king of England (1689–1702). As military commanders-in-chief and elite nobles, stadholders enjoyed great prestige and political influence. At the same time they were appointed by and in the service of the provinces, with Holland in the leading position. This meant that the Republic had complex political relationships in which power and influence had to be shared with changing factions of wealthy citizens who ruled the powerful towns and cities as regents. The conflicts this system gave rise to repeatedly became fierce and were typical of the political history of the early modern period. When the Republic was at its peak in the middle of the seventeenth century, the major provinces actually scrapped the post of stadholder (1650–72) and they repeated this for a significant part of the eighteenth century (1702–47).

Compared with the country's heyday in the seventeenth century, the eighteenth century can be classified as a period of political and economic deterioration (Chapter 4). The days when the Republic could secure its commercial and strategic interests using its own resources, or those of international coalitions it had forged, were over. There was no question of abrupt economic decay, but rather a gradual and relative decline that was accompanied by an inevitable weakening of the country's international position. By 1780, the Republic had become nothing more than a pawn in the chess game dominated by England, Prussia and France, resulting in its downfall and the flight of the last stadholder in 1795. This heralded a period of growing Dutch dependence on France, which ended with annexation by Napoleon's empire (1810–13). While the Netherlands' foreign political position during this period was marked by crisis and weakness, there was considerable innovative thinking and modernization in domestic politics. This trend was crowned in 1798 by the first Dutch constitution, which made a unitary state and the triumph of democratic Enlightenment principles a reality. Although these principles were to disappear from government again in subsequent years, there would be no going back on the unitary state.

On the contrary, after Napoleon's defeat in 1813, the Dutch unitary state acquired its definitive content during the nineteenth century (Chapter 5). The Netherlands became a kingdom under the House of Orange-Nassau. Initially, it was combined with Belgium in the United Kingdom of the Netherlands (1815–30). Thereafter it became the Kingdom of the Netherlands with borders that have remained essentially unchanged to this day. A liberal amended constitution in 1848 was followed, starting in around 1870, by a dynamic process of industrialization, urbanization and political modernization. The 1917 constitutional amendment was a milestone in this trend because it put an end to a few key late nineteenth-century political sore points. It also laid the foundations for the Netherlands of the twentieth century. The political landscape during the interwar years in the Netherlands was pillarized and essentially politically stable. The global economic depression during the 1930s hit the country hard. The government responded to growing international tensions by clinging tenaciously to a policy of neutrality in the hope that the Dutch would be able to remain outside the conflict, as they had during the First World War. That hope proved illusory in May 1940 when a five-year occupation by Nazi Germany began (Chapter 6). After 1945 the country developed from a neutral and relatively inward-looking nation into an active ally in Atlantic and European cooperation. This change of direction was ushered in by the Second World War, which also resulted in the decolonization of Indonesia. The transfer of sovereignty to Indonesia in 1949 signalled the end of the Netherlands' status as an important colonial power. There was a second watershed in the 1960s, when traditional political structures eroded, democratization was given priority and new political conventions made their appearance. This book ends with an analysis of what is happening in the early twenty-first century. Given the emergence of right-wing populism, changing global balances of power and crises in the European Union, this may well be considered in the future as the start of a new phase (Chapter 7). This Dutch political history concludes with a few key lines that are drawn from the sixteenth century to the present day (Chapter 8).

CHAPTER 2

OPPOSITION AND REVOLT: THE CREATION AND CONSOLIDATION OF THE UNITED PROVINCES OF THE NETHERLANDS, OR THE DUTCH REPUBLIC (1555–1609)

Introduction

Around the mid-sixteenth century, 'the Netherlands' was the term used to describe an area corresponding roughly to the present Benelux countries. Politically, though, the region had little more in common than a shared name on the map, and there was no legal or economic unity. Control of the many small states – known then as 'counties' and 'provinces' – was divided among rulers with diverse backgrounds. Around 1500, the most southerly provinces, as well as Holland and Zeeland, were ruled by Philip the Handsome, the son of Mary of Burgundy and Habsburg Maximilian I, Holy Roman Emperor. Bishops governed the provinces of Liège and Utrecht, and the sway of the latter extended as far as the present-day Dutch provinces of Drenthe and Overijssel. To the east, Duke Charles of Egmond was master of Guelders and parts of the present province of Limburg, while there was no central authority in the provinces of Friesland and Groningen.

It was during the reign of Charles V, born in 1500 to Duke Philip the Handsome and the Spanish Joanna of Castile, that these provinces united and became part of a major European empire. Joanna inherited the Spanish kingdoms of Aragon and Castile, but her husband's premature death in 1506 and her own mental illness saw the Spanish crown pass to Charles in 1516, after the death of the regent, his grandfather Ferdinand II of Aragon. A year earlier, the fifteen-year-old Charles had acquired power over the Netherlands, and in 1519, he succeeded his grandfather Maximilian as king of the German Empire.

In the 1520s he began to increase his influence in the Netherlands. Holland put an end to Friesland's independence in 1523, and in 1528, Charles V took over the secular power of the bishopric of Utrecht. In so doing he also assumed power over Drenthe and Overijssel. After coming to an arrangement with the pope, Charles V was assured of the support of the prelates in the bishoprics of Cambrai and Liège, and Groningen came under his sway during the 1530s. The conquest of Guelders in 1543 brought the number of provinces to seventeen, at which point the territory of the Netherlands corresponded pretty much with today's Benelux in terms of size. This contiguous territory was, however, interrupted by the neutral bishopric of Liège, leaving Luxembourg and parts of present-day Limburg without a common border with the other Netherlandish provinces. There were in addition a number of smaller enclaves, particularly in Guelders and along the border between Holland and Utrecht. Charles V's plan to add East Frisia and the bishopric of Münster to the Netherlandish provinces failed, but he did acquire the County of Lingen, which he likewise considered to be part of his possessions in the Low Countries.

Historians have rightly pointed out that the final eastern border of the Netherlands is not 'natural' in any way and that Dutch territory during the 1540s was similarly by no means 'complete'.[1] The outcome was in fact the fortuitous result of inheritances, wars and conflicts about power and influence. The struggle between the Habsburgs on the one hand and France and the Duke of Guelders on the other was crucial.[2] In 1548, the German Diet decided, in response to a request from Charles V, to group the provinces in an Imperial Circle, the *Kreits*, a self-governing administrative unit inside the Holy Roman Empire. This strengthened the bonds between the provinces, while the ties with the Empire became looser. This edict, known as the Pragmatic Sanction, stated that the seventeen Dutch provinces would continue to exist as a unified entity indefinitely and would not be divided up among different heirs. In 1549, the provinces ratified the Pragmatic Sanction, and in that same year Charles V's son, Philip II, the heir apparent, paid his respects by visiting the Netherlands for the first time.[3]

The Pragmatic Sanction did not survive for long. Things started to go wrong in the Northern Netherlands under Philip II. In the Act of Abjuration in 1581 the northern provinces declared their independence from his rule, and seven years later, they decided to go one step further as sovereign provinces, in what would become known as the United Provinces of the Netherlands, or the Dutch Republic. It was to endure, after gaining international recognition in the Peace of Münster in 1648, until its disappearance in 1795 as a result of French expansion. The southern provinces, on the other hand, remained under the rule of the Habsburgs until 1794, when Napoleon seized control of this area too. After Napoleonic domination in Europe came to an end in 1813, the former geographical Dutch 'unity' was briefly restored as the United Kingdom of the Netherlands at the Congress of Vienna (1814–15). Belgium and the Netherlands were united and put under the rule of King William I of the Netherlands, who also became Grand Duke of Luxembourg. Belgian–Dutch unity ended in 1830, and the link between the Netherlands and Luxembourg was severed in 1890 after the death of King William III. This brought the Netherlands back to its geographical position at the time of the Republic, which again corresponded more or less to the seven northern provinces of the Habsburg Netherlands.

This chapter focuses on the creation of the Republic. As we saw in the introduction, the Revolt that broke out during the 1560s was not about 'national independence', a misconception often asserted in later historiography and taught to generations of Dutch schoolchildren in the nineteenth and twentieth centuries. There was a multiplicity of factors that, through their interaction, unintentionally resulted in the formation of the Republic. Initially, it appeared that there was no way the rebels would have any chance of successfully challenging Spanish dominance, but in the course of the 1590s, the Republic drove the Spanish back and was able to consolidate its position. As the balance of power stabilized, a twelve-year truce was agreed in 1609.

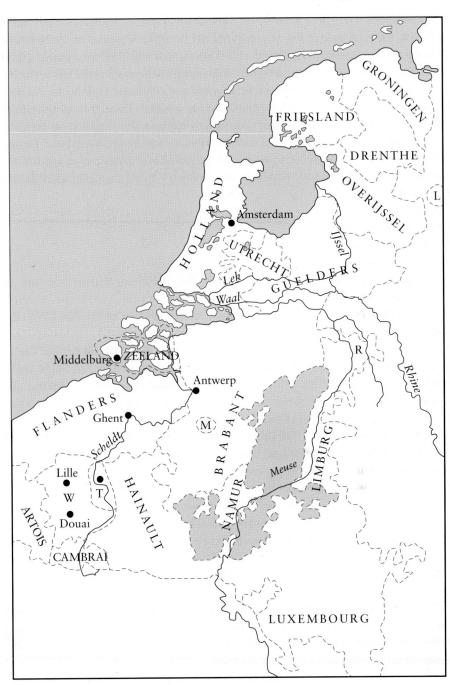

Principality of Liège   R Roermond Quarter in Guelders
L Lingen   T Tournai
M Mechelen   W Walloon Flanders

Map 1 The Netherlands around 1550.

The economic strength of the area was a key factor in the insurgents' success. During the Revolt, the economic centre of gravity shifted from the Southern to the Northern Netherlands. One reason for this was the flood of migrants who fled to the north in their tens of thousands after the Spanish tightened their grip on the south in the 1580s. During this period the northern economy started to grow, and continued to do so for decades. The successes in the different sectors reinforced one another. Trade, fishing, agriculture and industry all enjoyed spectacular growth, and expansion was driven by both the domestic market (population growth, urbanization, increasing prosperity) and foreign trade. This enabled the Republic to develop into a global mercantile power, and laid the foundations for the political, economic and cultural vigour that characterized the Republic during the Golden Age.

Economy, finance and the political structure

Around the middle of the sixteenth century, the Habsburg Netherlands was an economically and strategically important region, thanks primarily to the relatively densely populated and urbanized provinces of Flanders, Brabant and Holland. With the emergence of world trade, this part of Europe developed into a central international hub, with Antwerp as the most important city. This city on the River Scheldt became one of the greatest in Europe (from 40,000 inhabitants in 1495 to more than 100,000 in 1565), with increasing urbanization, particularly in the surrounding provinces. Holland had been evolving into a region with many small towns since the Middle Ages, and this structure remained a prominent feature of the province in the sixteenth century. In 1514, with a population of some 14,000, Leiden was Holland's biggest city and in that year 46 per cent of all the people in Holland lived in an urban environment, a percentage not significantly lower in Brabant (41 per cent). By European standards, these provinces had a very high degree of urbanization.[4] Throughout the sixteenth century, a key aspect in the north was the absence of one large city and the distribution of the population over a number of largish towns. This phenomenon would prove to be of great significance to the development of the economy and the form of government.

Population growth and urbanization swelled demand for commodities such as grain and wood from the Baltic, and in the north, it was Holland that took the lead. At the same time, agriculture became more intensive and specialized in the west of the Netherlands. The economic boom permitted population growth, with part of the increase coming through migration from other, poorer provinces. The economic dynamic of rising productivity in agriculture and increasing trade and urbanization drove up demand for timber, which was also imported from the Baltic.

Amsterdam developed into a major centre for trade in these commodities, and at the end of the 1550s, the ports of Holland were home to more seagoing ships than anywhere else in Europe. A significant difference between Antwerp and Amsterdam was that the former concentrated on high added value trade (textiles, colonial imports) whereas the later focused on bulk goods. As a consequence, Holland's merchant fleet had a large number of relatively big and cheaply built vessels suitable for transporting substantial quantities of cargo. The ships in the Antwerp fleet, on the other hand, were smaller and equipped for carrying more expensive products over longer distances. An additional difference was that the trading in Antwerp was predominantly passive; in other words, most of the traders sailing to the city came from other regions. Spaniards and Portuguese, for instance, brought cargoes from Asia, Africa and America to Antwerp, and the city was very dependent on shipping to and from Holland and Zeeland.[5] This luxury trade moved to the north after 1585, when Antwerp fell into Spanish hands and the northern provinces blockaded the Scheldt.

In the early sixteenth century, many types of commercial traffic thus came together in the North Sea, and the Netherlands took over Italy's central role in world trade. This was where the most important sea routes between the north and south of Europe, and between England and the Holy Roman Empire intersected. The area also had a good urban infrastructure, which gave economic development a powerful dynamic. Nevertheless, the Habsburg Netherlands could certainly not be described as a single economic unit in the first half of the sixteenth century. The historian Simon Groenveld characterizes the economy of the seventeen provinces at this time as 'unstable' and 'disjointed'.[6] Part of the Netherlands, particularly the sparsely populated northeast, still had a primarily agricultural structure with output intended solely for local and regional markets. The southeast was also poor and largely isolated from the growth in the western parts. Economic development in Antwerp, on the other hand, was modern, and this had a huge impact on the adjoining provinces. As yet, there was nothing like a 'national' economy, but a thriving economic and militarily strategic northern European hub was building up around Antwerp, and this was of key significance to the consolidation and expansion of the position of the Habsburgs in Europe and the rest of the world.[7]

The Habsburg expansion cost money – a great deal of money – which was spent mainly on waging war with France and the Turks. Charles V and Philip II, his son and successor in the Netherlands, relied on taxes from the Dutch provinces for part of the financing they needed, and they considered the highly developed western provinces to be particularly important targets. Under the Burgundies, there had been a system of land and property taxes, which obliged the ruler to request contributions from his provinces. This had always resulted in difficult debates between the ruler and the provincial states. The provinces tried above all to safeguard their own – regional – interests, whereas the ruler's primary objective was to alleviate his need for finance. We shall see how Philip II's efforts to abolish these local land and property taxes and set up a centralized taxation system were among the factors that sparked the Dutch Revolt. His plan would have eroded the fiscal independence of the provinces and consequently threatened to limit the freedom of the aristocracy and the citizenry – a development they fiercely opposed.

These differences of opinion about taxes point to both the contrast between the interests of the ruler and the provinces, and the different perspectives of the ruler and the population in the provinces. Charles V and Philip II took an overarching view and saw the Dutch provinces as a single entity that should, in due course, become a centrally governed kingdom between France and the Holy Roman Empire. From the point of view of Charles V in his court in Brussels, there was every reason to create a uniform government for the hotchpotch of counties, duchies, manors and independent towns that together made up the Netherlands. The move towards unification had started under the Burgundies and was in line with the general European pattern. Rulers elsewhere in Europe were also strengthening central and provincial authority, the power of regional nobility was being curtailed, and law and the administration of justice were being rationalized. An important reason for such a development in the Dutch provinces was the massive size of Charles V's dominions. He was the Holy Roman Emperor and was also monarch in his own right of two Spanish kingdoms and their overseas – American – possessions.

In the provinces themselves, however, people had a view from the ground, and resistance to the centralization policy emanating from Brussels arose among the existing regional nobility and bourgeois elite. These privileged classes were, after all, threatened with the loss of power and influence. In the northern and eastern provinces, the recent subjugation to the rule of Charles V was still fresh in people's memories and they were understandably reluctant to accept any further loss of power. This presented Charles V with a dilemma. On the one hand, he recognized that he needed the support of these elites to achieve his unification goals. He was also reliant on them to fund his costly wars. On the other, he realized that he would not get this essential support if he failed to take into account the interests of the most influential regional circles. The upshot of this fundamental contradiction between central authority and the regional elites was that the implementation of greater governmental unity was subject to clear limits. Unification therefore went hand in hand with significant tensions, which were to play a major role in fomenting the Revolt during the reign of Philip II.

In practice, this meant there was a hybrid of old and new, with Brussels adding a number of new central posts and institutions to the existing administrative network.[8] At the top, needless to say, was the Habsburg monarch, who exercised authority as the sovereign of each individual province. Since commitments elsewhere meant that he was frequently absent from Brussels, he was represented by a governor or regent, usually a member of his immediate family. From 1531 onwards, the governor remained in office even when the monarch was present, but was obliged to follow his instructions to the letter. That year also saw the establishment of three central councils, the Collateral Councils, all headquartered in Brussels. The most important was the Council of State, an influential central government advisory body that addressed international issues and 'national' matters of an ecclesiastical, financial and administrative nature. Originally, the members were drawn from the senior ranks of the nobility and the clergy, but it was not long before a new management group of lawyers appeared on the scene. By the time Charles V stepped down in 1555, there were already five lawyers alongside seven aristocratic representatives, very much to the displeasure of the latter, who saw their influence waning. Alongside the Council of State, there appeared a Privy Council consisting entirely of the new management group of career officials and lawyers. It met daily and was responsible for preparing and implementing policy. Finally, there was a Council of Finance, made up of three senior aristocrats and three legal-financial civil servants, which made preparations to collect land and property taxes and monitored provincial financial departments.

While the sovereign – in Brussels – had the governor as a deputy at a central level, he was represented in the provinces by a stadholder appointed from the upper ranks of the nobility. He was the commander of the troops in the province and was responsible for maintaining public order. He looked after the monarch's possessions and minded the interests of the church. He also played an important role in the appointment of urban office holders. Obviously he maintained regular contact with Brussels, either to account for his actions and to advise, or to receive instructions. Stadholders were usually responsible for more than one province. As we shall see later on, in the completely different circumstances of the Republic, the stadholder was to develop into a key figure in the political, administrative and military establishment.

The stadholder was also authorized to convene the provincial states, in which the nobility, the towns and cities, and the clergy had been represented since the late Middle Ages. The provincial states' most important job was to consider the sovereign's requests for money. The monarch was not able to impose taxes, and this gave the provinces the opportunity to bring forward their own interests and counterbalance centralizing tendencies. Another relic from the Burgundy era was the States General, the assembly of provincial representatives that was convened for the first time in 1464. Royal requests were the usual subject of discussion in the States General too. This body was convened regularly during the reigns of Charles V and Philip II. Having listened to the requests for taxation, the provincial representatives returned to their provinces for consultation before notifying the States General of their response. Like the provincial states, the States General increasingly became an independent political organ that attached conditions to its consent to the sovereign's requests and thus formed a counterweight to an excessive concentration of power in his hands.

Some provinces did not send representatives to the States General during the reigns of Charles V and Philip II. Friesland, Groningen, Drenthe, Overijssel, Guelders and Utrecht, the provinces that Charles V had added to the Habsburg Netherlands himself, had managed to negotiate an exemption and had only to attend a General Assembly in very exceptional circumstances – as, for instance, when Charles V abdicated in 1555 and when Philip II left for Spain in 1559.

Summarizing, the Habsburgs consistently pushed through centralization and the extension of bureaucracy. A new group of university-educated lawyers acquired influential positions in the various newly established councils, so that the old aristocratic elite lost power. At the same time, the pressure on the provincial states to centralize increased, and the monarch's needs for funding brought about rising tensions. In consequence, a tightly knit united Habsburg state, which is what Charles V and above all Philip II had in mind, was not yet within reach. As in other parts of Europe, the best that could be achieved was a composite state: a clustering of different units under one general administrative regime.[9] In this embryo nation the powers and the relationships between central, regional and local authorities had not yet taken shape. The accompanying tensions would come to a head during the years of the Revolt.

Reformation

The nature of the stress field between the growing power of Brussels and the provincial and local governing organs was not such that the process of unification was doomed to fail. On the contrary, such tensions are part and parcel of the road to greater unity. Jonathan Israel writes that in the mid-sixteenth century, the Habsburg Netherlands 'were to all appearances being successfully welded into a viable and coherent whole, with the support of both the magnates and the new elite of humanist-trained career bureaucrats'.[10] Van Deursen also asserts that unification could have succeeded 'had other causes not led to revolt and civil war'. According to Van Deursen, it was the issue of religion that made the problems of unification insoluble.[11]

The position of the church changed fundamentally during the first half of the sixteenth century.[12] Around 1500, an overlap between the Roman Catholic Church and society was still a matter of course, but by the middle of the century this unity had been lost. The credibility and moral authority of the Catholic clergy had declined as a result of Luther's growing influence in the Netherlands. Luther's writings spread throughout the country rapidly, thanks to the far-reaching degree of urbanization, the relatively high literacy rate, the large number of printers and intensive dealings with the German-speaking regions. As early as May 1519, Erasmus of Rotterdam reported that 'most of the Hollanders, Zeelanders and Flemish knew the doctrines of Luther'.[13] During the 1520s, however, Charles V pursued a vigorous and effective policy of repression and the first heretics died in flames at the stakes of the Inquisition. This was one of the reasons why the Reformation in the Netherlands lacked organizational drive and coordination, which soon impeded the spread of Lutheranism. It resulted in the internalization of the Reformation, and the development of a gulf between religious convictions and practice. While the majority of the population remained members of the church, they distanced themselves internally from the old beliefs and developed their own persuasions. Israel refers to early Dutch Protestantism as dogmatically pluriform and radically decentralized, a 'bewildering plethora of doctrines and standpoints'.[14] The Dutch historian J. J. Woltjer refers to a variety of nuances and prefers to speak of 'the reformations' rather than 'the Reformation'.[15] Many people were not thinking about breaking with the Catholic Church, but they did want scope for their own ethics and interpretation.

The Baptists were much more radical. Between the 1530s and the end of the 1550s, this small minority was the organizational vanguard of the Reformation in the Netherlands. They interpreted the Bible literally, and among the things they based on this was their view that infant baptism could not be recognized. They believed that only adults could consciously choose the religion and only they could be baptized. They also considered the other Catholic sacraments to be aberrations. Violent attempts to bring about the kingdom of God on earth even led to the occupation of the Westphalian cathedral city of Münster in 1534–5, and there were disturbances elsewhere too. The persecution of the Baptists was harsh and many of them paid for their radical views and violence with their lives. However, the Baptist aggression was over around the middle of the sixteenth century, by which time non-violence had actually become an important feature of the movement.

The roles of Menno Simons (*c.*1496–1561) and Dirk Philips (1504–68) were very important in bringing peace to the Baptist movement, which attracted a relatively large following among ordinary people, particularly in the north. The Baptists nevertheless remained a small minority who were not able to penetrate the governing elite even when they became economically successful. Their uncompromising obedience to God's commandments and their willingness to accept even martyrdom to that end remained unchanged. Many became victims of persecution even after the movement renounced the use of violence. It is estimated that altogether some three thousand people were put to death because of their faith between 1531 and 1574 and that two thousand of them were Baptists.

In the early 1540s, the voice of a third group that was relevant to the Netherlands began to make itself heard. The Calvinists abandoned the caution that many proponents of the Reformation had displayed in the preceding period, when they only supported the new persuasion in secret, avoided provoking a schism and hoped for renewal within the existing church. The Calvinists were no longer satisfied with that and demanded a fundamental choice between Rome or the Reformation, between the false and the true church. They absorbed some of the unstructured and fluid Protestantism that still existed, and initially attracted a greater following in the south than in the north. The spread of Calvinism began to accelerate in the early 1560s, and persecution increased. Tensions rose further because many Catholics abhorred the violent repression and the turmoil that went with it. The upshot was that many people became alienated from the Habsburg authorities and the Catholic Church, and sympathy for the Calvinists grew. This development was also a major factor behind the outbreak of the Revolt.

Around the middle of the sixteenth century, the religious map of the Netherlands presented a heterogeneous picture. The historians Groenveld and Gerrit Schutte refer to a 'sliding scale of religious convictions', ranging from orthodox to Protestantizing Catholics, Baptists, dogmatic and moderate Calvinists and a handful of Lutherans.[16] The turmoil around baptism was now a thing of the past and tranquillity appeared to have returned, but – as Israel sums up – by the end of the 1550s, the position of the Catholic Church had weakened to such an extent that its survival in its traditional form had become problematic.[17] The vehemence of the religious issue was to grow to an unprecedented degree from the 1560s onwards.

Loyalty, opposition and crisis (1555–66)

Charles V abdicated in October 1555 and the territory of the Netherlands came under the rule of his son Philip II. At the beginning of 1556, Philip also became monarch of two Spanish kingdoms, while Charles's brother, Ferdinand I, became Holy Roman Emperor. In the Netherlands, Philip had to face the same problems as his father. It was clear first and foremost that he was going to cling unrelentingly to the Church of Rome and that he would continue the persecution of heretics without mercy. Second, Philip had inherited an empty treasury from his father. The ongoing wars with France and other expenses meant that he soon ran short of funds. In 1556, he requested taxation from the provinces to alleviate his financial position, but the result – which did not come until 1558 after long and laborious negotiations – was an agreement hedged with numerous terms and conditions. A third source of tension arose from the relationship between the new monarch and the senior nobility. Philip depended on their support to implement his policy of centralizing the administration and making it more professional, but it was precisely this that provoked the resistance of the nobility. Equally unhelpful was the fact that Philip had surrounded himself with Spanish courtiers and advisors, while the Dutch had almost no access to him. He was a suspicious man who spoke neither French nor Dutch, and he rarely involved the Council of State in his political decision making. There was consequently a degree of relief when he left for Spain in 1559 to be crowned king. It emerged later that his departure was permanent; Philip II would never again set foot on Dutch soil. He appointed his half-sister Margaret, Duchess of Parma, as regent. She had little experience as a ruler, so this appeared to open up an opportunity for the senior nobles to increase their influence. This group of elite aristocrats was not large. William of Orange and the Counts of Egmont and Horn were the best known.

William of Orange was by far the richest and most distinguished representative of the upper ranks of Dutch nobility.[18] Born in Dillenburg, Germany, in 1533, he was the son of the Lutheran Count William I of Nassau-Dillenburg and Juliana of Stolberg. At the age of eleven, he inherited substantial family possessions in the Netherlands plus the French principality of Orange. This French inheritance brought him into the circle of reigning European royalty. Charles V, Holy Roman Emperor and hence the overlord of William's father, made it a condition for receiving this inheritance that young William would be given both a Catholic and a Dutch education at the court in Brussels. This led to close ties between the emperor and the young prince. When he abdicated in 1555, Charles V leant on the shoulder of William of Orange – by then twenty-two – as he entered the grand chamber of the palace in Brussels, where all the Dutch provinces were represented. In his biography of William of Orange, Olaf Mörke rightly points out that this gesture has to be interpreted above all as a sign that William enjoyed a high position in Dutch nobility, and at the same time as public confirmation of Orange's loyalty to the Habsburg ruler.[19]

Little changed for Orange when Philip II assumed power. William had served Charles V faithfully and he continued to serve his successor, to whom he gave key support in the war against France, which ended in a Spanish victory in 1559. When Philip left for Spain, he appointed William of Orange stadholder of the provinces of Holland, Zeeland and Utrecht. Egmont got the same job in the provinces of Flanders and Artois. The relationships within the central organ of power in Brussels did not improve, though, and the senior nobility failed to make its mark on political decision making.

The true power in Brussels, appointed by Philip II, was Antoine Perrenot (1517–86), better known as Granvelle. He was a lawyer, he did not come from the ranks of the nobility, and he represented the new administrative elite.[20] Granvelle had permanent access to Margaret of Parma and loyally carried out Philip's wishes and directions. Tensions between him and the aristocratic elite increased significantly in the early 1560s, largely fuelled by the issue of religion. A new ecclesiastical map of the Netherlands was announced in 1559. The seventeen provinces were divided into three archbishoprics with fifteen ordinary bishoprics below them. This represented major progress from the Catholic Church's point of view; before this there had been no archbishoprics in the Netherlands, and the number of bishoprics had remained small. This division was in line with the political unification of the Netherlands because between them the new archbishoprics more or less covered the territory of the seventeen provinces. During the implementation of the new ecclesiastical zoning, which proceeded with difficulty, Granvelle became Archbishop of Mechelen and was given 'primacy' in the Netherlands. His influential position was secured in 1561, when the pope made him a cardinal.

This ecclesiastical rearrangement in 1559 provoked resistance among various sections of the population. Both local clergy and senior members of the nobility lost influence as a consequence. It was laid down that newly appointed bishops must have completed a university education and hold a doctorate in theology. As was the case with the new government elite, they were now to be appointed on the basis of their education and dedication, not their background and connections. This was an attack on the traditional position of the nobility because ecclesiastical careers had until then been their prerogative. There was also resistance among large groups at different levels of the population because the new ecclesiastical configuration would lead to stricter supervision of religious issues and, as a result, there would be more severe persecution of unorthodox points of view and heresy. These concerns proved justified. Granvelle obediently pursued Philip II's tough line, while the spread of Calvinism grew.

William of Orange's position shifted in the opposite direction. In 1561 he married the Lutheran Anna of Saxony, sparking the mistrust of Philip and Granvelle. To his sovereign he swore loyalty to the Catholic Church, but he told his bride's family that his affinity for Lutheranism had not disappeared. Obviously, Orange had issues of prestige and political motives for this marriage, but his flexibility in matters of faith was not an expression of religious opportunism. In fact it indicated that he did not think in terms of denominational confrontation, and was prepared to accept religious pluriformity. Orange's marriage to Anna of Saxony also led to a breakdown of trust with Philip from a political point of view, not least because as a consequence William would have more dealings with Protestant German rulers, who were opponents of Philip.[21]

In the early 1560s, the upshot of the tensions with Cardinal Granvelle and the dissatisfaction among the nobles about the many decisions that were taken in Brussels without reference to them was the submission, in vain, of repeated complaints to Philip II. In 1563, the most important nobles, including Orange, Egmont and Horn, brought matters to a head by demanding the removal of Granvelle and by stepping down from their government posts. When Margaret of Parma, in her capacity as regent, also told Philip that she no longer had confidence in Granvelle, the king gave in and the cardinal left the Netherlands in 1564. While on paper this strengthened the position of the nobility, the king remained totally committed to his edicts against heresy and his policy of making government more professional and bureaucratic.

In December 1564, William of Orange made a lengthy speech in the Council of State in which he championed the principle of religious coexistence and freedom of conscience. A delegation from the Council of State led by Egmont travelled to Spain in an endeavour to persuade Philip in person to accommodate their wishes. The mission was unsuccessful. In October 1565, Philip let it be known – in what would later be called the Letters from the Segovia Woods – that the persecution of heretics had to continue unabated. Things rapidly went from bad to worse, and 1566 saw a critical escalation.[22]

At the end of 1565, members of the lesser nobility with a range of religious beliefs formed an association that they called the Compromise of Nobles.[23] They too had lost administrative and legal powers to the new professional civil servants and felt they had been driven into a corner. There was as yet no real collaboration with the higher nobles, who believed that their inferiors – who would not rule out resorting to violence – were too radical. William of Orange was, though, able to get the minor nobles to moderate their tone, and he channelled their protest into drawing up a petition.

In April 1566, some three hundred lesser nobles submitted a petition – which was indeed moderately worded – to Margaret of Parma. It was to become known as the Petition of the Nobles. In it, they asked her to suspend the anti-heresy edicts and convene the States General, which had not met since 1559. They were hoping to get support from the States General for a more tolerant policy, and they also wanted to see the restoration of at least some of the provinces' administrative powers so that their own influence would increase. The nobles did not attack the position of the king and his government; their petition was solely against the Inquisition. Legend has it that Margaret of Parma was very nervous when the petition was submitted to her, and her advisor Charles de Berlaymont tried to calm her down by saying, '*N'ayez pas peur, Madame, ce ne sont que des gueux*' ('*Fear* not, Madam, they're only beggars'). Shortly thereafter the lesser nobles adopted this name as a badge of honour and 'Beggars' became a synonym for those who turned against Spanish authority.[24] In the summer of 1566, a dozen minor nobles submitted a further petition to Margaret requesting general freedom of religion and expressing the desire to have the government put in the hands of elite nobles like Orange, Egmont and Horn – religious and political aspirations had come together.[25]

The regent, who now felt under pressure, promised to suspend the anti-heresy laws while a response from the king was awaited. Calvinist preachers were emboldened by the crumbling of central authority and started holding services openly in the countryside – hedge-preaching, as it was called. Throughout the summer of 1566, starting in the south and then spreading all over the country, huge numbers of people came to listen to Calvinist sermons in the fields and – to quote Israel – 'the surge of hedge-preaching released an accumulation of tension which had built up over four decades'.[26] It was only a small step from this to occupying church buildings and preparing them for services in accordance with other, modernizing beliefs. It was necessary, though, to strip churches of statues of saints and other 'papist superstitions'. That happened during an outbreak of iconoclasm that swept across the country in August and September 1566. This was not a rebellious plundering mass going from church to church. In fact, a relatively small minority efficiently purged church buildings, initially in the southern provinces and later on in the northern provinces too.[27]

It was striking that so little was done to obstruct this relatively small group of iconoclasts and in the north, in particular, many reacted passively. Apparently the majority of the population felt no great allegiance to existing ecclesiastical practice. The iconoclasm and the way it happened were primarily expressions of alienation from the old faith, its symbols, rituals and wealth. It was Calvinist leaders – ministers who were also town magistrates and lesser nobles – who initiated the iconoclasm. They were supported by sections of the population which at that time were faced not just with persecution for their faith, but with poverty and famine. The poor social and economic situation did not provoke the iconoclasm, but it did contribute to a radical and explosive mood among the people.[28]

Given these circumstances, the regent had no option but to accept the conciliatory proposals of Orange and his political associates, which meant that Protestant services would be permitted in the places where they were in fact already taking place. Margaret also appealed to Philip to convene the States General. In return, the association of lesser nobility was wound up. This agreement, the 'Accord' of 23 August 1566, proved extremely shaky and soon led to further confrontation. The regent decided to put an end to the unrest by using military force and Philip made it clear that this was what he expected of her. It was inevitable in such a climate of violent escalation that William of Orange's attempts to steer a middle course would come to grief. On the basis of the Accord, he negotiated local religious truces such that both Catholics and Protestants were allocated churches. Against the backdrop of an impending civil war, though, it soon became clear that there was no longer any scope for a conciliatory policy like this. Orange lost support, both in Brussels and among Calvinists, whom he did not want to help by supplying weapons. During the restoration of public order in Antwerp he even had a few iconoclasts hanged. Later, too, William of Orange would keep trying to reconcile implacable opponents. His position in the middle ground, so typical of him, became untenable, trapped between the two remaining possibilities: subjugation or violent revolt.

Meanwhile, Margaret of Parma's attempts to restore law and order by military means had been successful. There was no question of religious tolerance – the Protestant churches were closed – and she no longer talked about convening the States General. Sure of herself once more, in the spring of 1567 she requested the elite nobles to swear unconditional allegiance to the king. Egmont and Horn did so, but William of Orange refused and took refuge with his family in Germany.

The period from 1566 to 1567 was a key time in the build-up to the Revolt. Unrest increased in various social and religious groups. Yet there was no meeting of minds or any joint action; all that the different players had in common was their aversion to Philip II's policy, or certain aspects of it. Groenveld refers to a 'monstrous alliance' between the senior nobility, lesser aristocrats, citizens and the common people.[29] Some wanted restoration of their former privileges, others were concerned primarily about freedom of religion, and there were those who sought to make Calvinism the only permitted religious denomination. Orange had tried to calm the situation down and bring about freedom of religious conscience by mediating between the different groups, but he failed and in 1567 any compromise seemed to be further out of reach than ever. Spanish authority was restored and Philip sent the Duke of Alba to Brussels with the job of ridding the Netherlands of heresy once and for all. Since he left in 1559, Philip had concentrated primarily on the struggle with the Turks in the Mediterranean, but now his priority shifted to the north. According to historian Guido de Bruin, from a Spanish perspective, the Netherlands emerged as a touchstone for the way the empire should develop. The outcome of the conflict with the Dutch insurgents would, it seemed, determine the future of Philip's imperium.[30]

Radicalization, unsuccessful moderation and the road to the Republic (1567–88)

In August 1567, Alba arrived in the Netherlands with a large army of Spanish troops. One of his first measures was to establish a new court that would deal with the prosecution of rebels in the Netherlands.[31] Over the next few years, this Council of Troubles, soon called the Council of Blood in the vernacular, sentenced over a thousand people to death and expropriated the possessions of nine thousand citizens. The Counts of Egmont and Horn, who at the end of 1566 had obeyed Margaret of Parma's summons, sworn loyalty to the king and helped her to restore public order, were prominent victims of Alba's repressive policies. They were beheaded in the Grand Place in Brussels in 1568. Orange, who was stripped of his stadholdership in 1567 by Philip II, lost all his possessions and was also deeply afflicted when his twelve-year-old son Philip William was taken hostage and removed to Spain. He was not released until 1596. Tens of thousands fled the country, including many prominent citizens and representatives of the lesser nobility.

As well as prosecuting insurgents, Alba was tasked with strengthening centralized authority at the expense of the provinces and sidelining the States General. He had also been instructed to achieve a final resolution of the tax collection issue to the satisfaction of the Spanish. To that end, in 1569 he tried to introduce three taxes: a 1 per cent tax on assets, a 5 per cent tax on real estate transactions and a 10 per cent turnover tax on trade in movable goods. He had little success – in fact, the only effect was to increase resistance to his policies.

In 1568, William of Orange's first attempt to return by force of arms came to nothing. His brothers Louis and Adolph of Nassau initially achieved success in the north (at the Battle of Heiligerlee in 1568), but were soon afterwards defeated mercilessly by Alba. Orange himself tried an attack on Upper Guelders (the present North Limburg), but the absence of support among the inhabitants, lack of money and Alba's military strategy meant that he gained no ground at all and had to disband his troops. In his own words, William of Orange had not unleashed an armed revolt against the king. He wanted to return to the Netherlands not as a rebel against the lawful authority, but as someone who took a stand against the king's bad advisors. They, and not the king himself, were responsible for the poor governance and the conflicts of the preceding years. His motto was 'pro rege, lege et grege' ('for the king, the law and the people'), and so he presented his dispute as being not with Philip, but with Alba. In later years Orange was to revert to this line of reasoning in pamphlets and correspondence, in an attempt to get more support for his actions.[32]

The only threat from insurgents in the years immediately afterwards was from the Sea Beggars, a heterogeneous group of exiled nobles, seafarers, citizens and others. Armed with letters of marque from William of Orange, they carried out attacks and incursions from the sea. They also played a role in Orange's plans to risk another assault after the disastrous campaign of 1568. As before, William of Orange planned an attack from different directions; the Sea Beggars from the sea, Huguenots who supported Orange from France, and Orange himself from the east. Again things did not go to plan. The Sea Beggars, roaming around at sea after Queen Elizabeth I had refused them further access to English harbours, conquered the port of Den Briel in Holland on 1 April 1572 – more by luck than judgement and earlier than Orange had wanted. The mood among the population was now more anti-Spanish than in 1568, and other towns in Holland and Zeeland soon fell into the Beggars' hands. These bridgeheads were to form the basis for the ultimately successful outcome of the Revolt, while the struggle in the south and east once again went badly for the rebels. This was where Alba had concentrated his troops, and he had superior military strength. The decisive factor was that the advance from France failed to materialize – the Huguenots who were to have marched to Orange's side were slaughtered in the infamous St Bartholomew's Day massacre in Paris in August 1572.

Things went better in the provinces of Holland and Zeeland in the summer of 1572, and both fell almost wholly into the insurgents' hands. The States of Holland met in August in Dordrecht (The Hague was not yet safe). As he had done in 1568, William of Orange did not explicitly direct the rebels against the king and he tried to maintain the appearance of legitimacy. Acting as though Philip had not appointed another stadholder of Holland, Zeeland and Utrecht long before, the provincial states declared that William of Orange was still the king's representative in these provinces. A new feature though – and this was to remain the case later in the Republic – was that the stadholder was now given his authority by the provincial states. In Dordrecht, the States of Holland went one step further and recognized Orange as 'head and protector' of the whole of the Netherlands, as though Alba had not been appointed governor by the king. In making this move it was not the states' intention to create a subordinate position for itself under Orange. The German historian Mörke points out that they wanted a powerful partner in the person of the stadholder, who could drive Alba back and keep the Calvinist Beggars under control.[33] At the same time, the states did not want to relinquish any rights to the stadholder. That required a permanent process of negotiation and demarcation of powers between the stadholder and states. This situation would continue to exist in the Republic, and lead to considerable tensions.

The removal of the Huguenots gave Alba a free hand in the south. He started a campaign directed towards the north, where he inflicted painful defeats on the rebels. The brutality with which the populations of the conquered towns were treated was designed to dishearten the inhabitants of the town whose turn it was next and deter them from putting up any resistance. Mechelen, Zutphen and Naarden became synonymous with Alba's merciless strategy. Hundreds of residents were murdered after Zutphen fell, and virtually the entire population of Naarden was slaughtered at the

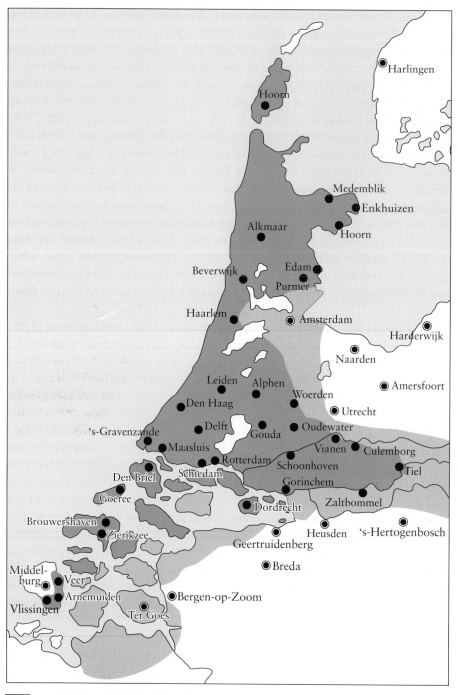

Map 2 Insurgent areas in December 1572.

Entirely in Orangist hands

Partly in Orangist hands

● Orangist towns and cities

◉ Royalist towns and cities

beginning of December 1572. In the summer of 1573, after a siege lasting seven months, Alba finally captured Haarlem, and in so doing drove a wedge between the rebellious towns of Holland. But that was as far as he got. In the short term, Alba's cruel methods were not without success, but in the longer term they proved damaging to Spanish authority because the will to resist grew stronger. Many towns in Holland were in low-lying areas with abundant water, and this was a strategic disadvantage for the Spanish. The insurgents only needed to breach a few dikes or open some sluices to flood large areas. This was a 'weapon' the Spanish besiegers could do little to counteract.

Finance was an even greater problem for Alba. Suppressing the rebels was a costly business, and so too was the war against the Turks that Philip had meanwhile started in the Mediterranean. From time to time during the Dutch Revolt, Spanish pressure would increase and then decrease again, depending on whether Philip was also waging war elsewhere. The huge cost of fighting the Turks meant that there was little or no pay for the soldiers in the Netherlands and they eventually mutinied. The Spanish advance became bogged down in the autumn of 1573 and Philip recalled Alba to Spain. Alba's successor, Luis de Requesens y Zúñiga, pursued a more moderate policy and was prepared to engage in a dialogue with the rebel provinces. And indeed, negotiations between him on the one side and the States of Holland and Orange on the other began in 1575. The Dutch let it be known that they wanted to be loyal subjects of the king, but only on condition that the king permitted Protestantism and would recognize the old 'rights and privileges' of the provinces. Philip II was not willing to consent to these requirements, so the probability of an agreement was virtually zero.

Nevertheless, conciliation did not appear to be out of the question. Short of money, the Spanish did not have their chronically underpaid and therefore mutinous troops under control. In these circumstances, the desire to see the back of the Spanish soldiers grew stronger in all the Dutch provinces, and Philip felt obliged to arrange a breathing space for financial reasons. In 1576, the Dutch provinces entered into a provisional settlement called the Pacification of Ghent.[34] The royalist and the rebel provinces had a meeting of minds when it came to the demand that Spanish troops must leave the Netherlands. On the issue of religion, they agreed that the status quo would be a starting point for a later definitive solution. Catholicism remained the only recognized religion in the south, and Calvinism had the same status in the insurgent provinces. However, dissidents would be left in peace in all the provinces. The States General, operating independently, set itself the goal of finding solutions to the political and religious issues for all the provinces jointly. Requesens died suddenly in 1576 and the new governor – John of Austria – had no choice but to accept the Pacification of Ghent; Philip II also recognized that he was obliged to tolerate it for a while.

The Pacification appeared to improve the chances of a moderate approach to the political and religious problems. William of Orange, whose goal had always been to maintain the cohesion of the seventeen provinces and embed religious tolerance in the Netherlands, tried everything within his power to strengthen the shaky basis of the Pacification. That proved impossible. John was waiting for the moment when Spain could seize the initiative again and force Holland and Zeeland into isolation. His interpretation of the Pacification – that the position of the Catholic Church could not be weakened – sent out the same signal and so, in no time, Holland and Zeeland, under the leadership of Orange, were engaged in a face-off with John.

As well as this, the moderates, who had built a consensus behind the Pacification, were a heterogeneous group, and the elites in the south were prepared to adopt an accommodating stance towards the new governor. Their objectives went no further than the senior nobles had wanted in the 1560s: a strengthening of their own power in the central organization in Brussels, an independent position for the Netherlands in the Habsburg Empire and the retention of Catholicism, but with a reduction in persecution. That was no longer sufficient for Holland and Zeeland. They wanted to see restrictions on the powers of the central authority, separation of the Netherlands and a dominant position for Calvinism.[35] A compromise between these two positions was effectively ruled out.

Yet when John went on the warpath, the provinces reached agreement again and the States General declared that the governor was the common enemy.[36] At the same time, they recognized Matthias of Austria as the new governor of the Netherlands. This was a revolutionary move since governors were appointed by the king. However, the States General hoped that Philip would accept Matthias because he was his nephew. William of Orange tried desperately to cling to his goals of unity and religious freedom, but radical Calvinists and many Catholics were not prepared to compromise. Orange's proposal, dating from 1578, under which permission would be given wherever at least a hundred families asked to be allowed to practise their religion freely, thus had no chance of being implemented. On the contrary, in many towns the confrontation between Catholics and Calvinists was such that the conflicts were more like a civil war. The chances for the solution that Orange was seeking quickly evaporated in the increasing polarization between Calvinists and Catholics, as well as within the group of moderates. Then, when John – with fresh troops from Spain – forced a few southern provinces to join his side, it was clear that the Pacification of Ghent had failed for good.

At the beginning of January 1579, the southern provinces of Artois, Hainaut and Lilloise Flanders united in the Union of Arras and started peace talks with Spain, while later that month a number of northern provinces joined forces in the Union of Utrecht. This created a defensive alliance against Spain in which joint and unanimous decisions were to be taken about war and peace. The provinces would continue to take decisions about 'domestic' matters, including religious questions. Holland, Zeeland, Utrecht and the Groningen Ommelanden were among the first signatories, and gradually other provinces joined them. William of Orange was not a proponent of the Union. He did not embrace it until May 1579, and only then on condition that the Union would strive for unification of the Netherlands and freedom of religion. Even though at that moment these objectives were further away than ever, Orange did not give up.

Now that moderation had failed and the north and south had been driven apart by the Unions of Utrecht and Arras, the struggle with Spain intensified. There was no longer any middle ground, and the choice was to support either the king or the Revolt. William of Orange took the initiative and asked the Duke of Anjou, the French king's brother, for military help. Philip excommunicated William of Orange shortly afterwards, and in 1581 the States General declared in the Act of Abjuration that it no longer recognized Philip as the ruler. This put an irrevocable end to the position that the rebels were not acting against the king, but against those who carried out his policy so poorly.

The States General, which now contained representatives of essentially all the provinces of the Union of Utrecht, brought in the Duke of Anjou as the new sovereign and the break between Spain and the provinces joined by the Union of Utrecht became definitive in 1580–1. Looking back, the Union of Utrecht and the Act of Abjuration mark the beginning of an independent Dutch federal republic, but at the time that was not the intention. As we saw earlier, it was not until 1588 that the Republic actually emerged, and even then it happened more or less in passing.

The Union of Utrecht proved unable to contribute much to stopping the advance of the Spanish under John's successor, Alexander Farnese, Duke of Parma. Philip, no longer plagued by a war on southern fronts, now had his hands – and money – free for a new offensive in the north. The southern provinces soon fell into Spanish hands. This was not due solely to the military force that Spain built up under Parma; the weakness of the rebel provinces was also a factor. The experiment with Anjou as the new ruler came to nothing. Rather than providing support against Spain, he proved to be interested primarily in increasing his own power. He quickly returned to France – in 1583 – without accomplishing his mission, and he died there in 1584. Soon afterwards, on 10 July 1584, William of Orange was murdered in Delft, and with his death the only person who was able to keep the divided provinces together was removed from the stage.[37]

William of Orange has gone down in history as the 'Father of his Country' and hence the founder of the Dutch nation. This is not incorrect, but when determining his historical significance we should bear in mind that his objective was very different from a Northern Netherlandish republic. During the 1570s, he became the key figure in a revolt, which was not what he wanted either. Initially, he was aiming above all for unity of the seventeen Dutch provinces under the Spanish crown, with influential positions for himself and other elite Dutch nobles. This later evolved into a union of provinces under a monarch, who would have to be William of Orange. The break with Philip II developed only gradually. Another important point is that the Pacification of Ghent was in line with his objectives, whereas the Union of Utrecht was not. Even after the Union of Utrecht had been signed, Orange did not abandon his goal of unity and he continued to hope for compromise, however, this was no longer realistic by then. His efforts to attain religious pluriformity and tolerance on the basis of equality also failed.

Viewed in this light, it could be argued that Orange failed to achieve his most important goals. He did, though, have a significant impact on the Revolt and its – unintended – outcome. Van Deursen concludes his biographical portrait of William of Orange with the comment that 'less than half of what William had hoped for' was achieved. 'But that smaller part continued to bear the stamp of its instigator.'[38] As a moderate man in the middle ground, he brought about collaboration between divergent groups, he adapted his approach pragmatically according to the situation and circumstances, as Mörke put it, and he became a key player in his own right. He also employed modern propaganda to create an awareness of Dutch unity. Orange's legacy

Figure 1 *William I, Prince of Orange*, Adriaen Thomasz. Key, 1579. Rijksmuseum Amsterdam.

was to become manifest in the political structure of the Republic: a form of government in which the rights and powers were divided in a complicated way between the stadholder, the provincial states and the States General. Serious tensions were to flare up repeatedly in this administrative arrangement, but it did provide the basis of the Republic's political system until the end of the eighteenth century.

Orange's legacy also made itself felt in the issue of religion, because a unique form of freedom of conscience was created under his leadership. State and church were not united, as was generally the case elsewhere in Europe. William of Orange laid the foundation for the policy of tolerance, which was a distinctive characteristic of the Republic, but the Dutch Reformed Church was the only one to be publicly permitted. Anyone in pursuit of power and influence had to be a member. Other denominations or religions were not officially allowed; adherence was tolerated, but not in public. This was not freedom of religion as Orange had wanted it, but for the times it went a long way.

These longer term effects could not be foreseen at the time of his death in 1584. On the contrary, in 1584 and for years thereafter it looked as though the achievements of the

Revolt would be lost. Even before Orange's death, large parts of Flanders, Groningen and Drenthe had fallen into Spanish hands. Brabant and parts of the eastern provinces followed between 1584 and 1590, so that the territory of the Revolt was reduced to the west and centre of the country (see Map 3, p. 29). One town after another fell to the Duke of Parma, who was a good general and an adroit politician and administrator. He was able to get towns on his side through his amnesty policy. Religious freedom was unthinkable under his rule, but he did offer Protestants the opportunity to sell up and leave town. Under these circumstances, many towns opened their gates without a shot being fired, with the result that the south became peaceful and Calvinism disappeared. In the north and the west, on the other hand, Calvinism spread without Catholicism being driven out. Although Catholic church services were officially banned, Catholics were still in the majority and, unlike Protestants in the south, the authorities could not throw them out of the country.

Parma's conquests – particularly the taking of Antwerp in August 1585 – also had major economic implications. The insurgent provinces retaliated by blockading the Scheldt, and Antwerp's importance as a port was lost for years. The exodus of Protestants also contributed to the city's decline. Over a four-year period, some 38,000 people – more than half the population – left for the north. Streams of migrants headed in the same direction from other towns and cities in the south. There was meteoric growth in the number of residents in many towns in Holland at that time. Thirty thousand immigrants settled in Amsterdam alone. The population of Leiden doubled to 26,000 and other Northern Netherlandish towns also grew by a factor of two or more. Initially, the mass departure from the south was prompted by religion, but the deteriorating economic conditions and the boom in the north saw people leaving for financial reasons too. This haemorrhaging of people and skills from the south represented a huge economic shot in the arm for the north, as we shall see later in this chapter.

The deaths of the Duke of Anjou and William of Orange again raised the urgent issue of who could be offered the sovereignty of the rebel provinces. As we saw earlier, the support that Anjou was supposed to provide had not materialized and, in view of Parma's successes, international help was a more urgent matter than ever. The French King Henry III refused to send the requested military support, so the States General looked to England and Queen Elizabeth I for help. She watched Parma's advance in the Netherlands with sorrow, but on the other hand she had her own agenda, and the independence of the rebel provinces was not on it. Her objective was the implementation of the old Pacification of Ghent: the Netherlands under Spain, but with enough autonomy to contain Spanish power on the continent. Given this goal, she was prepared to provide limited support. In 1585 she sent Robert Dudley, Earl of Leicester, to the insurgent provinces with troops and money. But, like the experiment with the Duke of Anjou, it was not a success. Leicester had no feel for relationships in the Netherlands, supported the tough Calvinist line, and became increasingly entangled in a power struggle with the States of Holland. In the end he lost Elizabeth's support too, and left the Netherlands unceremoniously in 1587.[39]

The fact that Leicester came off worst in the conflict with Holland was due primarily to Johan van Oldenbarnevelt, who worked his way up to become the most powerful man in Holland and the emerging Republic after Orange's death. He laid the foundation for this position very soon after William of Orange was murdered. Since 1576, he had been the Pensionary of Rotterdam. It was not a top job, but one that gave him a place in the powerful States of Holland as his city's representative. He established contact with William of Orange, organized his funeral in 1584, and carried out a number of important administrative tasks on behalf of the States of Holland. In 1586, when Leicester was trying to extend his power and the States of Holland were looking for a counterweight, they invited Oldenbarnevelt to become Advocate of Holland. Until then, advocates of provinces had had a supporting, civil service role. They represented the nobility in meetings of the provincial states, were their senior spokesmen and took care of correspondence.

Before Oldenbarnevelt accepted his appointment he insisted on a significant expansion of his powers. His tasks were to include setting the agenda for the States of Holland's meetings, writing draft resolutions and formulating the decisions that were taken. In addition, all contact with foreign countries had to go through him and he would become Holland's most important representative in the States General. The States of Holland agreed and a great deal of power came into the hands of the new advocate of the province.[40] Oldenbarnevelt became Leicester's most important adversary. On behalf of Holland, he fought a hard battle for power in the Republic – a fight that had some of the features of a civil war. Oldenbarnevelt settled things magnificently to the advantage of Holland and himself. After Leicester's impotent departure in 1587, it was clear that attracting foreign rulers to take over sovereignty of the Netherlands had failed.

In response, the provincial states of the northern provinces, with Holland in the lead, finished what they had started with the Act of Abjuration in 1581, and in 1588 finally took sovereignty themselves. They justified this by arguing that the states traditionally had sovereignty and had assigned it to a count (in Holland) or a duke (in Guelders). That same ancient right – so this line of reasoning contended – also included the right to turn against the count or duke if he harmed the province's interests. This was not, therefore, a case of a revolutionary declaration of independence or a new form of government. On the contrary, it was a matter of emphasizing the continuity of the provinces' own freedoms and privileges, and thus confirmation of the powers of towns, cities and nobles through the provincial states. In so doing, the states also assumed the rank of the former count, duke or lord whom they, in the person of Philip II, had stripped of authority in 1581 through the Act of Abjuration. In April 1588, they released the civil servants from their oath of allegiance to Leicester and these officials then swore an oath of allegiance to the provincial states. This can be considered as the actual creation of the Republic of the United Provinces,[41] and it laid the foundations for a unique political structure that would take shape in the years ahead.

Many of the developments during the Revolt had not been planned beforehand, and the same was true of the creation of the Republic. It was not proclaimed. It was simply the consequence of decisions deemed to be inevitable in a long-standing area of strain about provincial rights and powers in which tensions, sometimes of an extreme nature, arose inside and between the provinces. Holland set the tone in that process, and under the leadership of Oldenbarnevelt acquired the leading position in the emerging Republic.

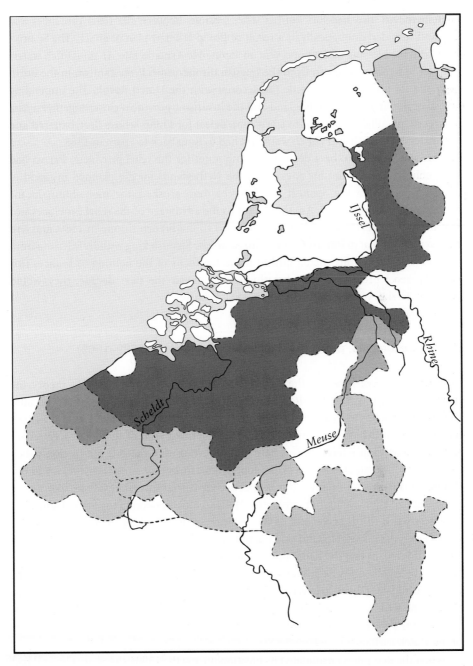

Territory controlled by Farnese in 1581

Spanish conquests up to 1583

Spanish conquests up to 1589

Map 3 Spanish conquests in the 1580s.

Oldenbarnevelt also had luck on his side. Tensions between the rebel provinces and England subsided dramatically as a result of Philip II's new plan of attack. The Spanish king, with the blessing of the pope, sent an 'invincible Armada' into Anglo–Dutch waters in order to remove Elizabeth from the English throne, crush Protestantism in the north once and for all, and finally settle the account with the Dutch Revolt. The impending arrival of the Armada drove England and the insurgent provinces closer together again. The resultant collaboration led to a crushing defeat for Philip, whose fleet, battered and decimated by English and Dutch warships, had to limp back to Spain in 1588.

This would prove to be a decisive turning point for the rebel provinces. Parma had been obliged to interrupt his advance in the Netherlands for the planned invasion of England, and when the Spanish naval forces were crushed, the momentum in the Netherlands also weakened. Another factor to the advantage of the rebel provinces was that the Protestant Henry of Navarre ascended to the French throne in 1589, and this represented a threat to Philip's Catholic mission. The Spanish king withdrew Parma from the Netherlands and instructed him to move the focus of the fighting to France. This gave the rebel provinces some breathing space. Over the next decade, they would recapture territory and give the Republic a stable basis.

Military successes, political consolidation and truce (1589–1609)

The new balance of power in the young Republic gradually crystallized. In theory, the power structure was clear. The Republic consisted of seven sovereign provinces because the provincial states had assumed sovereignty for themselves. The States General was the federal organ in which the provinces came together and each of them had a veto over matters of common interest. It was here that decisions were made about foreign policy and war, but the States General also developed into a forum for domestic issues – without this being laid down formally – that was above provincial sovereignty. On paper, all the provinces had equal rights, but in practice Holland took the lead in the States General. It paid nearly two-thirds of the cost of waging war and it was where the most money was made. From the outset, Holland was the only province that was entirely free of Spanish troops. This meant that the Republic's actual power base lay in the States of Holland, and thus in the eighteen towns and cities and the representatives of the aristocracy in this province. Initially, Oldenbarnevelt controlled everything within the States of Holland. To put it in modern terms, he was prime minister, minister of finance and minister of foreign affairs.[42] The power was concentrated in the Binnenhof in The Hague – currently the seat of the Dutch parliament – where the States General and the States of Holland met.

When the Republic consolidated its position during the 1590s, the States General had seven members and so there were seven votes. Voting was done in a set order: Gelderland, Holland, Zeeland, Utrecht, Friesland, Overijssel and Groningen. In view of its modest significance, Drenthe was not a member of the States General and only had the status of a county. The areas conquered later on in Brabant, Flanders and present-day Limburg were not members of the States General either. They were referred to as the Generality

Lands and were governed directly from The Hague. No matter how strong Holland's position was, however, it was impossible to rule the Republic with an iron fist from the centre. The decision-making process was always one of negotiation, of consensus building. People who had not mastered the art of 'persuasion' did not go far in the governance of the Republic.[43]

Maurice of Nassau, Prince of Orange (1567–1625), like Oldenbarnevelt, was inextricably linked to the initial successes and consolidation of the Republic.[44] Maurice was seventeen when his father, William of Orange, was murdered. The States of Holland and Zeeland appointed him as their stadholder in 1585, when he was eighteen, among other things to prevent Leicester from getting his hands on too much power. Unlike his father, who was both the political and military leader, Maurice only had command of the military. The States General had supreme command, which in fact came down to Holland and Oldenbarnevelt. Maurice strengthened his own position, though, in 1590 and 1591 by taking on the stadholdership of Utrecht, Gelderland and Overijssel. With his cousin William Louis of Nassau-Dillenburg (1560–1620), stadholder of Friesland and later also Groningen, he achieved remarkable military successes in the 1590s. This was not due solely to the breathing space that the Republic enjoyed because Philip II was actively involved in other wars. The Dutch military machine had also become more professional. Together he and William Louis modernized the army's organization and command structure and made the military strategies more 'scientific'. Above all, the systematic and carefully prepared sieges of towns and cities were successful and internationally renowned. Irrespective of whether or not the concept of 'military revolution' is applicable here, there is no doubt that – thanks to these developments – the Republic's army was the pre-eminent example of military competence in Europe for several decades.[45]

The Dutch historian Van Deursen writes that the period from 1588 to 1598 was the one in which 'the Revolt finally succeeded'.[46] The first major military success was the conquest of Breda in 1590, executed in spectacular fashion by smuggling soldiers inside the defences in a peat barge. Breda was soon followed by other towns and cities in the Republic, and this extended Dutch territory to approximately the present borders of the Netherlands, except for Limburg as it now is and the eastern part of Brabant. In 1594, Groningen and the Ommelanden became the seventh of the Republic's provinces. The dynamic of the military successes dissipated at the end of 1595, in part for financial reasons, but Spain no longer had the strength to mount a counteroffensive. The war with France had soaked up too much money, and in 1596, Philip went bankrupt for the third time, after earlier bankruptcies in 1557 and 1575. As a result of Oldenbarnevelt's diplomatic manoeuvrings, the Republic also achieved its first major foreign political success – the Triple Alliance with England and France in 1596, in which the three states formed a joint front against Spain. There were no actual combined operations, but this collaboration did ensure that Spain's options were subject to further constraints and it gave the Republic a significant window for its own consolidation.

Internationally, luck was on the Republic's side, and good cooperation – between Oldenbarnevelt as political leader on the one hand and Maurice and William Louis as stadholders and military commanders of their provinces on the other – contributed to

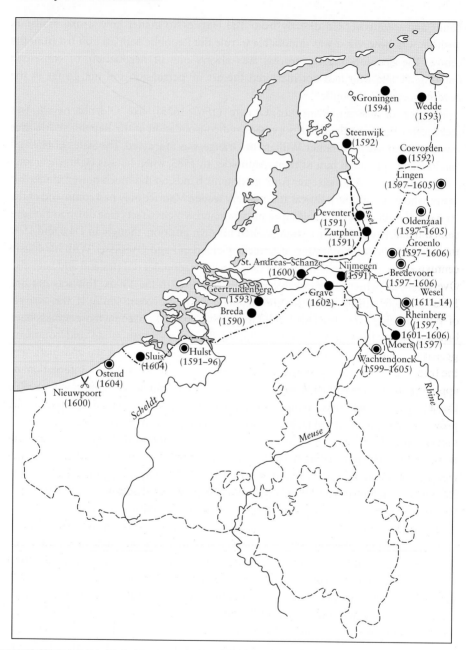

-------- Line of defence with redoubts built in 1605–6

—·—·—·— Front line in 1607–21

● Towns and cities that fell to the Netherlands, with date

◉ Towns and cities captured by the Netherlands and later retaken by the Spanish, with dates

Map 4 Military developments in the 1590s.

the success of these years. From the outset, Oldenbarnevelt played a major part in strengthening the position of Maurice, twenty years his junior, and for a long time they complemented each other extremely effectively. The roles of stadholder and Grand Pensionary of Holland – as the Advocate of Holland came to be called after 1621 – would also remain of key importance during the later Republic, and there were no infrequent disputes between stadholder and grand pensionary. One or other of them acquired superior power depending on their personal character, internal balances of power in the Republic and their success or failure in international affairs. Maurice and Oldenbarnevelt were also to be at daggers drawn, and in 1619, this actually led to Oldenbarnevelt's execution. This and other fierce quarrels are analysed in more detail in the next chapter. We are concerned here only with a general description of the two roles.

As we saw earlier, a stadholder's original office was as a deputy of the sovereign. This ceased to exist when rulers disappeared from the Republic, but the provincial states, as the new bearers of sovereignty, continued to appoint stadholders. In the late sixteenth century, it became standard practice for the provinces of Holland, Zeeland, Utrecht, Overijssel and Gelderland to appoint the same one. The same went for Groningen and Friesland in the north. Usually the stadholder in the five provinces above was a descendant of William of Orange, while the two northern provinces opted for an heir of Orange's brother John of Nassau-Dillenburg. Stadholders' powers differed from province to province, but generally speaking they held the highest military rank as captain general of the troops. In the western provinces the stadholder also had substantial influence on the appointment of local officials. Despite their exalted background and their power bases in the army and navy, though, the stadholders formally remained subordinate to the provinces that appointed them. The same was true of the grand pensionary, who was the second highest official in Holland after the stadholder. He could also emerge as a powerful man, but his success in this regard depended very much on his character and the circumstances. He had to work harder on acquiring standing and influence than the stadholder and, unlike the stadholder, in the Republic he was only the representative of the strongest province, which could give rise to friction with the others.

The potential for disagreement between Stadholder Maurice and Advocate of Holland Oldenbarnevelt was to develop into a serious conflict at the time of the Twelve Years' Truce (1609–21), but during the 1590s the two of them and William Louis were the ideal triumvirate to strengthen the young Republic. Diplomatic successes followed the conquests of the first half of the 1590s. When France made peace with Spain in 1598, and England looked as though it too would stop fighting them, Oldenbarnevelt was able to get additional covert support for the Republic from France and dissuade England from making peace with Spain. These were diplomatic results of considerable stature, and nobody else in the Republic operated on the international stage with Oldenbarnevelt's ease and prestige. It was through these accords with France and England that he was able to prevent the Republic from having to seek peace with Spain or use force to defend its territory.

Around the turn of the century, peace was still a long way off. At that time it was unthinkable that Spain would recognize the sovereignty of the provinces, and there was no solution to the religious question in sight either. Spain wanted to see the old rights of the

Catholic Church restored, while the Calvinists continued to demand exclusive rights for themselves. There were also internal considerations which meant that peace was still an unattractive proposition for the Republic. The tensions between and within provinces were too great, and would probably have led to an outburst as soon as the enemy would have disappeared from the scene. Philip II died in 1598, but even that brought about almost no reduction in the enmity between Spain and the Republic. Shortly before his death, Philip had married his daughter Isabella to the governor in Brussels, Albert of Austria, the Holy Roman Emperor's brother, and given her the seventeen Dutch provinces as a dowry. Philip formally withdrew from the Netherlands through the Act of Cession, but the new rulers in Brussels continued to be financially and militarily dependent on Spain. The man who had personified the enemy for decades might have gone, but the war continued unabated.

In 1600, at Oldenbarnevelt's instigation, the Republic mounted an expedition to the Flemish coast, where privateers sailing out of Dunkirk were causing considerable damage to Dutch shipping. Oldenbarnevelt hoped that this campaign would also help to incite the Flemish to rebel against Brussels. Maurice and William Louis were not at all happy at the idea of a military adventure of this kind, because it would leave the Republic too little to defend itself and they feared encirclement of the south. With great reluctance, Maurice set off for Flanders, where he narrowly won the Battle of Nieuwpoort. He returned soon afterwards without accomplishing his mission.

The Battle of Nieuwpoort would prove to be a turning point. Had Maurice lost and been taken prisoner, it would have jeopardized the very existence of the Republic. He had escaped by the skin of his teeth. It had also become clear that the south could not be part of republican ambitions. Oldenbarnevelt had staked a lot on the expedition, but Maurice had been proved right. Nieuwpoort was the first major dent in the relationship between the cautious Maurice and the less risk averse Oldenbarnevelt.[47] It would be going too far to claim that this was already the beginning of the later deep-seated conflicts, but damage was without doubt done to the trust between the two men. The relationship was to be tested again soon afterwards, when Oldenbarnevelt organized a new expedition to the south, which rapidly foundered.

Over the next few years, the Republic's prime concern was defending its own territory, and the Spanish were able to regain the initiative. In 1604, England too made peace with Spain and the Republic was on its own. Evaporating international support, lack of military successes, shortage of money and war weariness were some of the many factors that pointed towards peace talks. And yet there was no common desire for peace on the Republican side.[48] In the northeast, people wanted to put an end to the attacks and plundering by Spanish soldiers, Friesland and most of the towns and cities in Holland expected peace to bring economic benefits, and Oldenbarnevelt also began to steer a course towards peace. Maurice and William Louis were among the hawks. They feared that Catholic Spain would seize upon peace as an opportunity to regroup. Amsterdam and the province of Zeeland were also against ending the war. Negotiations nevertheless started early in 1608, but the positions on sovereignty and the religious question were too far apart to achieve peace. Spain also demanded that the Republic stop trading with the Far East and suspend its plans to found a West India Company.

A truce was the most that could be agreed. In April 1609, the two sides ac status quo and agreed to stop the war for twelve years. There was also an un that the sovereignty of the seven provinces would be recognized 'for always', which was interpreted by the Republic as 'in perpetuity' and by Spain as 'for the duration of the truce'. Trade with the Orient was not contested, but the Republic did promise not to set up a West India Company during the truce. The Republic retained complete control over matters of religion but failed to get agreement to freedom of religious conscience for Protestants in the south. Spanish troops would also remain in the south. In so far as the Pacification of Ghent had not been superseded long before, the truce implied further confirmation of the divide between north and south.

The truce began in the spring of 1609 and lasted, as agreed, until 1621. During these years the estrangement between Maurice and Oldenbarnevelt, who had been completely at odds with each other during the truce negotiations, reached its dramatic nadir. The differences of opinion became so severe that the Republic actually came to the brink of civil war.

Economic dynamism and expansion

Brief reference was made earlier to the economic potential of the infant Republic, specifically the self-propelling dynamic of population growth, urbanization, expansion of industry and the commercialization of arable farming, livestock farming and fishing. This encompassed the development of a trading network, where Antwerp had grown into a centre for luxury goods and Amsterdam had become a market for commodities – grain and timber from the Baltic and wine and salt from France and the Iberian Peninsula. This was a period when Europe's economic centre of gravity shifted from the Mediterranean to northwestern Europe and the Atlantic zone, and the Netherlands really cashed in on its position on the crossroads of the north-south and east-west trading and shipping routes. At the same time, it made a significant contribution to moving this centre of gravity to the northwest through its own economic expansion.[49]

Grain imports were a major stimulus of the Republic's synergetic commercial vitality. This development started with the late medieval rise in sea level and the cutting of peat in the Netherlands, which resulted in compaction of the soil. In consequence, the land became boggier and unsuitable for growing grain. Amsterdam merchants started importing Baltic grain as early as the fifteenth century, and during the sixteenth century Amsterdam became the heart of the European grain market. There was consequently almost always enough grain for domestic consumption in the Netherlands. At the same time it gave new initiatives in agricultural production a shot in the arm. Horticulture and industrial crops such as hemp, flax and oilseeds rose in importance, and large areas of arable land were converted into grazing for livestock. The self-reinforcing factors of population growth, bigger markets as a result of urbanization, expanding industry and rising prices created a lucrative agricultural diversity. Economic growth was interrupted temporarily by the Revolt and the military confrontations in the 1570s, but once armed conflict in Holland came to an end, the rise of prosperity resumed in the west. It heralded a period of economic expansion that did not end until the middle of the seventeenth century. This did not apply to the much less fertile eastern regions of the country, where there were only modest increases in prosperity, in part as a result of armed conflict that continued much longer and flared up regularly.

Demand for domestic agricultural products had risen to such an extent by the first half of the sixteenth century that a process of land reclamation started in Holland – a landscape dominated by water. This in turn became part of the dynamic of economic development. For many years the battle with water had been a matter of defence against flooding. Now, however, land was also being reclaimed. This allowed agricultural production to increase and also prompted the start of a technical development – the design and construction of windmills – that the Republic took to unrivalled heights. As early as the mid-sixteenth century there was a substantial increase in the number of drained hectares. After a temporary decline in the first decades of the Revolt, land reclamation activities continued at a faster pace after 1590 (see Map 6, p. 84).

Some of this reclamation was undone as a consequence of peat harvesting, which created lakes of various sizes in the lower-lying part of the Netherlands. Peat-cutting had been very widespread from the Middle Ages onwards, and was expanded in the sixteenth century. Technical innovations also made the process more intensive, and the upshot was a supply of relatively cheap energy. A beneficial side effect of peat extraction was the creation of a branched canal system in the both the west and north of the country. This represented a substantial expansion of the transport network, which in turn helped boost economic growth. As with land reclamation, substantial investment came from the towns and cities, which was made possible in part by the confiscation of land owned by the Catholic Church in the rebel provinces. When the province of Groningen became part of the Republic in 1594, for example, the extensive possessions of monasteries and convents were soon expropriated. Investors joined together to form peat companies to operate this lucrative business.

The result of these confiscations, which after 1588 also included land taken from senior nobles living in the south who had remained loyal to the king, was that more and more land was now owned by people living in towns and cities. This had been going on in Holland for some time, and since the sixteenth century the land owned by urban dwellers exceeded that of the nobility and the clergy. One reason underlying this urban preponderance was the relative weakness of the nobility, and so it was easy for an 'open, modern-looking bourgeois society' to develop. According to economic historians Jan de Vries and Ad van der Woude, independence, individuality and rationality were part and parcel of the mind-set of the population of Holland during the Republic.[50] This urban and bourgeois ascendancy was to become even more marked as a result of the Revolt. Roman Catholic clergy were no longer a factor, and in the ranks of the senior nobles – always rather thin on the ground in the north – only Orange-Nassau and Nassau-Dietz had survived. The minor nobility had also lost out in terms of numbers and influence, although their position in eastern provinces such as Gelderland and Overijssel had remained relatively strong.

Urban dominance was clear to see, particularly in Holland. The distribution of seats in the States of Holland changed during the Revolt, and the upshot was that eighteen of the nineteen seats (previously six) were reserved for that number of towns and cities, and only one for the aristocracy (previously also one). Towns and cities in the eastern provinces had about half the seats, so there was an extremely strong urban hold on power in the political structure of the Republic as a whole. City culture did not end at the city gates, and there were strong and observable ties between built-up areas and the surrounding countryside. This interaction was promoted by the relatively short distances and the good access to towns and cities. It should always be borne in mind, though, that there were significant differences between the prosperous provinces in the west and the much poorer regions in the east.

Herring fishing, also centred in Holland, was an important element in the growth of the economy. Catches were more than enough for the domestic market, and the lion's share was exported to the Baltic and German states. Herring exports slumped in the 1570s and 1580s, but boomed again in the 1590s; volumes remained at a very high level throughout the first half of the seventeenth century and Dutch salt herring monopolized the market in western Europe. There were several reasons for this upward trend. Fishermen started using larger boats, so they could sail further and return with bigger catches. A vertical integration process developed, bringing together catching, processing and trade, so businesses could work on the basis of a profitable annual commercial cycle. This all called for serious investment, coordination and supervision, and these were also present in the towns and cities of Holland. Even before 1600, herring fishing had consequently become a significant industry, which at that time had some 450 fishing boats and created jobs in other sectors too (for example, shipbuilding, salt extraction, smoking, packing and trade). Alongside the large-scale fishing for herring, there were also boats whose catches were on a smaller scale (cod for instance) and – from the beginning of the seventeenth century – whaling for whale oil and blubber. This was also important, but did not boom until around 1650.

Numerous factors that augmented and supported one another governed the spectacular economic growth that the Republic enjoyed from around 1580 to the middle of the seventeenth century. They resulted in internationally unique economic differentiation and interwoven activities that were the drivers behind the Republic's Golden Age. One of the trends fuelling the commercialization of the agricultural and fishing industries was population growth. By about 1560, the number of people in the Netherlands was 40 per cent higher than it had been around the turn of the century. The Revolt and military confrontations brought this development to a standstill, but in the north, growth started again in the 1580s. As we saw earlier, emigration from the south was a key factor. An estimated 100,000–150,000 people left for the north, although they did not all remain in the Northern Netherlands. The population grew fastest in the west and north, and by around 1650 these regions had three times as many inhabitants as in 1500. During this same century and a half, the number of people living in the territory that had become the Republic doubled.

Immigration from the south also provided a major stimulus for industry. According to De Vries and Van der Woude, from about 1580 the importation of workers, know-how and capital gave the urban economy an 'unprecedented boost'.[51] The relocation of significant parts of the textile industry from the south to Leiden enabled the city to develop into the most important European industrial centre, while Haarlem became the Republic's second textile manufacturing hub. Van Deursen writes that the economy of the Netherlands was 'Hollando-centric'.[52] Expropriated monasteries and convents were used as workshops and living accommodation. The large stocks of grain and the abundant supply of herring made it relatively easy to feed the newcomers, who with their knowledge and experience found new jobs primarily in the rapidly growing new industries. The fact that real wages in Holland rose sharply from 1590 onwards and that wage levels were higher than in the other provinces and neighbouring countries testifies to how well the growing supply of labour could be absorbed and was accompanied by rising production.

Shipbuilding was another key ingredient in economic growth, and in turn it stimulated other industrial sectors. One of the reasons why it was possible to modernize herring fishing was the construction of large boats. The launch of the first of a new type of vessel – the fluyt – in 1595 represented a major breakthrough for the cargo trade. This type of merchantman provided everything needed for expanding trade and industry. It had greater cargo capacity than existing merchant ships, it sailed faster, was more stable and needed fewer crew. While conventional vessels could make the voyage to the Baltic and back twice a year, a fluyt could make three or four return trips. An additional advantage of this ship was its pear shape when viewed from fore and aft. This meant it tapered towards its main deck, which was therefore relatively small, and so when it sailed through the Øresund it paid lower tolls, which were based on deck area. The design of the fluyt was a spectacular technological breakthrough and it made Holland (particularly the Zaan region and Amsterdam) the shipyard of Europe. The development of the sawmill – possibly the most important economical innovation in this period – played a major role in the success of Dutch shipbuilding.

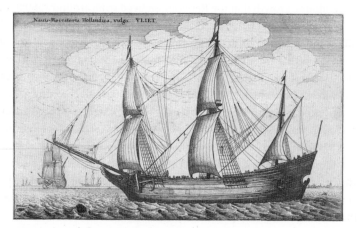

Figure 2 *A Fluyt*, Wensesclas Hollar. The Thomas Fischer Rare Book Library, University of Toronto.

The production of ships in Holland grew to unprecedented heights during the seventeenth century. Shipyards in Holland are estimated to have delivered between four and five hundred seagoing vessels a year between 1625 and 1700. Shipbuilding, with a workforce some ten thousand strong, was one of the biggest industries in the Republic and it also benefitted other branches of industry (including sawmills, windmill building and the manufacture of sails and rope). Imports of timber, an important element in trade with the Baltic, grew dramatically in consequence. This is yet another illustration of how closely interwoven the different economic sectors were.

These interrelationships were matched by developments in commerce and trade, and by the successful coordination of supply, processing, storage and sales. Holland – primarily Amsterdam – developed a commodities market which, thanks to its substantial stocks of goods, could deliver on request to the farthest corners of Europe (and beyond). Amsterdam was also a major hub for information about international markets. This knowledge of international commerce was one of the factors that led to the creation of a stable and reliable distribution system, which enabled the Republic to shake off international competition and emerge as the world's number one trading nation.[53] Before the Revolt, shipping to and from the Baltic and the grain trade had already made Amsterdam a major European trade centre. This trend was interrupted temporarily in the 1560s and 1570s, but from the 1580s onwards there was spectacular growth, and by 1620, the Dutch were trading twice as much seaborne freight with the Baltic area.

After the start of the Scheldt blockade in 1585 and the arrival of immigrants from the south, Holland also became the centre of a new network of trading routes that extended to virtually every continent – the Mediterranean, Africa, Asia and the New World. Amsterdam thus also took over Antwerp's central position in the luxury trade (high added value, expensive products), and so the extension of the trading range was accompanied by huge growth in the range of goods being traded. This trend was reinforced by the ongoing expansion of industry and the commercialization of arable and livestock farming.

Although Amsterdam profited greatly from the merchants coming from the south and their wealth, their contacts and their knowledge, the city did not simply continue what Antwerp had been doing. Amsterdam's success as an international commercial hub was based on a multiplicity of causes. Existing economic factors, such as a versatile supply of shipping capacity, low transaction costs and an efficient and effective market were enhanced by the political power and independence that the Republic acquired at this time. According to De Vries and Van der Woude, it was this combination of factors that equipped Amsterdam better than its rivals to satisfy the changing needs of the international market.[54]

The Dutch East India Company (Verenigde Oost-Indische Compagnie or VOC), which was founded in 1602 on the initiative of Oldenbarnevelt, held a key position in this global network. It laid the basis for the later extensive colonial empire that would be known as the Dutch East Indies.[55] The formation of the VOC came after the breakthrough into the trade in luxury goods in the Northern Netherlands, which also included colonial merchandise. This increased the need for a Dutch merchant fleet to sail to the Far East.

Starting in 1595, the Republic also had to contend with a renewed Spanish trade embargo and, faced with the loss of a large share in the trading of colonial goods, it needed more than ever to have its own vessels to make the voyage to Asia.

Around 1600, there were eight companies sailing out of various ports in Holland to trade in the East Indies. This plurality of activity called for greater streamlining and coordination. This was the primary purpose of the VOC. The intention was to sideline the competition (primarily Portugal, but also England) by combining forces and by taking control of supply and prices in the international trade in pepper and spices. This made the VOC a major factor in the struggle with Spain and how it was financed. The States General granted the new organization a monopoly on Dutch shipping and trade with the Orient and gave it the right to have its own troops, equip warships and exercise administrative authority in the Far East.

The organization of the VOC reflected the Republic's political structure, with its autonomous towns and cities and its balanced system of consultation and power sharing, in which local interests and those of the greater whole were thrashed out. The company was managed by the Lords Seventeen, who represented the investors and also had to maintain a balance between the six chambers from participating ports, which were both partners and potential rivals. Just over half the starting capital was raised in Amsterdam, but with eight of the seventeen seats on the board, the city was just short of a majority. A unique feature of this construction was that if investors wanted to sell their share, they had to do so on the stock exchange. The VOC became an enterprise with shareholders and was thus a completely new type of trading company. A governor-general had responsibility in the Orient and was assisted by the East Indies Council.

Trade with West Africa, South America and the Caribbean got underway at the end of the sixteenth century. But during the negotiations about the Twelve Years' Truce, the Republic had to make the concession to Spain that it would not establish a Dutch West India Company during the truce. This company therefore did not see the light of day until the war restarted in 1621 (West-Indische Compagnie or WIC). It became clear before the truce, though, that the Republic was claiming its right to develop its trading network in those areas. As we shall see in the next chapter, the WIC was much less successful than the VOC, which expanded rapidly, particularly from the 1620s onwards.

It should also be pointed out in this overview of economic development during the early Republic that there was a paradox. The prosperity described above was achieved in a period when the new state was involved in a very expensive war, yet some of the money involved was earned by trading with the enemy. The economic heart of the later Republic – Holland – saw no fighting after the mid-1570s, however, and so it could thrive in relative tranquillity. At the same time, the northern provinces profited from the conduct of the war, and the weakening of the south resulted in economic growth in the north. Trading with the enemy had economic benefits for both sides, and although trade embargoes were proclaimed with a degree of regularity, they usually did not last long or they were evaded because the economies complemented each other. Salt from the Iberian Peninsula, for instance, was very important to the Republic's fishing industry, while Spain was short of products from the Baltic (including grain and Swedish copper). There was also trading across the shifting border between north and south, where food and products from the Baltic were sold for large quantities of silver. The trade with the enemy was taxed through 'tariffs' that were paid to the Dutch admiralty, so part of the funding for the Republic's navy came directly from the Spanish enemy.

In summary, from about 1580, the young Republic developed into Europe's biggest trade centre and came to dominate world trade. That ascendancy would be maintained until the eighteenth century. From the late sixteenth century onwards, the Republic benefitted from a fortuitous combination of factors. These included the broadening and expansion of existing trade flows, population growth, urbanization, commercialization, technological developments, the declining economic significance of the Southern Netherlands, the increasing importance of the Northern Netherlands, and finally, the shifts in the international balance of power as a result of armed conflicts. All the elements contributing to economic growth came together in international trade, which provided the basis for the prosperity of the Golden Age. From about 1580 to the end of the Twelve Years' Truce, there was particularly dramatic commercial expansion. This was followed by a period of slower growth and consolidation, after which – from the middle of the seventeenth century – there were also setbacks. The next chapter explores these developments. We can conclude here with the observation that by the early seventeenth century, the Republic had become a major economic power.

CHAPTER 3
THE REPUBLIC IN THE GOLDEN AGE

Introduction

The internal tensions in the Republic increased during the Twelve Years' Truce (1609–21) and for a short time there was even a threat of civil war. The contentious issues included the relationship between church and state, theological questions and foreign policy. Stadholder Maurice emerged victorious from this struggle and enforced domestic political peace by staging a coup d'état. The war with Spain recommenced in 1621, and the Republic's territory expanded southwards under the leadership of Stadholder Frederick Henry (1625–47). The Peace of Westphalia was signed in 1648, and soon afterwards the First Stadholderless Period (1650–72) began. It was then that the Republic reached the pinnacle of its influence under Grand Pensionary Johan de Witt. In 1672, the Republic was briefly threatened with destruction after a combined attack by France, England and the bishoprics of Münster and Cologne. The House of Orange returned to the centre of power in the person of Stadholder William III. After the Glorious Revolution in 1688, he also became king of England. He spent many years waging war with France. One of the reasons behind the Republic's political and economic strength in the seventeenth century was the relative weakness of other European powers. Since the start of the 1660s, pressure from abroad and commercial competition had increased, however, and this was a contest that the relatively small Republic could ultimately only lose.

The growth of the economy, which had started in the 1580s, continued in the seventeenth century, and the Republic became the most prosperous and modern territory in Europe. There was further specialization and commercialization in agriculture, and land reclamation added substantially to the area of farmland. With a close-meshed canal system, the infrastructure was particularly modern, and meant that there could be seamless connections between urban and rural areas. The Republic was also an international leader in manufacturing. The Zaan region to the north of Amsterdam was the most important industrial zone in Europe, Leiden's textile output made it the major industrial city, and Holland developed into the biggest European sugar producer. Around 1650, the country's merchant fleet, which was responsible for the import, export and transit of products, was larger than that of England, France and Spain combined. The Dutch East India Company's trading posts gave the Republic a network of bases in present-day South Africa and throughout Asia. The Dutch were also active in Brazil, the Caribbean and North America for periods of various lengths; essentially the Republic had a worldwide trading network.

During the Golden Age, the Republic was a trend setter in painting, architecture and science. The Dutch School developed its own unique painting style and generated a huge output from countless studios and workshops in various towns and cities. Dutch architecture also acquired its own look. Most of the building commissions came from members of the ruling class and wealthy merchants, whose fondness for Dutch Classicism epitomized the Republic's bourgeois character. Technological advances flourished in shipbuilding and manufacturing, while the Republic's relatively generous religious and intellectual tolerance attracted philosophers from other countries, who were able to disseminate their work more easily and so during the Golden Age the Netherlands became a major centre of book production. These then are the political, economic and cultural developments that are the main themes of this chapter.

From the Twelve Years' Truce to the Peace of Münster (1609–48)

The Republic was still in an unstable state when the Truce took effect in 1609. Over the preceding decades, the internal differences of opinion had been muted by the struggle against the common external enemy. To make matters worse, the Republic's governmental structure, which took shape during the Revolt, was not equipped to resolve domestic tensions. In the ecclesiastical world, only the Calvinists were permitted to hold public church services, but religious relationships were still fluid and many people were looking for a religion in which they felt at home. Many Protestants were attracted to the beliefs of the Dutch Reformed Church but were not – or not yet – members, or held more moderate views. A significant proportion of the population had remained Catholic, while others were in fact Protestants, but they attended the services – to which a blind eye was turned – of other churches that had been formed as a result of the Reformation. So while the Calvinists had a leading position and their faith was the only one to be officially recognized, they were not in the majority. In Haarlem in 1620, only a fifth of the residents were members of the Dutch Reformed Church. Such figures, however, are less enlightening than their precision might lead one to think. Only adults who had been confirmed could become members of the church, but its services were attended by many people who were never confirmed or were only confirmed when they were older.

Internal tensions rose sharply during the Truce, both inside and between provinces. The subjects of dispute included the size of the provincial contribution to the communal treasury of the Generality and Holland's dominant position. On top of this, the Republic's administrative structure had no machinery for tackling the conflict between Oldenbarnevelt and Prince Maurice, which went beyond the question of whether a truce should have been entered into and was linked to religious, constitutional and international political issues.

Now that the weapons had been silenced, it was very much in Oldenbarnevelt's interests to find further legitimacy for the executive structure that had developed in the Republic, where the States of Holland was the power centre. He was supported in this by Hugo Grotius (1583–1645), who created a historical line from the Batavian leader Claudius Civilis and his victory over the Romans to William of Orange and the struggle against the Spanish. Grotius was not the first to make the Batavi the forefathers of the Dutch, but his *Liber de Antiquitate Republicae Batavicae* published in 1610 became

Figure 3 *The Conspiracy of the Batavians under Claudius Civilis*, Rembrandt van Rijn, 1661. Nationalmuseum, Stockholm.

the best-known work that put the Batavian myth into words. In a nutshell, it is that these freedom-loving and clever 'ancestors' were governed in the same way as their descendants in the Republic, namely by an oligarchy of the wisest men in the country. They had meanwhile assembled in the provincial states; Hugo Grotius thus constructed a centuries-long tradition of freedom and government continuity culminating in the Dutch regents and the States. This invention of tradition put into words a nascent national feeling that manifested itself in plays, poems and paintings (including *The Conspiracy of the Batavians under Claudius Civilis* by Rembrandt) that were a major influence on the historical self-image of the Dutch.[1] Successful as the creation of this self-image may have been, it did not, of course, represent a guarantee of political stability and the continuity of Oldenbarnevelt's central position.

The background to the domestic struggle that raged during the Truce, which Oldenbarnevelt ultimately lost to Maurice, was ecclesiastical and theological, but it was also about how best the Republic could be governed, what the relationship between church and state should be, and what direction the Republic's foreign policy should take. The immediate cause was the theological dispute between two Leiden professors – Franciscus Gomarus and Jacobus Arminius – about the issue of predestination. Gomarus, a strict Calvinist, took the view that God decided before someone was born whether that person would be given eternal life. The individual, even if he strove to do good, could exert no influence on this whatsoever because he remained a sinner and depended on God's mercy. Arminius criticized this Calvinist orthodoxy but shied away from addressing the issue of free will. He did, though, stress human responsibility, proclaiming that God's mercy applied to those who believed in him and lived their lives accordingly. He also stated that humans have the free choice to reject God's grace. This thinking was unacceptable to Gomarus and his supporters because it represented a violation of God's omnipotence and reduced the differences with the Catholic Church. The Arminians were a minority among Dutch Reformed Church ministers. In January 1610, they submitted a remonstrance or petition to the States of Holland asking for latitude for their opinions in the church. This act by the Remonstrants was followed a year later by a counter-remonstrance submitted by the Gomarists, in which the heresy of the other movement was condemned.[2] It also said that the state should not make decisions about theological disputes. Only the church could do that, and in order to establish the correct theological line the States General had to convene a national synod.

Oldenbarnevelt and the States of Holland were not concerned with theological rights and wrongs. The important issues for them were the primacy of politics, and peace in the official church, in which there had to be room for many movements – Remonstrants, Counter-Remonstrants, moderates and other Protestant groups. From that perspective, the official church should be regulated by the state, so the government was responsible for appointments and rules governing church life, and for monitoring doctrine. Yet it was precisely this primacy of politics that the orthodox Calvinists rejected. Their position was that the role of the state should be to protect the Dutch Reformed Church and effectively prohibit other denominations. Dogma, organizational issues and appointments, on the other hand, were internal ecclesiastical matters that the state should not be involved in.

Oldenbarnevelt's attempts to enforce calm and tolerance in the Dutch Reformed Church failed. In many places, the official church disintegrated into hostile camps and opponents were purged, depending on the balance of power. Neighbouring towns ended up on opposite sides and after 1616 this even led to serious disturbances in some places. The Gomarists were in the majority, and with increasing vehemence they demanded a national synod so that the Dutch Reformed Church could reconfirm its Calvinist roots and reject the Remonstrant point of view. Only the States General could convene such a synod, but it too was split into orthodox and moderate provinces. The polarization between the Remonstrants and Counter-Remonstrants had developed from a theological quarrel into a state affair. The character of the Dutch Reformed Church, the relationship between church and state, and even the stability of the Republic were at issue. Tensions ran high and in 1617–18 they were to bring the country to the brink of a civil war.

The ever increasing domestic polarization also came about because of concerns about foreign policy. Oldenbarnevelt clung resolutely to France as an ally, even after the French King Henry IV was murdered in May 1610 and France embarked on reconciliation with Spain. Many saw this as a potential danger to the Republic because they feared that a Franco–Spanish alliance would lead to peace terms detrimental to the Republic. They consequently believed it was necessary to find other allies. Maurice also came to this conclusion, changed course, and turned to England and the tense relationship with Oldenbarnevelt deteriorated even further.[3] The Advocate of Holland's opponents saw an increasingly strong link between his efforts to have an official church in which there was a place for Remonstrants and his tenacity in holding on to an alliance with France. After all, the Franco–Spanish rapprochement was bringing France back into the Catholic camp and, as a consequence of Oldenbarnevelt's views about the openness of the official church, the door would also be opened to Catholics. This combination of factors gave rise to the suspicion that Oldenbarnevelt was secretly scheming to make peace with Spain under terms that would harm the interests of the Calvinists.

The growing conflict between Oldenbarnevelt and Maurice came to a head in 1617, when the stadholder publicly sided with the Counter-Remonstrants. This overt preference for one of the parties prompted the question of whether Maurice would still be prepared to obey the States were it to order him to take military action. Oldenbarnevelt's response escalated the situation once and for all. In August 1617, on his initiative, the States of Holland officially came out against a national synod because it would be contrary to provincial sovereignty in questions of religion. More importantly, in that same resolution – which has gone down in history as the 'Sharp Resolution' – the States of Holland gave towns and cities permission to recruit soldiers. All the troops quartered in Holland and their commanders were reminded of their oath to obey the legal government in the town, city and province.[4] Oldenbarnevelt overplayed his hand in making these decisions because in effect he placed Holland above the Generality and undermined Maurice's position. Although as stadholder Maurice was only a 'servant' of the provincial states, he was also commander-in-chief of the province's army. After the 'Sharp Resolution', local armies were created alongside the 'national' army, and they did not come under Maurice's supreme command. As Van Deursen writes, Oldenbarnevelt had opted 'for a military solution but against the will of the military leadership'.[5] Jonathan Israel described the situation after the 'Sharp Resolution' as a civil war on the point of breaking out.[6]

The survival of the Republic was now at stake and there were disturbances in many towns and cities. Maurice seized the opportunity to isolate Holland and settled the conflict by grabbing power. With the support of the majority in the States General and using the threat of military intervention, he started – outside Holland to begin with – to replace Remonstrant town officials with Counter-Remonstrants. He also compelled Utrecht, likewise under the threat of military force, to disband their troops. This campaign was completed in the autumn of 1618 with the arrest of Oldenbarnevelt (and others, including his ally Hugo Grotius) and the further replacement of pro-Oldenbarnevelt town councils with Orangist magistrates. By taking these measures, which went beyond his formal powers, Maurice brought Holland and Utrecht into line and restored unity in the States General.[7] In the same way he had achieved military successes before, he had now defeated Oldenbarnevelt – cautiously, taking one step at a time, and striking when he was assured of victory.

In a political trial, Oldenbarnevelt was accused of betraying the country (handing over the Republic to Spain), high treason (seizing power), damaging the church and sidelining Maurice. A special court established by the States General condemned the deposed Advocate of Holland to death, and in May 1619 the sentence was carried out in the Binnenhof in The Hague. His supporter Hugo Grotius was sentenced to life imprisonment, but in 1621 he staged a spectacular escape in a book chest from Loevestein Castle, where he was being held. In 1618, shortly before Oldenbarnevelt's execution, the National Synod met in Dordrecht and in 1619 unity in the Dutch Reformed Church was restored by condemning Remonstrant error as heresy. An essential victory for the church was that it, and not the government as Oldenbarnevelt had wanted, had determined the basic rules of the faith. The church would remain subordinate to the government, but the government would not interfere with the content of the faith. This result allowed the Dutch Reformed Church to remain an orthodox bastion for a minority of the population.

Maurice had won the day by eliminating Oldenbarnevelt and condemning the Remonstrants, but he failed to capitalize on the victory to the benefit of the Republic. His biographer Van Deursen goes so far as to describe him as 'the victor who lost'. Maurice had probably prevented a civil war but, as Van Deursen writes, 'Someone who robs the Republic of its leader must know who can replace him, or otherwise fill the empty position himself.'[8] No replacement came for Oldenbarnevelt and Maurice did not have the qualities needed to fill the political vacuum that the Advocate of Holland had left behind. Maurice's great service to the Republic was that the struggle with Spain made decisive progress under his leadership, but he was not the man to run the country. He died in 1625, having achieved nothing of importance after 1618.

This gives rise to the question as to how profound the consequences of Maurice's coup d'état in 1618 were. They were without doubt substantial in the short term. The purging of pro-Oldenbarnevelt town councils in Holland meant that regents with a great deal of local government experience were replaced by less experienced men; inevitably, the towns and cities in Holland lost influence. Oldenbarnevelt's successors were also given fewer powers, and at first more inept individuals were deliberately appointed to the post, so that Holland's position was weakened to the benefit of the stadholder and the Generality. This had further deleterious implications for the power and cohesion of the Republic as a whole because Holland was, after all, the country's mainstay.

There were also purges in the militias, education systems and, above all, the churches. Only those clergymen who conformed to the pronouncements of the synod were allowed to remain in their posts. A number accepted the synod's outcome, but some 160 ministers lost their jobs, and about half of this group had to leave the Republic. Maurice's seizure of power also had consequences for the Orange-Nassau family's position. Although Van Deursen describes the 1619–25 period as Maurice's 'barren years', and Maurice did not want to become a cult figure, in the Counter-Remonstrant urban culture it became normal to honour the Orange-Nassaus with works of art in public buildings.[9]

As time passed, it emerged that the implications of Maurice's defeat of Oldenbarnevelt were less profound than they had appeared to be in 1618–19. Holland gradually recovered from its temporary debilitation and once again became the dominant factor in a consensus-seeking federal decision-making process. The year 1618 was not so much a systemic turning point as an abrupt change of power – by no means the last that would be seen in the seventeenth century. What did end for ever in 1618, though, was the principle of dividing tasks between the stadholder and the advocate of the province of Holland, as had come about under Oldenbarnevelt and Maurice and had worked well until about 1609. After 1618, only one of the two – stadholder or grand pensionary of Holland (previously advocate of the province) – would be the top dog. In the period up to 1650, it was the stadholders who wielded the power – Maurice until 1625, followed by Frederick Henry until 1647 and thereafter, until 1650, William II. This was followed by the First Stadholderless Period, when Grand Pensionary Johan de Witt set the tone

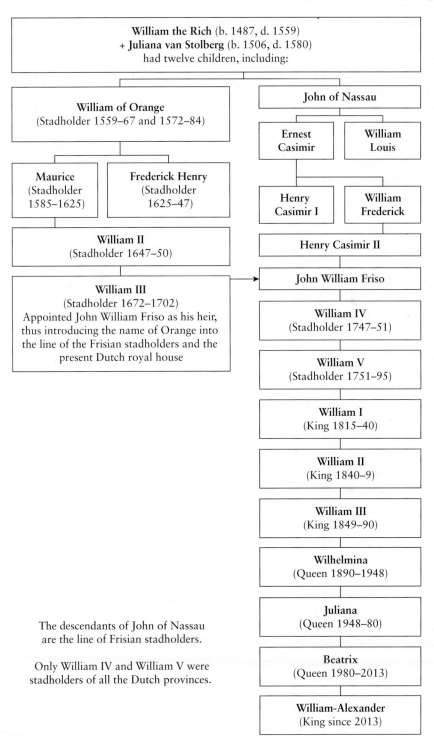

Illustration 1 The Orange-Nassau family tree.

between 1653 and 1672. After this, from 1672 to 1702, a stadholder – William III – had his hand on the tiller. Although more of the power in the Republic than ever before was concentrated in one person after 1618, characteristically there continued to be no formal personified centre of power with clearly specified authority. In this sense, the outcome of the conflict between Maurice and Oldenbarnevelt had no profound effect on the existing order in the Republic.

Oldenbarnevelt's defeat was also less far-reaching from an ecclesiastical perspective than one might have expected, given the result of the Dordrecht synod. While the Counter-Remonstrant triumph had been overwhelming, within a few years the efforts to combat the Remonstrants lost momentum in many places, despite protests from the orthodox Calvinist victors of 1619. These strict believers also had to accept that the rules governing church life approved in Dordrecht were only adopted unchanged in three provinces and that the States of Holland, for instance, specified its own rules. The net result was that the ecclesiastical situation continued as had been agreed in the Union of Utrecht. Every province organized its own religious affairs, which by and large were the same everywhere: only members of the Dutch Reformed Church could practise their religion publicly and other churches were officially prohibited from holding services.

Such bans were repeated regularly, but they were not put into practice consistently everywhere or for all churches. Although there were regional differences, the provincial synods did cooperate, for instance by exchanging representatives and respecting one another's decisions. The position of the churches in the seventeenth century will be discussed in greater depth later on. Here it is sufficient to note that the prohibitions were usually not enforced and the custom of turning a blind eye to services other than those of the Dutch Reformed Church, which had existed for some time, became a quintessential feature of the Republic's political and religious culture. In this regard, the Republic's policy differed from that of other European countries, where unity of state and faith was still the norm.

Developments in the Republic were monitored closely abroad, particularly since a major European religious struggle, known later as the Thirty Years' War (1618–48), erupted in 1618. This war was to have far-reaching consequences, above all for Germany, where there was an Evangelical Union under the leadership of Maurice's first cousin, the Calvinist Elector Palatine Frederick V, against a Catholic League under Ferdinand of Habsburg, who in 1619 became Ferdinand II, Holy Roman Emperor. Maurice had contributed to the outbreak of this war by promising his cousin troops and money for the imminent conflict. He reasoned that the growing tensions in Germany could be beneficial for the Republic. The Spanish Habsburgs could be expected to come to the aid of their Austrian relatives, relieving Spanish pressure on the Republic.

The Habsburg families did indeed join forces, but the expected advantage for the Republic failed to materialize. At the end of the Twelve Years' Truce, the Republic was surrounded by collaborating Habsburgs, and Madrid was out to restart the war. This did not mean that the Spanish king was still expecting to actually conquer the Northern Netherlands. His primary objective now was to weaken the Republic as a trading power. Maurice, who had never supported a ceasefire, also wanted to see armed conflict recommence. In his view, continuation of the war could not only strengthen the position of Calvinism in Europe, but could also counteract the resurgence of the Republic's internal differences of opinion. Aside from political and religious motives, there were economic interests at stake. The industrial towns and cities of Holland were in favour of resuming the war because it would reduce the competition from Flanders and Brabant, and the associated loss of business they had experienced during the Truce. Others were straining at the leash to set up a Dutch West India Company (WIC), which the Republic had agreed in 1609 not to do during the Truce.

When the Truce ended in 1621, Spain and the Republic once again locked horns, although the hostilities were relatively subdued and were conducted without clear military strategies. There was no straightforward resumption of the Revolt where it had stopped in 1609. The Republic was now seen as a major player on the international stage, and the Spanish–Dutch struggle had now become part of a much bigger European conflict. From 1621 onwards, the Eighty Years' War was part of the Thirty Years' War, which had broken out in 1618 and – through its complex alliances – involved virtually all the European powers.

The Republic did not profit from this internationalization at first. The situation remained worrying until the end of the 1620s, and the Dutch lost Breda in 1625 and a few military strongholds in German territory. There were also Spanish trade embargoes, and river blockades by Spanish garrisons, which surrounded the Republic from Flanders to the county of Lingen, cutting off transport along the Scheldt, Rhine, Waal, Meuse and Eems. The economic damage this caused was exacerbated by higher taxes, which were necessary to restore the Republic's defences. Compounding this, the Republic initially had no allies – for the first time since 1576 – and was thus completely alone. At the same time, however, the Republic had to provide financial support to friendly Protestant rulers. German Protestant armies were maintained to prevent the Catholic League in northwest Germany from getting the upper hand and from putting the Republic's defences under even greater pressure, and of course this cost money. In short, from economic, financial and military points of view, the Republic's position was difficult at the beginning of the 1620s, and the malaise was made even worse because there was no political leader. According to Israel, when Maurice died in 1625 the Republic was in the worst position since 1590.[10]

In this grim situation, the States General appointed Maurice's half-brother, Frederick Henry, as captain general.[11] He was then also made stadholder of Holland, Zeeland, Utrecht, Guelders and Overijssel. Like Maurice, Frederick Henry had an excellent understanding of military matters, but he had also inherited political and diplomatic skills from his father, William of Orange. He did not share Maurice's fierce Counter-Remonstrant sentiment and steered a central course that left room for the return of some Remonstrant regents who had been purged by Maurice. His conciliatory approach generated no enthusiasm, though, and tensions in Holland rose again in the second half of the 1620s. Nevertheless, Frederick Henry's statesmanship brought stability and he held the levers of political power. He made shrewd use of the divisions in Holland to strengthen his own position, and he was supported by confidants in the aristocracy outside this province. He also wielded substantial influence in the 'secrete besognes' – ad hoc States General committees set up on his initiative with the authority to take important decisions under conditions of strict secrecy. The absence of powerful grand pensionaries in Holland under Frederick Henry's rule is part of the same picture. Another characteristic of his stadholdership was a more aristocratic life at court than before, with his wife – Amalia of Solms-Braunfels – playing an active part. This manifested itself in several ways, for example the construction or refurbishment of prestigious palaces (Huis ten Bosch and Noordeinde in The Hague) and other residences appropriate to a stadholder. Frederick Henry was seeking to put himself on an equal footing with major European noble families.

His growing standing was of course also based on his military successes, which earned him the nickname of 'scourge of towns'. He overpowered a number of towns and strongholds in the border region. The conquests of 's-Hertogenbosch (1629), Maastricht (1632) and Breda (1637) were particularly important milestones and expressions of renewed military strength. In 1628, the Republic received a substantial financial shot in the arm thanks to Admiral Piet Hein. He was in the service of the Dutch WIC, which had been set up in 1621. In the Caribbean, he overpowered the annual Spanish treasure fleet while it was en route to Spain and brought home booty worth 11.5 million guilders. This sum – representing about two-thirds of the annual war budget – came as extremely welcome relief for the cash-strapped Republic.

The Republic also re-emerged on to the international stage from its isolation of the first half of the 1620s. Maurice had opposed collaboration with France during his struggle for power with Oldenbarnevelt, yet in 1624 he signed a new treaty with the French. Under this treaty, the French king, badly shaken by the Habsburg successes, promised to support the Republic again for a few years. In December 1625, Denmark, England and the Republic formed a coalition against the Habsburg emperor. The Republic feared an Austro–Spanish advance and so lent financial support to a Danish attack on the Holy Roman Empire. Earlier that year, England and the Republic made an agreement in Southampton about a combined Anglo–Dutch fleet to fight Spain; a treaty that England broke a few years later when it made peace with the Spanish.

The involvement with the Thirty Years' War became even more evident in 1635, when France and the Republic entered into an alliance and agreed to jointly conquer the Southern Netherlands and divide up the spoils. Each also promised the other that it would not make peace separately with Spain. Not everyone in the Republic supported this expansionist policy, which would make France a powerful neighbour immediately to the south. Things did not get that far, although under Frederick Henry the Republic did expand southwards; its conquests, as referred to above, included 's-Hertogenbosch and Breda in Brabant and Maastricht in Limburg.

At sea there were problems and successes. Privateers sailing out of Dunkirk were a major headache for merchant shipping. A small fleet based in the Flemish port of Dunkirk stopped and seized hostile vessels with the permission of the Spanish king. Attempts by Dutch warships to blockade the Flemish coast were only partially successful. A record number of 305 Dutch ships were lost in 1632.[12] On the other hand, Maarten

Harpertsz. Tromp, one of the seventeenth century's most important admirals, achieved a great deal. In 1639, he defeated a new Spanish armada off the English coast. The Spanish fleet in this part of Europe never recovered from the rout.

In this battle, English neutrality had been harmful and potentially dangerous to the Republic because it had given Spain the opportunity to sail north with its fleet and seek refuge in English waters. It was therefore very important to the Republic to prevent Anglo–Spanish rapprochement and create closer ties with England. That was achieved by successfully arranging a marriage: Mary Henrietta Stuart (1631–1660), the oldest daughter of the English King Charles I, had been lined up to marry the Spanish crown prince. But in 1641, at the age of nine, she married William (1626–1650) – the later Stadholder William II (from 1647 to 1650) – who was a good five years older and Frederick Henry's son. This major diplomatic coup for the Republic stopped any Anglo–Spanish overtures in their tracks.

In contrast to Maurice's last years, under Frederick Henry the Republic benefitted from the increased internationalization of the conflict, which gradually weakened the Spanish Habsburgs and reinforced the Republic's strategic position. This contributed to the growing number of voices in the Republic calling for peace during the 1630s, and the willingness to finance the army and navy declined dramatically. Support for peace came from the majority of the towns and cities in Holland, and the Provinces of Guelders, Friesland, Groningen and Overijssel. The opponents of peace were Zeeland, Utrecht and the industrial cities dominated by Calvinism, such as Leiden and Haarlem. Initially, Stadholder Frederick Henry was among the doves. He changed his position in the 1630s, but set a course for peace again in the 1640s. His son and successor William II, on the other hand, wanted to keep the war going. He was swimming against the tide, however,

Figure 4 *The Ratification of the Peace of Münster, 15 May 1648,* Gerard ter Borch, 1648. The National Gallery, London.

because the desire for peace had grown in other European countries too. Preliminary talks about ending this major European war opened in 1641. They led to complicated agreements about a key European peace conference, which began in 1644. During this conference, the warring parties negotiated in different combinations in Münster and Osnabrück.[13] The Spanish–Dutch negotiations started in 1646 in Münster, after Frederick Henry had also definitively declared his support for peace.

Meanwhile, Spain had become weaker internally and externally, and it was crucial for it to break the Franco–Dutch alliance. The upshot was that Spain wanted to placate the Republic by making sacrifices it had not previously been prepared to countenance. The peace terms negotiated in 1648 represented a huge success for the Republic. It consolidated its territory and was now recognized by Spain as a sovereign state. The area controlled by the Republic included the Generality Lands, which were areas taken over from Spain and governed directly by the States General (States Brabant, States Flanders and States Limburg) (see Map 5, p. 55). Agreement about the Republic's borders was finally reached in supplementary treaties in 1661 and 1664. There was reciprocal recognition of the status quo in the East and West Indies, and Spain accepted the charters of the VOC and WIC. The Scheldt remained closed and nothing was recorded about religious freedom for Catholics. Broadly speaking, these terms confirmed what had been agreed temporarily in the Truce of 1609.[14] The Peace of Münster had finally brought the Republic a recognized position in the international community of nations, and it was in this that the importance of peace to the Netherlands lay.

However, the 1648 peace treaty meant the Republic broke the alliance with France. In 1635 the two states had promised one another that they would only stop the war with Spain jointly. Now the Republic said it was entitled to make peace if France only wanted to continue the war to serve its own interests and maintained opposition to reasonable peace terms. When France withdrew from Dutch attempts to mediate, the States General considered proof of this to have been supplied, and issued instructions to go ahead alone and sign the peace treaty. This was done on 30 January 1648 in the current Haus der Niederlande in Münster (see Figure 5, p. 56), and the peace was ratified that May in the city's town hall. Peace was ceremonially announced and celebrated in the Republic in June 1648. The joy, though, was not equally unconfined everywhere in the country. Zeeland had resisted peace until the bitter end and Leiden was among the cities that saw no reason to join in the merrymaking.

Stadholder Frederick Henry died in 1647 and so did not live to see peace. His son William II, who became stadholder of six provinces and captain general of the Union in that same year by hereditary succession, had not been a supporter of peace. Ending the war in 1648 did nothing to change his views, so behind the scenes he set out to resume the joint struggle with France against Spain. He also hatched plans to give his English family military support in recapturing the English throne after his father-in-law, King Charles I, was deposed and beheaded in 1649.[15] Looking at the family history, William II came to the conclusion that the only way to achieve fame and influence was by waging war. But he failed to see that times had changed and there was no longer a majority in the Republic in favour of armed conflict.

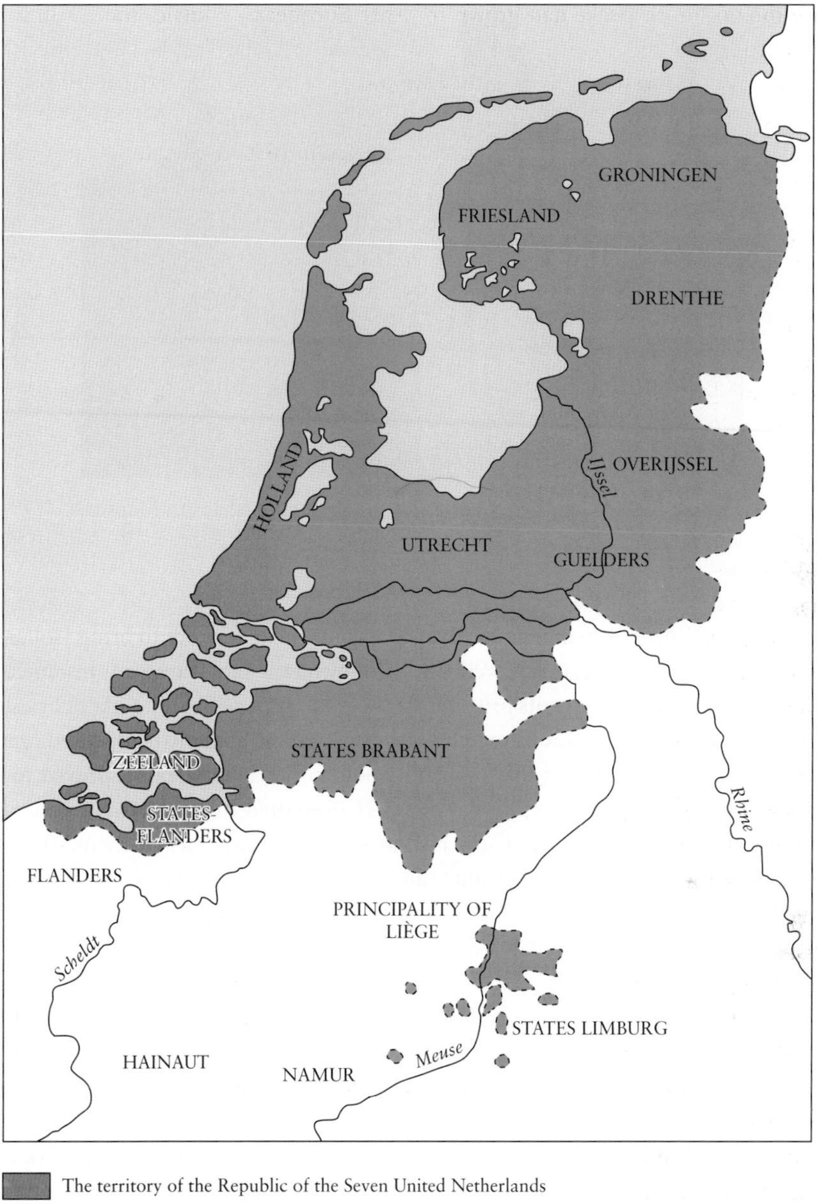

Map 5 The Republic in 1648.

The struggle came down to the question of how much money would have to be spent on the army. Holland, which had always provided about 60 per cent of the funding, was a particularly strong advocate of dramatic troop reductions. The other six provinces were more restrained and supported William II in his goal to hold off cutbacks. There was consequently a danger of repeating the situation in 1618, when Stadholder Maurice –

Figure 5 The Haus der Niederlande, in Krameramtshaus in Münster (2012).

supported by the other provinces – had staged a coup d'état in order to bring Holland to its knees and secure his own power. William II followed the same course as his uncle and took a number of Holland regents prisoner. At the same time, the stadholder of Friesland, William Frederick, and his troops marched on Amsterdam. Initially it appeared that the stadholders were winning, and that Holland would come around, but it proved to be a pyrrhic victory. When the impetuous William II presented his real plans in the States General in the autumn of 1650, it was not just Holland that resisted them. The other provinces were also opposed to resuming the war. The struggle for power in the Republic that was then ignited between the States General and the 24-year-old stadholder came to an abrupt end with his sudden death at the beginning of November 1650.

There was no successor waiting in the wings because William II's son was born a week after his father's death. Holland decided not to appoint a temporary successor and resolved the stadholder issue in a manner as simple as it was radical – the province just abolished the position. No law had to be swept aside or promulgated to do this because the post of stadholder was based on customary law and had never been embedded in a constitution. Holland consequently considered itself entitled to take this step, but it did feel the need to discuss it with the other provinces. That need was all the greater because after the Peace of Münster the question arose as to whether and how the 1579 Union of Utrecht should be developed further. The Union had been set up as an alliance during the conflict with Spain, but this had now been won and thus it seemed sensible to amend the old basis of collaboration to fit the significantly changed circumstances. On the initiative of Holland, in January 1651 the General Assembly met to deliberate on the matter. This was a special gathering of the States General to which all the provinces sent large delegations. The advantage was that there was no need for a complicated and time-consuming process of being bound by a mandate, so binding agreements could be made within a relatively short time. The agenda covered important issues, among them the position of the church, the organization of the army and the design of the political system.

The General Assembly, which continued to meet until August 1651, produced no clear decisions. Nothing changed on the ecclesiastical front, and every province retained its own freedom of action to allow churches other than the Dutch Reformed Church by more or less turning a blind eye to them. In military matters, Holland successfully resisted the appointment of a captain general of the Union and brought about decentralization of the national army by dividing it among the different provinces. Troop movements between the provinces would thus only be allowed with the agreement of the provinces concerned. Holland got its way in the political arena to the effect that each province could decide for itself whether it would appoint a stadholder or not. In so doing, the General Assembly legitimized what had in fact already started in Holland, Zeeland, Utrecht, Overijssel and Guelders after the death of William II in 1650 and would go on until 1672 – a period without stadholders. Later historiography has called this era the 'First Stadholderless Period' (1650–72); a name that underlines the historical dominance of Holland because in the north the Nassau-Dietz branch of the Oranges remained stadholders in Friesland. All in all, nothing came of a political renewal of the Union, and the General Assembly resulted in little more than confirmation of the status quo – a federation of sovereign provinces with Holland as its political and economic heart.

All the same, something fundamental had changed and the year 1650 should be seen as a turning point in the Republic's political history.[16] The disappearance of the stadholder also removed the person who could embody the cohesion between the provinces and, since there was no constitutional head of state, could actually lead the country – something that the Nassau-Dietz branch of the Oranges in Friesland did not have the power to do. The absence of the House of Orange meant there was no longer any counterweight to the dominance of Holland, which consequently increased in the years that followed.

The First Stadholderless Period ushered in an era that regents in Holland described as 'true freedom'. They no longer needed to share power with a stadholder, and the path to a semi-monarchical system with a Prince of Orange at its head was blocked – a development that William II would have so much liked to pursue. Johan de Witt, Grand Pensionary of Holland, was to emerge as de facto leader of the Republic starting in 1653 and, until 1672, the embodiment of the 'true freedom' of the regents of Holland in the republican structure.[17]

The Republic around 1650

By the mid-seventeenth century, the prosperous Republic's fame and power had reached an extraordinary level. The Peace of Münster had confirmed the Republic's international position, and in the years that followed, it consequently played a major role in the arena of European power. It consolidated its position as an economic powerhouse and trading nation, and its culture and science attained great heights. Israel describes the years between 1650 and 1672 as the period in which the Republic was at its greatest. Prak says that from 1650 the Republic was 'a top ranking power', notes that a decline started after 1672, and dates the end of the Golden Age to a point somewhere between then and 1715.[18] There are thus good grounds for Willem Frijhoff and Marijke Spies to choose 1650 as the focus for their standard work on the Netherlands in the Golden Age – *Dutch Culture in a European Perspective, 1650: Hard-won Unity*. Although, of course, it is impossible to reduce the Golden Age to one particular year or one particular image, 1650 is a good moment to interrupt the chronological account in this book and to ask what the Republic was really like in the seventeenth century. What was the population, what was the social stratification like, who governed the Republic and – given its diversity – how unified was it?

If we look first at the size, regional distribution and stratification of the population, we find that around 1600 some 1.5 million people lived in the territory of the current Netherlands. By 1650 this number had grown to approximately 1.9 million. This was followed by stagnation until around 1750, when it started to grow slowly again, to 2.1 million in 1800 or thereabouts. It did not begin to increase rapidly until the first half of the nineteenth century.[19] Holland remained the most densely populated and urbanized province. About half of the population lived there during the seventeenth century, and from 1650 around 60 per cent of them lived in a town or city. If we take the area of the Republic as a whole as a starting point and also include the small towns, for example Sloten in Friesland with about 450 residents, around 1670 nearly half of the total population lived in an urban environment, whereas this percentage was generally not greater than fifteen in other countries.

This made the Republic, with the Southern Netherlands, the most urbanized region in Europe in the seventeenth century, as it had been in the sixteenth century. There were, though, always big differences in the numbers of inhabitants in each town or city, and the rates of growth also varied. Amsterdam grew from 140,000 in 1647 to 200,000 in 1672, and by 1700 the number had increased slightly to 205,000. Other major cities in Holland – Leiden, Rotterdam and The Hague – also expanded significantly during the third quarter of the seventeenth century. This growth ended in most places in 1672, after which there was stagnation. Then, from the late 1680s, the population actually began to fall, and quite quickly. In Leiden, the Republic's second city, the population rose from 60,000 to 72,000 between 1647 and 1672. This number held steady until 1688, and then dropped to 63,000 in 1700.

The substantial population increase up to the middle of the seventeenth century was primarily due to the stream of migrants coming to the Republic. The demographic and economic significance of the immigration from the Southern Netherlands in the late sixteenth century was discussed in the previous chapter. Now migrants were coming from other points of the compass, and they made up for the high death rate that existed in those days. Armed conflict caused relatively high mortality in the east and south of the Republic during the first half of the seventeenth century, while elsewhere dike collapses, poor hygiene and disease – malaria for instance – also contributed to high mortality figures. Epidemics of plague also took their toll. There were many deaths in the merchant fleet too, particularly that of the VOC. It is estimated that of the 300,000 men who signed on as sailors on VOC vessels during the seventeenth century, fewer than 100,000 returned alive.

The countries that migrants came from included Germany (Westphalia, Lower Saxony and the Rhineland), Scandinavia, Poland, England and France, attracted chiefly by the employment opportunities and the better living conditions in the Republic. As a result, the proportion of foreigners in the population was substantial. During the seventeenth and eighteenth centuries, an estimated 6–8 per cent of the population in the Republic as a whole had foreign origins, and this percentage was considerably higher in Holland.[20] The prosperity of the Golden Age would have been unthinkable without these many tens of thousands of foreigners. Large numbers worked as seasonal labourers in agriculture or gravitated to industry and commerce. Textile factories in Leiden attracted many Walloons and Germans from 1647 onwards, and this catalysed explosive growth in textile manufacturing. Over 40 per cent of the seafarers who signed on to serve on VOC ships in the 1650s were born outside the Republic. Such percentages were likewise not uncommon on other vessels, and De Ruyter and other admirals would never have achieved their dramatic successes without foreign seamen. In the seventeenth century there also arose a small black-African community in Amsterdam, also partly employed by the VOC and WIC (for WIC see p. 89).

Migration also meant that many people had spouses with foreign origins. There was a significant excess of women in the Republic – estimated at 39 per cent among the Amsterdam working class – so this was not so surprising. In 1640 in Leiden, only 44 per cent of bridegrooms came from the Republic. Migrants made their mark in many areas, and many towns and cities in Holland consequently had a marked international character.

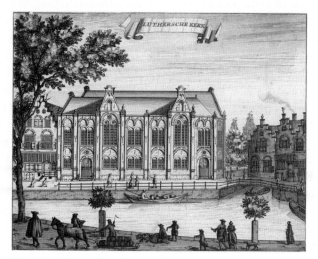

Figure 6 *The Old Lutheran Church on Spui in Amsterdam,* etching, 1723. Amsterdam City Archives.

Without the arrival of German emigrants, the conspicuous Lutheran churches in Amsterdam, consecrated in 1633 in Spui and 1671 in Singel, would never have been built (see Figure 6). By the end of the seventeenth century, some 17 per cent of the people of Amsterdam belonged to the Lutheran congregation, making Lutherans the third largest group in the city after members of the Dutch Reformed Church and Catholics.

Migrants were attracted by the booming labour market and the relatively high wages, but they had other motives too. During the Thirty Years' War, the Republic was a safe haven for many Germans, and at the end of seventeenth century tens of thousands of French Protestants (Huguenots) came to the Republic because of its tolerant religious climate. Jewish immigration was also very important. The decline of Antwerp after 1585 provoked the departure of Portuguese–Jewish merchants to northern towns and cities. During the first decades of the seventeenth century, this was followed by the migration – indirect and direct – of Sephardic Jews from Portugal. For economic reasons, some towns and cities in Holland attached so much value to their arrival that they tried to steal a march on one another by offering favourable conditions for establishing a business.

Some Portuguese Jews were very successful commercially and were to join the wealthy elite, primarily in Amsterdam. It was different for the Ashkenazi Jewish inflow from Germany during the Thirty Years' War and the Eastern European Ashkenazi Jews (mainly Polish) who fled to the Republic after 1648. Like the Lutherans, around 1650 the Jews were permitted to have their own places of worship, visible for all to see. However, immigration policy varied dramatically from province to province and town to town. Amsterdam developed into the most important Jewish centre in the Netherlands (in 1675 about 4 per cent of the population was Jewish), and that would remain the case until the Second World War. Yet even there the Jews did not have equal rights. In common with others who were not members of the Dutch Reformed Church, they were excluded from jobs as public officials. They were likewise not admitted to the guilds, which meant that many urban occupations were also beyond their reach.[21]

The Republic's urban population is generally divided into different social layers and classes.[22] The 10–20 per cent right at the bottom of the social ladder lived in poverty and deprivation with little chance of improving their living conditions. They included vagrants, beggars and unskilled labourers with irregular casual work. Not far above them were the wage earners (manual workers, servants, soldiers and sailors), but the boundary between these two nethermost social levels became blurred in periods of economic decline. On the third rung was the lower middle class, predominantly the self-employed (artisans and shopkeepers). Between them, these three strata represented about 90 per cent of the urban population. Above them was the middle class proper, a group that included businessmen, wealthier retailers, junior officers, some civil servants and a number of clergy. The second highest level was the upper middle class, whose members had more wealth and greater status. These were the leading merchants, owners of large businesses, senior officers, high ranking officials and the like. At the top of the social ladder – the upper class – there were some two thousand regents. They and their families accounted for around 1 per cent of the population. The executive power of the Republic was in their hands. It goes without saying that they all enjoyed citizenship. This concept did not mean the same thing in all towns and cities. It was often inherited, sometimes it was bestowed by the town or city, but in most cases it had to be purchased. Only those with citizenship could join a guild, and more often than not membership of a guild was a requirement if one wanted to set up in business or open a shop. Only citizens were eligible to become civic guardsmen – members of militias tasked with maintaining peace, order and safety. In many towns and cities citizenship was only open to Protestants, whereas Catholics and Jews were excluded. Although the rules varied from place to place and also changed over time, anyone who wanted to get anywhere in business or local government had to hold citizenship.

The number of people with citizenship fell as one descended the social ladder. Even among the riffraff at the bottom of the pile there were nevertheless still a few townsfolk who were citizens. During the seventeenth century, an individual's personal assets became progressively more important. Regents who lost their wealth also lost their government positions and disappeared from the upper crust. The clergy had lost their social standing some time before, and during the Golden Age it was the turn of concepts like 'aristocracy' and 'commoners' to lose their significance in social stratification. In the seventeenth century, the old social hierarchy was gradually replaced by a class society with growing social inequality.[23]

The picture was much the same in rural areas. Vagrants, farm workers and smallholders made up a large group living on or below the poverty line. Above them was a more successful farming middle class, and at the top were the rich, successful farmers and the nobility. The number of noble families varied from one province to the next – relatively few in Holland and more in the north and east – and remained constant until about 1650, but after that it dropped everywhere in the Republic. Although the rural aristocracy and the urban patricians had frequent dealings with one another in political, governmental and economic areas, there was barely any merging. Some wealthy regents purchased manors and land in the countryside, and in the summer many spent time in their places in the country, which often had aristocratic pretensions. Conversely, a number of nobles had prestigious houses in town, and there too the paths of the patricians and the nobility often crossed. Nevertheless, the aristocracy kept its ranks closed and accession to them from outside was rare.

The 'true freedom' of the First Stadholderless Period meant that Orange's role had been played out, at least for the time being. Power was now in the hands of the urban patricians, and this group very largely determined the Republic's character. For a long time, historians writing about the Netherlands of the seventeenth century have painted a simplified picture of the existence of an Orange party, supported by the nobility and the lower classes, opposed to the republican party of regents and the more prosperous classes. In fact, though, there were no two 'national' parties, each with clearly defined political views, but a multitude of factions and groups of local rulers together with their supporters who – depending on the circumstances – determined their own positions. Local factions often had contact with factions elsewhere, however, so sometimes configurations that looked like parties were created.

The regents' power base was in urban areas. Here they divided up the government posts among themselves and were the legislative, judicial and executive authorities.[24] Regents also played an influential role in ecclesiastical matters (including the appointment of clergy), in education and in caring for the poor. Essentially, all important political, judicial, economic and social areas came together under their control. In many cases this did not stop at the town or city limits. Thanks to the acquisition of manors – be it on a personal basis or by the town or city – their authority usually extended to the surrounding rural areas where, for example, they were on water authority boards. The towns and cities also sent representatives to the provincial states, where the urban areas – and thus the regents – took the lead, particularly in Holland. Finally, there were also regents in the States General, the Council of State, the Admiralty Boards and on the boards of the VOC and the WIC. It went without saying that the top government jobs were reserved for a small proportion of the regents, and powerful and prominent families rose to the upper ranks of the executive hierarchy faster and more easily. If there was a stadholder, he had the 'right of recommendation', which meant that he could make the final selection of new council members and magistrates from a list of candidates. But the list of names from which he could choose was drawn up in advance by the regents.

During the years of 'true freedom' the latitude of the small group of powerful regents was even greater, and the Dutch historian Joop de Jong tellingly describes them as 'the only players in a game with no referee'.[25] It comes as no surprise that when the influential government posts were shared out, the losers were dissatisfied and got together in their own factions, so tensions frequently ran high. It is obvious from which groups the stadholders recruited their supporters when they ousted public officials who were not of their mind, something that happened from time to time. Maurice did just that during his coup d'état in 1618 and William II tried it in 1650. As we shall see, in 1672, 1748 and around 1788, stadholders abruptly and collectively replaced officials in many towns and cities.

The regents' standing and political power would have been unthinkable without their wealth, which most of them had originally acquired through trade and industry. Until the first half of the seventeenth century, many were actively involved in commercial matters, and wielding political power was still a secondary activity. During this period, the differences between the families of regents and the upper middle class were not very significant. Yet even before 1650, a trend had appeared: success in business had made some of the regents very much richer. This put them in a position to give their government posts priority and put their economic activities on the back burner. After that, increases in the value of assets through investments, for example in the VOC, land reclamation and purchasing land, and the income from their government jobs were the primary sources of their continuing affluence.

The result was that about a third of Amsterdam regents withdrew from active involvement in commerce between 1618 and 1650. This proportion grew to two-thirds between 1650 and 1672, and then dropped to around a half. A side effect of this trend was that regents' children were no longer groomed for a position in trade and industry but for a career in government service. This was less marked in smaller towns, where a larger percentage of regents continued to take an active part in economic activity. Social mobility from the wealthy upper middle class to the circle of patricians was possible. Their lifestyle was comparable, there were marriages between the two social groups, and government officials were also recruited from the numerous members of the upper middle class.

The modest power of the aristocracy – by international standards – the relatively prosperous middle class, the wealth of the upper middle class, and the ubiquitous power of the patricians combined to make the Republic a decidedly bourgeois place, something that was evident in all sorts of areas. The local militia, with its military and policing role, also embodied the bourgeois urban society, as the many militia group portraits attest.

Much of the economic and social life in towns and cities was organized through guilds, whose members, as mentioned above, had to be residents with citizenship. Urban neighbourhood organizations were another important ingredient. They set the tone for the social life in their districts and were led by citizens. This structure of civil society, supported by local church councils in religious matters, was the backbone of society which, with its high degree of urbanization, was a quintessential feature of the Republic as a whole.

Many historians in search of other key aspects of the Republic use the concept of 'diversity'. Frijhoff and Spies identify three basic types of diversity during the period around 1650, against each of which there was a movement preferring unity.[26] First, there was diversity in government administration. The traditional urban and provincial particularism, encapsulated under the umbrella of the Union of Utrecht as 'harmony in diversity', was opposed by the 'national aspirations' of the stadholders. This should not be thought of in terms of a nation state ahead of its time, but as the growing claim by the House of Orange – given its increased prestige and its military significance to the Republic as a whole – to an enduring, supra-provincial position. And indeed the Oranges were an important continuous presence in the Republic's political and social culture.[27] But the governmental administrative structure did not have monocratic leadership, which meant that political power always had to be organized and legitimized. Power had

Figure 7 *The Governors of St Elisabeth's Hospital*, Frans Hals, 1641. Frans Hals Museum, Haarlem.

been in the hands of the stadholders from Maurice's victory over Oldenbarnevelt in 1618 to the death of William II in 1650. But after the General Assembly in 1651, diversity in government administration – under the leadership of Holland – seemed to have definitively triumphed over Orange and the Orangist factions. Grand Pensionary Johan de Witt, who was the Republic's strongman between 1653 and 1672, likewise did not have a formal legal power base. He was dependent on the States of Holland's consent and hence on the Holland regent. As we shall see, he was obliged to manoeuvre carefully to attain his goals. From 1660 onwards, not least of his concerns was the permanent exclusion of the still youthful William III, in an endeavour to block any return of the House of Orange.[28]

Even without this tension it was difficult enough to keep the ship of state on course. The desire to retain local and regional 'freedoms' had been a significant driver of the Revolt against Spain, and the creation of the Republic was a 'triumph for this particularism', as Prak puts it. Yet at the same time, the struggle against Spain had made it necessary to work together. As a result, the Republic had to perform a permanent balancing act between unity and discord.[29] This remained the case after the end of the conflict with Spain, and there was no constitution to channel the permanent tensions between local self-government and coordination at a national level. There was no powerful political centre, and towns, cities and provinces derived their identities primarily from their own independence.

'All authority in the Republic was fragmented and was contested from different sides,' writes Prak in his monograph on the Golden Age. This could involve confrontations between Orangists and those opposed to the stadholder, but also between towns, cities and provinces. The upshot was that conflicts were usually resolved through laboriously reached compromises, after which new squabbles soon arose and the negotiating process had to continue.[30] However, the centrifugal forces were never strong enough to pull the fragile structure apart because the common interest was too great, and the potential external threat also kept towns, cities and provinces together. During relatively quiet times on the international scene, though – during the Truce, for instance, and after 1650 – internal tensions became more acute. The conflicts that existed during the Johan de Witt era, the compromises that were worked out, and the dramatic end of this stadholderless period in the 'Disaster Year' of 1672 will be explored later. It is sufficient here to observe that diversity in government administration and divisions continued unabated during the Republic's heyday.

A few examples serve to explain how this led to awkward regional differences when it came to practical cooperation. Throughout the seventeenth century, the Republic had two different calendars – the Gregorian and the Julian. This meant it was always ten days later in Holland, Zeeland and Brabant than in the other provinces. Coinage was also a provincial matter, and there was even greater diversity in weights and measures. Even the gauges for carts and wagons varied from region to region. Anyone travelling in the Republic would have been lost without almanacs and conversion tables.[31]

Reflecting governmental diversity and the often wearisome decision-making process, the Republic developed its own uniquely Dutch 'discussion culture', which can be regarded as a second basic form of diversity. A characteristic feature of the Republic's debating climate was not just the wholehearted involvement of the middle class, but the fact that a specific consensus and unity was embedded in it. It was not about the substance of an agreement – opinions and interests were often diametrically opposed – but about the way the decision making should take place and about the fact that this method was an essential element of the common identity. Meeting, discussing and consulting became key aspects of the Republic's political culture. Time after time they confirmed the high degree of diversity and the centrifugal governmental structure. On the other hand, according to Frijhoff and Spies, it was in this very 'horizontal consultation model' that the 'society's strength and cohesion' lay.[32] In other words, while there were divisions in this form of diversity, there was at the same time a specific form of Dutch unity. This climate of discussion became such an essential feature of the Netherlands that to this day it is usually referred to as a characteristic of the Dutch decision-making culture.

The third basic form of diversity lay in the major religious differences.[33] The Republic's religious pluriformity arising from the Revolt was perpetuated by provincial sovereignty in spiritual matters and also by the horizontal organization of the official church, which amplified local and regional variations and ruled out strong central leadership. One of the reasons why the Dutch Reformed Church did not develop into an established Calvinist church for the whole population was the attitude of many of its members. They believed that membership of this church was reserved for a select group of worshippers who lived their daily lives in strict accordance with God's word and whose conduct was unimpeachable. This view was opposed by moderate members, who advocated broader admission to the church and resisted Calvinist orthodoxy.

This conflict came to a head in the mid-seventeenth century in the dispute between Gisbertus Voetius (1589–1676) and Johannes Coccejus (1603–69). The former was a member of a Pietist movement that wanted to strengthen personal religious life, advocated stricter discipline being imposed by the Calvinist church, and sought to initiate a Further Reformation. This was necessary to avoid God's wrath, which would manifest itself in lost wars, dwindling trade and other symptoms of decline. They rejected any government involvement in ecclesiastical matters and saw it as the church's task to guard and disseminate true Calvinist doctrine.

Coccejus, on the other hand, opposed Puritanism and dogmatism, was less strict about Sunday observance, and was also prepared to accept a degree of government influence in the life of the church. The dispute between the Voetians and Coccejans in the middle of the seventeenth century did not become as heated as the quarrel between the Arminians and Gomarists at the beginning of the century, although the differing positions were comparable. The Coccejans tried to prevent the Calvinist orthodox church from dominating politics and society, as had the Arminians, and their primary support came from the Holland regents. The Voetians' supporters, like those of the earlier Gomarists, were mainly Orangists. However, this is not the place to delve into these theological wrangles and their political and social implications. The key point here is that diversity was also significant inside the official church and created multiple tensions.

As we saw earlier, in 1651 the General Assembly had once again ratified the privileged position of the Dutch Reformed Church. It was the only one to be officially permitted and in principle only members of this church were eligible for government posts. The authority of each province to set the limits of freedom of other churches was also confirmed. This type of tolerance was typical of the Republic, but it was unique from an international perspective and it always surprised foreign travellers. In practice, there was far-reaching pragmatic tolerance around 1650, and other churches were permitted to hold their services, although there were differences from town to town and province to province. Most adherents of other faiths were not allowed to have churches recognizable as such from outside, and passers-by were not to be aware of services. This is why clandestine places of worship were created; Our Lord in the Attic – a Catholic church constructed on the top three floors of a canal-side house in the 1660s in the centre of Amsterdam – is a well-known example. The situation was more difficult for Catholics than for the countless Protestant movements, but if enough money changed hands, they too were usually left in peace to worship.

Orthodox Calvinists frequently protested about such tolerance but, as far as most regents were concerned, pragmatism and maintaining peace and quiet had priority.

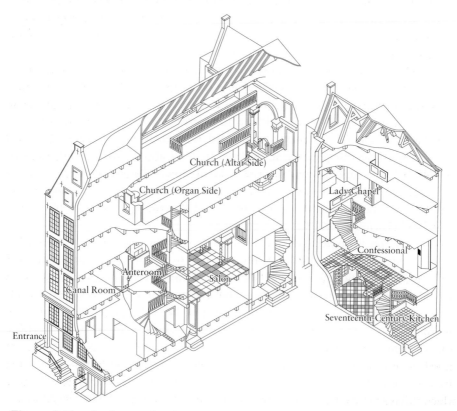

Figure 8 The clandestine church of Our Lord in the Attic, Oudezijds Voorburgwal, Amsterdam. Our Lord in the Attic, Amsterdam.

Provided that the other churches did not threaten public order and behaved with restraint, little was done to interfere with them, particularly in Holland. The ideal values of tolerance and freedom existed, but pragmatism like this was more important. As they had been during the Revolt, the members of the Dutch Reformed Church were a minority of the population and it was recognized that the Republic's political stability and prosperity were not helped by the heavy-handed exclusion of dissenters – quite apart from the issue of whether the Calvinists had the means to do so.

This pragmatism is understandable because around 1650 there was still no religion that dominated in terms of numbers of adherents. Religious pluriformity was not evenly spread over the Republic either. It is generally assumed that during this period about one-third of the population belonged to the Dutch Reformed Church – a share that gradually grew to some 55 per cent by around 1800. Most of the members of the Dutch Reformed Church and other Protestants (mainly Mennonites, Remonstrants and Lutherans) lived to the north of the Rhine and Meuse. The percentage of Protestants in Groningen, Friesland, Drenthe and Zeeland was 85 or higher, but Catholics represented between 45 and 55 per cent in Overijssel, Guelders and Utrecht, and approximately 30 per cent in Holland. During the 1650s, about a quarter of the urban population of Holland was Catholic, and this proportion dropped to only some 14 per cent by around 1725. By way of contrast, essentially the entire population of the Generality Lands in the south was Catholic, and this was not to change until the twentieth century.

Taking the population of the Republic as a whole, in the middle of the seventeenth century about 40 per cent was Catholic. This proportion gradually decreased to about a third by around 1725. After that, the number of Catholics slowly increased and around 1800 they once again amounted to 40 per cent of the population. Finally, in 1650 or thereabouts, there was a group of believers who were 'undecided' or 'neutral'. They had still to choose between Catholicism and a Protestant church, and now and again they attended services of one or other persuasion. Visitors to Dutch Reformed Church services who were not yet members were called 'dabblers'. As soon as they let it be known that they wanted to join, their conduct and religious beliefs were scrutinized. If the result was deemed positive, they could be confirmed.[34]

Although there were slight shifts in the relative numbers of Protestants and Catholics after 1650, the religious situation had largely crystallized since the Peace of Münster and the General Assembly. Individual Christian identity was now increasingly linked to an individual's church and religious beliefs, and people's day to day lives increasingly focused on their own ecclesiastical environment. There was a fall in the number of mixed marriages and social care was largely provided within people's own circles. So while there was a degree of religious compartmentalization on the one hand, a form of interdenominational exchange developed – in spite of all the theological conflict and divisions – that Frijhoff and Spies describe as 'ecumenical dealings in the public domain', which blunted the sharp edges of religious diversity. Collaboration in politics and society was not hampered by denominational differences despite the clear religious hierarchy, with its Calvinist dominance. Tolerance of other persuasions for reasons of pragmatism grew into what Frijhoff and Spies describe as the national interest, or in other words the Republic's secular ideology.[35]

Around 1650, a common 'fatherland' was also clearly developing alongside the Republic's religious and political multiformity. The seven sovereign provinces, non-sovereign Drenthe, the Generality Lands and the towns and cities were a hotchpotch with differently stratified loyalties and factions struggling with one another. Yet at the same time, there were self-images that transcended towns, cities, factions and provinces, and these formed the basis of an emerging shared identity.

We saw earlier how Oldenbarnevelt and Hugo Grotius spread the Batavian myth – a historical construct of the Dutch sense of freedom and republican governance. A second myth promulgated by the Calvinists testifies to their strong self-esteem and sense of being chosen. They claimed that God had given the members of the Dutch Reformed Church the task of converting the Republic in line with God's intentions, and in so doing to shape a 'second Israel'.[36] The historian Schutte, a leading authority on Calvinism in the Netherlands, rightly points out that this way of thinking was not unique to the Netherlands, and that similar convictions of having been selected and providential calling emerged in other parts of the Christian world. He also stresses that the Dutch Reformed Church's seventeenth-century theologians used the concept of a 'Dutch Israel' to refer to their own church only and not to the Republic as a fatherland.[37] Nevertheless, given the Calvinist hegemony in politics, the church and society, this myth also had a unifying effect. Like the Batavian myth, it was fed by the broader self-image of the heroic struggle against the wicked Spanish, and also by what Frijhoff and Spies call 'translation' or conferment. Around 1650, many of the Republic's residents considered their territory and themselves to be the place on earth where the former power and knowledge of the Mediterranean would be taken forward. Classical Athens, ancient Rome and Renaissance Italy remained valuable historical resources, but in this scenario Holland owned the future and continued the old traditions. There was no doubt about it because, so people believed, the Republic had God on its side.[38]

A new self-image was created after the Peace of Münster. The armed conflicts in which the Republic was involved in the 1650s and 1660s were not about recognition of the Netherlands' right to exist, but to secure and augment its opportunities. From the dominant Holland-centric perspective, this meant free trade and unrestricted seagoing shipping. This led to the development of the Republic's self-image as a prosperous, trading and peace-loving nation that had a primary interest in international peace, stability and maintaining the status quo. Johan de Witt said that 'the interests of this state are completely bound up in calm and peace so that trade is not impeded'.[39] This love of peace did not, though, mean a lack of willingness to employ military means. On the contrary, if the international balance of power was disrupted or its own latitude was threatened with restrictions, the Republic took firm action. The navy's successes in the 1650s and 1660s were consequently viewed as confirmation of the self-image of valour that had emerged in the past. Many believed that these successes and the associated vigour had only been possible because of the Republic's decentralized governmental structure and discussion culture, so these characteristics also became part of the 'national' self-images.

A common feature of these various self-images was that they considered the Republic and its population to be special – a miracle on earth. This admiration and reverence for their own country was matched by the praise that English, French, German and other foreign visitors heaped on Holland in the seventeenth century – the highly commendable freedom and tolerance, the independence and sovereignty won from Spain, the flourishing economy and culture, dominance in trade and seagoing shipping, and scientific inventiveness. And all this had been achieved by a country with a very modest land area and a decentralized governmental structure that was out of step with the broader European trend towards centralized nation states ruled by a monarch.[40] Surely this oddly structured small country, with its religious tolerance, should be a simple pawn on the international chessboard? Was the Republic not an anomaly in a royal Europe? In other words, foreign admiration was also based on amazement. This apparent contradiction between assumed weakness and actual strength in many areas is exactly what Prak describes as the 'enigma of the Republic'.[41]

The 'true freedom' (1650–72)

The circumstances leading to a stadholderless period that began in most provinces after William II's sudden death in 1650 have been discussed above. The Republic was starting in a strong position in the new international relations that emerged from the Peace of Westphalia, and its economy was the strongest in the world. But during the years of 'true freedom', England and France would develop their economic potential, grow their international power and eventually bring the Republic to the brink of the abyss.

France played an important role in this development. The Franco–Spanish war that had recommenced in 1648 ended in 1659. Peace between Spain and France also changed the situation on the continent for the Republic, and during the 1660s France ceased to be an ally and became a potential enemy. That became a reality in 1672 when – as part of a joint Anglo–French attack supported by the bishoprics of Münster and Cologne – a large body of French troops marched into the Republic. The catastrophic outcome of this war – 1672 has gone down in Dutch history as the 'Disaster Year' – was the end of the stadholderless era and the return of the House of Orange to the country's centre of power. In that year the 21-year-old William III became captain general of the Union and stadholder of Holland, Zeeland, Utrecht, Overijssel and Guelders.

The first confrontation in the Stadholderless Period, however, was with England, which as a maritime power had the same trading objectives as the Republic. Initially, Protestant England set out to form an alliance, but it wanted the Republic to be very much the junior partner. The English approaches were therefore politely brushed aside. In 1651, England responded by promulgating the Navigation Act. Under its terms, goods from a particular country could only be carried to England in vessels from their country of origin or in English ships. The Republic was the leader in world trade and this measure was primarily designed to contest that dominance. This English legislation did not have major implications, however, because there was not much trade between the Republic and England.

The First Anglo–Dutch War (1652–54) broke out the following year. It was about who ruled the seas, and the Republic's fleet was no match for the more modern English navy, which had purpose-built men-of-war. The Republic's fleet was weak – a random assortment of mostly hired-in armed merchantmen.[42] The Dutch also paid the price for not having a general admiral who, as supreme commander of the navy, could have led the five geographically dispersed admiralties. This lack of overall leadership also meant that the fleet was dominated by particularism. The Republic was forced on to the defensive to such an extent that merchant shipping and fishing came to a virtual standstill, and the people began to turn against the 'true freedom' recently implemented by the regents, because they had proved incapable of stopping the English threat. This led to disturbances in some places, and there were also voices calling for the return of an Orange, even though the only one eligible was still a toddler. All in all, this was a difficult situation for 'true freedom' before it had got properly under way. It was in these circumstances that Johan de Witt became Grand Pensionary of Holland in 1653. All the Republic's political strands would come together in his hands and under his leadership the country would successfully fend off English and French challenges until the 'Disaster Year' of 1672.

Initially, during the war with England, this had not seemed a likely prospect, but after Oliver Cromwell assumed complete control, English strategy changed. Cromwell was prepared to put an end to the war and even returned to the idea of a union with the Republic under English leadership. Above all, he wanted to prevent the Stuarts regaining the English throne, and this had implications for his attitude to the Republic. William II's widow, Mary Henrietta Stuart, was the daughter of the English King Charles I, who was beheaded in 1649, and the sister of Charles, the pretender to the throne. It was therefore not out of the question that the Republic would develop into an operating base for the Stuarts, particularly given the swelling chorus calling for the return of the House of Orange.

It was consequently very much in Cromwell's interests not to endanger the 'true freedom' of the regents and to support them in their anti-Orange policy. He was prepared to make peace with the Republic, but on condition that the still very young Prince of Orange would be excluded from the posts of stadholder and captain general (the Act of Exclusion). Johan de Witt secretly agreed to this condition on behalf of Holland, thus succeeding in achieving peace with England. There was great indignation when it emerged that De Witt had done this on his own authority and had acted behind virtually everyone's backs. His opponents felt they had been put on the spot because they had to choose between continuing a war that was already lost and accepting the Act of Exclusion aimed against Orange, and hence against the Stuarts, so they were left with little choice but to resign themselves to the Treaty of Westminster (1654) that Johan de Witt had negotiated.[43] This reinforced De Witt's position of power, but Orangist supporters would never forget that he had sidelined William III.

In 1653, the catastrophic outcome of the naval battles in the war with England prompted ambitious plans to build a substantial standing fleet.[44] The Republic began to catch up quickly, establishing the basis for a powerful maritime position, which enabled it to secure its interests in trade and seagoing shipping. While there were substantial investments in a strong and permanently deployable navy under De Witt's leadership during this period, there were at the same time drastic cuts in spending on the army, and this was to prove catastrophic for the Republic in the 'Disaster Year' of 1672. De Witt's core objective was to create the conditions for the further expansion of trade and seagoing shipping, which meant that international peace and a stable balance of power were in the Republic's interests. To this end, De Witt pursued a policy of active neutralism, based on a well-thought-out array of international treaties. As soon as international peace was threatened with disruption and the Republic's trade and seagoing shipping were exposed to danger, however, the Republic had to be able to act to restore equilibrium. It intervened in the Second Northern War (1655–60) between Sweden and Denmark, which threatened to disrupt the balance of power in that area in favour of Sweden. At stake was the passage through the Øresund (the Sound) to the Baltic, which was absolutely vital to Dutch trading. A balance of power in the region was essential to keep the route open, so when it looked as though Denmark was going to lose, the Republic came to its help. Sweden was forced to accept peace terms and Dutch interests were safeguarded.

Relations with England and France were key to De Witt's aim of creating a balanced international power equilibrium, with the best possible opportunities for the Republic to flourish. At that time, the links between these three countries determined political relations in Western Europe. The relationship with England changed after the Stuarts returned to the English throne in 1660 in the person of Charles II. The new English king was the uncle of William III, who by then was ten, and although Charles did not make immediate efforts to restore the Oranges' position in the Republic, it did mean the end of Cromwell's anti-Orange policy. It was thus important for De Witt to make overtures to Charles II, but that proved difficult and things soon went wrong after the renewal of the Navigation Act in December 1660. In 1662, De Witt entered into a treaty with France in which the two countries promised to help each other in the event of an attack by other countries. They also agreed to a trade treaty. These two treaties eliminated a possible danger from the south and so trade could flourish. In that same year, England entered into a Treaty of Friendship with the Republic, although this was of little significance. The English did it to send a warning signal to the French rather than out of sympathy for the Republic. These treaties did not bring lasting stability, but De Witt's policy of maintaining equilibrium by focusing on France and England prolonged the Republic's key role in international relations.[45]

Given their competing interests on the world's oceans, however, confrontations between England and the Republic were inevitable. In 1664, England overpowered the Dutch settlement of New Amsterdam, which became New York, and there was also fighting in western Africa. The Second Anglo–Dutch War, which broke out in 1665, went badly for the Dutch initially, but ended in 1667 with a great victory when Admiral Michiel Adriaensz. de Ruyter sailed up the Thames and destroyed the English fleet moored at Chatham. Typical of De Witt's policy of balance was that the Republic did not humiliate England through the Treaty of Breda, and moderate peace terms were reached. 'The Republic,' writes Van Deursen, 'was unable to maintain its position as a great power

Figure 9 *Johan de Witt (1625–72), Grand Pensionary of Holland*, Jan de Baen. Rijksmuseum Amsterdam.

for long, but Breda was the pinnacle in that brief glorious period, and it had De Witt to thank for it'.[46] As we shall see below, there was another reason why the peace terms that emerged in Breda were moderate: the French invaded the Spanish Netherlands in 1667, and the expansion of French power in a northerly direction was not in the Republic's interest. Under these circumstances it was not prudent to make England eat humble pie, and possibly drive it into the French camp as a result.

During the Second Anglo–Dutch War, it also became clear where the Achilles heel of De Witt's security doctrine lay. Bernhard von Galen, Prince-Bishop of Münster, invaded the Republic from the east and conquered a few towns. It was then that the Dutch paid the price for De Witt's policy of ploughing all the resources into the navy, because the army was in a deplorable state. The Republic called on France to help, peace was made with Münster's prince-bishop in 1666 and the pre-war status quo was restored.[47]

French claims to the Spanish Netherlands after the death of the Spanish King Philip IV in 1665 represented a much greater threat. When Louis XIV advanced into the Spanish Netherlands in 1667, an attack that later became known as the War of Devolution, he met with little resistance. In 1668, De Witt signed a Triple Alliance with England and

Sweden in an attempt to restore balance and force France into a more moderate position. This was successful, but also risky. It was successful because France was kept in check – although this was not the only reason – and it agreed to a modest territorial gain in the Spanish Netherlands. It was also risky because Louis XIV did not want to leave the Republic's anti-French conduct unavenged. Tensions also increased in the commercial arena. France's mercantilist policy was intensified, with the result that the Republic increasingly had to contend with two economic rivals. One of them, France, had the biggest army on the continent while the other, England, had the biggest fleet. If they were ever to form an alliance against the Dutch, the Republic would not stand a chance.

And that was exactly the danger that threatened when England made clear what its intentions had been by signing the Triple Alliance and soon disclosed the secret clause in it against France. It stated that the parties to the alliance would – under certain conditions – actually take action against France. Louis XIV considered this as a violation of the defensive treaty he had concluded with the Republic in 1662 and felt betrayed. This French anger with the Republic was exactly what Charles II intended, so that he could eliminate Dutch competition by teaming up with France. The next step to that end was a secret pact made between England and France in Dover in 1670. In it, they agreed to jointly attack the Republic and divide the conquered territory between them. What remained would be transferred to Charles's nephew, William III. France also promised the financially weakened Charles II substantial sums of money. In exchange, the English king undertook to convert to Catholicism.

Johan de Witt, the brilliant diplomat and master of balance, did notice that cooperation with England was getting more difficult, but he could not imagine that the Republic's two rivals were ganging up on it. Such a pact was alien to his rational view of international politics, in which states only acted in their own, objective interests. In De Witt's thinking, France and England were rivals, and it could not be in English interests if France were to increase its power at the Republic's expense. As he saw it, an Anglo–French alliance was unthinkable. The magnitude of this miscalculation became clear in 1672. In fact the Anglo–French attack was to have taken place in 1671, but Louis did not want to advance on the Republic through the Spanish Netherlands because that would reignite the conflict with Spain. He therefore asked the permission of the bishops of Münster and Cologne to let his troops make for the Republic through their territory. A combined attack by these four parties in 1672 brought the Republic to the edge of the abyss, and ended the First Stadholderless Period.

Orange's return in 1672 was not completely unexpected. While the Orangists had suffered major defeats with the abolition of stadholdership in 1650 and the Act of Exclusion in 1654, there was still a large group of people looking for a counterweight to the dominant regent factions, particularly in Holland. This group did not want an Orange as a monarch, but a *republica mixta*, a mixed form of government involving regents and the House of Orange. This view was supported by people in the lower classes who still had a soft spot for Orange leadership. Initially, there was little more to discuss than the upbringing of the young William, but there were considerable differences of opinion about this during the Stadholderless Period. William's mother, Mary Henrietta Stuart, was hoping above all for a joint return of Orange and the Stuarts, and preferred English-oriented schooling. But his grandmother, Amalia of Solms-Braunfels – the widow of Frederick Henry, wanted rapprochement with the regents and was convinced that only a Dutch education would keep alive the chance of Orange's return to the Republic. Johan de Witt and the regents of the 'true freedom' did everything they could to obstruct the latter alternative; of all things, they did not want William to be prepared for government tasks.[48]

Johan de Witt had little to worry about in this regard until 1660, when a Stuart returned to the English throne and the balance of power changed. William, now aged ten, increasingly became a factor influencing the relationship between the Republic and England. De Witt came under greater pressure than during the 1650s to take the prince's upbringing into account in his national and international political calculations. This was the background to De Witt's willingness to make concessions. The Act of Exclusion was set aside and responsibility for educating the young prince was given to the States of Holland, which was charged with grooming him for high, but unspecified, office. Not that De Witt had an important post for William in mind; what led him to take this step in 1660 were the internal relationships in the Republic and the expectation that the States of Holland – by taking the prince under its wing – could in any event counteract undesirable English influence on him.

Everything changed a year later with the sudden death of Mary Henrietta Stuart. In her will she specified that her son's schooling should be put in the hands of her brother Charles II. The latter played his trump card cleverly in 1665 by offering the Republic – initially in a tight spot because of the Second Anglo–Dutch War and the attack from Münster – peace, provided that William III would be offered high offices. Things did not go that far, but in 1665 the fifteen-year-old William became the 'Child of State'. From that moment, Johan de Witt took a close personal interest in the prince's education and gave him a weekly lesson. Nonetheless, the overall objectives of De Witt and the supporters of 'true freedom' remained diametrically opposed to those of the circles around the young William. The former group wanted to safeguard 'true freedom' as far as possible while the latter wanted the prince to follow in his forebears' footsteps.

Although it was still not clear by the middle of the 1660s which group was going to come off best, the prince's position gradually became stronger. In 1667, a new page was turned when the States of Holland abolished the office of stadholder in its own province in the Perpetual Edict and declared that in other provinces the office should be separated from that of captain general. On the face of it, this looked like a victory over the Orangists, but upon closer examination it was actually a compromise that strengthened the prince's position. If the other provinces agreed with the Perpetual Edict, Prince William could become a member of the Council of State and captain general of the Union on his eighteenth birthday. Initially, therefore, De Witt opposed the Perpetual Edict because it could give the prince an undesirable position of power. After the Treaty of Breda his own position appeared so unassailable, however, that he could agree to it.

De Witt's successes also generated opposing forces and this benefitted the factions pushing for restoration of the old *republica mixta*, in which there had to be a place for

Orange. The advance of Louis XIV in the Spanish Netherlands in 1667 demonstrated once again that arrangements for the supreme command of the Republic's army were unsatisfactory, and this was one of the factors that confirmed the urgency of the issue. Prince William became a member of the Council of State after all provinces had ratified the Perpetual Edict in 1670. He was also given the right to vote, against the wishes of De Witt. In the same year, William visited his uncle Charles in England, which made the rift between De Witt and the prince even greater.

Contrary to what De Witt presumed, this visit did not result in a relationship of trust between Orange and Stuart. Charles II continued to look on his nephew as a useful pawn he could use in his own power game, while William was not inclined to play this role for his uncle. When the threat of war with France increased in 1671, the pressure on De Witt to appoint the prince as captain general rose too. This eventually happened in 1672, but the decision making surrounding it had taken so long that the urgently needed reinforcement of the army came too late. Besides, the lengthy period of neglect the Republic's army had endured could not be undone in an instant. As the 'Disaster Year' proved, the Republic's land forces were no match for the French army – superior and four times the size – which marched into Utrecht in June 1672. The carving up of the Republic by the attackers was only a matter of time, or so it seemed. If Louis XIV had wanted to, he could also have overrun Holland, but the French king believed he had already achieved his objectives. He was also aware that the long supply lines from France and the fact that Holland would defend itself by flooding land were not without risks. Another factor that might have played a role was that his offensive capability had decreased because some of his troops had remained behind to occupy the conquered towns and cities. The Republic was thus spared from complete annihilation.

The blame for the military collapse of the Republic was laid squarely at the door of Johan de Witt, his brother Cornelis and all the other 'true freedom' regents, and a serious hate campaign against him began to grow. At the same time, there was a call for Orange to save the situation and by the beginning of July 1672 the 'true freedom' had been pushed aside by a coalition of Orangist regents and other groups. The void was filled by the 21-year-old William III, who became stadholder of Holland and captain general and admiral general of the Union. Johan de Witt, who was wounded in an attack in June, could do little else in these circumstances but submit his resignation, which was accepted at the beginning of August 1672. The political rupture of 1650 – the start of the Stadholderless Period – was healed.

The nadir of the emotional tsunami that swamped the Republic came in August 1672 with the lynching of the De Witt brothers by an infuriated crowd in The Hague, close to the Binnenhof, where the grand pensionary had been the most powerful man in the Republic for nearly two decades. Traditional historiography has long perpetuated the story of an angry mob that had this gruesome lynching on its conscience. In fact, it was a case of citizens applying the principle of an eye for an eye and a tooth for a tooth, and punishing the men they held responsible for the Republic's desperate situation.[49]

The internal political developments of 1672 were not unlike those of 1618. Then too a powerful official – Oldenbarnevelt, Advocate of Holland – had been at odds with an Orange – Maurice – and Orange had won. Maurice was not prepared to spare Oldenbarnevelt's life in 1618, and neither was William III willing to do anything to stop the murder of the De Witt brothers in 1672. In fact, he even rewarded the ringleaders afterwards. In both 1618 and 1672, there was strong Orangist support among the common people and, although the circumstances were very different, many saw Orange as a beacon of hope at a dramatic moment for the Republic. The fact that the Oranges were able to settle matters in their favour on both occasions was also directly related to the military resources they controlled in their positions as commander-in-chief. Finally, both years heralded the beginning of a phase of the Republic's history dominated by an Orange. In William III's case it would last until 1702. Unlike the position in 1618, in the 'Disaster Year' many people turned on the 'bad governance' of the incumbent regents and demanded they face the consequences personally. The threatening language of the many political pamphlets that were published in the summer of 1672 and the physical intimidation of many regents showed that there was a powerful popular movement with its own political agenda, which also set limits to the power of the young stadholder, William III.[50]

The Republic had flourished economically and in international politics during Johan de Witt's term as grand pensionary. Although the times of spectacular economic growth were over and it was more a matter of continuation, the Republic's economy remained very strong and the Dutch retained their dominant position in world trade. De Witt's policy of active neutrality contributed significantly to this and prolonged the status quo in international power politics – as long as it lasted, for ultimately it was inevitable that the Republic would lose out to the potentially much stronger rivals of England and France.

In the same way as the emergence of the Republic in the late sixteenth century was only conceivable against the backdrop of the weakness of other powers, so the problems of 1672 were unavoidable because of the rise of two countries that – given their size, population and economic potential – had been less strong than they could have been. According to historian Luc Panhuysen, the Republic had attained a high position among nations but, when faced with competition from France and England, it proved ultimately to be nothing more than 'a small country living above its means'. As the Dutch statesman Johan Rudolf Thorbecke was to comment in 1836, Johan de Witt fought 'a battle against the fate of the Republic'.[51] Although William III was to successfully extend that battle, he too would have to face facts. By the end of his rule in 1702 the Republic was virtually spent as a great power.

The return of Orange: The Republic under William III (1672–1702)

The year 1672 has gone down in Dutch history as the 'Disaster Year' for good reason. For a few months, the Republic's existence and affluence were at stake because of its rapid military collapse, trade paralysis and domestic political instability.[52] This was not really surprising, given the huge military might that France and England, supported by Münster and Cologne, represented. The Republic's rapid recovery afterwards is much more remarkable. Under Stadholder William III it became the linchpin of a broad European coalition against French domination in subsequent decades. Combatting French power in Europe would also become the young stadholder's main aim in life – a goal that he continued to pursue until his death in 1702. His domestic policies were to be completely subordinate to this aim.[53]

The stadholder's top priority in 1672, though, was to drive foreign troops out of the Republic's territory. That summer, the majority of the Republic was in enemy hands. The French had conquered areas in the south and centre of the country, and the Bishop of Münster in the east and north. The situation was dramatic, but in hindsight it is clear that the worst was over by August. William III, the new political and military leader, gradually brought calm to domestic politics. At the same time, the Bishop of Münster's advance ground to a halt and, as we saw above, Louis XIV's push towards Holland came to a standstill after the capture of the city of Utrecht. Before that, Admiral Michiel de Ruyter was able to thwart the combined English and French fleets at the Battle of Solebay. The battle proper was indecisive, but the numerically inferior fleet of the Republic emerged as the moral victor and the threat of a seaborne invasion or a blockade was warded off for the time being.[54]

The fact that the enemy advance was not carried through to the bitter end had nothing to do with the military prowess of the young stadholder. There had simply not been enough time since his appointment as commander-in-chief at the beginning of 1672 to improve the condition of the national army. The significance of his actions that summer lay primarily in successfully tackling defeatism inside the country, while at the same time refusing to accept French and English peace terms. Had he accepted them, the Republic would have survived as not much more than an Anglo–French protectorate. William III was able to persevere by gaining support from other powers concerned about French efforts to expand. Cooperation with Brandenburg and the Habsburg emperor started as early as the summer of 1672. He gradually forged an international coalition that was formalized in 1673 as the Quadruple Alliance between the Dutch Republic, the Holy Roman Empire, Spain and Lorraine. This forced Louis XIV to divide his forces between a number of fronts and William III was able to take the offensive on Republic territory.

At sea that same year, De Ruyter (1607–76) inflicted three serious defeats on the Anglo–French fleet, which in each case was numerically stronger. In 1673, he also had defensive successes that rank among the greatest tactical achievements of the admiral's life.[55] His contribution was critical in bringing about peace with England, which King Charles II was forced to accept for financial reasons in 1674. Peace was also made that same year with the bishoprics of Münster and Cologne, and the Republic was given back all the areas captured by Münster.

Meanwhile, William III had transformed the national army, which had been so weak in 1672, into a large and effective fighting force, and France had retreated further and further. By October 1674, Maastricht was the only prize Louis XIV retained from his conquests in the 'Disaster Year'. It was too soon, however, to make peace with France because William III continued to support the alliance's fight against French expansionism.

Nevertheless, under pressure from the regents of Holland and against the wishes of the stadholder, in 1678 the Republic and France made peace and signed the Treaty of Nijmegen, whereupon the Dutch withdrew from the anti-French coalition, which at that time comprised the Holy Roman Empire, Spain and Brandenburg. Holland – Amsterdam in particular – which had suffered particularly badly during the war, had been pressing for peace with France for some time and could be happy with the very favourable peace terms in 1678. The return to the Republic of all the areas conquered by France in 1672 was certainly important, but the decisive factor for Holland was Louis XIV's promise to abolish the trade tariffs that France had imposed since 1667. That was an offer that Holland could not afford to refuse, particularly since the end of the war would reduce the huge expense of maintaining the army. From this perspective, peace was a resounding success for the Republic. William III, however, was less satisfied. Louis XIV had used the Peace of Nijmegen to torpedo the anti-French coalition and paint the Republic as an unreliable ally concerned solely with its own commercial interests, and this was not consistent with William's paramount foreign policy objective: permanently weakening France.[56]

Although the Peace of Nijmegen demonstrated that William III's power in the Republic was not unlimited, there can be no doubt that he could pull many strings. In 1672 he had rapidly filled the domestic and foreign policy vacuum created by the resignation and death of Johan de Witt. That summer, the confusion among the population and their fury with the incumbent regents were so intense that 'true freedom' disappeared with breathtaking speed and all hope was pinned on the stadholder. It is therefore not surprising that William was able to purge the regents and replace a large number of De Witt's followers with his own supporters. He also built up a substantial informal network that operated independently of existing channels and was accountable solely to him. Although William III developed a strong power base in the States of Holland as a result – and with the skilful support of the new Grand Pensionary, Gaspar Fagel – his policies ran into opposition and it was difficult for him to keep Amsterdam in line. As a political realist he was well aware, however, that Amsterdam's support in the States was indispensable. In the 1680s, after a period of confrontation, he opted for rapprochement and collaboration, which benefitted the Republic's political stability.

William III's power base in Utrecht, Guelders and Overijssel became even stronger after the departure of French troops in 1674. Governance regulations gave William III the power to appoint people to all the important executive bodies, giving him complete control in these provinces. Guelders was prepared to go even further and in 1675 it offered to make him the duke – the first step for the prince on the road to sovereignty of the whole Republic.[57] But by aspiring to the ducal title he had overplayed his hand. Holland and Zeeland opposed it, and this made it necessary for him to decline the honour. In spite of this he acquired an impressive degree of power. One of the contributing factors was the States General's decision in 1675 to declare the supreme command of the army and navy hereditary in the Prince of Orange's male line. The States of Holland had done the same thing the year before for the province's stadholdership. The power that William III built up in just a few years was greater than that of any stadholder before him. However, he could not be an absolute monarch in the Republic's structure. In practical terms, though, his position was not that much weaker than that of his great bête noire, the absolutist monarch Louis XIV.[58]

As far as the stadholder was concerned, the Peace of Nijmegen was no more than a compulsory breather in the conflict with the French king. Nijmegen was only a ceasefire for Louis XIV too, and in subsequent years he continued to pursue his expansionist policy, but without its leading to another war with the Republic. In the early 1680s, William III tried in vain to get support in Holland for mobilization to help Spain against France because he was personally profoundly insulted by Louis's annexation of the principality of Orange in 1682. Once again he found that Amsterdam in particular was standing in his way, although elsewhere in the Republic, too, people had little enthusiasm for new martial adventures.

A military victory over Louis XIV was thus not on the cards for the time being, but meanwhile, William III had hit him where it hurt in another area. In 1677, the 26-year-old stadholder married his 15-year-old cousin Mary Stuart (1662–94), daughter of James, the heir to the English throne. This strategically important move was to form the basis of the English monarchy that he and his wife would assume after the Glorious Revolution of 1688. In 1677, that coronation was still a long way off, but what did become clear immediately was that this marriage had made the anti-French coalition very much stronger.

William III was never loved by the people, nor did he make any effort to be so. He did not have an engaging personality and was moody, tight lipped and suspicious. In the 'Disaster Year' he had certainly turned the Republic around and was admired for having done so. Under his leadership the country had, moreover, become a major military power, and this earned him respect. But after the immediate danger had receded, his ongoing pursuit of war, for which he employed all his domestic instruments of power, met with resistance. His attempts to acquire the title of Duke of Guelders in 1675, and in so doing to reinforce his formal power base, also gave rise to a great deal of criticism and did his standing considerable damage.[59]

In 1685, two events ratcheted up international tensions dramatically. First James II, William III's father-in-law, became king of England in February of that year. In principle, the Republic and England came closer together through the strategic family tie but James, who was a practising Catholic, soon instigated a pro-Catholic religious policy, which from the Republic's perspective was alarming. In so doing the English king was making it clear he was not prepared to form an alliance against France, and so in fact drove England and the Republic further apart. Second, the situation in Europe deteriorated in 1685 because Louis XIV revoked the 1598 Edict of Nantes. Under it the Protestant Church in France had been given the status of a tolerated minority, albeit without the same rights as Catholics.

The position of Protestants in France had worsened during the course of the seventeenth century, and in 1685 Louis XIV put an end to what still remained of the Edict of Nantes. From that moment there was no longer any place for Protestantism in Catholic France. As a consequence, a stream of Huguenot refugees left France en route to a number of Protestant states. According to a cautious estimate, some 35,000 Protestants fled to the Republic over a short period. They settled primarily in the towns and cities of Holland and increased the overall population of the country by 2 per cent. The persecution of Protestants in France and the refugees' accounts of it made it abundantly clear what a Europe dominated by the French could lead to, and the upshot was growing anti-French sentiment. William III profited from this because it was now simpler for him to get support for his struggle against France. This support became even greater when in 1687 Louis XIV scrapped the trade clause in the Peace of Nijmegen and reinstated the high trade tariffs of 1667. Amsterdam now also abandoned its resistance and was prepared to help the stadholder in his anti-France war policy.

This policy was pursued first and foremost via England and was not without risk. Although James II's pro-Catholic policy had given rise to concerns in the Republic, initially it could still be assumed that his rule would end sooner or later and that the Protestant Mary Stuart, William III's wife, would then – as first in line to the throne – become monarch. That positive picture of the future changed in 1688 into the threatening prospect of an English Catholic dynasty when a male heir to the throne was born at the English court. This made the probability of Mary Stuart becoming queen of England remote in the extreme, and opened the door to enduring cooperation between France and England, which without doubt would have more dramatic consequences for the Republic than the ad hoc alliance between the two countries in 1672. At the same time the trade dispute between the Republic and France flared up and renewed war had become inevitable.

It was in these circumstances that William III, in the strictest secrecy, made preparations to invade England; in the autumn of 1688, at the request of the English opposition, he drove his father-in-law from the throne. The fact that he met with little resistance does not detract from the huge military success he achieved. Israel describes the invasion and its preparations as marking 'the high-point of the Republic's effectiveness as a European great power'. Taking all military, maritime, financial, logistical and diplomatic factors together, this was 'one of the most impressive feats of organization any modern regime ever achieved'.[60] The change of power in England in 1688 – the Glorious Revolution – reached its zenith at the beginning of 1689 when Mary Stuart and William III became queen and king of England. As stadholder-king William III now had greater opportunities than ever before to play the leading role in a grand anti-French coalition, comprising the Republic, England, the Holy Roman Empire, Spain and a number of German principalities. No Dutch national before or since ever played such a prominent part on the European stage. This coalition defined the sides in two major wars that were to rage in Europe for the following twenty-five years, with a brief intermission between 1697 and 1702.

The first, the Nine Years' War (1688–97), ended with the Treaty of Rijswijk and did not lead to any significant loss of French power. It was favourable for the Republic, though, because Louis XIV no longer laid claim to the Southern Netherlands and he evacuated a number of conquered towns there, so the Republic could feel more secure about its southern border. The principality of Orange was also returned to William III and Louis

XIV recognized him as King of England, Scotland and Ireland. France also once more withdrew the 1667 trade tariffs that were so deleterious for the Republic. These were certainly beneficial peace terms for William III and the Republic, but once again it was only a breathing space, which ended in 1702 with the beginning of the War of the Spanish Succession. This new war, which was to last until 1713, will be discussed in the following chapter. William III was intensively involved in the preparations for it but did not live to see its outbreak because of a fatal fall from his horse.

It would be beyond the scope of this book to analyse in detail William III's strategic military and international political activities after 1688. It is important, though, to consider the position of the stadholder-king in England and the Republic. In this context it should be pointed out that after his accession to the English throne, William III only went to the Republic on occasion and surrounded himself with Dutch advisors at the English court. This led to resentment on the English side, which was exacerbated because Dutch officers set the tone in the army. Furthermore, William III was a Calvinist. He pursued a tolerant religious policy, but nevertheless made many Anglicans mistrustful. As he had done in the Republic, he took little trouble to make himself liked by the population; he avoided public gatherings and enjoyed little popularity. This did not, though, mean his kingship was threatened. After he had defeated James II once and for all at the River Boyne in Ireland in July 1690 – a victory that Northern Irish Protestants still commemorate every year – he remained firmly in the saddle until his death in 1702.[61]

The initial delight in the Republic when the stadholder took the English crown rapidly diminished, and dissatisfaction grew there too. The two navies operated in concert. England acquired the upper hand in this combined fleet, which was commanded by an English admiral. The Republic was thus relegated to the second division as a maritime power, below England, and was never to recover from this. Many regents were furious that the English navy had taken the lead because they – true to tradition – wanted a strong fleet to protect trade and shipping. William III, in contrast, wanted the army to be the centre of gravity in the Republic's armed forces, so that it could protect the southern border against France. Further irritation was created in the Republic because William III did nothing about the Navigation Act, which harmed Dutch trade with England and so was seen not to be making sufficient efforts to support the Republic's commercial interests. Despite all this, his position was never in jeopardy. On the contrary, in the 1690s the power of Orange and his favourites was actually greater than ever.

This was not just because of his foreign policy, for which there was no alternative, but was without doubt also the result of his tolerant religious policy. He himself belonged to the strict Calvinists in the official church, but he made sure there was room for moderates too. Outside the official church he made a point of ensuring that there was a place for Catholics, Jews and Baptists. This policy defused a source of criticism traditionally used by the anti-Orangist opposition, and enabled him to present himself as a defender of liberty and broadmindedness. And lastly his position was strengthened by the efficient and effective performance of Grand Pensionary Anthonie Heinsius in the States of Holland and the States General. Grand Pensionary Fagel, who had been so important to

William III, died in the year he crossed to England, but Heinsius developed into a pillar of support as stable as his predecessor.[62]

The exertions during the Nine Years' War left deep financial and economic scars. Unremitting warfare meant high taxes, and developments in other areas made it clear that at the end of the seventeenth century the Republic was losing its leading position. The economic stagnation and deterioration will be discussed in more detail below. Here, looking back at William III's stadholdership, it is important to note that under his leadership the Republic acquired the greatest power in international politics that it had ever possessed, but at the end of his career the country was nevertheless weakened. One could also say that the Republic ultimately paid a high price for its huge efforts during this period; by overreaching during the late seventeenth century it brought about its own decline as a top-ranking power.

Without doubt William III's greatest achievement was to save the Republic from destruction in 1672. His crusade against Louis XIV was certainly understandable from the Republic's perspective, but it is fair to ask whether he overestimated the aggressiveness of the French king's policy of expansion, blinding himself to the opportunities for rapprochement.[63] William III left no important marks on the Republic itself. His exploitation of formal and informal instruments of power enabled him to acquire a virtually unassailable position, but the existing political structures remained intact. The stadholder-king was childless, and his sudden death in 1702 brought an end to the House of Orange in the direct line of descent from William of Orange (1533–84). Thus a new stadholderless period began in 1702; it was to last until 1747. This and the definitive end of the Republic's position as a major power after the War of the Spanish Succession (1702–13) will be discussed in the next chapter.

The economy in the Golden Age

During the seventeenth century, the Republic was a great power and played a key role in international relations. Its aim was not territorial expansion in Europe, but consolidation of its independence, and the defence of its interests in trade and seagoing shipping. The Republic obtained definitive international recognition after the Peace of Münster in 1648, and during the years of 'true freedom' (1650–72) it reached the zenith of its international standing. More than ever before it was in a position to secure its commercial and maritime interests through diplomacy and power politics. Even after Johan de Witt's 'system' came to an end in 1672, the Republic went through a torrid, if brief, phase before re-emerging on the international stage as a major player. From the point of view of power politics, it reached a new high point under stadholder-king William III, although upon closer examination England gradually outstripped the Republic during this period.

This international political development of the Republic in the seventeenth century can only be understood against the backdrop of the economic might it had built up since the sixteenth century, which peaked in the Golden Age. An overview of the economic development until the early seventeenth century was presented in the previous chapter.

The period between about 1580 and 1621 was one in which many economic growth factors reinforced one another, and the early Republic became the wealthiest and economically most modern region in Europe. Particularly favourable economic trends also continued in the decades thereafter, although there were shifts in the relative importance of different sectors.[64]

Specialization in agriculture started in the late Middle Ages. The import of cheap grain from the Baltic was one of the elements leading to the development of horticulture, industrial crops and stock breeding. Population increases, urbanization and the growth of manufacturing strengthened this process, and agriculture also profited greatly from new technologies that enabled higher yields. The modernization of agriculture can be well illustrated by the history of the tulip, which originally came from Turkey. Initially, tulips were collectors' items for the rich, and huge sums were spent on them. During the 1630s, there was even a brief period of tulip mania. Certain tulip varieties became objects of speculation, and in some cases thousands of guilders were paid for individual bulbs. When this craze came to an end in 1637, the tulip became a mass-produced product for the market, and formed part of the foundations of the Dutch floriculture industry, which is still important today.

The commercialization of agriculture reached its peak in the first half of the seventeenth century and led to a spectacular increase in the area of agricultural land through reclamation. The area of North Holland, for instance, grew by one-third between 1610 and 1635 (see Map 6, p. 84). Urban investors spent at least ten million guilders on new polders – more than the total amount of capital subscribed to establish the Dutch East India Company (VOC) in 1602.[65] This land reclamation in coastal provinces brought about a sharp rise in the number of farms. There was also an increase in scale, and regional specialization and technological innovations produced higher yields. Despite the significant increase in agricultural acreage, ground rents continued to rise steeply until 1650, and so too did productivity and profits, which is a further indication of how important agriculture was in the economy of the Golden Age. This industry also benefitted from the Thirty Years' War (1618–48). Large areas of Germany were devastated, keeping foreign demand for agricultural products at a high level. Besides producing food, farmers were also an indispensable link in the supply chain of raw materials for industry in the towns and cities, including flax, hops, hemp, madder root and oil-rich plants.

This interweaving of urban and rural areas and of towns and cities with one another was raised to new levels in the seventeenth century by the construction of a dense network of canals, particularly in Holland, Utrecht, Friesland and Groningen. This created a modern transport system for goods and passengers, and on some routes there was even a barge timetable with fixed journey times. In the years immediately after the opening of the canal between Amsterdam and Haarlem in 1632, passenger numbers on this route reached thirty thousand a month.[66]

The period of prosperity in rural areas in the coastal provinces came to an end around the middle of the seventeenth century. The prices of agricultural products started to drop all over Europe in the early 1660s, and as an exporting country the Republic was

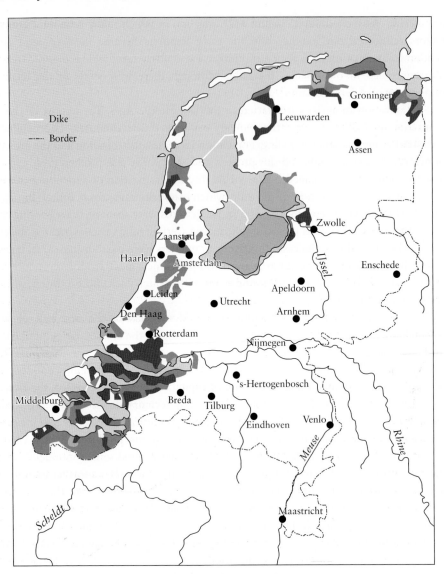

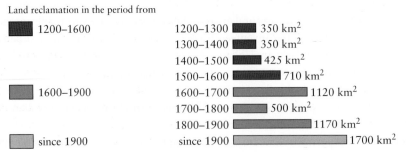

Land reclamation in the period from

▓ 1200–1600	1200–1300 ▓	350 km²
	1300–1400 ▓	350 km²
	1400–1500 ▓	425 km²
	1500–1600 ▓	710 km²
▓ 1600–1900	1600–1700	1120 km²
	1700–1800	500 km²
	1800–1900	1170 km²
▓ since 1900	since 1900	1700 km²

Map 6 Polders created since about 1200.

particularly badly hit. Profits came under even greater pressure because taxation increased, and many farmers ran into financial problems. Small farmers sold their land and headed for the towns and cities. The richer ones bought more land at knockdown prices, so there was a concentration of land ownership; even so the crisis had an impact on them too. Land and lease prices sank along with those of agricultural products, and urban investors lost interest in putting any more money into rural areas as financial returns shrank. Many landowners in the towns and cities consequently sold their holdings and put their money into bonds issued in Holland. This was a portent of developments in the eighteenth century, when the vast majority of regents lived off interest instead of investing their capital productively. The agricultural crisis became even more severe at the end of the seventeenth century, descending to a nadir in the first half of the eighteenth century. Farming in the coastal provinces did not get back on its feet until around 1750.

The situation in the inland provinces was even worse. They had profited less from the boom in agriculture during the first half of the seventeenth century. There had been much less modernization, specialization in occupations and harmonization between the urban and agrarian economies. Nevertheless, there had still been some agricultural commercialization. Farmers in Drenthe bred cattle that were sold to Holland, and in the first half of the seventeenth century tobacco growing developed on the Veluwe – a rural area in Guelders – likewise for a larger market. Unlike the coastal areas, during the second half of the seventeenth century the rural population of the inland provinces increased slightly, while their urban areas lost residents. The upshot was that waste land in these relatively infertile provinces was cultivated and agricultural acreage increased. Many small farmers and landless poor led a miserable existence, and the very labour-intensive cultivation of tobacco was the only alternative available. It flourished.

There were also changes in fishing around the middle of the century. Herring fishing had grown rapidly at the end of the sixteenth century, and this expansion continued during the first decades of the seventeenth, with Enkhuizen as an important centre. During this period, the Republic's herring fishing sector had the monopoly on the herring trade in the Baltic, but the emergence of the Scandinavian fishing industry knocked back the Republic's share in the second half of the seventeenth century, and demand in other markets dropped too. Eighty per cent of the herring catch was for export, so the decrease in international demand had immediate consequences for this sector. As was the case in agriculture, herring fishing declined during this period, although dramatic deterioration did not set in until the eighteenth century. This reversal was partially compensated by catches of other fish, including cod, on the Dogger Bank and off Iceland. This activity grew in significance and the catches were also intended mostly for export. Whaling remained very important. It emerged early in the seventeenth century, started to grow rapidly from about 1640, and reached a high point in the middle of the 1680s. At that time there were ten thousand fishermen on whalers, and the catch was much greater than the domestic demand for whale oil, so here too export was vital. The disadvantage of this industry was that the size of the catches fluctuated wildly, so profits alternated with losses and investments were usually speculative.

Finally, looking at the significance of fishing as a whole for the Republic's economy, despite the decline of herring fishing it was still of great importance in the second half of the seventeenth century. Around 1670, the Republic's entire fishing fleet numbered at least seven hundred ships, and this represented about a quarter of the total number of seaworthy commercial vessels in Europe.[67] Bearing in mind that fishing boats were expensive because of their equipment and that fishing also accounted for substantial employment on dry land, this sector remained a vital element in the Republic's economy until the end of the seventeenth century.

Add to this the merchant fleet, the navy and the vessels of the VOC and WIC, and it is not surprising that shipbuilding was one of the biggest branches of industry for many decades of the seventeenth century. We saw earlier that shipyards in Holland delivered four to five hundred vessels a year between 1625 and 1700, and that some ten thousand workers were employed to build them. The lion's share of the output – about three hundred vessels – was destined for use in the Republic, and the rest was exported. Ships were built primarily in the Zaan region, but many towns and cities also had large shipyards, such as those of the VOC and the Admiralty in Amsterdam. Much repair work was also done in Rotterdam and Amsterdam.

The Zaan region also developed into the centre of timber processing. At the beginning of the eighteenth century, this area had 584 windmills, nearly 450 more than in 1630. There was thus a very substantial increase during the second half of the seventeenth century. Most of them were sawmills for shipyards, house building, water management works and export products. The main shipyard activity was the mass production of the well-known *fluyt* and herring buss – important innovations from the late sixteenth century. It is remarkable that there were no further technical developments or innovations in shipbuilding in the seventeenth century. England and France caught up in the later decades of this century, helped by a protectionist policy that obstructed imports from the Republic. Consequently, shipbuilding in the Republic had peaked by the end of the century. But the success of the sawmills lasted much longer, and they did not start to decline until about 1730.

The water-dominated landscape of the Zaan region was not just home to the country's greatest concentration of shipyards, it was also the most important industrial area in Europe. Windmills supplied cheap energy for the sawmills and countless other industrial activities. Many windmills pressed oil from oil-rich seeds, while others husked grain, beat hemp or supplied pulp for the paper industry. This illustrates important characteristics of the Republic's seventeenth-century industry: versatility, differentiation and regional specialization.[68] Manufacturing flourished in many sectors and specialization was facilitated by specific measures taken by local authorities. Thanks to its high added value textile industry, Leiden became the most important industrial city in Europe. Expansion continued until the middle of the century, but prices came under pressure and this was followed by a turning point in production levels in around 1670. Haarlem was internationally renowned for weaving and bleaching linen. Around 1700, Gouda had a population of approximately twenty thousand, of whom four or five thousand earned a living making pipes. During the 1650s and 1660s there was explosive growth in Delft's potteries and they flourished for some fifty years, from the 1670s to the 1720s. The paper industry was concentrated primarily in the Zaan region and on the Veluwe. High-quality paper was manufactured for a range of applications using improved technology.

This is not the place to give a comprehensive overview of manufacturing activity, but this summary would be incomplete without referring to the importance of the processing or finishing industry. This involved taking raw materials, largely from abroad, and turning them into end products, such as refining South American sugarcane to produce cane sugar. Amsterdam was the most important refiner, and during the seventeenth century Holland emerged as the number one sugar producer in Europe. The salt works, tobacco cutting shops, soap factories and Dutch gin distilleries in Schiedam were also important.

It is not easy to provide a concise overview of Dutch industry in the seventeenth century. While there were ups and downs, until the middle of the century there was growth and prosperity in virtually all sectors. International prices started to drop between 1650 and 1670, and this heralded a change. The picture of the decades after 1672 is not without ambiguity: some branches of industry lost ground but survived at a lower level, others suffered reverses that were either continuous or incremental, while yet others prospered and grew. There was also a shift of some production from the expensive coastal provinces with their high wages to the cheaper inland provinces. This was not a case of decline, but rather of stagnation at what was still a high level.

The tremendous growth manufacturing had enjoyed in the late sixteenth century was closely linked not only to advances in agriculture, but also to trade and shipping. The huge significance of trade with the Baltic, the Iberian Peninsula, France, England, the Mediterranean, Asia and the Atlantic countries was discussed in the previous chapter. As we saw, between around 1585 and 1621, the Republic – and Amsterdam in particular – acquired a key position in global trade. Trade with every part of the world flourished particularly dramatically during the years of the Revolt (1609–21). After decades of rapid expansion, the rate of growth slowed down somewhat after the 1620s, and a long phase of gradual strengthening and consolidation began.

By the middle of the seventeenth century, the Dutch merchant fleet was larger than those of England, France and Spain combined. At that time 20 per cent of the Republic's population was living in the port towns and cities of Holland and Zeeland, further underlining the joint importance of trade and fishing. From about 1650, however, the Republic entered a new phase in which it was still the dominant trading power in Europe, but the obstacles became greater. In 1650, the Republic's share in trade with the Baltic was over 60 per cent, but by about 1690 this had dropped to 47 per cent.[69] After 1672, there were growing difficulties in a number of areas, but the timing and extent of the decline varied. It is fair to say that, starting around the middle of the seventeenth century, there was a gradual drop in the trading of important products like grain, herring, salt, textiles and timber. A number of factors lay behind this, among them falling prices, English and French mercantilist policies, changed consumption patterns, the relocation of production centres, and the emergence of direct trading links that bypassed the Amsterdam commodities market.

These setbacks were partially offset by the expansion of colonial commerce. The VOC grew rapidly for decades after it was founded in 1602.[70] Under Jan Pietersz. Coen, Governor-General of the Dutch East Indies from 1619 to 1623 and from 1627 to 1629, there was particularly rapid expansion of trade with Europe and also within Asia, with a string of settlements that ultimately extended from Persia to Japan. In 1619, Coen established the city of Batavia on the site of the current and then Jakarta. It was to become the centre of the VOC's trading network in Asia. During this period, the VOC developed into the biggest European commercial and political powerhouse in Asia. However, Coen's actions have not earned him an uncontroversial place in history.[71] Until well into the twentieth century he was praised for his robust approach which ensured success for the VOC successful, acts. The second tunnel named after him ('Coentunnel') under the North Sea Canal in Amsterdam was opened as recently as 2014. Over the years, however, the brute force with which he expanded the VOC's power base became an increasing issue. The establishment of Batavia was preceded by burning the then Jakarta to the ground and in 1621 he undertook a punitive expedition on the Banda Islands because the population had supplied the British with nutmeg in defiance of the VOC's ban. Safeguarding the VOC's monopoly position on the islands cost 15,000 natives their lives. One of the results of the recent focus on the violent side of his deeds was a new inscription on his statue in Hoorn, where he was born. Since 2012 it has been, 'Jan Pieterszoon Coen (Hoorn 1587- Batavia 1629) . . . Architect of the VOC's successful commercial empire in Asia. . . . Praised as an effective and visionary administrator. But just as strongly condemned for the violent way he acquired trading monopolies in the Orient'.

The establishment of Batavia was followed by other new trading posts, including Zeelandia in what is now Taiwan (1624), Deshima (near present-day Nagasaki in Japan; 1641) and Malacca (1641). Outposts were also set up elsewhere, including a staging post in South Africa in 1652 that would become known as Cape Town. In 1656 Colombo was founded in Ceylon, present-day Sri Lanka, bringing several hundred thousand Sinhalese and Tamils under Dutch rule. The number of trading post residents could remain limited because the VOC was primarily a trading organization and had no intention of conquering a large colonial empire. As a rule there were a few hundred people at most. The settlements in Batavia and Ceylon were the only ones that were significantly bigger, but even there the Dutch community, including Germans and Scandinavians, was not much greater than 2,500. The Dutch also went exploring under VOC direction to Australia (New Holland), New Zealand and the island of Tasmania, named after the Republic's explorer Abel Tasman (1603–59). No matter how far apart some of these areas were, or how small some of the settlements, if we consider the role of the Dutch patricians who, from a considerable distance, ultimately determined the local asymmetric balance of power and profited from it, it is fair to say that there was colonial rule in this phase too.[72]

The period between 1630 and 1670 was one of stability, big profits and handsome dividends because the VOC was highly successful in the international trading of pepper and other spices. But the VOC's profits came under pressure, as they did in other commercial sectors. Falling prices, international competition and sharply reduced income from trade inside Asia forced the VOC to change course in the 1670s. The company expanded the fleet significantly and the number of ships per year sailing to Asia nearly doubled between 1680 and 1720. The new vessels were also larger, so the decline in trade within Asia could be offset by carrying bigger cargoes on the return voyage. Another important factor was the broadening of the range of goods for the European market (including coffee, tea, porcelain, textiles and saltpetre). But here the Republic ran into competition with England and France, and profit margins were lower than in the past.

A characteristic feature of this new era of expansion was that in the 1720s the VOC operated on twice the scale of sixty years before, but profits remained essentially the same in absolute terms. Between 1630 and 1670, the VOC's average annual profit was 2.1 million guilders, and between 1680 and 1720 it was about the same at two million guilders. The number of VOC employees, on the other hand, increased during this period, with many crew members of German origin. By 1690 or thereabouts the company employed some 22,000 people. This made the VOC the Republic's biggest company and possibly also the largest European enterprise in the whole of the seventeenth century.[73] Although the heyday of massive dividends was over, VOC shares continued to be particularly attractive, even after 1680, because alternative investment opportunities had become less lucrative. No matter how impressive the VOC's figures were, the company's importance to the Republic's overall trade in the seventeenth century should not be exaggerated. Around 1640, the volume of business done in the East Indies represented about 6 per cent of all Dutch trade; over the subsequent decades it rose to 10 per cent, and was slightly higher at the turn of the century.[74]

The Dutch West India Company (West-Indische Compagnie, WIC), which was founded in 1621, was much less successful.[75] When it was set up, the States General gave it a monopoly on trade with the entire New World and the west coast of Africa south of the tropic of Cancer. But the Spanish, Portuguese and English had beaten the Dutch to it, so a great deal of money and energy was needed to establish a foothold. The voyage to the west was shorter and less dangerous than the trip to the east, so merchants could undertake the journey using their own resources. This meant that the WIC did not acquire the monopoly it was supposed to have. In consequence, it also had to cope with competition from within its own country, which put downward pressure on profit margins.

The main reason why the WIC was less successful than the VOC, however, was the difference in the level of economic development between the west and the east. Asia had an advanced economy that could satisfy European demand, whereas this was not the case in the Americas, and the Europeans had to develop the economy there themselves.[76] Prior to 1621, most South American sugar reached the Republic thanks to privateering and smuggling. The Republic became more aggressive after resuming the war with Spain, and hence also with Portugal, which had been ruled by Spain since 1580. One of the objectives of the WIC was to have its own plantations. They came close to achieving that goal in 1628 when Piet Hein overpowered the Spanish treasure fleet (see p. 52). This brought immediate relief to the Republic's financial concerns and enough was left over

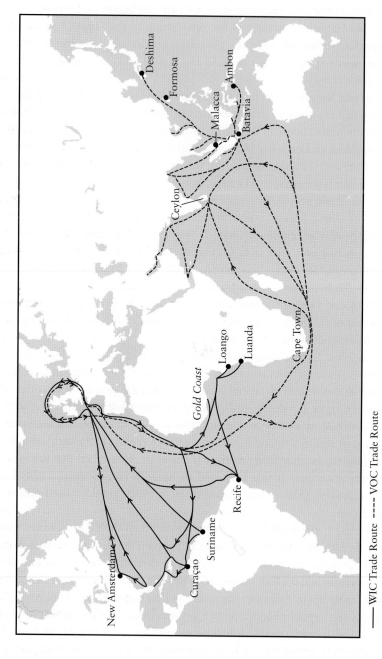

Map 7 Routes sailed by the VOC and WIC.

—— WIC Trade Route   ----- VOC Trade Route

to finance driving the Portuguese out of the lion's share of the sugar growing area in northeastern Brazil in the early 1630s.

In 1636, John Maurice of Nassau-Siegen, a cousin of stadholder Frederick Henry, was appointed governor of New Holland – the name given to this part of Brazil. In the same period the WIC captured a number of bases on the west coast of Africa in the Gold Coast and Angola, from where it transported large numbers of slaves to the conquered area in Brazil. Although this trade expanded significantly and amounted to some four thousand slaves a year in the 1640s, it did not prove profitable. The customers were mainly Portuguese who had remained on their plantations after the Dutch arrived, and they bought the slaves on credit. The dissatisfaction of the Portuguese planters with Dutch administration grew after Portugal regained independence in 1640, and the result was a revolt in 1645. The WIC, which was neither prepared nor equipped to intervene, was left with bad debts. The last piece of land in Brazil was ultimately lost to the Portuguese in 1654.

WIC shares had meanwhile lost most of their value, but Dutch trade in the Atlantic did continue. Curaçao became a major centre for the slave trade, and the Netherlands continued to play an important part in it until the nineteenth century.[77] Dutch merchant shipping also transported most of the raw sugar to Europe and supplied European products to the Caribbean. Part of this raw sugar came from Suriname, which the Republic finally acquired from England in 1674. Between 1683 and 1713 the number of sugar plantations there increased from 50 to 200. In the same year – 1674 – in exchange for Suriname, the Republic definitively relinquished New York. Established in the 1620s as New Amsterdam, it had grown into a relatively large settlement, but it had never had much economic significance.

Finally, if we draw up a balance sheet of the Republic's overall economy in the seventeenth century, it is striking that during the first half it profited from the relative weakness of the surrounding countries.[78] But starting in the 1660s, the pressure from France and England increased, and there was more competition and interference with trade. As long as the Republic still had sufficient means of exercising power to ward off this pressure – as it had during the Johan de Witt years – this trend could be contained. But as the other powers grew stronger, the Republic's vulnerability increased, all the more so because its domestic market was small and people were dependent on international trade. Also, particularly after 1672, there were the harmful effects of virtually permanent warfare and the heavy financial burden it brought in its train. When the Republic emerged as a great power, the enmeshment of all economic sectors had been a positive factor that resulted in cumulative growth across the board, with international commerce as the driving force. Then, starting in the 1660s, prices started to fall and demand for services and products from the Republic dropped. These negative trends fed into one another. Yet this did not lead to immediate decline because the country's economic resilience remained strong, and reverses in one sector could still be compensated by growth in another. The purchasing power of many people furthermore went up during this period because their wages stayed the same but prices fell.

The overall picture was thus one of healthy growth between about 1580 and 1621, followed by a second phase of consolidation and strengthening until the middle of the century, followed by a gradual decline in the 1650s and 1660s. When the upheaval of the 'Disaster Year' of 1672 was over and recovery started, there was a long era that can best be described as stagnation at a high level.[79] It lasted for virtually the whole of the eighteenth century, as we shall see in the following chapter.

Art, architecture and science

The international political might and the economic strength that the Republic emanated in the Golden Age were reflected in art, architecture and science. To this day, the cultural vigour of the seventeenth-century Republic is still a major element of the Dutch self-image and of the way foreigners see the Netherlands. It was above all the Dutch school of painting that determined these images. In the sixteenth century, there was little Northern Netherlandish painting, and the centre of art output was in the southern provinces, primarily in Bruges, Ghent and Antwerp. The success of the Revolt and the arrival of tens of thousands of people from the Southern Netherlands in the 1580s and 1590s changed that. There were many artists among the refugees from the south and they had a significant impact on the development of painting in the North. The character of painting changed at the same time and a completely original Dutch school emerged.

The traditional patrons for works of art had been the Catholic Church and the nobility, but they played only a minor part in the emerging Republic. Artists had to seek another market, and they found it in the wealthy towns and cities of Holland. Regents, as well as ordinary citizens with a more modest budget, proved to be potential buyers. Demand really took off after about 1620, when it became increasingly common for people with any money at all to have one or more paintings on the wall.[80] This enabled an important new branch of commerce to develop, and by around 1650 between 63,000 and 70,000 paintings a year were coming on to the market. Taking the Golden Age as a whole, it is estimated that more than five million paintings were produced – a figure achieved by well-nigh industrial methods and a high degree of specialization. Many artists had workshops with large numbers of apprentices and assistants essentially mass producing paintings, and there were towns and cities that specialized in a particular genre. There were important landscape painters and portraitists in Haarlem, architecture artists in Delft and 'fine' painters of domestic scenes in Leiden. During the seventeenth century, Amsterdam developed into an important European art market. It was also home to a number of specializations working alongside each other, for instance historical, maritime, landscape and portrait painting.[81]

Figure or genre pictures were particularly popular. They were usually small works depicting scenes from daily life that everyone recognized, often with a moralizing or narrative message. Such paintings were intended for a wide public and were therefore relatively cheap. Some painters, such as Gerrit Dou (1613–75) and Gerard ter Borch (1617–81), evolved this into a highly polished style that was in fact very expensive.

Portraiture became immensely important around the middle of the century. Individuals and groups had themselves immortalized. Proud citizens in the militias, self-assured regents on their governing bodies and on the boards of charitable organizations all posed for their portraits. The most famous example of a group portrait is the Night Watch painted by Rembrandt van Rijn (1606–69) in 1642. This work did not receive the admiration from the clients who commissioned it that it has enjoyed since the nineteenth century, when it was extolled as the most brilliant example of seventeenth-century painting.[82] Frans Hals (*c.*1580–1666) was another leading portraitist. Born in Antwerp, he lived and worked in Haarlem (see Figure 7, p. 63).

Landscapes and, from the 1650s, townscapes were genres that were very much in demand and were painted and copied on a big scale. Around 1670, Jacob van Ruisdael (1628/9–82) embarked on a long series of panoramic views of Haarlem that actually acquired their own nickname – the 'Haarlempjes' (views of Haarlem) (see Figure 10, below).[83] Paintings depicting the successes of the fleet and its admirals were also very appealing. Urban and provincial patrons searched for other subjects to underline the dignity of their positions and status. Regional and local historical events were given pride of place in town halls and government buildings. From the middle of the century one could also admire mythological and allegorical depictions reflecting the authority and good governance of the different government institutions. Such works were done in

Figure 10 *View of Haarlem from the North-West, with the Bleaching Fields in the Foreground,* Jacob Isaacksz. van Ruisdael, ca. 1650–ca. 1682. Rijksmuseum Amsterdam.

a baroque style, expressed even more powerfully in the stadholder's palaces built for Frederick Henry (1625–47).

The stadholder and his wife wanted to keep up with the baroque of the international court culture. The zenith was the decoration of the Orange Hall in the royal palace Huis ten Bosch in The Hague, which was later the residence of Queen Beatrix (1980–2013). After Frederick Henry's death, his widow had this domed room decorated with frescoes and ceiling paintings that glorified the deceased and his family on a grand scale in mythological and allegorical depictions. This huge project was without doubt inspired by comparable scenes that the Flemish artist Peter Paul Rubens (1577–1640) had painted for some European courts, and indeed a number of Flemish painters worked on it. Artists from the Republic received commissions thanks to the Oranges' contacts, particularly with German royals, among them the Elector of Brandenburg Frederick William I, who was married to Louise Henrietta of Nassau, Stadholder Frederick Henry's daughter. Some of these contacts went via Cleves, where John Maurice of Nassau, the former governor-general of Brazil, had become the Elector's stadholder. The Oranges' network weakened during the First Stadholderless Period, but regained its charisma after the Glorious Revolution in 1688, thanks to Oranges at the English court.

By then the heyday of painting in the Republic was already at an end. The 1670s were a watershed here too. The art market was caught up in the general upheaval that overwhelmed the Republic in the 'Disaster Year'. Instead of buying art, everyone wanted to sell. Prices plummeted and many artists found themselves in dire financial straits. The art market never recovered from this blow. The number of painters is estimated to have fallen during the 1670s to about a quarter of what it had been in the 1650s and the era of the big names was over. It is striking that when the art market showed some signs of life again, it was not the work of late seventeenth-century artists that was in demand, but the work of the great masters – who had died in the meantime – painted in the glory years up to about 1670. Although the Republic was still producing more art at the end of the seventeenth century than anywhere else in northern Europe, the Golden Age of Dutch painting was history.

Summarizing, it can be said that the painting of the Golden Age was more than a reflection of what the Republic represented. Thanks to its very widespread internal distribution it also confirmed and sustained that self-image. Dutch painting was pre-eminently bourgeois, depicting as it did the physical, cultural and social reality of the Republic's citizens, and encompassing urban and provincial pride. Yet at the same time it was more than a simple record of urban and rural daily life, of the upper crust regents, of militias and soldiers, of trade and shipping. Using themes from the Bible or Greek and Roman mythology, it transformed that reality into an artistic fantasy world designed to enhance the clients' prestige. Even the apparently realistically painted landscapes often featured stretches of unspoiled countryside that no longer existed in intensively cultivated Holland. These paintings thus also project an imagined world in which past and present were brought together in harmony.[84]

Alongside a completely individual painting style, the Republic also developed its own architecture, which was likewise very much interwoven with economic and political factors. This was evident in Amsterdam's cityscape. The seventeenth century saw the construction of the famous semi-circular canals and their elaborate architecture – initially in Renaissance style, which was followed from the 1620s by the more austere Dutch Classicism. The use of this architectural style began with stadholder Frederick Henry, who had a number of palaces built in classical style to bolster his regal ambitions. This quest for international style was coupled with a need for practical utility and also found its way into the building of smaller, but nonetheless grand town houses and the luxurious country seats of rich regents. The architectural style that developed caught on at the stadholder's court and among regents. The Mauritshuis in The Hague is a well-known example of the Dutch classicist style. It was built in 1644 as a residence for John Maurice of Nassau and is now a museum. It houses one of the most famous collections of seventeenth-century Dutch masters.

The architects involved in the construction of the Mauritshuis included Pieter Post (1608–69) and Jacob van Campen (1595–1657), who were from Haarlem. The latter also designed Amsterdam's town hall, known these days as the Royal Palace in Dam Square (see Figure 11, below). Construction started in 1648 and it was officially inaugurated seven years later, but it was not actually completed until 1665. This town hall, with its sober monumental exterior and opulent baroque interior, was the biggest public building project of the seventeenth century and demonstrated the self-confidence of the regents and merchants of the trading metropolis. It accommodated all the city departments, and the imposing Citizens' Hall was open to the public. Its floor consists of a huge map of the world, with Amsterdam as the centre of heaven and earth. The style of the architecture in other town

Figure 11 *The Town Hall in Dam Square in Amsterdam*, Gerrit Adriaensz Berckheyde, 1672. Rijksmuseum Amsterdam.

and cities was less imposing but reflected a comparable pride. There was a building boom in the first half of the seventeenth century, particularly in Holland, Zeeland and Utrecht. Town halls, public buildings, expensive town houses and country mansions sprung up everywhere. Stadholder Frederick Henry was an important patron until his death in 1647, but it was undeniably the regents and rich merchants who determined the look of the Republic's towns and cities. They left the stamp of their bourgeois taste and power on classicist structures, be they private houses or government buildings.

Dutch architecture also had a degree of international prominence, thanks primarily to the Oranges' network. During the 1650s, Frederick William I, the Elector of Brandenburg, had Oranienburg Castle built in the Dutch style, followed in the 1660s by the castle and pleasure gardens in Potsdam.[85] This influence was also manifest in other north German courts. The same applied to landscape gardening, which was not to approach its refined zenith in the Republic, in part under French influence, until the end of the seventeenth century.

The culture of the Golden Age was shaped not least by the high literacy rate, which was in all probability the highest in Europe.[86] The Reformation had contributed to reducing illiteracy in the sixteenth century by emphasizing the importance of individual Bible study. The flood of political pamphlets published during the Revolt was an additional stimulus. The growth of the reading culture was likewise encouraged by developments in trade, industry and shipping. Urbanization, the political structure of the Republic, and maintaining international contacts were factors that made it necessary to put things in writing, which promoted literacy. By the middle of the century Dutch had developed into a very largely standardized language. The authorized translation of the Bible into Dutch, which was decided upon at the Synod of Dordrecht (1618–19, see p. 47 ff.) and completed in 1637, was very widely distributed and also had a significant impact. Unlike France, for instance, the Republic had no central guiding authority to promote the development of the standard language. The situation in the Netherlands was characterized by the individual dynamic of the involvement of relatively large groups of people in economic, political, religious and cultural life. Consequently, the obvious significance of the common language soon grew rapidly for virtually everyone.

This development was fostered by the existence of a close-knit educational network – for basic education (up to the age of twelve) and for secondary education at the Latin or grammar school, which prepared students for university and the Athenæum Illustre ('illustrious school'). By the middle of the century, almost every town of any significance had a grammar school, and this high degree of coverage was probably unique in Europe. The oldest university in the Netherlands, Leiden, was founded during the Revolt at the instigation of William of Orange in 1575. Between 1626 and 1650 it had some 11,000 enrolments, which made it the biggest in Europe in the first half of the seventeenth century. The universities of Cambridge in England and Leipzig in Germany were the largest in their countries during that period, with 8,400 and 6,700 enrolments, respectively. This was followed by the foundation of universities in Franeker in 1585 and Groningen in 1614. Just below the level of these universities were the illustrious schools, two of which developed into universities in the early decades of the seventeenth century

(Harderwijk, Utrecht). By about 1650, the Republic had six universities and eight illustrious schools. During this same period the number of enrolled students peaked at some 1,600–2,000 Dutch and a slightly lower number of foreigners (primarily from German states, England, Scandinavia and central Europe).

Although the universities were important as places to prepare for the professions (theology, medicine, law and classics) and for cultural development, innovative scientific research was done elsewhere. None of the celebrated Dutchmen who made important contributions to international scientific development were university professors. This was true of Christiaan Huygens (1629–95), internationally renowned physicist and astronomer and the inventor of the pendulum clock, and the self-taught Antonie van Leeuwenhoek (1632–1723), famous for his discoveries in the biology of cells and microorganisms using microscopes he made himself. It was the same for the two most eminent seventeenth-century Dutch scholars, Hugo Grotius (1583–1645) and Baruch de Spinoza (1632–77).

During the Twelve Years' Truce (1609–21), Grotius supported Oldenbarnevelt in his struggle against Prince Maurice (see p. 47) and in 1619 was sentenced to life imprisonment. After his spectacular escape from Loevestein Castle in 1621 he went to Paris, where he spent the greater part of his life. He returned to Holland when the climate in the Republic became more tolerant under Frederick Henry, but he was in danger of being arrested again because he refused to submit a request for a pardon, so he left the Republic once more. Grotius acquired his international fame primarily for his work *De Jure Belli ac Pacis* (1625), in which he laid the foundations for modern international law. His *Mare Liberum*, in which he formulated the right to free access to seas and oceans, is likewise renowned. Grotius was also a theologian and he wrote tragedies, poems and historical works in Latin. As became clear at the beginning of this chapter, in the last of these he promulgated the Batavian myth of the spirit of freedom and good government, and in so doing he was closely associated with a self-image projected primarily in Holland.

The philosopher Baruch de Spinoza, born in the Portuguese–Jewish community in Amsterdam, became a major innovator in the thinking about the relationship between God and man, and he departed so radically from existing Jewish ideas that he was barred from the synagogue in Amsterdam. But Spinoza also collided with the official church. In essence, he rejected the idea that God intervened in people's lives and he denied the existence of Satan or other devils. Building on the thinking of René Descartes (1596–1650), Spinoza realized his philosophy went beyond the bounds of the permissible and was therefore cautious about publishing his ideas. In 1670, his *Tractatus Theologico-Politicus* was published anonymously. Among other things it contained a radical plea for freedom of expression and religion. It caused an uproar,[87] as did his magnum opus *Ethics*, which was published as part of his collected works after his premature death in 1677, but without stating the place of publication and the names of the publisher and translator. A year later the States of Holland banned all Spinoza's publications. This did not, though, mean the end of his influence on intellectual life in the Republic and on theological discussions, because his philosophical ideas would live on in the eighteenth century in the thinking of the Dutch Enlightenment.

Even though the two most famous Dutch seventeenth-century scholars – Grotius and Spinoza – were confronted with the limits of freedom, compared to other countries there was a tolerant and liberal intellectual climate in the Republic. This Dutch freedom was not a matter of principle. It was a case of pragmatic tolerance, and intellectual latitude varied depending on place and time.[88] Nevertheless, religious and political pluriformity was at all times greater than anywhere else in Europe. René Descartes, the founder of rationalism and the mechanistic world view, settled in the Republic in 1628 for this very reason. But his rationalist scientific work brought him into conflict with orthodox members of the Dutch Reformed Church, who feared that their theological dogmas would be impugned. He wrote his most important works during his lengthy stay in the Republic, and his ideas were first taught at Utrecht University. The Huguenot Pierre Bayle (1647–1706), an important pioneer of the early Enlightenment, was also attracted by the Republic's relative freedom and taught at the Rotterdam École Illustre. Well-known English philosophers like John Locke (1632–1704) and Thomas Hobbes (1588–1679) stayed in the Republic for extended periods or published their works there. The Republic thus became a focus of international science and philosophy, and Dutch publishers enjoyed considerable esteem and were among the most important book producers in Europe.

Most books were published for the national market, though, which was uniquely large in Europe because of the high literacy rate.[89] Around 1650, the Republic had 265 printers, publishers and booksellers – twice as many as in about 1630 – spread over thirty-eight locations. They produced books, almanacs, pamphlets and newspapers for professions, trades, government, education and science, as well as literary works for the reading public. A select group would meet in Muiderslot Castle, near Amsterdam, where the host Pieter Corneliszoon Hooft (1581–1647) created an intellectual climate that transcended religious and political differences and in which there was a quest for new literary forms and creativity. Hooft was the son of an Amsterdam burgomaster and was appointed sheriff of Muiden by Prince Maurice. He wrote poems, plays and a lengthy but unfinished history of the Revolt.

The most authoritative seventeenth-century poet and writer was Joost van den Vondel (1587–1679), who was also often to be found at Muiderslot. He wrote in the style of classical tragedies. In one of his plays, *Palamedes*, he criticized the execution of Oldenbarnevelt (1619) in allegorical form. He was fined for penning this work, which appeared shortly after Maurice's death in 1625, but was otherwise left in peace because the Amsterdam regents were also proud of him. The play was not staged until the First Stadholderless Period, when it was a great success. Vondel used a historical setting to put across a topical message in other dramas too, for example in *Gijsbrecht van Aemstel* (1637), in which he presented the history of Amsterdam in a form that the city's regents, with their decidedly independent attitude towards the States of Holland, supported. He was commissioned by Amsterdam council to write a poem in praise of the city to mark the opening of the new town hall. His words also rang with the proud urban self-confidence that was so characteristic of the culture of the Golden Age.

Jacob Cats (1577–1660), long-time Grand Pensionary of Holland under stadholder Frederick Henry, was the most popular poet and author of the seventeenth century. Cats was best known for his didactic and moralistic *emblemata*: small allegorical prints with a proverb and a legend designed to convey a moral message. They were published in huge numbers and reached a less sophisticated readership, which was presented with moral and religious lessons about life and death, as well as proper conduct in everyday situations in marriage, running a home and raising children.

Dutch scientists, scholars and publishers played a major role in the emergence and dissemination of new trends in science, technology and philosophy in the seventeenth century. The relatively high degree of religious and intellectual tolerance was also attractive to foreign academics, which gave an additional boost to the Republic's significance to developments in Europe as a whole. The Republic's literature and poetry, on the other hand, met with little response abroad, although Vondel and Cats had a degree of fame in Germany and Scandinavia. Apart from the language barrier, this was probably because of the different character of the Republic's literature. While an expressive baroque style with extravagant verbiage dominated in other European countries, the tone in the Republic was more restrained and less theatrical. This was indicative of a more general cultural difference between the Republic and the rest of Europe in the seventeenth century. Dutch art and architecture also reflected much less baroque exuberance. The absence of an absolutist court and a powerful Catholic Church, which played such a key role in the development of baroque art and culture elsewhere, could explain this.[90] In the Republic, by contrast, the bourgeois and Protestant character of society generated a more pragmatic and down-to-earth environment across the board. Yet this was no barrier to self-assurance and pride, as the cultural legacy of the Golden Age attests.

CHAPTER 4
A SECOND-RATE POWER: THE DECLINE OF THE REPUBLIC IN THE EIGHTEENTH CENTURY

Introduction

The heyday of the Golden Age was followed by a period of reversal. This was not a case of sudden and rapid decay, but of relative economic and political decline and an inevitable shift of the centre of power politics to England and France. This trend had emerged at the end of the seventeenth century, but was still partially masked by the position of King-Stadholder William III. During the first half of the eighteenth century, however, it became clear to everyone inside and outside the country that the Republic's era of prominence in international politics was over and that it had to accept a place in the second division. While the Republic mobilized an army that was bigger than ever in the War of the Spanish Succession (1702–13), it was no longer a leading player, and during the course of the eighteenth century it increasingly became a political football in the international arena.

It also lacked the power to shape domestic relationships. Political reforms failed to appear in the Second Stadholderless Period, which started with William III's death in 1702 and ended in 1747. Hopes that Stadholder William IV (1747–51) would be prepared to do something about it disappeared soon after he assumed office, and changes in this area would not occur until the Patriot era of the 1780s. Yet again reforms were stifled, this time by the Prussian invasion of 1787, which brought Stadholder William V, who had fled to Nijmegen, back into the centre of power in The Hague. William V was forced to withdraw permanently eight years later, at the beginning of the French period (1795–1813). Then, there followed a period of fundamental reforms. The Netherlands got its first constitution, known as the *Staatsregeling*, in 1798. Although many democratic elements soon disappeared, this move made the Netherlands a unitary state – a major milestone in the country's history.

The Republic lost the dominant economic position it had developed in the seventeenth century, although the decline varied dramatically from one commercial sector to another. Generally speaking, there was no decline in an absolute sense for many years, but rather relative deterioration compared with other countries. At the same time, the differences between the Republic's rich and poor grew sharply. One factor that explains this economic degeneration was the Republic's weakened international position, but of course, as we shall see, other aspects played a role as well. The glory and aura of the Golden Age were in the past, and eighteenth-century artists tended to follow foreign trends rather than generate their own creative, individual work.

In this sense there was a decline in all areas compared with the Republic's zenith in the seventeenth century, although not to the same degree nor at the same time everywhere. Contemporaries were aware of this deterioration, but their desire to turn the tide and bring back the country's heyday remained an illusion. As the eighteenth century progressed, the Republic gradually accepted a position that matched its size – that of a minor power. In 1795 it went under, and the Batavian Republic, which was dependent on France, emerged. After a number of regime changes, the Netherlands was absorbed into the Napoleonic Empire in 1810. Following Napoleon's defeat, the Netherlands regained its independence in 1813 and the House of Orange returned.

International relations: The end of a great power

In 1702, when William III died suddenly and the War of the Spanish Succession broke out, the Republic was still a major international player. William III had once again forged a coalition to combat French expansionism, this time to prevent Philip, Duke of Anjou and the grandson of Louis XIV, from succeeding Charles II, the Catholic king of Spain who died in 1700. Were this clause in Charles's last will and testament to be implemented, it would mean a serious threat to the Republic and to William III's main aim in life – to weaken France. If honoured, the late Spanish king's wish would unite France and Spain and create a concentration of Catholic power that would menace the Republic's southern border and its overseas interests.

In 1701, French troops marched into the Southern Netherlands and the Republic was forced to withdraw its garrisons from its strongholds there. The upshot was that the buffer between France and the Republic disappeared, and the Dutch could no longer restrict commercial traffic along the Scheldt. The Republic's trading position in Latin America was jeopardized because France and Spain started to work together in the region. All this meant that William III could count on support from Holland in his attempts to weaken Spain and France. Holland resolutely maintained this policy after his death in 1702.

The Republic was no longer the linchpin of international coalitions it had been during the heyday of the Golden Age and so could not have much impact on the outcome of the struggle and the peace terms. That era, it became clear during the War of the Spanish Succession (1702–13), was gone for good.[1] Besides debilitating Spain and France, the Republic also sought to prevent England – an ally in this war, as were Austria and Prussia – benefitting from victory by strengthening its already powerful position as a maritime and colonial power at the Netherlands' expense. These tensions escalated after William III's death and the end of the personal union between England and the Republic, and cooperation between the two states soon became difficult. England wanted France humiliated and the whole Spanish inheritance to go to Charles of Habsburg, son of the Holy Roman Emperor. The Republic, on the other hand, would have been satisfied with a division of Spanish possessions, with the Southern Netherlands under Austrian rule, and the return of its border fortresses.

There were also disputes with its ally, Prussia. After William III's death, the king of Prussia, Frederick I, annexed the counties of Lingen and Meurs on the Republic's eastern border, justifying his action by citing the last will of Stadholder Frederick Henry, who died in 1647, and William III's lack of an heir. The legality of this claim is not the issue here. The key point is that the Republic could do nothing to stop the Prussian annexations and had to accept that a major power was emerging on its eastern border.

The extent and duration of the Republic's military efforts in the War of the Spanish Succession were at levels never before seen in its history. The army was bigger and costlier than ever. Yet even these exertions could not disguise the fact that the Republic was falling behind. England was in the driving seat of the coalition facing France and Spain, and when London and Paris decided it was time for peace, it was they who determined the peace terms, and the Republic was then permitted to agree. The Peace of Utrecht in 1713 brought the Republic a modest territorial gain (the city of Venlo). Two years later, a Barrier Treaty was entered into with the new Austrian rulers of the Southern Netherlands. It restored the Republic's right to garrison troops in a number of strongholds along the border with France, and contained agreements about a joint Austro–Dutch defence against any renewed French aggression.

This last aspect appeared to be not unfavourable, but nearly forty years of war with France had exhausted the Republic's finances. After 1713, Holland had to spend about 70 per cent of its income on servicing existing debt. This monetary situation, plus the much stronger position of other states, meant that the Republic emerged from the War of the Spanish Succession as a minor power. There was not enough money to invest in the army and fleet because much of the taxation went to pay interest on the huge national debt. An additional factor was the continued existence of the division of expenses between the provinces agreed in 1616. Under this arrangement, Holland paid 58 per cent of the Republic's defence expenditure, but in practice the other provinces often failed to fulfil their obligations, knowing that Holland would shoulder the responsibility if the worst came to the worst. However, Holland's mountain of debt meant that insufficient resources were available. The Republic could not break out of this vicious circle during the eighteenth century.

The country's foreign policy objectives were comparable to those in the seventeenth century. Safeguarding maritime trading interests and national security in a European balance of power was the priority. Collaboration with seafaring powers, particularly England, remained very important, but the country also had to remain on friendly terms with the Austrians in the Southern Netherlands. There had, though, been a major change. Under William III, active alliances had been forged against France, whereas now the Republic sought the shelter of neutrality and tried as far as possible to keep out of impending confrontations between others. The contrast with the glory days of the seventeenth century was manifest. The Republic was no longer capable of protecting its interests by force and had become dependent on others.[2] The Republic's army was still no smaller – 40,000 men – than it had been in peacetime in the seventeenth century, but major players like France, Prussia and Austria now had substantially larger standing armies and English supremacy at sea had meanwhile become unassailable.

A fortunate side effect was that England and France did not pursue aggressive foreign policies in the years immediately after the Peace of Utrecht in 1713, and the Republic's new dependence was more theoretical than practical. During the 1720s, however, Prussian pressure on the eastern border grew and tensions arose with Austria about the Republic's commercial and security interests in the Southern Netherlands. This relatively peaceful period lasted until 1747, when the Republic was harshly confronted with its own weakness. At the outbreak of the War of the Austrian Succession (1740–48), the Republic tried to remain neutral, but even as a weakened state it was still part of the array of alliances. In the mid-1740s, its four powerful neighbours – France and Prussia on one side and Austria and England on the other – were at war over the succession in Austria. The Republic was obliged by treaty to support Austria and England, but it feared possible Prussian reprisals and had no desire to offend France either. The result was a rather ineffectual support of the Austrian Netherlands. Starting in 1744, the Dutch border fortresses capitulated without any great resistance and by 1746 essentially the entire Austrian Netherlands was in French hands.

A year later, the Republic suffered a dramatic setback when France occupied a small part of Zeeland. The objective of this limited military exploit was to prevent the Republic from giving further support to Austria and England, but the consequences of the French action were primarily domestic and raised the spectre of the 'Disaster Year' (1672). Then, too, there had been French troops in the country and the future existence of the Republic appeared to be at stake. As in 1672, 1747 saw a groundswell of popular opinion calling for the return of Orange to rescue the country in its hour of need. And so the Second Stadholderless Period (1702–47) in the Republic's history came to an end. But there was no repeat of 1672, when William III swiftly set matters to rights and the Republic re-established its international position. It emerged that William IV (1747–51) was not capable of doing so. This had less to do with his personal qualities than with the fact that the Republic no longer had the power to be a significant continental player. The areas conquered by France were returned to the Republic under the Peace of Aachen (1748), but that was certainly not thanks to William IV because he had not raised an army of any significance. There were other reasons why France was prepared to offer the Republic favourable peace terms.[3] Restoration of the status quo consequently did little for the Republic, which remained dependent on the major powers of England, France, Prussia and Austria.

In the second half of the eighteenth century, the Republic tried harder than ever to further its commercial interests from a neutral position. After 1756, this became a virtually impossible task. That year saw the outbreak of the Seven Years' War (1756–63) with France and Austria on one side, and England, Prussia and initially Russia on the other. England and Austria – two former allies – were now enemies, and the Republic could not afford to take sides. Now that France and Austria had joined forces, the barrier of defensive positions in the Austrian Netherlands had essentially lost its significance. Supporting this Catholic coalition rather than Protestant England and Prussia, however, was unthinkable. Aside from religious considerations, the Republic did not have the resources to protect its eastern border against Prussia and to resist England at sea. The

English would have had little difficulty in doing irreversible damage to the Republic's overseas trade. The Republic was, moreover, actually still bound by the 1678 support treaty with England, an obligation it preferred not to be reminded of. Yet siding with England and Prussia was equally undesirable because the southern border, already severely weakened, would become even more vulnerable. The flourishing trade with France would be seriously harmed and the Republic would become completely dependent on England.

So the Republic remained neutral, but it had meanwhile become so feeble on land and at sea that in fact it could not even defend that neutrality. Lack of money and the dispute between the coastal and inland provinces about whether the army or the navy should be strengthened resulted in neither benefitting. During the Seven Years' War, England therefore paid little heed to the Republic's neutrality and detained many Dutch merchantmen. This did serious damage to trade with France and North America.

The Republic's powerlessness and dependence had become irreversible and would reach a new nadir in the 1780s. During the 1770s, widespread sympathy arose for England's rebellious colonists in America. The American War of Independence, which had broken out in 1774, reminded many in the Republic of their own struggle against Spain, and they had a bond with the rebels' Protestantism. The form of government that the Americans chose was also similar in many ways to the Republic's. The Confederation Act of 1776 was even based on the 1579 Union of Utrecht. Less idealistically and in fact more importantly, many in the Republic were pleased to see a setback for England as a trading rival. There were also fat profits to be made from the illegal arms trade with American insurgents, who were able to build up an army of their own as a result.[4] The Dutch island of Sint Eustatius in the Caribbean was an important link in this unlawful commerce. There were hopes, particularly among Amsterdam merchants, that American independence would change the maritime balance of power to England's disadvantage, and that the Dutch commercial and colonial position could improve again. This sympathy for America's struggle for freedom was not universal. In Orangist circles there was aversion to the rebels, and Stadholder William V also remained loyal to his preference for the English.

Despite the Republic's formal neutrality in the American War of Independence, there were incidents involving the English, due in part to Dutch trade with France, with which England had been at war since 1778. Matters came to a head for England in 1780 when it learnt that two years earlier Amsterdam had entered into a trade treaty with the Americans that could only be interpreted as support for the American cause. The Republic was furthermore on the point of joining the League of Armed Neutrality. Initiated by Catherine the Great of Russia, the goal of the League was to protect the rights of neutral maritime states, which in practice meant an alliance against England. The other members were Prussia, Sweden and Denmark

These, then, were the factors that precipitated the Fourth Anglo–Dutch War (1780–84), which was a disaster for the Republic. The Republic's shipping soon came to a standstill, and England impressively confirmed its naval supremacy all over the world. It captured Sint Eustatius, and virtually all the WIC's African forts and various bases in the

Far East. These blows were so severe that the long period of economic stagnation and relative deterioration was abruptly followed by a phase of headlong decline. Before examining this, let us review domestic political developments after William III's death in 1702.

Stagnation in domestic politics (1702–80)

Although the childless King-Stadholder William III had put forward his distant relative John William Friso (1687–1711), stadholder of Friesland, as his successor and also designated him in his will as Prince of Orange, the regents of Holland elected to follow a different course. Once again they opted for the 'true freedom' of a stadholderless era, and their lead was followed by Zeeland, Utrecht, Overijssel and Gelderland.[5] In Holland, this redistribution of power and the return of control by regents went ahead with relative ease. Things were different in provinces where the wheels of government had been completely in the hands of Orangists over the preceding decades. A great deal of dissatisfaction had built up, and after 1702 there were disturbance s, which in Gelderland even took the form of a civil war. These conflicts between incumbent regents (the 'Old Crew') and the 'New Crew' have gone down in Dutch history as the 'Plooierijen'.

The combatting 'Crews' were in no way units: these were local and regional power struggles with Orangist and anti-Orange factions taking the leading roles. After Stadholder William III's death, the provinces of Gelderland, Utrecht and Overijssel abandoned the provincial regulations that he had used in 1674–75 to appropriate virtually all the power relating to appointments (see p. 78). Yet there was little or no new division of power with regent families that had been excluded for many years, which explains the vehemence of the disputes. At the same time, they were more than a revival of the old squabble between Orangists and Republicans. In many towns and cities, part of the New Crew's support came from middle class people in guilds and militias who were dissatisfied with the autocratic and oligarchic conduct of the sitting regents. They wanted participation in council elections, a fairer and less severe tax system, and greater control of local government and financial management. From this perspective the New Crew represented a bourgeois, early democratic manifesto. But the middle classes were not successful. Where they did play a role in the appointment of regents from the New Crew, they were soon sidelined, sometimes with the help of Generality troops. The outcome was the restoration of control by regents after years of unrest (the wrangles in Gelderland lasted until 1707–8).

Although new factions had gained the upper hand in some places, in the first half of the eighteenth century there was nevertheless a closed elite of regents who shared out power among themselves and kept Orange-Nassau out of Holland, Zeeland, Utrecht, Overijssel and Gelderland (until 1722). As was to be expected in this era of relative decline, the regents at that time tried neither to modernize the Republic nor effectively counteract deterioration. Admittedly, they had few opportunities to do so because the decay was too structural, but the regent class during these years also had little ambition other than keeping an eye on things and taking care of their own family interests.

It is consequently not surprising that the regents who were in office during the first half of the eighteenth century are not spoken of highly in history books, and that for a long time this period was pejoratively described as the Periwig Era. This was an allusion to the fact that the regent elite had distanced itself from its governmental and social responsibilities, had withdrawn into its own oligarchic world, harked back nostalgically to the Golden Age, and looked primarily to France in matters of language, culture and fashion (hence the wigs). This is certainly an oversimplification and a cliché, but the fact remains that government at this time was weak and seen to be such, both then and now.

This was illustrated, for example, by the extraordinary meetings of the States General in 1716–17 – also referred to as the Second General Assembly – about the effectiveness of provincial cooperation (see on the First General Assembly p. 56–7). All attempts to create a new executive structure, in which provincial particularism would be suppressed in favour of reinforcing the Generality, failed. Measures to reform the Republic's finances and reduce the large deficits were consequently not taken. The only important decision taken by the Second General Assembly was to make further reductions in the size of the army. Simon van Slingelandt, later Grand Pensionary of Holland (1727–36), led the energetic lobbying of the General Assembly in favour of giving the Council of State and Generality greater powers. Instead, however, during the first half of the eighteenth century, the ties between the provinces actually became less strong. During the Republic's heyday, the unusual federal executive structure had not been a problem and dominant Holland had directed and driven the Republic. Now, during the period of deterioration – not least in Holland – this government structure emerged as an obstacle to stopping the rot.

This was compounded by the fact that the tensions between Orangist and anti-Orange factions started to flare up again in the late 1720s. In the period since 1702, Holland and other provinces had successfully excluded the Frisian stadholder, John William Friso. They had furthermore given him little or no support in his negotiations with the king of Prussia about the inheritance of the king-stadholder William III. Friction with the Frisian stadholder came to an end in 1711 when he was drowned while crossing the Hollands Diep at Moerdijk.

His son William Charles Henry Friso – the later William IV – was born shortly afterwards. He was automatically regarded as the future stadholder of Friesland because in 1675 the States of Friesland had declared the stadholdership hereditary in the male line. Obviously it was quite a while before he could build up a position of power, but by around 1730 he had made significant progress. First, he became stadholder of Friesland, Groningen, Drenthe and Gelderland in 1729 at the age of eighteen. In 1732, he reached an agreement with the king of Prussia that settled the dispute about William III's inheritance. Under that agreement, William IV accepted the Prussian annexation of Lingen and Meurs, and in return, the Prussian king dropped his claims in the Republic and the Austrian Netherlands. They also agreed they could both use the title Prince of Orange. Now that the inheritance issue had been resolved, the regents of Holland were faced with the potential danger that Prussia and Orange-Nassau would team up and together threaten the regents' hold on power. Shortly afterwards, in 1734, William IV strengthened his position still further by marrying Anne, Princess Royal (1709–59), the eldest daughter of the English king, George II. Grand Pensionary van Slingelandt and the regents of Holland tried, and failed, to prevent this marriage.

While the position of the stadholder and his supporters grew stronger, the regent regime weakened. The energetic Grand Pensionary van Slingelandt managed to slow down this decline, but he too was faced with systemic economic and financial problems and waning military and maritime power. After his death in 1736, the feeling of malaise among large sections of the population grew and so too did the resentment they harboured against the regents, who had proved unable to stop the decline, let alone turn the situation around. While there was no question as yet of poverty on a mass scale, many people were becoming visibly impoverished and were being subjected to high taxes. Many of the regents, on the other hand, continued to do extremely well. Their huge wealth stood in stark contrast to the situation of the middle classes who were struggling to cope with the financial strain and the population as a whole sinking into destitution. Regents' capital was invested in securities and they could share out the influential posts among themselves. These social contradictions played a role when a rerun of the 'Disaster Year' of 1672 threatened in 1747, and Orange was brought in by a popular movement as a saviour in the country's hour of need. Once again Orange was seen by many as a protector of the people against the oligarchic regime of the regents.[6]

William IV also became stadholder of Zeeland, Holland, Utrecht and Overijssel soon after the French invasion in 1747. He was consequently the stadholder of all the provinces – the first time this had happened in the Republic's history. In May 1747, the States General also appointed him captain general of the army and admiral of the fleet. There were consequently great expectations of William IV. He embodied more than the hope that the war could be settled to the Republic's advantage and the country's shattered self-confidence could be restored. Many people also looked to him to implement domestic reforms, get the economy to flourish again, destroy the power of the regents and suppress Catholicism. The power he was given to achieve these objectives was vast. The 1675 provincial regulations in Utrecht, Gelderland and Overijssel were reinstated so that the stadholder had complete control over government posts and councils in these provinces. The important executive reins gradually came together in his hands in other provinces too, and this was crowned by the declaration that stadholdership would be hereditary throughout the Republic. In 1747–8, William IV thus accumulated more power than any stadholder before him. While William III had acquired an almost monarchical position in the Republic, William IV's position was even stronger. The only thing he did not have was the title of king.

However, the stadholder failed to use this power to push through reforms. He was no innovator. Van Deursen describes his preferred approach as 'unimaginative conservatism' and he did nothing to rein in the regents' influence.[7] He did not respond to proposals to centralize or modernize the machinery of government, and he similarly did nothing to get the economy going again. Many people, particularly in the middle class, were soon disillusioned.[8] Their desire for a say in government was even stronger than during the struggle between the Old Crew and New Crew at the beginning of the century, and initially they looked on William IV as an ally in achieving this goal.

Their grievances about the taxation system were very specific. The collection of most taxes was outsourced to private individuals who, on payment of a fee, were granted the right to collect taxes. The high level of taxes, the lack of transparency about the activities of the private tax collectors and the feeling among the general public that they were more heavily taxed than many regents fomented social and political unrest in several provinces, and the homes and belongings of private tax collectors were looted. The focus of these tax riots was Amsterdam, where the movement started in the militia headquarters – the *Doelen* – on Kloveniersburgwal and has gone down in Dutch history as the *Doelisten* Movement.

The tasks of the militias, the archetypal representatives of the bourgeoisie, included maintaining law and order, but now they themselves were a major source of unrest. There was much more to this than changing the taxation system. Now, for instance, the militia members wanted to appoint their own officers rather than have them put forward by regents. In many towns and cities the inhabitants also wanted to have an influence on the composition of the local council, monitor decision making, have an insight into regents' privileges, have a different way of assigning public sector posts, and have a national postal service instead of private ones. This was not yet a movement with a detailed and structured programme. The demands were too varied and there was little unity. Many of the *Doelisten*, disappointed with William IV's lukewarm support, turned against him and radicalized. The key issue was a desire to broaden the basis of government and stop the excesses of regent rule. In reality, though, they were thinking more about an idealized past than formulating a future political objective.[9]

The *Doelisten* Movement was transitory and had little success, although private tax collection was abolished and a form of national postal service was introduced. There was also no direct line to the reform and democratization movements of the 1780s and later

tering der PATRIOTTEN op de groote BURGERZAAL in de CLOVENIERS DOELEN te Amsteld: in Aug: A° 1748

Figure 12 *Doelisten* Movement 1748. Atlas Van Stolk, Rotterdam.

(which will be discussed below). The *Doelisten's* view of society was too conventional for such things. It nevertheless became clear that something had changed. Not only had the bourgeoisie risen up of their own accord for the first time, they had also appealed to the stadholder in the hope that he would take the lead and implement political reforms. But the stadholder had done little more than facilitate the movement and even fan the flames to a degree for his own purposes. 'He changed the government to serve his own ends, and did nothing for us,' wrote a contemporary about the disappointment among the population, and he was certainly not wide of the mark.[10] This betrayal of their hopes left deep scars. It was the last time in the nation's history that political reformers looked to the House of Orange for support to attain their goals.[11]

In hindsight it is, of course, easy to conclude that William IV squandered these opportunities to modernize government and strengthen his position among the middle classes. From his point of view, however, his actions were logical and consistent. He looked to the past and saw William III as his great exemplar. Like his predecessor, he had no desire to change the system of government. He sought to achieve a strong personal position of power within the existing one. William IV hoped in this way to restore the Republic to its former glory – a hope that was to remain an illusion and one to which harking back to the old system of government could contribute nothing.

When the sickly William IV died in 1751 at the age of forty, the regents resumed their independent positions with little or no difficulty. For the time being there was no prospect of a stadholder with a forceful personal impact on appointments and other decisions. William IV left a three-year-old son, who succeeded him as hereditary Stadholder William V, but did not actually take office until he reached the age of eighteen in 1766. His mother, Anne of Hanover, Princess Royal, deputized for him until her death in 1759, but she had no power or authority. Behind the scenes the influence of one of her advisors grew. He was Louis Ernest, Duke of Brunswick-Wolfenbüttel, who also became captain general. After Anne's death, Brunswick became the young William V's guardian and continued to play a key part after William started to discharge his role as stadholder in 1766. They even signed a secret Instrument of Consultancy under which Brunswick would continue to advise the stadholder but could never be held liable for his advice.

William V underwent long and thorough preparation for his position and, with a two-year hiatus between 1785 and 1787, he remained in office until 1795, but like his father he achieved little of lasting value. He was a man of the old school, who wanted to bear sole responsibility and was not interested in any change whatsoever in the Republic's existing order. At the same time, he was too indecisive and too unsure of himself to act resolutely, and he took no advantage of the opportunities to implement bold policies that existed in the Orangist system of patron–client relationships. He was influenced on the one hand by Brunswick, and on the other by the energetic Prussian Princess Frederika Sophia Wilhelmina (1751–1820), whom he married in 1767.

Wilhelmina of Prussia, as she is known, was a niece of both King Frederick the Great of Prussia and the Duke of Brunswick, with whom she soon clashed because she tried to reduce his influence, although with little success.[12] Brunswick's role did not end until 1784 when, after the existence of the Instrument of Consultancy became known and after the calamitous war with England, he had to leave the country. William V also had little effect on foreign policy. His sympathies and Wilhelmina's lay with England, but attempts to remain neutral in the American War of Independence were undermined and, as we saw earlier, tensions with England flared up in the 1770s. The stadholder likewise had little success in addressing the deadlock between the inland and coastal provinces about reinforcing the army or the fleet and putting an end to the deplorable condition of both.

It is therefore not surprising that the Republic succumbed to a feeling of stagnation and paralysis. When the country was unable to take a stand after the outbreak of war with England in 1780 and the stadholder came across as helpless in his position as captain general and admiral general, the people's fury was also directed at him. Unlike William III in 1672 and William IV in 1747, who were both brought in as a saviour when the country was in dire straits, William V was held responsible for the crisis. Compounding this, William V, despite his political indecisiveness and weakness, had controlled the system of stadholder patronage and created a network of loyal regents throughout the Republic. This 'informal unification', as Maarten Prak describes it, had the reciprocal effect that protests against local abuses also had national dimensions, directed 'at the stadholder and the way in which he had appropriated the system of government'.[13]

The Patriot era and the restoration of Orange (1780–95)

Tensions in domestic politics rose as a result of the war with England, and the stadholder's authority came under progressively greater pressure. The opponents of William V and the Orangists came together in the Patriots, a collective name for a heterogeneous group that can be considered as the Dutch version of the revolutionary movements in late eighteenth-century Europe. Profoundly disillusioned by the Republic's internal and external weakness, they sought restoration of its former power. To that end, they wanted participation in local government, but they also developed national pretentions at the same time. In international affairs they were opposed to England and sympathized with France.

At first the movement had no clear social profile, and all strata of the population were represented. But the bourgeoisie soon became more prominent – and some of them were radicalized in the political dynamic of the 1780s – while many regents recoiled from actual influence by the general public. For the first time in the Republic's history, this was no longer a factional squabble about 'for or against Orange', but a real political and ideological battle of ideas about the structure of the state. The Orangists found themselves on the defensive, yet they had more to offer than the simple rejection of patriotism and they developed a conservative dissenting option. Thus, a modern political debate took place for the first time in the Netherlands of the 1780s.[14]

The climate in which it was conducted has to be viewed against the backdrop of the Dutch Enlightenment – a variant of the European Enlightenment of the eighteenth century. Universal enlightenment ideals such as integrity and knowledge were combined with traditional national values as early as the 1730s, and a positive national sentiment was disseminated – through Justus van Effen's journal, the *Hollandsche Spectator*, for instance – together with great pride in the nation's culture and demarcation with regard to foreign countries. Underlying this were concerns about the weakening of the Republic, which people observed in many areas and which contrasted sharply with the glorious seventeenth century. Apparently, so the argument went, traditional merits had disappeared in an instant as a result of foreign, primarily French, influence. This explained why the virtuous, hardworking merchants who had made the Republic prosperous and influential had been pushed into the background. In their place, according to the criticism in spectatorial magazines, there was now a social elite that looked down on trade, lived off interest, flaunted its wealth and gave its children a French-oriented education.[15]

Contrasting with that perceived moral decline, the Dutch Enlightenment broadcast the optimistic message that this putative deterioration and reduced social cohesion could be stopped and turned around through national reflection. Counteracting this was thus among the central themes of the Dutch Enlightenment.[16] And precisely because there was a desire to restore a past that was not so long ago, it was possible to hark back to almost 'tangible' traditions, and a radical schism in thinking was not on the agenda. Reason and the re-establishment of bourgeois virtues in a moderate Protestant framework were the ingredients of the Dutch Enlightenment. It consequently maintained a restrained tone. People were striving for reconciliation between reason and Christianity instead of making them confront each other. A further explanation of the Dutch Enlightenment's moderate character is that in the Republic, unlike the situation in France, for instance, enlightenment ideals such as freedom and tolerance did not have to be wrenched from an absolutist monarch and an established church. They were already a part of its specific Dutch tradition.[17] It has also been pointed out that the Republic's market of authors and readers was simply too small for magazines and pamphlets that disseminated radical views. But there was broad distribution of writings that – full of concerns about the conditions in the Republic – wanted the country to regain standing and prosperity in an atmosphere of harmony, fairness and a sense of public responsibility.[18]

The optimism of the Dutch Enlightenment in the 1760s that solutions could be engineered developed rapidly, and all over the nation reading and discussion groups sprung up and expressed this thinking through countless activities.[19] A characteristic feature of all these initiatives was the absence of any desire for a new political system, so in this phase these associations can even be described as apolitical. Similarly, they did not aim to stir up contradictions among the population. On the contrary, the goal was moral rearmament on a national scale within the existing order so that restoration of the Republic to its former glory could be achieved through collaboration. A well-known example is the Economics Branch of the Holland Sciences Society, which was founded in 1777 and, through dozens of local departments, aimed to contribute to a new economic élan. A better-known organization, founded in 1784 and still in existence today, is the Maatschappij tot Nut van 't Algemeen (the Society for the Public Good) or Nut for short, which sought and seeks to promote self-improvement among the population and to educate and train the poorer classes. Modernization of science and popular enlightenment had to go hand in hand, so the Nut was an organization that wanted to involve the entire nation in its activities. Around 1800, it had more than fifty local chapters and thousands of members.

When the Nut was established, this enlightened, apolitical, fatherland cult had already been partially displaced by the politicized nationalism of the Patriots. There were consequently also many people in the Nut who came together and played a key role in the politicization that took place in the 1780s. A famous example of writing in which the new political message was disseminated is the pamphlet *Aan het volk van Nederland* (To the People of the Netherlands), which was distributed anonymously in many of the Republic's towns and cities in September 1781. It was not until the nineteenth century that it was discovered that it had been written by the Overijssel noble Joan Derk van der Capellen tot den Poll. It was a fiercely anti-Orangist diatribe in which the author laid the complete responsibility for the Republic's dramatic situation at the door of William V. 'Yes, Prince William, this is all your fault!' he railed. In so doing, he created a clear distinction between Orange and his supporters on the one hand, and true Patriots on the other. But the latter were not calling for the overthrow of the existing system. In fact, they wanted to ensure that the 'old privileges' would be reinstated.

This raises the issue of what Maarten Prak refers to as the 'corporative revolution' of the Patriots.[20] His concept of 'corporative' does not have the current meaning of cooperation between the state and civil society organizations, but instead the historical sense of local communities, trading companies and bourgeois institutions such as guilds and militias, social care organizations and even churches and universities, which were all part of a much more broadly based institutional system. Such organizations also functioned in rural areas, for example in the form of councils of nobility, water boards and manors. A characteristic feature of this corporatism was the high degree of independence these organizations enjoyed and the privileges that membership brought. Between them they made up the historically formed institutional structure of the Republic, with its many levels and domains of decision making.[21]

The Patriots' goal was an idealized image of that old institutional structure. Translated into specific political demands, this meant that the abuses of Orange's patronage system and the regents' oligarchic power cartel that had gradually developed had to come to an end. As far as the Patriots were concerned, in principle the regents were not opponents but potential allies who would, however, have to be supervised and elected with the participation of the middle classes. And local corporative organizations such as guilds and militias would be ideal candidates to fulfil that role. In the interests of underlining the importance of these demands and also demonstrating bourgeois self-awareness, arming the citizenry and organizing democratically controlled volunteer corps were popular instruments in many towns and cities. At the same time, the Patriots were making it clear that they were prepared, if necessary, to defend their own community against the stadholder's troops. A last important point is the mixture of local and national aspirations among the Patriots. They operated within a small radius and their social composition and precise demands varied from place to place. Yet the Patriots were a movement of a national nature too, as the title of Van der Capellen's pamphlet clearly illustrates. This nationwide character was facilitated by the development at this time of pamphlets and newspapers into an interurban political forum in print, which was a new phenomenon.

There has been a great deal of debate as to whether the Patriots were a modern movement or were more concerned about the past. Their demand for reinstatement of lost supposed rights and privileges of the corporative organizations that existed during the Revolt against Spain – as expressed in the important 1783 Patriot document *Grondwettelijke Herstelling* (Constitutional Recovery) – indicates a conservative slant. The same could be said of their primarily local focus. Yet such an approach does not do justice to the renewal that they stood for and that was hidden behind the demand for the restoration of rights.[22] After all, much of what they sought was rooted in the ideas of the Enlightenment, indicated a completely new type of self-awareness among the middle classes, and was presented in a similarly new and politicized way. Some requirements for participation by the citizenry also went far beyond what would ever have been thinkable in the context of old rights and privileges, which in fact points to radical objectives.

They thus mixed old and new political patterns, in which what was new and modernizing emphatically dominated. There was no sudden upheaval and, quoting historian Niek van Sas, the sought-after renewal was a process of 'piecemeal innovation, leading to piecemeal revolution'. No matter how modern the Patriots may have been in some regards, their renewed thinking remained within the Republic's political framework.[23] They did not seek to establish a new order, although they did create a new political culture with robust political mobilization and fierce debates in the press, societies and corporative organizations.

The Patriot movement started to radicalize in 1784, and cracks appeared in the front against the stadholder and his supporters. Many Patriot regents believed their objective had been achieved with the visible weakening of William V and had little desire to share their power with the middle class. And so a significant polarization developed between radical Patriots on one side and Orangists on the other, and some of the regents who initially leaned towards the Patriots changed their views and likewise started to look to the stadholder. Finding himself in a tight spot and isolated in the politics of Holland, William left The Hague in 1785 and retreated to Nijmegen in the hope that the political climate would change in his favour. Meanwhile, the Republic became increasingly fragmented into Patriot and Orangist zones. The Patriots had the upper hand in Holland, Utrecht and Overijssel, while the stadholder's supporters were stronger in Friesland, Zeeland and parts of Gelderland. There were clashes between Patriot volunteer corps and the stadholder's troops in a number of towns and cities, and there were fears of an impending civil war.

This was the climate in which the decisive Wilhelmina of Prussia left Nijmegen for The Hague in June 1787, supported by England, to encourage the Orangists to call for the return of the stadholder. But she never got to The Hague because a Patriot volunteer corps stopped her near Gouda (see Figure 13, p. 115). The States of Holland did not give her permission to continue her journey to The Hague. The princess's brother, Frederick William II, who had become King of Prussia in 1786 and had no sympathy with Patriot

De aanhouding van Prinses Wilhelmina aan de Goejanverwellesluis.

Figure 13 *Wilhelmina of Prussia Detained at the Goejanverwellesluis,* J. R. R. Wetstein Pfister, 1787. National Museum of Education, Dordrecht.

ideas whatsoever, used this 'insult' to the House of Hohenzollern as a pretext for a Prussian invasion of the Republic. The Prussian army pushed the Patriots aside without meeting any serious resistance, and the stadholder's authority was restored in September 1787.

This was the start of a difficult period for the Patriots. Thousands fled the Republic, mainly to the Southern Netherlands and France, demoralized by the counter-revolution of the stadholder and his supporters, anti-Patriot plundering and the associated repression. At the same time, there was an unprecedented purge of government office holders. Almost half the regents were dismissed, many clergymen were driven out, and there were hundreds of court cases. This restoration was rounded off with an obligation on all civil servants to swear an oath of allegiance to the hereditary stadholdership of the House of Orange.[24] Ultimately, though, William V's victory was a pyrrhic one because no stable political situation emerged.[25] The brutally executed restoration had generated a great deal of discontent, and actually cost William V and Wilhelmina support. Many with Patriot leanings withdrew to apparently apolitical societies and reading clubs of the kind that had existed prior to 1780. Behind this façade, however, Patriot views persisted.

As happened on several occasions in the Republic's history, events abroad and their implications were to fundamentally change the domestic political situation. After the French Revolution broke out in 1789 and revolutionary France became embroiled in war with Prussia and Austria in 1792, further hostilities also broke out in 1793 between France on one side and England and the Republic on the other. These developments gave the Patriots hope that the time for a revolution in the Republic had arrived and they could once again play an important part. To that end, a Batavian Revolutionary Committee was set up in 1792 with French support to act as a provisional government should the need arise. In France, the Patriot Herman William Daendels even raised a volunteer foreign legion, which marched north with French troops in 1793. The first attack was warded off with support from Prussia and Austria, but by the end of 1794 the region south of the Waal, Rhine and Meuse had fallen into French hands. At the beginning of January 1795, the rest of the Republic was wide open after the rivers froze over, and these natural barriers were easily crossed. Wilhelmina and William V fled to England in a fishing boat shortly before the French marched into The Hague.

The departure of the stadholder marked the end of the Republic – as it had existed since the Revolt – and the stadholdership disappeared for good. Orange returned to the Netherlands in 1813 in the person of William Frederick (1772–1843), William V's oldest son, who shortly thereafter was to become the first king from the House of Orange-Nassau as William I. But the country's political structure had changed fundamentally since his father's departure in 1795. Before examining these years of political transformation, 1795–1813, we shall review the economic developments in the eighteenth century, arriving at the point where the history of the Republic – the United Provinces of the Netherlands – can be concluded.

The economy in a century of stagnation and decline

It became clear in the previous chapter that a long period of high-level economic stagnation started in the 1670s and did not actually descend into decline until the end of the eighteenth century. Economic historians long disagreed about the exact trends in the eighteenth century and even came to contradictory conclusions. Jan de Vries, for instance, believed that the economy of Holland deteriorated significantly between 1670 and 1750, and then recovered somewhat. J. C. Riley, on the other hand, concluded that there was growth from 1695 to 1860. Johan de Vries adopted an intermediate position, seeing stagnation between 1700 and 1780, followed by dramatic decline. Jan Luiten van Zanden investigated these different views, compared them with new sources, and concluded that the situation in Holland agreed closely with the opinion of Johan de Vries. He deduced there was persistent stagnation between the 1670s and about 1800, and in this period the estimated volume of production fell by a total of 10 to 15 per cent.[26]

The picture in some economic sectors was much more turbulent – sometimes even dramatic. Manufacturing output fell by about a third and the fishing industry lost 90 per cent of its turnover. By contrast the service sector – trade and transport – had its ups and downs, but remained at a relatively high level. We see the same picture in agriculture, although there was a depression in the first half of the eighteenth century. Losses in manufacturing and fishing were offset to an extent by profits from investments. Rich people put their money into foreign countries, government loans and the VOC. Given the ongoing building of large country houses and the construction of ornamental gardens and parks in the French geometric style, these individuals did very well out of their assets, but the Republic was less fortunate. Although the country as a whole was among the most prosperous regions of Europe during the eighteenth century, many in the middle and lower classes descended into poverty. Among other things, they were faced with the decline of industry in the towns and cities, and the consequent loss of jobs and income. The result was that in the eighteenth century, the gap between rich and poor was greater than in the seventeenth century.

So although economic development in the eighteenth century was not as bad as the terms 'deterioration' and 'decline' suggest, the Republic unquestionably had to relinquish its position at the top. During the seventeenth century, there was dynamic commercial growth in which manufacturing, trade and transport boosted one another, but in the eighteenth century, this collaborative resonance disappeared and economic equilibrium remained stationary. The limited domestic market was one of the reasons why expanding international markets had been essential to seventeenth-century growth. When international trade could no longer grow because of the mercantilism and competition of larger neighbouring countries, stagnation was inevitable.[27] This manifested itself very clearly in the shifting relative size of the Dutch merchant fleet. Around 1670, it represented about 40 per cent of the European fleet, but by about 1780, it was only 12 per cent, while the number of Dutch vessels had not dropped. In other words, the Republic proved unable to benefit from market growth in the eighteenth century and in an absolute sense it marked time.

In trying to explain this relative decline, it is necessary to look first at the weakening of the Republic's political power discussed above. The result was that in the eighteenth century, the Republic was no longer able to settle trade conflicts to its own advantage by military means, and had to take its cue from the positions of more powerful nations. Later in the century, during the Fourth Anglo–Dutch War (1780–4) and above all during the French period after 1795, the waning of the Republic's political power became even more apparent when many colonial outposts fell into English hands. The leading international trading nations of the eighteenth century were thus powers that had outrun the Republic. Amsterdam lost ground as a trading metropolis to rivals such as London and Hamburg, and also to business that bypassed the commodities market, which meant that many products were no longer traded via Amsterdam but were transported directly from producer to customer. On the other hand, Amsterdam and Rotterdam could offset part of this loss, thanks to the growing transit trade of colonial merchandise to the German hinterland.

A second significant factor that explains the relative weakening of the Republic's economy is what economic historians identify as the penalties of the pioneer.[28] Part of the Republic's commercial might in the seventeenth century came from the technological lead it had developed in many fields – cheap energy (peat and wind), using modern windmills as a power source in a range of manufacturing processes, cheap and efficient inland transport, modern shipbuilding and a sophisticated financial services system. All of these lost dynamism from the end of the seventeenth century because, from the perspective of this lead, there was less incentive to invest in new and expensive production technologies. Windmills continued to be an important source of power for industry, for instance, so less money was spent on more modern technology using steam power. Putting it another way, the former lead generated too little stimulus to innovate.

The Republic's institutional structure represented a third factor inhibiting the economy. The country reached great heights during the seventeenth century because it successfully resisted the centralization policy of the Habsburgs and was able to integrate a modern economy and an efficient decentralized government system. These advantages turned into drawbacks when a top-down 'national' modernization framework was created in other European countries, in which there was also scope for freedom of religion and conscience. In the Republic, on the other hand, people became trapped in an institutional inability to implement innovations. Local and provincial regulations covering manufacturing, quality control and taxation, for example, had little flexibility, and this institutional rigidity stood in the way of change. Maarten Prak's concept of the Republic as a corporative system clarifies and underlines this bureaucratic gridlock. The absence of strong central authority gave all local, regional and provincial special interest groups a substantial degree of independence and they operated in a complex stress field. The interests of only a few players in this system were served by centralization, so stimuli for innovation on a national scale remained weak.[29]

This institutional impotence played a key role at every point in the eighteenth century when changes to the country's political structure were on the agenda. There were no real attempts to alter the Republic's institutional configuration during the Old Crew/New Crew conflict in the early eighteenth century, the period of the *Doelisten* Movement around 1750, the Patriot era or after restoration of the stadholder's authority in 1787.[30] There were repeated attempts to bring greater unity, coordination and effectiveness into decision making, but all those remained rooted in provincial and urban particularism. This was true of the regents and of the different popular movements, which sought to restore or reinforce traditional local corporative associations. Some of the drive behind reforms was thus focused on the past. Stadholders William IV and V did little or nothing to centralize and strengthen the nation's political structure. Generally speaking, their role was limited to perfecting the stadholder's traditional patronage system. The institutional impotence that left its stamp so clearly on the eighteenth century did not end until the Batavian Revolution of 1795 and the unitary state that followed it. Yet a stable and durable construction for the relationship between central, provincial and local authorities was not to emerge until the constitutional amendment of 1848.

A lack of innovation stimuli, which in turn was closely linked to the Republic's permanently high national debt, is a fourth factor in the explanation of the relative economic degeneration. We saw earlier that the wars of the late seventeenth and early eighteenth centuries were the prime reason why Holland's debt, in particular, soared so dramatically. In 1795, Holland accounted for three-quarters of the Republic's total debt. As had been the case after the War of the Spanish Succession in the early eighteenth century, almost 70 per cent of this province's tax revenues went to pay interest. The figure was below 35 per cent in other provinces, which therefore had no reason whatsoever to support a more equal distribution of the burden across the whole country. Attempts were made at the beginning of the eighteenth century to create more equilibrium in financial policy, but they were unable to overcome resistance from the provinces. Taxation systems consequently remained a matter for the provinces. They continued to cling to their political autonomy and refused to cooperate in centralizing the Republic's executive powers, which could have fostered modernization in other areas.

High interest charges had yet another inhibiting effect in Holland, bringing a fifth factor of relative economic decline into play. Many rich citizens invested most of their money in government loans and lived on the interest paid for by high taxes. It meant that a substantial proportion of the available capital was invested unproductively, and the financial elite were spending their time primarily on managing public debt and barely if at all on economic renewal. Income in the form of interest was largely invested in foreign enterprises, so capital flowed out of the Republic. The vast amounts of money that accumulated in the hands of a small group contributed significantly to making Amsterdam the most important financial centre in Europe in the eighteenth century. The Dutch guilder developed into an international currency, comparable to sterling in the nineteenth century and the dollar after 1945. Banks made a lot of money, but only a few people profited and little employment was created. As has been said, little or nothing was invested in domestic manufacturing and commerce, and this could only lead to stagnation or decline. There was no drive to break out of this vicious circle because a system that earned the highest returns at the lowest risk was in wealthy regents' interests. From the perspective of members of the rich upper crust, they acted rationally in the eighteenth century and there is no point in 'reproaching' them for living on interest and contributing too little to economic renewal and maintaining dynamism.[31] There were simply too many obstacles in the path of such development.

Amsterdam, however, lost its leading position on the international capital market during the 1780s. The reasons included the Fourth Anglo–Dutch War and the Republic's dramatic political and military deterioration it revealed, the debt mountain, political instability, flight of capital and mismanagement at the Bank of Amsterdam (the Wisselbank). London took over its role as a financial centre.

The VOC was also dragged down in this decline.[32] In the eighteenth century, the VOC and trade with America had expanded to become cornerstones of Holland's economy. But profits had been dropping fast since about 1730 and structural cracks had appeared. To begin with, the VOC was increasingly losing out on trade within Asia. Its declining military might was one of the reasons. This business had been very profitable in the seventeenth century, but it was no longer financially feasible in the eighteenth and the losses it was making had to be offset by returns elsewhere. The English and their East India Company also responded more successfully than the VOC to the development of new products and markets – cotton for instance – and they reacted more effectively to political changes in Asia. The English also typically had more sophisticated and faster ships, while the technical improvement of the VOC vessels was lagging behind by the middle of the eighteenth century. Finally, in the 1790s, it was decided to introduce a new merchantman class, but by then it was too late to save the company.

There was corruption everywhere and at all levels, and the ships' crews were increasingly inexperienced and underpaid. The living conditions of VOC personnel in the Orient were also a concern. There was a sharp increase in deaths after 1740, probably from malaria, and many more were weak and debilitated. The VOC's decentralized structure, based on its local chambers, hampered a prompt response to problems and was also relatively expensive. Local chambers were so closely tied to their respective urban economies that they had no interest in centralization, in Amsterdam or Rotterdam for example. This was not surprising. When manufacturing in Holland slumped in the eighteenth century and many urban economies went into a steep decline, VOC chambers were still large employers in their respective cities, for instance in shipyards, warehouses and delivering goods. From the perspective of the VOC as a whole, there was a lot to be said for more centralization and streamlining, but chambers in the smaller cities – Hoorn, Enkhuizen, Middelburg and Delft – were concerned primarily with local interests. The VOC was thus also a prisoner of corporatism and the Republic's decentralized structure, and was incapable of making the necessary organizational reforms. That inability to make changes in its own structure was also linked to the split that grew during the eighteenth century between the political and financial elite of the regents on the one hand and merchants on the other. The oligarchization of the regents and their alienation from traders resulted in a growing degree of ignorance among the VOC directors about buying and selling, and the quality of the management deteriorated.[33] From this perspective, in the eighteenth century the VOC increasingly developed into 'an instrument of the conservative patrician elite' who were primarily concerned with their own financial interests.[34] In practice this meant that the VOC was living above its means, and during a lengthy period in the eighteenth century it paid high dividends that were out of proportion to the actual trading results. The VOC consequently ate into its capital and its debts rose sharply. Even in the 1780–95 period, when the VOC was making substantial losses, it still paid out a dividend of 12.5 per cent for many years.

The Fourth Anglo–Dutch War (1780–1784) exposed the severity of the situation. Around half the VOC's fleet fell into English hands and valuable cargoes were lost. Rapid bankruptcy was only prevented by subsidies and credit guarantees from the States General and the States of Holland, and the VOC was put under state control in 1790. The death blow followed in 1795, when the Republic – by then in the French sphere of influence – went to war with England and lost virtually all of its colonial possessions. Nothing remained but to liquidate the VOC. It was declared bankrupt and its debt, which had risen to 120 million guilders, was taken over by the state. This resulted in a substantial increase in the already huge national debt. No real prospect of trading with colonial possessions emerged again until after 1813 – and this would be limited to the Indonesian Archipelago, because important former possessions elsewhere, including Ceylon and the Cape Colony, were to remain in British hands.

The WIC met with the same fate as the VOC as a result of the Fourth Anglo–Dutch War. We saw in the previous chapter that the WIC was not very successful in the seventeenth century. It came to grief in 1675 and was re-established later that year, but did not flourish thereafter either. The WIC lost its last monopoly in 1738 and was less important than trading across the Atlantic by independent merchants who circumvented it. Slavery played a not insignificant role in transatlantic trade both during and after the WIC monopoly. In the course of the seventeenth and eighteenth centuries, Dutch slave traders brought some 600,000 Africans to the other side of the Atlantic Ocean; this represented about 5 per cent of the total African slave trade conducted by European powers. The slave trade had a huge number of victims. Apart from the principle of the system itself, many also died early deaths as a result of their treatment on board and on the plantations. The transmission of diseases not known in Africa, and against which Africans had insufficient resistance, was another factor. The upshot was that about a quarter of the slaves in the West Indies died within three years of their arrival. From the point of view of the slave traders, the business was only moderately lucrative, with an average annual profit margin of 2–3 per cent.[35] Aside from the slave trade, the major business of the Atlantic trade was transporting sugar and coffee from the Caribbean to Europe. This trade increased on average by 2 per cent a year from about 1710 to the 1770s, but this growth rate was modest compared with the performance of England and France. Dutch plantation output was also smaller and became less significant even in relative terms. During the 1680s the Republic produced about 8 per cent of the sugar in the Caribbean, but by 1775 even this unimpressive share had shrunk to 5 per cent.[36] Nevertheless, trade with the Caribbean in the eighteenth century was a much more important source of income for the country than the permanent losses incurred by the WIC would lead one to suspect. Here too, however, the Republic paid the price for its military weakness and dependence on international relations. When England made short work of the Dutch trading network in this area during the Fourth Anglo–Dutch War, it was soon all over for the WIC. The States General 'nationalized' it in 1791. After 1795, the plantations in the west met the same fate as the colonial possessions in the Far East – they came under English rule. Suriname was returned in 1815, but what is now Guyana remained English. During this period the Dutch slave trade also officially came to an end. This was not a consequence of a powerful movement in the Netherlands opposing slavery. No action was taken during the French period, and the 1798 Constitution made no mention of abolishing the slave trade or slavery. It was not until August 1814, coinciding with the Restoration under William I (see p. 134 ff.), that significant English pressure put an end to the Dutch slave trade. London threatened, if the Netherlands did not decide upon abolition, not to give back the Dutch colonies that had come under English rule after 1795.[37] The reason behind this threat was that in 1807 England had prohibited the slave trade on pain of a fine of a hundred pounds for every slave found on an English ship. This situation obviously made it extremely difficult for English planters in the Caribbean to buy new slaves and threatened their competitive position. England was therefore pressing for the abolition of the slave trade at an international level.[38]

Manufacturing had declined sharply earlier in the eighteenth century. As we saw in the previous chapter, there had been deterioration in some industrial sectors since the 1670s, while there had been growth in others, and so the overall picture has to be broken down into its constituent elements. The textile industry in Leiden and Haarlem, for example, went seriously downhill from the late seventeenth century, as did the building trade and breweries in many towns and cities. The number of industrial windmills in the Zaan region, on the other hand, continued to grow until 1730, and the paper industry, sugar refineries and tobacco and silk sectors expanded. Shipbuilding also remained healthy. From the 1730s onwards, though, there was a downturn in most areas of manufacturing and production, and production for export ran into problems. The high production costs were a major weakness in Holland's manufacturing sector. Wages that were very high in relative terms had not been an obstacle in the prosperous seventeenth century, but increasingly became so in the changed circumstances of the eighteenth century, with its growing competition, falling prices and political weakness. All this was compounded by the high taxes in Holland. The upshot was the loss of labour-intensive manufacturing in many towns and cities in the province.

Industrial cities that had flourished in the seventeenth century, for example Leiden, Haarlem and Delft, saw their populations shrink dramatically between 1720 and 1750. In 1720, Leiden had 65,000 residents, but by about 1750 there were only 36,000. During this same period the number of people in Haarlem fell from 45,000 to 26,000. Contrary to the European trend of population growth and urbanization, during these decades the number of Holland's inhabitants fell; the percentage living in urban areas also dropped in the eighteenth century. While the coastal provinces lost out, the inland ones became relatively stronger. Some industry moved away from the coast because of the lower production costs, which compensated somewhat for the decline in manufacturing in the Republic as a whole.[39] The sharp drop in the populations of towns and cities in Holland and changes to the economic structure obviously had implications for the urban way of life. No new migrants arrived while others left. Many unemployed labourers escaped impoverishment by signing on as seamen on VOC ships, and this – in part because many did not return – acted to a degree as a safety valve that restored equilibrium.[40]

In the Golden Age, agriculture in coastal provinces had seen tremendous growth, entirely in line with the dynamism of the economy at that time, when increasing business in one sector generated prosperity in others. But after 1670 the sector sank into a depression that lasted until about 1750, and the production of crops and animals fell considerably as a result. The relative stability in the inland provinces compensated in part for the serious decline of farming in Holland. There was recovery in the second half of the century and agriculture benefitted from population growth elsewhere in Europe, so that the Republic's share of the international agrarian market actually increased significantly. Agriculture was not hampered by the high production costs that were hurting manufacturing and it was able to hold its own against international competition. It – with the trading and financial sectors – prevented the economy falling into serious decline during much of the eighteenth century.

In the end, the rot could not be stopped, and the collapse came in the 1780s. Although the commercial problems arising out of the Fourth Anglo–Dutch War were serious, the conflict was more of a catalyst than the cause of the economic decline. The dramatic and rapid course of events during the war demonstrated once and for all what had happened in the eighteenth century. The once mighty Republic of the seventeenth century had become a minor power, with huge government debt and weakened defences. All attempts to turn the tide had proved illusory. The international balance of power had changed for ever, and the Republic had too many inherent obstacles in its system to achieve institutional renewal without external pressure. So the Republic remained a captive of the structures that had made it great, but were no longer fit for the purpose of generating political and economic modernization.

This did not happen until after 1795, when the Batavian Republic was created under French supervision. No matter how important the political and institutional changes during the French period (1795–1813) were to be, from an economic point of view this era was even more dramatic than the 1780s. The new Republic increasingly became a French colony, deployed in the Napoleonic wars and robbed of its maritime and colonial sources of income. There would be no scope for economic recovery until after the Napoleonic era and the return of a sovereign Dutch state in 1813.

The Batavian Republic and the French period (1795–1813)

The advance of the French army across the frozen Waal, Rhine and Meuse, the collapse of the Republic, and the flight of William V and Wilhelmina of Prussia to England in January 1795 created a rebellious mood in many towns and cities. Reading clubs emerged as revolutionary cells, which seized power locally. Some were supported by Batavian militias, made up of refugees who had returned with the French troops. In January 1795, France recognized the 'Batavian Republic' as a sister republic. It was independent in name only; in reality it was a French satellite. The Treaty of The Hague of May 1795 stipulated that the Batavian Republic would pay France substantial 'liberation costs' and, among other things, would relinquish a number of fortified towns. The Scheldt also had to be opened up completely to seagoing shipping, French troops would be stationed in the country, and the young Republic would have to bear their costs. In addition, the Batavian Republic became an ally of France, which meant it was automatically at war with England. Historian Remieg Aerts tellingly describes the Batavian Republic's freedom as no more than that of a 'kite on a string'.[41]

It would not be correct to conclude, however, that the Republic's internal relationships were completely in French hands. What happened was a Dutch revolution within French parameters. Based on the French example, the rallying cry of the new Dutch rulers was 'Liberty, Equality and Fraternity', but opinions about the content and political substance were seriously divided. While it was clear that the old state institutions and the social structure were in the past and that democratic principles had to replace them, how far did democratization have to go and, above all, what government structure should the new Republic have? Political decision making was often slow in the old federal Republic because local and provincial positions had to be included. It was no different in the Batavian Republic's political debates. The upshot was a velvet revolution, characterized by years of discussion, without violence and without appreciable repression. Even determining the exact rules for elections to a National Assembly, which was to replace the States General, took over a year. It was not until March 1796 that the assembly met to define the constitution. The members were elected indirectly by all men over the age of twenty provided they were not receiving charity and had renounced the stadholder under oath.[42]

This parliament failed to reform constitutional law because insurmountable political differences soon arose. During the 1780s, the Patriots had fought for their local political rights and resisted centralizing tendencies. A number of delegates continued to take this position after 1795 and wanted no more than a few changes to the old federal structure. Others, influenced to a degree by the French Revolution and the failure of the Dutch Patriots in the 1780s, wanted a unitary state and an end to the corporatist basis of the former Patriot demands.[43] So Federalists squared up to Unitarians and they obstructed each other. The Moderates, a third group, supported the principle of a unitary state but were more pragmatic than the Unitarians. There were opposing views in other areas too, for instance about suffrage and the extent of democratization, but the dividing lines were not the same as those about government centralization. The result was that no one was satisfied with the 1797 draft constitution, which was referred to as the 'big book' because of the many amendments added in the National Assembly. When the population rejected the new constitution in a plebiscite in January 1798, the Unitarians staged a coup d'état with French support.

The coup was intended to force a breakthrough after years of talking and create a constitution, but the French also had a foreign policy objective. In October 1797, the English inflicted a major defeat on the Batavian Republic's fleet, and France wanted its sister republic to make a more significant contribution in the conflict with England. To that end it was necessary to actually have a functioning government. The goal of the coup was achieved. The Constitution for the Batavian People was drafted in April 1798 and approved in a referendum, after care had been taken to ensure Orangists and Federalists were not entitled to vote.[44] An example of the radical unitarian character of the Constitution was the abolition of the seven provinces, cornerstones of the old Republic. They were replaced by eight departments with new names and new borders, which only had administrative powers in the new unitary state. Another new feature was the introduction of agencies, which were like ministries, headed by agents tasked with creating centralization. There had been 'national' policies for the army, navy and foreign policy in the old Republic, but now national targets were formulated for education, poor relief, water management and the economy. The Netherlands thus became a unitary state in 1798 with a central government in The Hague, and so it was to remain. This is what made 1798 significant.

This first Dutch Constitution did not last long. It was to be replaced as early as 1801 by a more moderate version, which in turn was supplanted by a third a few years later. The 1798 Constitution's implementation gave rise to resistance because the Unitarians took too radical an approach and did not reach out to more moderate forces. The result was a second coup d'état in June 1798. It was a domestic Dutch matter, but the instigator – Herman William Daendels – knew he had France behind him because a more moderate regime had also assumed power in Paris. Daendels did not brush the Constitution aside, just the radicals who were implementing it. New elections gave the moderates a majority, and the new government saw its task as promoting national unity and putting the Constitution into effect. In practice, though, the transition from federal republic to a unitary Batavian state was difficult, in part because old mechanisms and the new system repeatedly clashed. As a result, genuine renewal lagged behind the written reforms in the Constitution. Many Batavians, disappointed by the coups and purges, simply turned their

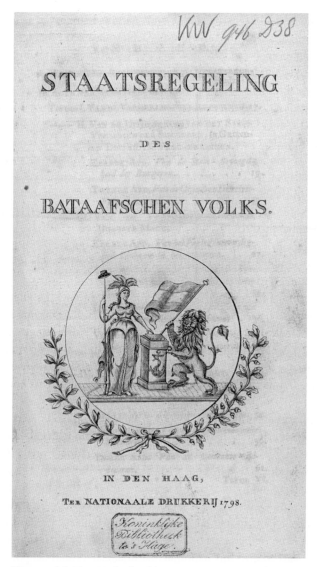

Figure 14 The Netherlands' First Constitution: the 1798 *Staatsregeling*. The Hague, Royal Library, Signature 010097002888.

backs on politics, and the feverish political zeal of the 1795–8 period disappeared. All the revolutionary rhetoric notwithstanding, there was consequently a surprisingly high degree of continuity with the old Republic's system of government in the Batavian era.[45]

Nevertheless, the 1798 Constitution can be seen as a milestone in the political and constitutional history of the Netherlands, and its essential components would no longer be undone. The fundamental significance of the 1798 Constitution is comparable to the 1814 Constitution and the constitutional amendments of 1848 and 1917, which will be discussed in the next chapter. The Netherlands became a unitary state in 1798, with the people as sovereign. The characteristic urban autonomy and provincial sovereignty of the old Republic disappeared. The privileges of social status were abolished and from then on all inhabitants were equal under the law. Civil rights such as freedom of expression, association and religion were guaranteed. Previously, civil rights had been linked to a town or city and did not apply to everyone, but now they were granted to all residents by the nation state. Everyone was now a citizen – a fundamental difference from the previous select group of citizens of a town or city. At the same time, the word 'citizen' changed from a purely legal, exclusive and local concept to 'an open, dynamic and inclusive category' for everyone living in the Republic's territory.[46] This equality also meant the end of the Dutch Reformed Church's privileged position. Public sector jobs were now accessible to all citizens regardless of their religion. The National Assembly had already decided that in 1795, but the separation between church and state was now established in law. In line with enlightened thinking about forms of government, the principle of separation of powers was introduced with independently operating legislative, executive and judicial branches.

The Constitution also heralded a new era for the economy. The intention to abolish the guilds, which had been an important element in the former corporatist structure, was a radical idea that was executed with moderation. Initially, there was no actual abolition – that did not happen until 1820 – but the guilds became less important and influential, to an extent because central government assumed more powers. There was furthermore consensus that a new taxation system was needed, but its content was not hammered out until 1805.

The Batavian Republic inherited the old problem of Holland's huge debt mountain from its predecessor. It was in Holland's interests – although not those of the other provinces – to convert this provincial liability into a national one.[47] This required a completely new taxation system under which the provinces would have to relinquish their old financial autonomy and the privileged position of the guilds and their members would have to come to an end. This is not the place to discuss in detail the financial position of the Batavian Republic and the pathway to a national taxation system. The key point is that after the Netherlands became a unitary state by virtue of its constitution, a process had to start to give this nation actual financial, economic, political and social substance. But implementation was difficult because opinions about how exactly this substance should be shaped were sharply divided and because there was still no strong central government. Daendels's coup d'état in June 1798 was intended to start this implementation, but the Executive Authority – as the government was called – was only partially successful in achieving it.

Despite the dissatisfaction about the political deadlock in which the Batavian Republic once again found itself, and about the ongoing war with England and its economic consequences, the revival of Orangist sentiment remained muted. Even so, England and the exiled stadholder William V had developed plans for a return of Orange. To that end, in 1799 they attempted, with Russia, to occupy a number of towns in the north of Holland and march on Amsterdam and Haarlem. William V called on his former supporters to seize power. His son William Frederick, later King William I (1815–40), fought with the invading army. But the populace remained passive and in October 1799 Franco–Batavian units forced the Anglo–Russian troops to withdraw and capitulate.

This episode had nonetheless demonstrated just how vulnerable the Batavian Republic still was. Napoleon thought so too. He came to power in France that same year and wanted greater Batavian support for the French side. That was more important to him than implementing the Constitution, so restoring political peace and order was his first priority. If the Batavian Republic's regime could be reconciled with the Federalists and Orangists, it would be easier for the sister republic to become the colony that Napoleon had in mind. In 1801, when England no longer insisted upon the restoration of the House of Orange and William V proved willing to abandon his claim to the Republic in exchange for a few areas in Germany, Napoleon took it as a sign that the time was ripe for national reconciliation in the Netherlands.

Quite apart from this, the Executive Authority was now prepared to involve former adversaries in the political process again. The absence of an Orangist uprising during the Anglo–Russian invasion in 1799 was one of the factors underlying this. But for such a reconciliation to take place it was necessary to suspend the Constitution and draft a new one. A few members of the Executive Authority wanted this, but the Representative Assembly – as the parliament was called – refused to cooperate. In 1801, there was a new coup d'état, with French support, and the Representative Assembly was dissolved. A new constitution was submitted to voters soon afterwards. Although the number of opponents (some 52,000) was greater than the number of supporters (about 17,000), the new Constitution was nevertheless considered to have been approved simply by counting the vast number of voters who stayed at home (around 330,000) as supporters. The Batavian Republic was renamed the Batavian Commonwealth and was to be governed by a body known as the State Council until 1805.

The new regime's 'national reconciliation' resulted in the reversal of many of the democratic reforms introduced since 1795, and the restriction of political freedoms led to the creation of an autocratic executive. The new Constitution contained many federalist elements that had been incorporated in the 'big book' of 1797. The old provincial boundaries and names were restored and the agencies were scrapped. Many former regents returned, including Orangists who had been given permission to do so by William V from his new residence, Oranienstein Castle in the Duchy of Nassau. The former stadholder hoped that this would lay the foundations for his possible return. What happened was therefore more a restoration of conservative forces than an actual reconciliation between the different political movements.

Despite all this, there was nevertheless a real national rapprochement during this period. Scope for it was also created as politicization weakened, albeit the differences were covered up rather than resolved. In the climate created around the turn of the century, people harked back to the former apolitical fatherland cult of the Dutch Enlightenment, while at the same time work could continue on the national framework, which had been strengthened since 1795. The role model here was not the politically aware Batavian citizen, but the industrious and virtuous Dutchman, proud of his history, his cultural heritage and his language.[48] This new awareness of nation was also strengthened by external pressure. Initially, the Batavians had welcomed the French as liberators, but this changed because France was increasingly behaving as an occupier. In such a situation, national solidarity made more sense than pursuing internal political differences. Furthermore, many people realized that there was little choice but political accommodation of the mighty France and a form of moderate cultural nationalism. According to Van Sas, this deepening of nationalistic feelings, this reinforced consciousness of the border between 'us' and 'others', would have a profound influence on the further development of national awareness in the nineteenth century.[49]

As far as international relations were concerned, the Batavian Republic was stuck fast between French continental domination and English maritime and colonial power. Bound hand and foot to France and so permanently at war with England, after 1795, the Batavian Republic lost one colony after another. Exiled stadholder William V had given the Dutch regents instructions to collaborate with the English. Some did indeed do that, while others refused. It made little difference. The Republic's colonial trading empire, from the Caribbean via South Africa and Ceylon to the Indonesian Archipelago, disintegrated and the English took over virtually everywhere. The economic consequences were huge. The VOC failed in 1795, and the loss of the colonial settlements in the years that followed put a temporary end to Dutch shipping and overseas trade. Shipyards and ports in Holland and Zeeland came to a virtual standstill, manufacturing slumped and many town and cities again lost large numbers of inhabitants. Even Amsterdam, which had a stable population in the eighteenth century, saw it shrink from 217,000 to 180,000 between 1795 and 1815. The economy had been badly hit in the 1780s, but now – in the French period – it went into freefall.

The fighting stopped briefly after the Anglo–French Treaty of Amiens in 1802, but hostilities resumed the following year and Napoleon again demanded substantial sums from the Batavian Commonwealth, which it was barely able to pay. To start with, the national debt had increased since 1795 and the need to pay interest put even greater pressure on expenditure. Second, there was still no effective national taxation system, so the state's income was too low and more and more money had to be borrowed. Third, the collapse of the economy made it even more difficult to find the sums being demanded.

Napoleon was consequently not satisfied with the support he received from the State Council and so he decided to make another regime change. Rutger Jan Schimmelpenninck, an important spokesman for the Moderates between 1795 and 1798 and ambassador in Paris thereafter, was given the assignment of drafting a new constitution based on the authoritarian French model. Napoleon then appointed Schimmelpenninck as grand pensionary, deliberately reverting to this title from the history of the old Republic. Schimmelpenninck's rule only lasted until 1806, but he left a positive legacy. Government finances were centralized, a modern system of national taxes was introduced, a nationwide postal service was set up and an education act created the basis for national public education. Democracy along the lines of the Batavian model was long gone, but Schimmelpenninck made a significant contribution to the unification of the Netherlands that many had been advocating since 1795.

There was as yet no end to the regular regime changes and coups. In 1806, Napoleon made short work of the Batavian era and appointed his brother Louis Napoleon Bonaparte as ruler of a new state – the Kingdom of Holland. Napoleon was once more dissatisfied with the effort made by the Batavian Republic against England, this time because Schimmelpenninck did not cooperate sufficiently with the introduction of the Continental System, which was intended to block the entire coast of Europe from English products. Louis Bonaparte, aged twenty-eight, was the first King of the Netherlands and at first had no rapport with the Dutch people, who in turn were oddly passive and let matters take their course. Many people were dispirited after the coups and regime changes of the preceding years, while others harboured pragmatic hopes that the centralization of politics and government would be continued. There were also those who accepted the situation in the realization that the new kingdom was in any event better than Napoleon's alternative – annexation by France.

Louis, who was an enlightened ruler, disappointed his brother but has gone down in Dutch history as a 'good' king. Rather than making the Kingdom of Holland subordinate to Napoleon's plans, Louis proved sensitive to the interests of his subjects. His room for manoeuvre may have been modest, but he implemented only some of the measures imposed by his brother. The unification of the Netherlands also made progress under his regime. He built on the national reconciliation that had come about since the turn of the century and surrounded himself with advisors representing a range of political viewpoints. He had no sympathy with democratic ideas, however, and his style of government displayed a number of Bonapartist characteristics.[50] Never before in the history of the Netherlands had so much power been in the hands of one person. He expressly projected himself as a *majesté nationale* and in that role he tried to associate the new monarchy with Dutch national awareness. He established a national public holiday, for example, and went out of his way to show his royal sympathy when there were floods and other disasters. He encouraged the organization of national exhibitions and in 1807 a national coinage system was introduced under his rule. A scheme was also set up to return to Catholics church buildings they had lost during the Revolt. They had been demanding this since denominations were given equal status in the Batavian Revolution. Other steps of lasting significance were the drafting of the Dutch Civil Code and the Dutch Penal Code. While these may have had evident parallels with the corresponding Napoleonic legislation, they certainly cannot be considered as simply translations from French into Dutch – there were too many rules that arose from Dutch customs and traditions in these new codes and the role played by Dutch jurists in their drafting was too great. The National Library and Art Gallery, which were established in 1798 and contained the exiled stadholder's book and art collections, were extended and reorganized under Louis Bonaparte. His name remained associated with them because in 1806 he granted them the right to use the designation 'royal', resulting in the Royal Library and the Royal Museum – the present Rijksmuseum in Amsterdam. In 1808, he also promoted the establishment of the Royal Institute of Sciences, Literature and Fine Arts (the present Royal Netherlands Academy of Arts and Sciences).[51] He lives on, too, in the name of Amsterdam's most famous building: the Royal Palace in

Dam Square. Louis moved into this monument of the old Republic – the former town hall – in 1808.

The last phase of the French period began in July 1810, when Napoleon's frustration with his brother's disobedience prompted him to abolish the Kingdom of Holland and annex the Netherlands as part of France. Until 1813 the country was flooded once more with centralizing measures, but now no account was taken of national traditions. Justice was organized strictly in accordance with the Napoleonic *code civil* and *code pénal*, the registry of births, deaths and marriages (with surnames for everyone – a requirement that had not previously existed) and the land registry were introduced, and the French metric system put an end to regional differences in weights and measures. The huge national debt – part of which had been caused by the massive burden of payments to France – was lightened to a degree because the interest on government borrowing was reduced to one-third of its old level. As a result many people who had invested in government bonds lost a substantial part of their wealth, but there were few alternatives to this radical step.

The introduction of compulsory military service was extremely unpopular. The *départements réunies*, as the annexed Netherlands was called, were obliged to provide a certain number of soldiers for Napoleon's campaigns. Over 10,000 Dutchmen died in the 1812 Russian campaign alone. Initially, sons of prosperous families could pay instead of joining the army, but in 1813 Napoleon alienated this part of the population too by setting up the *gardes d'honneur*, an army corps for sons of the wealthy elite. Thanks to the Continental System, which was now strictly enforced, the economy declined rapidly and the detested military service also caused unrest and local riots. Although the French occupation was increasingly perceived as oppressive and humiliating, it did not lead to manifest anti-French nationalism. Love of country was expressed primarily through culture in the traditional societies and literary circles.[52] A characteristic of the prevailing apathy was that no initiatives were launched to seize power until November 1813, after Napoleon's defeat at the Battle of Leipzig and after Prussian and Russian units had entered the Netherlands.

The rapid collapse of the French administration was followed by Orange's return, which had been prepared and well managed by a small group. On the very beach at Scheveningen from which Stadholder William V and his wife Wilhelmina had fled headlong to England in 1795, their son William Frederick landed in November 1813. He was to become sovereign ruler and, in 1815, the first Dutch king of the Netherlands. He found a very different country from the one his father had left. Nothing remained of the democratic reforms during the years immediately after 1795 and many plans from that period had not been implemented or had been reversed. Nevertheless, something fundamental changed during the French period. Original Dutch thinking had merged with French influences. The federal Republic, with its autonomous towns and cities and sovereign provinces, had been replaced by a unitary state in which government, taxation, legislation, culture and education were centralized. The associated modernization was still at an early stage in many areas, but the era of the *ancien régime* was definitely a thing of the past. Whereas the Patriots of the 1780s acted in a corporative spirit, the Batavians'

1795 velvet revolution created a national framework different from that envisaged by the Patriots. The old locally rooted corporative organizational structure, with its guilds, militias and urban-related citizenship, had disappeared. Not by decree in a radical upheaval, but in steps – both large and small – over a period of more than twenty years.[53] That new national framework, tied to a new sense of nationhood, also formed the backdrop against which Orange returned in November 1813. That result of the French period was the foundation on which the new kingdom would be constructed.

CHAPTER 5
FROM RESTORATION TO THE LIBERAL ERA (1813–1917)

Introduction

The Dutch regained their independence in 1813 and the United Kingdom of the Netherlands came into being at the Congress of Vienna (1814–15). The former Northern and Southern Netherlands were joined to form one kingdom under King William I, who also became Grand Duke of Luxembourg. The integration was successful to a degree, but the kingdom broke up after the Belgian Revolt of 1830, although the Netherlands did not accept Belgium's secession until 1839. Disappointed and embittered, William I stepped aside in 1840 to make way for his volatile son William II who, fearful of a revolution, agreed to a liberal amendment to the constitution in 1848. Under its terms, the introduction of ministerial responsibility restricted the king's power, which meant that ministers were now accountable to parliament, not to the king.

After that, the Netherlands gradually developed into a liberal state. The first political parties were established in the 1870s. The main issues concerning them were the extension of electoral suffrage, social legislation and equal entitlement to government financing for non-denominational and Christian primary education (the school funding controversy). The upshot of this development was the constitutional amendment of 1917, under which the right to vote became universal and secret. This made the country a modern parliamentary democracy. At the same time, the school funding controversy was resolved and equal entitlement to state funding of primary education was adopted. This amended constitution created a framework for further political developments in the twentieth century.

Economic progress in the nineteenth century was defined primarily by relatively late and slow industrialization. A phase of modern economic growth started in 1870. Structural changes resulted in a smaller workforce on the land and more employment in trade, manufacturing and services. Many people moved from rural to urban areas, and towns and cities grew significantly. Economic expansion in the late nineteenth century came from growth in the domestic market and increased commercial activities in Germany. Then, as now, relations between the two countries were significantly shaped by the broad range of economic interaction.

In international relations, after the failed experiment of its United Kingdom, the Netherlands was once again a small country with a modest position in continental Europe. To safeguard its interests as a trading nation and colonial power as best it could, the country steered a neutral course that was also in the interests of the major European players. For this reason, the nation was able to remain neutral during the First World

War, but this could not prevent the dramatic deterioration of economic and social conditions in the last phase of the war. Nevertheless, there were no major political earthquakes, and the constitutional amendment facilitated the peaceful creation of political reforms in 1917.

Last, the nineteenth century bore the clear stamp of an ongoing process of national unification. The fall of the federal Republic and the creation of a unitary state in 1795 signalled the start of a process of political and economic modernization that brought with it an acceleration in nation building. This manifested itself particularly clearly in the second half of the nineteenth century, although answers to questions about the character of the Dutch nation depended on whether an individual was a liberal, orthodox Protestant, Catholic or social democrat. At the end of the century the royal house was used more often and more successfully as a symbol of national unity. Summarizing, for the Netherlands – in common with other European countries – the nineteenth century was an epoch of ongoing unification in many areas. This development went hand in hand with political and economic modernization.

The failed experiment: The United Kingdom of the Netherlands (1815–30)

The end of the Napoleonic era was the start of an era of restoration in Europe, which in some ways was a return to the period before the French Revolution. Democratic principles, which had so markedly informed late eighteenth-century political thinking, appeared to have been nothing more than an intermezzo, and autocratic political structures controlled the political scene virtually everywhere in Europe. 'Restoration' as a concept does indeed suggest that the legacy of the French Revolution and the Napoleonic era had been swept away and there was significant continuity with the years preceding them. This also corresponds with the image that the political elite projected in its behaviour after 1813. This was most certainly the case in the Netherlands. In the proclamation he wrote upon the return of Orange, Gijsbert Charles van Hogendorp put it as follows: 'Orange forever. Holland is free. . . . The seas are open. Trade is reviving. All discord is at an end. Everything in the past is forgotten and forgiven. . . . The good old days are back. Orange forever!' Van Hogendorp was not just looking back to the age of the Republic of the United Provinces of the Netherlands, but – as will emerge – even to the Burgundian period of the late Middle Ages. That history and that supposed historical continuity were, for him, what legitimized the construction of renewed Orange authority.

But that past had little to do with the reality of the times. A new form of government was emerging which, although harking back to supposed historical traditions, was in fact fundamentally different from that former political structure. While some of the Republic's stadholders had developed royal airs, none of them ever became monarchs. Now the Netherlands became a monarchy under the House of Orange-Nassau. There had been a federal republic of sovereign provinces with powerful towns and cities until the French period, but now it was definitively a unitary state.

Figure 15 *The Arrival of the Prince of Orange at Scheveningen, 30 November 1813*, Nicolaes Lodewick Penning, 1813. Rijksmuseum Amsterdam.

This also had implications for the States General. While the name of the representative body did not change, it was now composed of individuals elected by the people rather than delegates from the provinces. These new parliamentarians certainly had little in common with politicians towards the end of the nineteenth century, but they were the basis for later parliamentary development. And the same was true of the constitution. During the Republic, there had been little more than the Union of Utrecht, and the first constitutions came into effect during the Batavian French period. These provided the foundations for constructing a constitution that established the most important rules of the political order. There was little evidence of the democratic achievements in the Batavian period and the monarch could govern as he saw fit. The political basis was nonetheless different from that during the Republic.

The power vacuum created in the Netherlands in November 1813 by the collapse of the French empire soon disappeared, thanks to Van Hogendorp's firm action. This former pensionary of Rotterdam, out of office since the Batavian Revolution of 1795, spent years working on a draft constitution that could guide the orderly return of Orange in such a vacuum. Even before the French had left the country he, with a handful of other Orangists – but in the name of the 'whole population' – called on the Prince of Orange to return and accept sovereignty over the country. The prince was in London trying to drum up English support for precisely that purpose, and he sailed from there to land on Scheveningen beach on 30 November 1813. Meanwhile, Van Hogendorp and his political friends had formed a General Executive, which they now handed over to 'William the First, sovereign prince of the Netherlands'. The new ruler was not yet king. He wanted to strengthen his position with the population first. He expressly reached out to the people, who barely knew him, and held out the prospect of a constitution that would guarantee their freedom. It comes as no surprise that Van Hogendorp's draft was the basis of that constitution.

According to Van Hogendorp, the old stadholders did not have enough power to protect the 'ordinary people' from the regents' oligarchy. That was why the Netherlands should now become a constitutional monarchy with a king at the centre of political power. This would put an end to the old dualism between stadholders and regents from the time of the Republic. This interpretation of the stadholder's position in the eighteenth century was a simplification of reality – William IV and William V in fact had quasi-monarchical powers – but Van Hogendorp used it to clear the way for the creation of the monarchy. He sought historical legitimacy for this, too, and he found it in the late Middle Ages and during the time of Charles V, when there was said to have been harmony between the ruler and the people – harmony that was lost in the Republic and now had to be restored under an Orange sovereign.

The Dutch historian Henk te Velde rightly refers, freely rendered from Eric Hobsbawm, to 'one great invention of tradition' which was nonetheless not 'a concoction based on nothing'.[1] Something new was created from a collection of sometimes contradictory historical fragments on the one hand, and recent modern experience with the constitutional unitary state on the other. In consequence, Van Hogendorp is sometimes referred to as a conservative reformer. It was at his instigation that the modern principle of a constitution was fleshed out with restorative substance in which there was no trace of ideas about popular sovereignty and equality. In their place were royal sovereignty and elitist thinking.

In 1814, the Netherlands thus became a constitutional monarchy in which the clientelism of the political culture predating 1795 was revived and the ruler was given great power.[2] Ministers implemented his policy and were accountable to him, not to parliament. Many fields, for example foreign affairs, colonial matters and finance, were kept virtually in their entirety outside the States General and left to the king. The States General did not yet represent the people in the modern sense. The members were indirectly elected by the Provincial States, which in turn consisted of the newly established classes (noble, urban and rural). The aristocratic element was more strongly represented in the representative bodies than in the bourgeois-dominated Republic prior to 1795.

The new constitution came into effect at the end of March 1814, but behind the scenes William I was concentrating primarily on foreign policy – an area in which he had great ambitions. As well as retrieving colonial possessions that had fallen into English hands during the French period, he wanted to extend the kingdom's territory on the continent. In particular, he was thinking of the Southern Netherlands, Luxembourg and areas of Germany as far as the Moselle. More important than William's aspirations were the interests of Britain, which wanted a strong buffer state to the north of France. Dutch territory did not expand to the extent William I had hoped, but after Russia, Austria and Prussia had also given their approval, on 1 August 1814 he accepted sovereignty over the Southern Netherlands. William I was soon able to prove the value of the new buffer state against France after Napoleon escaped from Elba at the beginning of March 1815, and troops were needed to defeat him again. William I announced he would adopt the title of king to underline the importance of his own role in this regard. He then gave his son command of a united Netherlands army, which contributed to Napoleon's final defeat at Quatre Bras and Waterloo.

The creation of William's United Kingdom, incorporating the former Northern and Southern Netherlands, was ratified by the Congress of Vienna (1814–15). He also became Grand Duke of Luxembourg, so he ruled the area of the current Benelux countries (see Map 8, p. 138). This new territorial situation and William I's kingship made it necessary to amend the 1814 constitution. A bicameral system was introduced at the request of southern representatives. From then on the States General was to comprise Lower and Upper Houses, where the Lower House was a continuation of the former popular representation. Although the south had many more inhabitants than the north (about 3.4 million and 2 million, respectively), each was allotted the same number of delegates (fifty-five) who, as under the 1814 constitution, were elected indirectly through the Provincial States. The members of the Upper House, numbering between forty and seventy, would be appointed directly by the king, who – as before – could govern without any appreciable influence from parliament.

There were, however, modern features: the sessions of the Lower House would be open, freedom of the press was guaranteed, and the people were given the right to submit petitions to the monarch. These measures even led Austrian, Prussian and Russian diplomats to regard William I as progressive and liberal.[3] But the way the king declared that the constitution had been adopted revealed a different picture. Among other things, people in the south resented the assignment of seats in the Lower House and the combining of the national debts, a move that was highly disadvantageous to them. More important, though, was Catholic resistance to equality for all religions and William I's attempts to acquire influence over the ecclesiastical organization. The upshot was that a majority of the group of southern dignitaries convened to vote on the constitution rejected it. Nevertheless, thanks to some political and arithmetical trickery, the king declared the constitution adopted. This *arithméthique hollandaise*, as history has dubbed his manoeuvring, created a great deal of bad blood in the south and put a huge dent in the constitution's legitimacy.

Although the creation of the United Kingdom was hailed as a contribution to peace and order on the continent, and although Van Hogendorp also stressed the historical significance of the 'reunification' of the north and south, the citizens of the new state were lukewarm about it. 'People were not opposed to it,' according to the Dutch historian Piet de Rooy, 'but hardly for it either.'[4] The decisions had been made by a small group and there were no feelings of solidarity whatsoever between north and south. According to the historian Aerts, the man in the street and the elite accepted the new nation under strong monarchical leadership, anticipating and apparently wanting calm after the many regime changes since 1795.[5] William I was able to build on the 'national reconciliation' that had started in the north around 1800, had covered up the differences between the Batavians and the Orangists, and had created a depoliticized climate. The early years of the United Kingdom were no different. Harmony, stability and domesticity were what

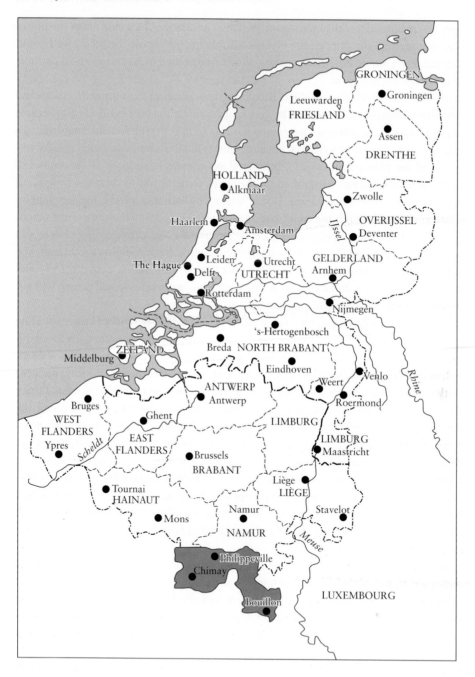

Territory returned by France in 1815

—·—·—·— Border of the United Kingdom of the Netherlands 1815–30

—·—·—·— Border between the Netherlands and Belgium 1830

Map 8 The United Kingdom of the Netherlands 1815–30.

was needed. Politics were not a matter of hammering out controversial issues, but promoting unity and community spirit. William I appeared to fit the bill perfectly.

The United Kingdom experiment lasted only fifteen years and ended in 1830 with the Belgian Revolt, which led to secession. This outcome does not seem surprising given the indifference of the population at the beginning and the rancour in the south about the constitution. But such a conclusion is too hasty because in the mid-1820s integration of the north and south had progressed to such an extent that stable national unity did not appear unthinkable. William I had pursued unification with great vigour. The language policy – getting everyone to speak Dutch – was implemented without compulsion at first. But the pressure was gradually increased. In 1819, for example, it was announced that from 1823 onwards government and the administration of justice in the Flemish provinces would only be permitted in Dutch, although bilingualism would be allowed in the Walloon provinces for the time being. The king's language policy did not meet much resistance, but the situation was quite different when it came to his measures for education – an ideal instrument for promoting unity. In 1821, the North Netherlandish school model was also introduced in the south, which meant the creation of rigidly uniform public primary education. This had a major impact on the spread of the Dutch language because primary education in the Flemish provinces was given virtually entirely in that language as a result.

The sensitive aspect of the education policy, however, was not linguistic but religious.[6] It went without saying that education should also foster Christian virtues but – according to the government – they should be general in nature and not denominational. The government thus curbed ecclesiastical independence in teaching, and it was precisely this that ignited the resistance of the Catholic Church in the south. Since 1815, it had founded a number of junior seminaries, which prepared students to study for the priesthood, but they were also attended by children who would not become priests. The government took action against these preparatory seminaries in the 1820s. It withdrew the church's right to establish schools without permission and even closed some of these institutions. The government founded its own Collegium Philosophicum as the only place permitted to teach aspirant clergy. Anti-clerical liberals in the south gave their support, but this policy antagonized many Catholics. Looking at the results of the education programme, success in improving literacy was certainly achieved. As an instrument for nation building, however, it was a failure.

William I's educational policy was closely bound up with his religious policy. As far as William was concerned, the churches were autonomous when it came to doctrine, but they had to be loyal to the government and contribute to educating the people as moderate and enlightened citizens.[7] William's attempts to obtain influence over the ecclesiastical organization when the constitution came into effect had already led to intense dissatisfaction among Catholics, and these tensions were to increase during the 1820s. William I had successfully brought the Protestant churches together in 1816 under the Department of Protestant Worship, thus putting an end to the many Protestant churches and subjecting them to one unifying hierarchical organization. Although the state did not officially concern itself with doctrine, the fact that the regulations stipulated that the Dutch Reformed Church should enforce morals and disseminate love of the monarch and the fatherland pointed clearly in the direction of state influence. Initially, Protestants approved of William's unifying church policy, in part because the king reinstated remuneration of clergymen by the state.

Things were very different on the Catholic side. The king also endeavoured to introduce regulations for the Catholic Church that brought unity to the ecclesiastical organization. This objective was obvious. Unlike the Catholic South, the Protestant North had no episcopal organization. As a relic of the Protestant-dominated Republic, it did, however, have a mission. William I was dependent on cooperation with the pope in order to establish regulations for Roman Catholic worship, but the latter was not interested. The 1827 Concordat did not put an end to the tensions, and at the end of the 1820s Catholic critics accused the king of trying to be a 'Dutch pope' and provoke a schism in the Catholic Church. Discontent rose to such a serious level that it was a factor in the failure of the United Kingdom. Compounding this, the Catholic majority – some three-quarters of the population – already felt they had come off second best as regards the shared sense of nationhood that had been propagated from the top down. The dominance of Protestant Northern Netherlandish traditions was unmistakable. In a general sense, too, the northern elites considered the south to be more an extension of their own territory than a partner with equal rights in a new entity. This rather arrogant northern attitude came up against a gradually growing sense of self-awareness in the south.

William I's reign has been described as that of an 'enlightened despot', which is an unfortunate portrayal because it gives the impression that he ruled like an absolutist eighteenth-century monarch, and this was not the case.[8] Even though he had considerable constitutional scope, there was no question of a monolithic government structure because there were very real opposing forces that he had to take into account. Up to a point, that also applied to the States General. Although there was no ministerial responsibility, the Lower House had no right of amendment and only very limited budgetary authority, popular representation did have some influence. It was not that members of the Lower House wanted to check the king and his ministers. Their view of their primary task was more modest. It was to rise above conflicting interests and support the government as good patriots and contribute to moderate and prudent policies. However, this did not eliminate tensions and criticism, a fact that emerged during the debate on the first ten-year budget in 1819.

The 1815 constitution stipulated that, starting in 1819, the government would always submit a ten-year budget to parliament. The underlying idea was that this would make it easier to sort out the national debt, which was still considerable. But the Lower House was unhappy about the planned high level of expenditure on the army. They were also critical of the way the government presented its intentions. Last but not least, there was growing resistance to the marginalization of parliament associated with a ten-year budget, because if it were to be approved, the Lower House would be sidelined from monitoring finances until 1829. The upshot was the rejection of the budget, and the king and his ministers found themselves in opposition to parliament. In a modern democracy, a parliamentary result of this kind would lead to the fall of the government and new elections, but that was unthinkable in the United Kingdom's political system. The constitution did not provide for it because there was no ministerial responsibility, and such a consequence was not part of parliament's understanding of its task. A few months later, the king decided to submit a virtually identical budget, and this time it was approved. It was typical of parliament's position in the existing political order that this approval was given because of a sense of responsibility for a 'national policy', and also because of the king's promise to pursue the Lower House's wish to make changes to the taxation system. Although the Lower House's power was limited and its view of its own role bore no resemblance to a modern parliament, in some areas it was able to exert real influence.[9]

Nevertheless, the king remained the central factor, and that was how William I wanted it. His biographer Jeroen Koch pointed out that the king was prepared to be a constitutional monarch, 'but only on his own terms'. He wanted to remain in command of everything: 'Ruling, governing, deciding, managing – he even considered administration to be his task, almost as though it was a royal prerogative'.[10] Until the mid-1820s, in particular, he had substantial political elbow room and he was also given scope to bypass parliament on many decisions by issuing a Royal Decree. He was at the heart of the system and, as the historian Van Sas describes it, 'he initiated, intervened and arbitrated'. In addition to his strong constitutional position, he also had a widespread informal network that only he oversaw.[11] In the end, this system of William I's was not successful. Where so much was geared to him as an individual, the king proved incapable of getting and keeping a firm grip on all the reins of power. And, despite all his good intentions, he was not really willing to respond constructively to critical signals from the people. The consequence was that at the end of the 1820s, his regime came to grief in a political crisis. Before we explore this any further, however, it is appropriate to take a look at William I's economic and financial policies.

William I went to work on the economy with great energy and left a clear stamp on the developments. The challenges facing the United Kingdom were very daunting. The north emerged from the French period economically weak and with a huge national debt. That could have been compensated for by the south, which was not in such dire financial straits and had a relatively highly developed industrial infrastructure. In theory, the two parts of the new country could complement each other, provided that the north's trading tradition and the south's industrial strength could be harmonized. To that end, the first priority was to create unity in the respective taxation systems. This was not simple because the north's interests lay in a tax system that promoted international trade, while the south benefitted from the protection of industry. At first, the tax measures taken to create unity primarily favoured the south, a move on the king's part designed to strengthen his position in that part of the country, which was still not undisputed.

But in the early 1820s, the pendulum swung back the other way, and although the king tried to maintain a balance between the north's and south's interests, the north received preferential treatment. There was no equality between north and south in government spending, for instance. Only just over 20 per cent benefitted the south, whereas its contribution to tax revenues was 40 per cent in 1816 and as much as 50 per cent in 1829. There was thus a substantial transfer of finance from the south to the north every year. According to economic historians Van Zanden and Van Riel, it increased from some 17 million guilders in 1816 to 31.5 million in 1829. The latter sum represented between 5 and 6 per cent of the entire country's gross domestic product.[12] Not surprisingly, this created a great deal of discontent in the south and contributed to the split in 1830.

Any analysis of the financial policy's consequences for the treasury must conclude that it was deleterious. The national debt continued to grow while William I was on the throne – from 575 million guilders in 1814 to over 900 million in 1829 and to 1,200 million by the end of his reign in 1840. He furthermore increasingly withdrew the oversight of the financial situation from any kind of audit, and an impenetrable system of income and expenditure that provoked growing resistance was created under his direction. The Amortization Syndicate was given an important place in the king's financial policy. Originally set up as an organization to coordinate repayment of the national debt, it developed into a royal financial labyrinth with secret funds and hoards of cash that William I used exactly as he pleased. Resistance to it was a major factor behind the political tensions that flared up during the debate about the second ten-year budget in 1829.

While William I's financial policy may not have been a success, he achieved better results with his handling of the economy. The king made vigorous attempts to breathe new life into trade and industry and a national prosperity policy to reinforce the unification of the kingdom. Substantial investments in infrastructure were designed to benefit the integration of the north and south and improve access to economic centres throughout the country. This programme resulted in more roads, ports and above all waterways, including improvements to existing routes, as well as coining one of William I's many nicknames – the Canal King. Although the significance of the canal construction programme should not be overestimated and the degree of success was not the same everywhere, some important waterways were indeed created.[13] The speed of this process was not just the result of royal initiatives; the fact that the Netherlands had become a unitary state played a role too. Far less account needed to be taken of regional and local special interests, which had often delayed decision making in the former federal Republic.

The Fund for National Industry was set up to foster manufacturing. It was part of the king's proactive industrial policy, which also included low interest rates between 1823 and 1830 to encourage investments in the sector. The south was the primary beneficiary, while the north profited greatly from the Netherlands Trading Society (Nederlandsche Handel-Maatschappij or NHM), which was set up in 1824. The king took the initiative to found it after attempts to resurrect trade with the East Indies, which had been returned to Dutch sovereignty in 1816, met with little success. Unlike the earlier VOC, the NHM was not given a monopoly on merchant shipping to and from Asia and it would not play a role in colonial administration. Its primary goal was to foster Dutch commerce, particularly in regard to the competition from Britain. To that end it was given a broad portfolio of tasks and was involved in many economic sectors, including manufacturing, shipbuilding, agriculture and fishing. The king personally guaranteed an annual profit distribution of 4.5 per cent on the shares and he also invested a substantial sum himself. This helped generate considerable public interest in NHM shares. And the NHM would indeed play an important part in the revival of trading. The king's involvement in this area earned him another nickname – the Merchant King.

So what impact did William I's proactive policy have on the United Kingdom's actual economic development? After the economic slump during the annexation by France (1810–13) there was a slight recovery, followed by a recession. But after 1819, there were two decades of economic dynamism and structural growth. The economic situation in the Netherlands during this period was very different from the economic stagnation of the eighteenth century. The financial sector – a key element of the eighteenth-century economy – had disappeared and during the 1820s agriculture became a major contributor to economic expansion. Together with the service sector, which was in turn driven by colonial trading, these two areas were the engine of commercial development in the decades after 1814. Rhine shipping grew spectacularly, primarily because of a sharp increase in the trading of colonial products that started in the 1830s.[14]

The explanation for this lies in developments in the Dutch East Indies. At the Congress of Vienna (1814–15) England had promised to return virtually all the Dutch colonies that had come under English rule during the French period. In 1816 there was an official handover of the East Indies territories in Batavia at which the colonial state of the Dutch East Indies formally came into being. On paper it extended over a substantial part of the archipelago that is present-day Indonesia. In practice, however, the Netherlands did not have the resources to exercise its colonial authority over large areas. Dutch power was greatest on Java, where there was also internal friction between various Javanese courts. Tensions increased, culminating in the Java War (1825–30). The hostilities were primarily between the charismatic Javanese leader Pangeran Diponegoro and Dutch troops. In the end Diponegoro lost. During that period, war and starvation caused the deaths of some 200,000 Javanese, while the Dutch sustained around 15,000 fatalities. The Javanese elite had embarked on the struggle to regain its traditional position of power, but suffered a significant defeat. The Netherlands established its colonial authority by very violent means.[15] Additional areas in the East Indies archipelago were conquered by brute force later in the nineteenth century.

The Cultivation System introduced in the Dutch East Indies in 1830 was of great importance to the Dutch economy from then on. Under this system native farmers were forced to grow crops like coffee, sugar and indigo, and sell them at low prices. This system put great pressure on the colony's rural population and generated a large surplus for the Netherlands. In addition to the huge growth in trade in colonial products, there was also expansion in related business activities in the Netherlands and exports to the Far East. By about the middle of the nineteenth century, the colonial surplus was so big that it was rightly dubbed 'the cork' that kept the Dutch economy afloat during this period. Prior to 1850, income from the East Indies represented on average 19 per cent of Dutch state income. During the 1850s it rose to about 31 per cent. During the following decade it was some 24 per cent before dropping to 13 per cent between 1871 and 1877.[16] At the centre of the web was the NHM, whose profits were often diverted by the king personally into his financial–economic labyrinth. In fact these profits were used to subsidize no end of companies at the king's discretion in his attempts to win support in certain towns, cities,

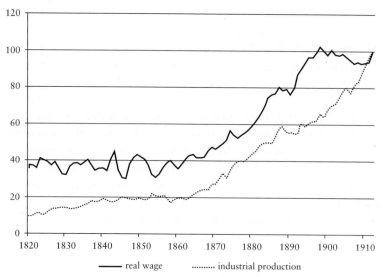

Illustration 2 Industrial production and wage trends 1820–1913.

regions or parts of the population. This may have been politically effective and economically useful for William I in the short term, but in the longer term it was not. This subsidy system was in fact nothing other than a form of protectionism for Dutch commerce and industry; it resulted in underinvestment in many business sectors and later had a damaging effect on Dutch competitiveness.

Against this background, industrial development lagged behind. In the 1820s and 1830s, manufacturing extricated itself from the slump it had suffered during the French occupation but, compared with surrounding countries, industry in the north remained relatively small beer. As Illustration 2 shows, Dutch manufacturing did not start to grow rapidly until the 1860s. Obviously, it is impossible to say how the economy of the Netherlands would have developed had Belgium not seceded in 1830. Probably the much more advanced industrialization of the south would have driven the entire country. Instead, though, the Dutch economy was propped up by three cornerstones – colonial revenues, trade and agriculture.

When one looks at the economic development of the United Kingdom of the Netherlands an ambivalent picture emerges.[17] The king's energy led to successes and rising prosperity. But – more significantly – his opaque subsidy system meant that he did not build stable foundations for economic modernization. As we have seen, there was no real parliamentary or other counterweight, so all the reins were in his hands and no consistent policy that could count on broad support emerged. After Belgium's secession, royal obduracy brought about a dramatic turn for the worse in state finances, which reached a nadir during the 1830s.

Despite political, economic and religious tensions, the fall of the United Kingdom was not preordained in any way and its end in 1830 was unexpected. Historians agree that in the mid-1820s, stable unity between north and south appeared to be feasible, even though there was still no meeting of minds. But during the late 1820s, widespread discontent with William I's form of government grew, and liberal forces in both north and south demanded political reforms. Liberal publications in both parts of the country started to agitate, pressing, among other things, for a form of ministerial responsibility and the separation of legislative, executive and judicial branches. While such a demarcation existed on paper, it was different in practice. A complication for the king in the south was that liberals and Catholics, who had very different political views, were united in their joint criticism of the absence of freedom under William I. In addition, a petition movement developed in 1828 and 1829, primarily in the south, and people submitted their wishes to parliament about all sorts of subjects (the economy, language, religion, press freedom and education). In 1829, some petitions had more than 300,000 signatures on them, indicating that politicization was growing rapidly and the earlier 'national harmony' no longer existed.

The crisis of authority to which William I's reign had led reached a new low point during the parliamentary deliberations about the second ten-year budget in 1829. Essentially all the southern members of the Lower House and about half of the northern ones rejected the budget, and in so doing demonstrated their indignation about the king's scant willingness to implement political reforms. William I responded to the indications from the Lower House with a few minor concessions, but he remained stubborn about basic political ideas and retained the existing political model. Remarkably, the northern and southern reactions diverged. Many northern delegates shrank from a confrontation with the king and so their political behaviour remained within the existing conventions, but in the south criticism did not die down, and this engendered irritation with their southern neighbours among the political elites in the north.[18] The unity of the United Kingdom may have advanced in economic and administrative terms, but the mind-sets were still very different. Attitudes diverged very quickly in 1830.

The cause was relatively trivial. At the end of August 1830, a group of excited theatregoers paraded through the streets of Brussels after a performance of Auber's opera *La muette de Portici* (*The Mute Girl of Portici*) about a popular Neapolitan uprising against Spanish authority in 1647. The unrest after the performance intensified, and there were disturbances and rioting in the streets, swelled by poorer members of the population who were suffering as a result of unemployment and high food prices. All the same it was not yet a real revolt; it was the dynamic of action and reaction that soon led to an insoluble political crisis. In seeking an explanation, it is important to record that initially the army and police did not intervene in the disorders because of concern that the situation would escalate, as had happened in the July 1830 revolution in France, leading to the overthrow of the king. An armed civilian force formed in Brussels and Liège to restore order. It seized power and then presented the king with political demands, some of which were general and liberal (introduction of ministerial responsibility, freedom of the press and the like), and some were specific to the situation in the south (education and language issues, more southern representatives in the States General).

The responses of William I and Crown Prince William Frederick (later King William II, 1840–49) were ambivalent and contradictory. The king made it clear he did not want to give in to the demands and would not shrink from using military means. But the crown prince, who was dispatched to the south to resolve the situation, proved to have his own political ambitions and – not for the first and last time – to have his eye on becoming king of Belgium.[19] Before secession requirements had been properly formulated in the south, the crown prince let it be known he was in favour of an administrative division of the kingdom. In so doing he made an entirely personal contribution to the disintegration of north and south. Shortly thereafter the king was prepared to listen to the States General's opinion. At the beginning of September 1830, he asked for its views about the future of the national institutions and the United Kingdom. Most of the northern and southern delegates proved to support liberalization and weaker national links between north and south, but no clear answer or programme for solving the crisis was forthcoming.

At the same time, the disturbances escalated, and they were particularly serious in Brussels. The king sent his son Frederick to the south at the head of a body of troops to restore calm. The street fighting in Brussels lasted three days and more than a thousand people were killed. When the army withdrew from the city again at the end of September 1830, strong anti-northern feelings were unleashed and the insurgents set up a Provisional Government, yet the States General still broadcast conflicting signals. While a slim majority of parliamentarians had supported the separation of the two parts of the nation in late September, the position of the delegates was not that clear. Had there been a constructive decentralization and liberalization programme, it would probably also have got a majority. The Provisional Government presented William I with a fait accompli, while he – flip-flopping between implacability and compromise – had no real answer. He tried to get support from the major powers for military intervention, instructed a government committee to prepare changes to the political system, and sent some of his ministers to Antwerp as a signal to the Provisional Government that he would not give up the south without a struggle.

On that same day, 4 October 1830, the Provisional Government declared Belgium's independence, and a month later called elections to a National Congress. By early 1831, Belgium already had a constitution – from a European perspective a very liberal and democratic one. The new state became a constitutional monarchy, albeit that the House of Orange was excluded from the throne.[20] The great powers, Britain, Austria, Prussia and Russia, which had been involved in the inception of the United Kingdom, convened the London Conference at the end of 1830. Together with France their intention was to prevent a general European crisis.[21] As early as December 1830, they made it clear that they accepted Belgian independence and at the beginning of 1831 they laid down that Belgium would be neutral 'in perpetuity'. During the course of that year they put forward three proposed lists of conditions for a permanent settlement, but Belgium and William I could not reach agreement about them.

The secession of Belgium in 1830 was not the consequence of a nationalist revolt of the south against the north, but the unintended outcome of a political crisis, which was made deeper by the counterproductive crisis management of King William I and Crown Prince William Frederick, who was acting in accordance with his own political agenda.

The more deeply rooted background of the crisis was the failure to introduce political reforms in preceding years and the unwillingness of William I to make his governing style more liberal. There had been a desire in both parts of the kingdom for liberal change that tied the north and south together and appeared to enable further unification. Yet the two drifted apart because they responded differently when the crisis intensified as a result of the conduct of the king and the crown prince. The more romantic and expressive liberals and Catholics in the south wanted their freedom, and clashed with the more introvert and moderate liberals and Protestants in the north, who distanced themselves from the 'inordinate' and 'uncontrolled' insurgents. According to many in the north, there was a need for a reasonable, cautious approach embedded in political experience and a sense of national responsibility, not emotion, passion and the accentuation of differences.[22] The political and cultural divide that thus manifested itself between the two sections of the country amplified fierce mutual antagonism between northern and southern nationalism, and propelled the secession process forward in October 1830. Viewed in this light, nationalism was not the basis for secession, but rather arose out of it in both the north and the south. The speed at which secession happened reveals there had been little integration of mind-sets since 1815.

Political stasis and malaise (1830–48)

The outrage about the 'ungrateful' and 'unreliable' Belgians led the States General, which had consisted entirely of northern delegates since October 1830, to agree to secession without any objections. But the question did arise as to whether political reforms were desirable as part of amending the constitution, which was now necessary because the 1815 version related to the United Kingdom. It is typical of the political climate in the 1830s that the debate about ministerial responsibility, electoral reform and finances (including the ten-year budget) dragged on without liberals being able to agree on joint plans. The discussion soon died down, and any opposition and dynamism that had emerged in the late 1820s disappeared. The moment to implement political reforms in the north, too, had passed. The concept of 'good nationalism' was once again reduced to adapting to the king and his government. They and the country manoeuvred more and more in isolation.

William I was unhappy about the list of conditions for the dissolution of the United Kingdom drawn up by the London Conference in June 1831. Shortly thereafter he opted for force and undertook a military expedition to Belgium, where he achieved successes during what came to be known as the Ten-Day Campaign. This intervention left it in no doubt that he wanted to hold on to the United Kingdom and the European role assigned to it during the Congress of Vienna. He was also speculating on an early end to the new kingdom of Belgium, which he assumed would be too vulnerable to survive in any European conflict. William I's international political ambitions could not be reconciled with a small Netherlands, which – without a role and gravitas – was only a second-class power. The king had to accept that in the system of European states the Netherlands was not much more than what the great powers considered it to be: a client state of England. The British, in cooperation with the French, put a swift end to William's military adventure, but even after the 1833 armistice the king refused to agree to the secession settlement, even though it had been amended in the Netherlands' favour after the campaign. He stubbornly kept the army mobilized in order to exact a more advantageous settlement for the north.

At first parliament, the press and public opinion rallied round the throne, and feelings of national solidarity and the desire to maintain national honour dominated. Gunboat Captain Jan van Speyk was upholding this view in February 1831 when he blew up his ship, including the crew and himself, near Antwerp in order to prevent it falling into the hands of Belgian insurgents. The wave of unanimity this generated in the north was typical of Dutch nationalism at that time. Offended and complacent, many turned their backs on the evil foreign countries that had deserted the Netherlands so treacherously. This was not about getting Belgium to come back into the kingdom, which virtually nobody wanted and was not in line with the nationalism that had developed, but about rehabilitation and recognition that they were in the right.

Criticism did not thrive in this political climate, and the message was to adapt. The few who did not accept this – the remaining critical parliamentarians, as well as critical representatives of the press and the church – were subjected to royal pressure. In 1834, a group of orthodox Calvinists split with the Dutch Reformed Church in what became known as the Secession. They were opposed to the advent of the Groningen theology, which advocated the influence of the Enlightenment in the Dutch Reformed Church. The 1834 Secessionists wanted to return to the principles of the Synod of Dordrecht (1619), and in so doing to an idealized Calvinist past. They withdrew from the oversight of the Dutch Reformed Church that William I had established in 1816. They were consequently treated as troublemakers and schismatics, and were thwarted with prohibitions, fines and the like. The persecution did not stop until 1840, by which time thousands of them, alienated from their own country, had emigrated to the United States.

The political stasis engendered by this repressive climate, in which the king ruled in his old, familiar, unchecked way, ended in the late 1830s with a new crisis. The financial consequences of the policy of persevering with regard to Belgium were disastrous. The national debt, which was already high, rose rapidly because of the years of mobilization, and resistance to the high burden of taxation increased. In 1839, the king had no choice but to accept the October 1831 secession settlement. The constitutional amendment that was now necessary did not deliver a real new beginning. Under pressure, the king proved willing to accept ministerial responsibility under criminal law (ministers would now have to sign laws but were still not politically responsible for them), the introduction of a two-year budget, and publishing government finances. But there was no actual progress towards a more liberal system. Things came to a head when the king was faced with a barrage of public indignation about his intention to marry a Catholic Belgian countess. In September 1840, a month after the promulgation of the amended constitution, he stepped down and moved to Berlin, where he died in 1843. His volatile son William

Frederick, with whom he had always had difficult political and personal relations, succeeded him as King William II (1840–49).

The new king's governing style matched his character and behaviour. There was no clear message and William II was a ruler who acted in a volatile, unpredictable and often impetuous way in both domestic and foreign politics. He certainly had a degree of sympathy for liberal thinking as crown prince and during the early years of his reign, but these convictions were not very profound. To an extent they could be considered a response to his father's regime and the opportunistic desire to become popular with the people. In practice, though, the changes in governing style were not great, particularly from 1844 onwards when William II set a more clearly conservative course.[23] The fact that the Netherlands turned its back on a royal regime in 1848, relatively suddenly, and replaced it with a modern, liberal constitution was due more to his caprice and impulsiveness than his political insights. The 1840s thus did not reflect a linear progression from the half-hearted 1840 amended constitution to the 1848 liberal breakthrough. This period was in fact dominated by malaise, in which politics had no direction. Few were satisfied with the existing political order, which differed hardly at all from the years before 1840, but the political will to put an end to it was lacking. The tenacity with which the Lower House clung to pre-liberal thinking emerged in 1844 when one of the members – Johan Rudolf Thorbecke (1798–1872) – with support from a few other delegates attempted to introduce a fundamentally more liberal constitutional amendment through the so-called Nine Men's Proposal. The Lower House did not even debate it because a majority took the view that only the king was entitled to take such initiatives. It is consequently not surprising that historian Aerts describes this period as the 'aimless years' when the old system was no longer satisfactory and there were as yet no new principles.[24]

The composition of the Lower House, comprising 'fifty-eight honourable eligible gentlemen', explains this. Broadly speaking, there were three main groups – conservatives, conservative liberals and liberals. There were no parties or strictly divided factions. Political parties did not appear until the late nineteenth century. With the exception of the small liberal group, political cooperation of like-minded members was still extremely disjointed. The conservatives, with just under twenty-five members, were mostly from aristocratic and former regent families. They were opposed to a fundamental revision of the constitution and clung to the traditional trade policy and the existing colonial establishment. The centre group of conservative liberals, estimated at twenty-five plus, were primarily interested in getting parliamentary control of government finances and were generally in favour of free trade. Their power base was in Holland (particularly in Amsterdam) and by and large they represented the prosperous financial and commercial elite. Their goal was gradual political change and above all securing their own influence within the bounds of 'national traditions'. Here they differed from the small group of doctrinaire liberals – with between five and nine members – who sought to have a radically different constitutional system and advocated the principles of the free trade system more emphatically. Thorbecke became the most important representative of this liberal movement after the Nine Men's Proposal in 1844.[25] A few years later he was to play a decisive role in the 1848 amendment to the constitution. Thorbecke was a lawyer who had studied at various German universities and was strongly influenced by German romanticism. He was a professor in Ghent between 1825 and 1830, and after Belgium seceded he moved to the north to become a professor in Leiden.[26]

In 1844, Thorbecke and his supporters had not been counting on a positive response from William II or the Lower House. They were primarily interested in mobilizing public opinion, which indeed became more strongly politicized again in the years thereafter than had been the case in the preceding decades. The greatest support came from the liberal cultural news magazine *De Gids*, founded in 1837, and the older liberal *Arnhemsche Courant*.[27] At a slightly greater distance, there was also support from the *Algemeen Handelsblad*, with its roots in Amsterdam, and the *Nieuwe Rotterdamsche Courant*, established in 1844. These bourgeois–liberal newspapers did not have big circulations, but as a mouthpiece for a small group they made it abundantly clear that opposition was taking shape. There were also radical papers with small circulations that agitated, but did not usually last long. However, the liberal opposition was still too weak to seize control. As has happened several times in Dutch political history, it took an external stimulus to bring about change. This time it was the European revolutions of 1848.

The political renewal of the 1840s essentially stalled until that year. A further problem was the debt mountain left behind by William I, a major burden on the country. The king's shadowy national bookkeeping no longer existed, but sorting out its consequences required drastic spending cuts. In the early 1840s, a depression in trade with the Dutch East Indies caused a drop in income from the colony and the urgency increased. The pressure on the Dutch East Indian population was increased (higher rents, lower prices) in order to keep the colonial surplus at its old level, despite falling prices for colonial products on the Amsterdam market. In consequence, rice cultivation was neglected, food prices rose and the people of Java were threatened with famine. This impoverishment also led to the collapse of Dutch textile exports to the East Indies, which made the economic malaise even worse. But national bankruptcy could be prevented by prudent financial policy and the burden of interest on the debt could be reduced.

In the mid-1840s, however, major economic and social problems emerged. The general business depression meant that jobs were scarce, and living conditions deteriorated still further as food prices rose dramatically. Much of the potato harvest in 1845 and 1846 was lost to blight, and in 1846 the grain harvest was more than halved by a plague of mice. Epidemics (malaria, influenza and cholera) and long, hard winters between 1846 and 1848 added to this doleful picture.[28] During the 1840s, more people than ever before turned to poor relief, but the help it could provide was limited. There were food riots and looting in different parts of the country, and the death rate rose. In 1847 there were more deaths than births.[29] The situation in the Netherlands was certainly no worse than in other European countries, but in Britain and Belgium the poverty issue was closely linked to the rising industrial proletariat in an expanding economy, while the Dutch were suffering from economic stagnation.

There was also malaise and uncertainty in foreign policy. Recognition of Belgian secession reduced the size of the Netherlands to more or less that of the Republic in the eighteenth century. Save for a few minor corrections, the borders fixed in 1839 are still the same today. Belgium relinquished a few parts of its province of Limburg and got part of Luxembourg in return. The area concerned was detached from the German Confederation, and as compensation essentially the entire current Dutch province of Limburg joined it. What was left of Luxembourg remained a member of the German Confederation and was actually governed by Grand Duke William II, and so the Netherlands remained in a personal union between two areas directly involved in developments in Germany. Limburg's position was particularly worrying in the 1840s. The population of Limburg, supported by other Belgians, had resisted its inclusion in the Netherlands, and consequently a separatist movement emerged during this period. Rejoining Belgium was out of the question given the international circumstances, so initially Limburg separatists sought to make Limburg an independent duchy in the German Confederation. They received support from German liberals during the European revolutions of 1848, and with them tried to incorporate Limburg in a new German republic. Although the danger of such a secession disappeared after the failure of the 1848 German revolution, it had become clear that the Netherlands was vulnerable to developments inside the German Confederation – an issue that was to re-emerge during the 1860s.

This vulnerability also extended to commerce. Tensions with Prussia had arisen as far back as the reign of William I, when the Dutch tried to keep a monopoly on trade with Germany and blocked free Rhine shipping as much as possible. Prussian irritation with the Netherlands' attitude resulted in the construction of the Iron Rhine – the railway line between Cologne and Antwerp – whose effect was to seriously weaken the Dutch position in trade with the German hinterland. Trade policy measures by Prussia and the German Customs Union sent the Netherlands a clear message that the European balance of power was shifting. In 1851, Prussia and the Dutch reached a settlement on Rhine shipping that reflected Prussia's stronger position and caused irritation in the Netherlands because it was the weaker party.

There was also friction with England. Disappointment about the lack of support from this 'natural ally' during the Belgian secession was followed by tensions about Dutch expansionism in the East Indies, the NHM's position and the Cultivation System. All told, in its foreign relations, the Netherlands was repeatedly faced with its position as a small, susceptible power.[30] The approach to foreign policy was consequently to retain the nation's position for as long as it could, while avoiding conflicts as much as possible. This caused uncertainty, but there was no clear alternative. Whereas William I had tried – unsuccessfully – to get support from the Northern Alliance of Russia, Austria and Prussia in the 1830s, commercial and shipping interests now indicated that the best policy was to maintain strict neutrality in international conflicts.

The impulsive William II, however, was the last person to pursue such a sober policy. At the beginning of the 1840s, he manoeuvred the Netherlands into an isolated international political position through involvement in a conspiracy against the Belgian King Leopold I, which in diplomatic circles earned him a reputation as 'an unpredictable and impetuous conspirator', to quote his biographer Jeroen van Zanten.[31] Between 1841 and 1843, his unfortunate and volatile manoeuvrings during Luxembourg's accession to the German Customs Union caused unnecessary problems in relations with Prussia. At that time he also lost sight of a good balance by adopting a strongly pro-French course, and then – acting on the conservative recommendations of his brother-in-law the Russian Czar Nicholas I – he started to focus more on Britain once again. Historian J. C. Boogman describes the 'political capers' of an 'emotional, unbalanced king' who repeatedly clashed with his ministers about foreign policy.[32] Van Zanten is no less critical when he stresses the loss of Dutch international prestige under William I and talks about 'failing foreign policy'.[33]

The fact that the Netherlands adopted a liberal constitution in 1848 was directly linked to the king's political waywardness. Reference was made earlier to William II's frequent change of political plumage during his reign, and 1848 was no different. At one moment he seemed willing to permit liberal reforms, the next he would put the brakes on again. He took a radical step in March 1848: without informing his ministers and parliament he instructed Thorbecke to draft a modern constitution. Historians have speculated long and hard about why he took this step. Later the king himself declared that fear of revolutions in other European countries spreading to the Netherlands had converted him 'from being very conservative to very liberal within twenty-four hours'. Recent research points to several explanatory factors. The fear of being pushed aside in a revolution certainly played a role, but his previous sympathy for liberal ideas and his desire for popularity were also important. Blackmail probably also played a part in the king's U-turn. He had been blackmailed some years before in connection with conspiracy plans in Belgium and because he had stirred up a witch hunt in the press against his father at the end of his reign. Now, in 1848, he was faced with blackmail because of his homosexual tendencies, and in Van Zanten's biography of William II the author presents a plausible case that threats to expose these sexual proclivities also influenced the king.[34]

In fact, the king was hoping that he could turn back the clock to politically less troubled times. That was not to be, and 1848 proved to be a clear watershed in Dutch political history. As political scientist Siep Stuurman rightly contends, this non-violent revolution was unexpected and should not be considered as the logical conclusion of a process that was on the cards.[35] At the beginning of 1848, the consensus view was that the existing political system was stable. Not long afterwards this thinking was superseded and a new political culture emerged.

The constitutional amendment of 1848

Thorbecke was able to start where he left off with his 1844 Nine Men's Proposal, and managed to present a draft new constitution within ten days. That same year, the Netherlands had an amended constitution that would form the structure for the political, social and economic developments in the decades thereafter. Thorbecke was no democrat, but he did support the constitutional state, good government and a clear separation of

Figure 16 *Johan Rudolf Thorbecke (1796–1872). Minister of State and Minister of Home Affairs,* Johan Heinrich Neuman, 1852. Rijksmuseum Amsterdam.

powers.[36] According to Thorbecke, good government meant understanding the signs of the times; he believed that the state should create a framework that enabled people to develop into free citizens of the political nation. If they used this opportunity, they would be able to contribute to good government and reinforcement of the constitutional state, as a result of which broader suffrage would also be possible. Thorbecke had an organic concept of nationhood and saw his constitution as a backdrop against which the Dutch state and nation could gradually achieve greater unity. Given the durability of this constitution, the principles of which have remained unchanged to this day, the Netherlands did indeed seize that opportunity.[37]

The key points in the 1848 constitution were the definitive separation of church and state, the establishment of such liberal values as freedom of association and a free press, and the introduction of systems for direct elections and ministerial responsibility. This last point meant that ministers were politically accountable to parliament for all government decisions and the king could no longer take political decisions as he saw fit or have complete control over ministers, although constitutionally he remained part of the government. In the constitution's terminology, which is still in use, the king 'can do no wrong' and the minister is 'responsible'. Although it was to take years before this system was definitively and fully adopted in political practice and the king's political influence remained strong, it was clear in 1848 that the position of popular representation had been fundamentally strengthened vis-à-vis the king.

The new suffrage was another fundamental step forward. The indirect class-based right to vote was scrapped and direct male suffrage was introduced for the Lower House, Provincial States and local councils – although only a small proportion of the male population was given the right to vote. This was in line with Thorbecke's liberal view that electors should be independent in order to be worthy of suffrage. In practical terms, this meant that the right to vote was linked to a certain level of direct taxation paid by an individual (suffrage based on tax assessment). Despite a few changes in the 1887 constitutional amendment, this system would in fact remain until 1917. It is remarkable that initially the 1848 electoral reform reduced rather than increased the number of voters. Before 1848, some 90,000 people were entitled to vote in elections to the Lower House; afterwards there were only 80,000. This meant that out of a total of some three million Dutch subjects, initially 10.5 per cent of the male population had the right to vote.[38] Elections to the Upper House also changed fundamentally. Until 1848, the king appointed the members, but after that they were elected indirectly by the directly elected Provincial States. This indirect system was a vestige of the old structure and is still in place today.[39]

Parliamentary democracy did not start in 1848. Suffrage was still far too limited for that. It is better, in the words of historian Te Velde, to talk about a parliamentary system in which an era of 'constitutional politics' began.[40] The 1848 amendment to the constitution provided a framework, and during the years thereafter the issue was how it would be given substance in practice. This was not confined to the powers of regional and local authorities, laid down in provincial and municipal legislation, or the exact formulation of electoral law. It also covered the positioning of the Lower House and the development of parliamentary instruments (motions, amendments, inquiries and so on).[41] The liberals were now at the centre of power, as a result of circumstances rather than their own efforts, and it was they who took the lead in structuring the Netherlands.

At first there were no political parties or sharply demarcated political movements, and virtually no electoral associations. The predominant view, which was also Thorbecke's, was that a member of parliament should be elected in his personal capacity and take decisions on the basis of his own judgement and insight, without any ties to voters. According to Thorbecke, 'the truth' could emerge through rational discussion between the individual members and the best legislation would be created.[42] Obviously, there was collaboration between like-minded colleagues. Thorbecke, for instance, regularly held meetings at home with a group of 'Thorbeckians'. But in so far as there were 'groups', the boundaries were very fluid and forming factions was regarded as unseemly. The creation of parties or groups was similarly not encouraged by the electoral rules because members of the Lower House were elected according to the constituency system. Local electoral associations were not political parties ahead of their time, but organizations in a constituency that organized elections and counteracted too much fragmentation. Political organizations in a modern sense did not appear in the Netherlands until the 1870s, as they did elsewhere in Europe.

The king also had to find a place in the new machinery, and how this happened depended on the ministers, the members of parliament and, of course, the king himself. There was too little time for William II, who instructed Thorbecke to draft a new constitution in March 1848, to turn the clock back. He died in 1849 after an unstable and largely unsuccessful nine-year reign. His son William III succeeded him that same year and remained on the throne until 1890. He was volatile, like his father, and did not think much of the liberal system. This had emerged immediately after the new constitution came into effect in October 1848, when he let it be known in his inner circle that he no longer wished to become king under this constitution, and therefore renounced his right to succeed to the throne and left for London. He remained there when his father died in March 1849 and announced from London that he did not wish to govern 'because my father swallowed that ridiculous 1848 constitution'.[43] In the end he let himself be persuaded and remained king till his death in 1890. His conservative, anti-liberal views did not change. This became apparent in 1853, when there was a major conflict about the content of the constitution between liberals on one side and conservatives, orthodox Protestants and the king on the other.

The separation of church and state was defined more strictly than ever before in the 1848 constitution, and every church was given the opportunity to organize in accordance with its own wishes and tradition. The Vatican took advantage of this possibility in 1853, planning the reintroduction of the episcopal hierarchy in the Netherlands, but was anything but tactful, describing the Netherlands in papal documents as the land of 'Calvinist heresy'. Some Protestants, who feared for the future of 'their' Protestant Netherlands, took serious action, which has gone down in history as the April Movement.[44] There were disturbances, particularly in the future archiepiscopal city of Utrecht. In excess of two hundred thousand people – more than double the number entitled to vote – signed a petition addressed to King William III, asking him to block papal plans in the Netherlands. If the king had sided with the protest movement, he would have broken openly with the new constitutional ministerial responsibility. He did not want to go that far, but when the new episcopal order took shape, the king did express clear sympathy for his Protestant subjects and implicitly criticized the plans of Thorbecke's government. The latter considered this damaging to government unity and so tendered his resignation. The liberals sustained a painful defeat in the subsequent elections and a moderate conservative government was formed.

It is evident that the struggle to give the constitution a really liberal content had still not been definitively won in the 1850s. Conservative networks such as *King and Country* did not want a different constitution as such. They were concerned with how existing laws should be put into practice and how the relationship between ministers, parliament and king should crystallize out. A unanimous answer to such issues was not forthcoming from the conservatives either and unity was not appropriate in their individual positioning. If one nevertheless wants to identify a conservative common denominator, it was that they looked on parliament primarily as a sounding board for the government, as had indeed been the case before 1848. According to them, the king should continue to play an important part, not as an autocratic ruler but as a symbol of national unity and guardian of the existing order. William III, though, was not an appropriate person for such a role. Cautious collaboration with parliament and ministers, as called for by the new constitution, clashed with his unpredictable nature and ever changing moods – and hence, his views. William III was consequently not the right man in the right place for conservatives who attached importance to a steadfast monarch who acted independently. A number of historians have referred to William III, who would have preferred to follow in the footsteps of his autocratic grandfather William I, as a 'tragic' monarch. Whether ministers during his long reign were conservative, moderate or liberal, few of them could get on with him and most chose to take decisions without involving him.[45] His antipathy to change and his many conflicts with ministers and members of parliament of varying political persuasions did result, however, in the assertion that William III contributed to the development of parliamentary democracy in the Netherlands in his own very particular way. His biographer Dik van der Meulen formulated it slightly differently but no less crushingly. He summarized William's performance as king thus: 'William's primary contribution was to be the first Dutch king in a country that was governed by others'.[46]

In political history books, the years 1866–1868 are often identified as the period when the liberal interpretation of ministerial responsibility finally took shape. Twice the king and ministers tried to get around insufficient support in the Lower House by dissolving parliament and calling new elections. At the same time the ministers remained in post and during the elections the king expressed his personal political preference. When the Lower House rejected government policy for the third time in 1868, the king and ministers acknowledged defeat and the government at last stood down. Since then there has been an unwritten parliamentary rule that a government steps down as soon as it can no longer count on a majority in the Lower House.

However much this result decreased the visible power of the king and increased that of parliament, it is too simplistic to consider it as a victory for the 1848 system. To be sure, between 1866 and 1868 the liberals had turned against the position of the king and ministers, who ultimately yielded. Yet it was a victory that at the same time heralded the end of the liberal political self-image as shaped by Thorbecke. He believed that politics was a matter for qualified gentlemen who debated the structure of the state without ties to voters. Now voters had been given the opportunity to vote twice in a polarized climate, so that the distance between politics and the community grew smaller and politics, which was becoming more turbulent, lost some of its independent dignity. That was no reason for a liberal celebration. Leave-taking of a period would have been more appropriate.[47]

Politicization and the creation of parties around the school funding controversy, social question and suffrage issue

Change in the status of politics and the way it functioned did indeed come about during the 1870s. Before then, men gained support in elections primarily in their personal capacities. Now, though, key individuals were increasingly labelling themselves liberal, conservative, anti-revolutionary or Catholic.[48] The orthodox Protestant Abraham Kuyper (1837–1920) was the primary driving force behind this trend, and this is why he is sometimes called the first modern political leader of the Netherlands. Important as Kuyper and the successive foundation of political parties may have been in the political modernization of the country, it should not be concluded that the formation of groups around political issues did not exist until the advent of political parties.

The historian Maartje Janse has convincingly demonstrated that a number of single-issue movements emerged after 1840. Initially, expressly outside parliament, they set the agenda and gave direction to the development of public opinion on such matters as the temperance movement, slavery, colonial policy and primary education. While information and informed debate were the main activities to begin with, the distance from politics started to shrink in the late 1860s. There were now deliberate efforts to influence political decision making and there was no longer any hesitation in making recommendations about how to vote in elections to the Lower House.[49] From 1860 – in other words, long before political parties appeared – people gathered in associations, for instance during the school funding controversy, and often engaged in vehement disputes.[50] The debating culture also changed in the polarized climate that existed after 1866, in which a younger generation took the lead and a fiercer tone became more commonplace.[51]

The distance between politics and people decreased, which meant that so too did the gap between parliament and society. It also meant that members of parliament took a different view of their own role. As Abraham Kuyper saw it, members of parliament were not independent wise men who served the general good without obligation and consultation, but representatives of groups of the population with shared principles and interests. Members should behave as 'men of principle' and act as spokesmen for like-minded individuals who made politics a joint undertaking and brought political passions into play. To that end he founded the daily newspaper *De Standaard* in 1872, wrote a party manifesto (*Our Programme*) and in 1879 brought local electoral associations together in the first national Dutch political party, the Anti-Revolutionary Party (ARP).[52]

The name 'anti-revolutionary' was not new and had been used in prior decades by Guillaume Groen van Prinsterer (1801–76) in his political and religious activities both inside and outside the Lower House. The concept referred to the rejection on principle of the ideas of the Enlightenment and the French Revolution. This was the basis for Groen van Prinsterer's opposition to the 1848 constitutional amendment, and he and his sympathizers had challenged the policy of the liberals and moderates. Following in his footsteps, Kuyper became the leader of the anti-revolutionary persuasion. Kuyper's thinking on religious matters was in line with the tradition of the Secession (1834), a movement which – as we saw earlier – wanted to return to the basic Calvinist principles of the Synod of Dordrecht (1619). He had a comparable goal in 1886 when he brought about a new schism in the Dutch Reformed Church. Six years later, Kuyper brought his followers and the supporters of the 1834 Secession together as the Reformed Churches in the Netherlands. This orthodox Protestant congregation represented about 8 per cent of the population and also formed the hard core of the ARP.

Kuyper's political crusade was directed primarily against the liberal school policy. For decades, orthodox Protestants had resisted mixed state schools in which children of different denominations were brought together and the teaching served to foster general Christian and social virtues. They had argued – unsuccessfully – that each religious grouping should be able to provide its own education within the walls of its own school, paid for by the state. This difference of opinion intensified in the second half of the nineteenth century, when the liberals discovered education as an engine of progress and social development. The 1857 Education Act was an initial cautious step. While it became somewhat easier to found private denominational or free schools, the act also confirmed the mixed state school as the standard and improved the regulation of education. Orthodox Protestants abandoned their original hope of state schools for each denomination and started to work towards their own entirely independent schools. It was to be a long and difficult path. In the 1870s, the Netherlands had 3,800 primary schools, of which only two hundred were orthodox Protestant.[53] There was no unanimity among orthodox Protestants about the route that had to be followed to achieve their own education. During the 1870s, there were increasingly heated arguments between those who, like Kuyper, politicized the education issue and wanted to force a solution through their own political party, and those who wanted keep beliefs and politics separate because they feared their faith would be defiled by politics.[54]

It was not just orthodox Protestants who wanted their own education – Catholics felt exactly the same. They had supported the liberal amended constitution of 1848 to improve their own position, but afterwards disagreements between Catholics and liberals became increasingly evident. Tensions rose in 1864 on the publication of the papal encyclical *Quanta Cura* with the famous appendix *Syllabus Errorum* – the syllabus of errors condemned by the Church, which unequivocally included liberalism. This was followed in 1868 by a declaration from the Dutch bishops fiercely opposing non-denominational state teaching and demanding Catholic education. In the years thereafter Catholics and Protestants found they had a joint objective – their own schools financed by the government – and a common opponent: the liberals.

The gradual cooperation in the school controversy did not mean that the mutual distrust between Catholics and Protestants had disappeared. On the contrary, while Catholics felt their rights had greater protection under the 1848 amended constitution, the traditional strong antithesis of many Protestants towards popery remained, as the 1853 April Movement had demonstrated once again. This Protestant outburst had furthermore reinforced the Catholics' tendency to act in public with great caution. At the same time, when reintroducing the episcopal hierarchy in the Netherlands, the Vatican had operated more offensively than before and Catholics felt the authority of their church more strongly than previously. This all added up to a Catholic world that was more sharply delineated from that of Protestants and liberals. The Catholic Church in the Netherlands was thus becoming increasingly self-aware, and Protestants perceived in this the necessity of continuing to protect the 'Protestant nation'. Their own schooling was an effective means for doing this. Students could learn the national Protestant perspective of history that orthodox Protestants had cherished since the sixteenth-century Revolt, which, as far as they were concerned, contained the essence of the Dutch nation.

The struggle for an equal financial footing for education rose to new heights in the 1870s after a liberal government led by Johannes Kappeyne van de Coppello (1822–95) enacted primary education legislation in 1878, which was a painful defeat for Protestants and Catholics.[55] Based on the liberal principle that the state should create conditions for the education and development of individual citizens, this law was a major step on the road to centralization, uniformity and improvement of primary schooling. Tougher requirements were set for teacher training and school buildings. The importance of good teaching staff was underlined by increasing teachers' salaries.

This produced a huge improvement in the quality of education, but also a substantial increase in cost. Central government shared these costs for the non-denominational schools by providing part of the financing of education. Since the liberal government had expressly rejected subsidizing separate Protestant and Catholic schools, but these schools were nonetheless obliged to meet the new, tougher quality standards, the 1878 Education Act threatened to be a serious setback for private denominational education. The upshot was a storm of objections from the religious parties. Kuyper took the decisive step on the path to his own party, but more importantly he organized a broadly based extra-parliamentary protest, which was a further clear indication that a new type of political leader had emerged.[56] He swiftly set up a sizeable petition movement intended to stop King William III from signing the act. More than 305,000 Protestants and 164,000 Catholics signed the petition, which was a huge mobilization of religious grassroots support, particularly considering that the total number of men entitled to vote in the Netherlands at that time was about 100,000.[57] The petition movement did not achieve the hoped-for success, however, and the king signed the act. Given the constitutional rule of ministerial responsibility, in fact the king had no other choice.

The year 1878 had far-reaching implications for Dutch political culture that continued to have an impact until well into the twentieth century. The confrontation between liberal and religious politicians over the Education Act highlighted a political dividing line between the Christian and non-Christian parts of the Netherlands, which Kuyper would later accentuate in his 'antithesis'. Liberals, socialists and the neutral state, Kuyper contended, were exponents of the modern world that represented a threat to Catholic and Protestant religious life. Protestants and Catholics should therefore join forces to defend the Christian nation and secure their joint interests. That did not mean the end of interdenominational tensions – Protestant and Catholic opinions about what this Christian nation should look like diverged significantly – but it covered them up. Kuyper realized that his orthodox Protestants were a minority of the population and consequently it would be impossible to get his ideas accepted in general across the Christian nation. His primary goal was to organize his own support and, starting from this strong basis, acquire important positions in society and politics.[58]

At the same time, his own grassroots support had to be shielded from government influence. The state should not get involved with parts of society that functioned independently. Kuyper fervently believed that groups organized along ideological lines could be responsible for themselves. Obviously, Kuyper's concept of 'sovereignty in your own circle' also applied to other communities, which could also take steps to counteract state influence. In 1891, the 'subsidiarity principle' in the encyclical *Rerum Novarum* gave Catholics a comparable concept – anything that could be organized at local or regional level should withdraw from central government regulation. Despite their differences, Catholics and Protestants found common ground, while recognizing that the gap between their religious principles could not be bridged.

Kuyper introduced new political and social dividing lines with the concepts of 'antithesis' and 'sovereignty in your own circle'. They were the forerunners of the compartmentalization along sociopolitical lines which, in the following decades, would become so typical of the political culture and split the Netherlands into Protestant, Catholic, social democrat and 'neutral' or liberal segments. Vertical dividing lines were thus established before industrialization and social and economic modernization had created new horizontal ones. The result was that the Dutch political structure would later be characterized by both.[59] The vertical partitioning, in particular, was to leave deep marks on politics and society. Many historians and political scientists have written at length and had contentious discussions about this 'pillarization' as a theoretical concept and a historical phenomenon, but that is beyond the scope of this chapter (see p. 184 ff.). Here it is sufficient to say that the pillars, which took shape gradually, were to have several functions. For example, they provided security and identity, they were vehicles for forming parties, emancipation and social mobility, and they gave the elites an instrument for social control of their own supporters and for demarcation against state meddling. The pillars also gave protection against the shock waves caused by the social and economic modernization that started in 1870. Industrialization, urbanization and other forms of modernization took place within the tried and trusted frameworks of people's own pillar, which could put a check on undesirable side effects and use the positive achievements (science, technology and so on) to the benefit of their own group. Protestants and Catholics created the foundations for constructing pillars. They were followed by the social democrats and – unwillingly – the liberals.

Important as the phenomenon of pillarization was during the period when political parties were being created and well into the twentieth century, it is necessary to avoid the impression of too systematic a classification of politics and society. First, the pillarized system did not include the whole population, and for many others there were different group ties that informed their lifestyles (philosophical, religious, social, regional and the like). Second, pillars were not homogeneous units and the divisions were great, particularly in Protestant circles. Taking a broad view of the history of Protestant churches and groups in the nineteenth and twentieth centuries, one is struck by the far-reaching fragmentation and the large number of different denominations.

Needless to say these divisions had political implications too.[60] Kuyper's modern political style also rubbed people up the wrong way and created resistance even in his own anti-revolutionary backyard. Some clung to the conventional view of an independent member of parliament's task – in other words, without any obligations to voter or party line – and during the 1890s they were fiercely opposed to extending suffrage. This led to the formation of the Free Anti-Revolutionary Party, which, together with a few other small Christian groups, founded the Christian Historical Union (CHU) in 1908. During the following decades, the CHU, reflecting the values of orthodox members of the Dutch Reformed Church, would continue to differentiate itself from the ARP as a rather classier, less strictly organized and more anti-Catholic party.[61] During the twentieth century, additional small orthodox splinter groups would form alongside these two medium-sized Protestant parties, but the only really relevant political players were the ARP and CHU. That remained so until the 1970s, when the Christian Democratic Appeal (CDA) was formed by these two parties together with the Catholic People's Party (KVP).

The way Catholics formed a party was different from the approach taken by Kuyper's orthodox Protestant ARP, which had 'ordinary people' as the basis of the movement and organized from the bottom up. The more assertive Catholic stance since the 1860s was primarily a reflection of the church's attitude, as was the idea of a mainly top-down organization. The leading Catholic politician, the priest Herman Schaepman (1844–1903), moreover had multiple simultaneous goals in mind. He had to follow the papal line that was passed on to him through the bishops, wanted to achieve emancipation for the Catholic part of the population in a country that had been dominated by Protestants since the late sixteenth century and aimed to reconcile the social differences within the Catholic community. It was not until the 1890s that Schaepman was given somewhat more support in this area through the papal encyclical *Rerum Novarum* (1891). His efforts to form a national Catholic political party, using the German Centre Party as an example, also had little success. He ran up against resistance inside the church. As a priest in the bishopric of Haarlem, he was actually banned from preaching for an extended period.

Initially, the interest in a national party was muted in the Catholic dominated south of the country – virtually all Catholic members of parliament were from the provinces of North Brabant and Limburg – and regional interests were at the top of the agenda. Furthermore, many conservative Catholic parliamentarians from these provinces did not want to give up members of parliament's traditional independence. In their view, it was the church and the social organizations associated with it that were central, not the party. Against this backdrop it is not surprising that a party was not formed until relatively late. By 1897, most Catholic electoral associations were prepared to accept a national manifesto, but it was not until 1926 – by which time Catholics had for years been the largest group in parliament – that the Roman Catholic State Party (RKSP) was formally founded.[62]

As we saw above, the school controversy and the creation of religious parties were inextricably linked. The defeat of religious politicians in the 1878 debate about primary school legislation drove Protestants and Catholics together. The first exclusively religious government was formed in 1888,[63] but it was not of one mind, nor was it powerful. This government's most important achievement was the 1889 Primary Education Act, which enabled state funding of private denominational education. Even then, the schools still did not have completely equal status, although considerable progress was made and from then on denominational primary schools were able to recover about 30 per cent of the costs from the government. The liberal victory of 1878 was thus largely undone, but it was not until 1917 that completely equal status for denominational and non-denominational schooling was implemented.

Abraham Kuyper's political style was one of the factors that gave Dutch politics a new look in the 1870s. The first socialist leader, Ferdinand Domela Nieuwenhuis (1846–1919), was made of comparable stuff but was less successful.[64] He too embodied the new form of politics that emerged in the late nineteenth century. Like Kuyper, Nieuwenhuis was a clergyman – Lutheran in his case. Kuyper's charisma with anti-revolutionary grassroots support was matched by Nieuwenhuis's appeal to the emerging workers' movement. He was both its leader and its prophet. He left the church in 1879, and in 1881 he was one of the founders of the first Dutch socialist party, the Social Democratic League (SDB). Initially, this party was the driving force behind demands for universal suffrage, but the SDB's political agitation shifted towards an anarcho-syndicalist agenda, and in 1893 it decided not to take part in any more elections. In 1894, others established the Social Democratic Workers' Party (SDAP). Its manifesto was essentially a literal translation of the *Erfurter Programm*, the program of the Socialdemocratic Party of Germany (SPD). The new party retained the goal of universal suffrage, but without renouncing revolutionary objectives and weapons. The SDAP thus provided no solution for the dilemma between revolutionary theory and reformist practice. As in other countries, pragmatic reform policy was not to push revolutionary principles out of the manifesto until well into the twentieth century.[65]

At first the SDAP was not a significant political player, and had only a slender parliamentary basis because of the prevailing suffrage based on tax assessment. The religious ties of many Dutch workers also hindered its growth. The party did not become a serious political factor, with fifteen of the hundred Lower House seats, until the eve of the First World War. Despite this weakness and the relatively late advent of the workers' movement, the social question had been a political theme for some time. The liberals had adopted this issue in the 1870s and, thanks mainly to the activities of the young and the later social liberals, a system of social legislation – albeit very modest – was gradually created. The 1878 Education Act discussed earlier was also an indication that some liberals wanted to assign more duties to the state. They discovered their responsibility for fighting poverty, protecting the weaker members of society, and educating and developing disadvantaged parts of the population. Liberals believed that citizenship was not determined in the first instance by culture and politics, and that it had a significant social and economic dimension. If one wanted to increase the number of citizens, as the liberals did, working to improve the social position of the lower classes was an obvious step.

It therefore comes as no surprise that the first trade union in the Netherlands, the General Dutch Workers' Association (ANWV), was established by social liberals (1871) and that the first proposals for improving working conditions, social housing and social legislation came from this liberal group. The poor and 'needy' had to be educated to become fully fledged citizens, and that meant having to instil such values as thrift, devotion to duty, order, tidiness and hygiene. The promotion of measures to improve the social and economic position of the poorest groups in the population would not only prevent declining morals, it would also enable them to improve their position and thus reinforce the nation's bourgeois character. This thinking certainly had an element of national integration. The lowest social strata were also counted as part of the nation in principle, and citizenship should serve as an expectation for them too. They had to learn to make independent judgements in order to achieve that. An improved social and economic position was a requirement for this, and so the social question on the one hand and citizenship and broader suffrage on the other were directly linked.[66]

Social liberals shrunk back, however, from actual active government intervention in social and economic relationships, so the practical results of their activities initially remained very limited. The way Sam van Houten, the well-known social liberal, acted during the 1870s was typical. He published regularly on the social question, he fiercely criticized doctrinaire liberals for their restraint and he demanded reforms. He contributed to the creation of the 1874 Child Labour Act, which curbed – on a modest scale – the use of children as workers. At the same time he also opposed any increase in state influence on the economy. The historian Dirk Jan Wolffram therefore rightly asserts that in the 1870s the social liberals were still not providing a feasible alternative.[67] The results also remained limited in the decades thereafter. While some social legislation came into effect around the turn of the century, including the Housing Act and the Industrial Injuries Act, and steps were taken during the First World War to set up pension and unemployment benefits, minimal state intervention remained a key feature of social policy in the Netherlands.[68]

In addition to the school controversy and the social question, there was also political conflict in the late nineteenth century about the suffrage issue. As we have seen, suffrage based on tax assessment was introduced in 1848. According to the predominantly liberal thinking until then, parliament was not *of* but *for* the people, as Jasper Loots writes in his study of the development of suffrage.[69] Citizens could only be granted the right to vote, and thus be admitted to the political nation, if they reached a given level of prosperity and paid a certain percentage in direct taxes. The liberals were working on the assumption that the number of citizens should increase and that one day all Dutch nationals would be worthy of the right to vote. But the liberal suffrage policy was not without internal tensions and objections. The liberals supported the principle of equal rights, but they also had to be fearful of the consequences. They benefitted from both suffrage based on tax assessment and the constituency system and continued their political dominance, yet the majority of the population was not liberal.[70] Wider suffrage and the introduction of voting rules that reflected the actual political balance of power would almost certainly result in serious damage to the powerful liberal position. As a result, opinions were divided in liberal circles about the pace and type of broader suffrage. The upshot was that little changed for many years and the number of men entitled to vote during the 1870s stagnated at around 12 per cent.

Among progressive liberals, the view that there was a very real link between voters and elected members and that parliament was a forum for airing important differences of opinion gradually gained ground. According to this modern view, parliament should no longer be for but of the people. This pointed in the direction of wider suffrage, but no agreement was reached on a broadly supported answer to the question of what form it should take. Another factor was that Protestants and Catholics opposed amending the constitution to change suffrage rules unless the liberals agreed to their demands in the school controversy. In 1887, the religious parties agreed to a liberal constitutional change that enabled a substantial expansion of suffrage in exchange for the liberal declaration that the constitution did not exclude subsidizing denominational education (the liberals had asserted the opposite in 1878).

The 1887 constitutional amendment scrapped the old suffrage based on tax assessment introduced in the 1848 constitution and 1850 elections act, but blocked the establishment of universal suffrage.[71] It stipulated that all men aged twenty-three and older were entitled to vote provided they demonstrated certain characteristics of prosperity and suitability. Parliament could define these characteristics in detail in simple election legislation. This opened the door to a significant expansion in suffrage, which would be implemented in a number of steps in the years thereafter until ultimately universal male suffrage was achieved in 1917, with a new amended constitution. The proposal put forward by left-wing liberals in 1894 – an election year – to exclude only illiterates and the poor from entitlement to vote provoked massive resistance. The differences of opinion cut across all political groups – not just between religious and liberal politicians. Among the Protestants it resulted in a split between Kuyper and his anti-revolutionary colleague A. F. de Savornin Lohmann, which in the end was to lead to the creation of the CHU.

The liberals were also divided over the issue. A minority within the Liberal Union – a national liberal organization founded in 1885 – was opposed to the proposal of the left-wing liberals because it was considered as going too far, and those involved formed a separate group. In 1906, this faction became the conservative League of Free Liberals. The social liberal Free-Thinking Democratic League (VDB), which had a progressive agenda for social legislation and suffrage, was established in 1901. This means that around the turn of the century, the liberals broke up into three camps. This, with the further extension of suffrage, would ultimately lead to severe erosion of their position in parliament.[72]

The left-wing liberals' proposal of 1894 did not get a majority, but the compromise that was hammered out nevertheless increased the number of voters substantially.[73] This process continued, and by 1913, 67 per cent of the male population were entitled to vote. The primary beneficiaries of this extension of suffrage were the religious parties and – on the eve of the First World War – the socialists. The 1890s could still be labelled as a liberal decade, but at the start of the twentieth century the liberals lost ground, and the Netherlands was governed primarily by religious parties until 1913. Liberal political influence remained considerable despite this loss of power. Protestants and Catholics were at loggerheads to such an extent that their normally stronger electoral position was not converted into permanent political dominance. Moreover, most liberals and religious politicians had a common loathing of the emerging socialist workers' movement. In this sense the religious politicians blended well into the bourgeois–liberal Netherlands that took shape in the second half of the nineteenth century. For the time being there was no effective political alternative.

Economic growth and modernization

Late and slow industrialization is a striking feature of the Dutch economy in the nineteenth century. Although recent research presents a more positive assessment of industrial development in the first half of the nineteenth century than was often the case before, there can be no doubt that the Netherlands lagged behind Belgium and Great Britain, among others, and the gap widened between the 1840s and 1870s. Economic historians Van Zanden and Van Riel point out that in the Netherlands the liberalization of international trade, which began to make rapid advances in the 1840s, stimulated agriculture rather than industry.[74] In Belgium, a few branches of manufacturing already had a strong position, and consequently industry could easily benefit from foreign and domestic orders. Furthermore, the Belgian government's finances were healthy, and so there was a good investment climate in the country. The Netherlands had none of these advantages, but on the other hand the productivity of Dutch farms was high, thanks in part to far-reaching specialization. Agriculture also profited from growing international trade. Rising demand contributed to higher prices, so farming was usually lucrative at this time. Yet the group benefitting from it remained small and increasing agricultural land prices – under pressure after a few failed harvests among other things – had deleterious consequences for many. The cost of living climbed, so the population's purchasing power felt the effects. The long period of low real wages – which did not start to increase again until the 1860s (see Illustration 2, p. 144) – also put the brakes on industry, which was producing primarily for the domestic market. Add to this the dismantling in the 1840s of trade barriers resulting from William I's protectionist policy and the exposure of Dutch manufacturing to fiercer international competition, and it is not surprising that industry lagged behind and net imports of manufactured goods continued to rise until about 1870.

The prosperity in the agricultural sector was not enough for it to function as an engine to drive the whole economy. In the end it was the services sector, which benefitted greatly at this time from international liberalization of trade and industry that fulfilled this role. Although the Netherlands had tried to protect its own position in Rhine shipping until the early 1850s and trade with the Dutch East Indies was not liberalized until the 1860s, the irreversible growth of free trade in the 1840s meant that the country was caught up in the dynamic process of international economic integration. While the Dutch share of Rhine shipping fell, the absolute volumes increased hugely – to such an extent, in fact, that it became one of the Dutch economy's most important growth sectors. Elsewhere in the transport industry, from the late 1850s the Netherlands also began to invest more heavily in building railways and the first steamship companies were founded. Until then the Dutch rail network had remained relatively limited, but between 1860 and 1880 an integrated system linking the most important towns and cities emerged. It was some 2,000 kilometres long and provided a significant boost to the national economy.

A period of 'modern economic growth' started in the Netherlands around 1870. In their standard work on the Dutch economy, Van Zanden and Van Riel define this concept as virtually permanent high growth combined with structural economic changes such that agriculture became relatively less significant, while manufacturing's share of national income increased.[75] The figures for Dutch economic output between around 1860–1870 and 1900–1910 show that this is exactly what happened. At the beginning of the 1860s, some 40 per cent of the Dutch population was still working in farming or fishing, whereas around 1910 this figure had dropped to about 30 per cent. During this period, the number of people employed in industry, trade and services rose by approximately 10 per cent.

This change in the occupational structure was reflected in the movement of people to towns and cities. Amsterdam, Rotterdam, The Hague and Utrecht grew particularly strongly. After stagnating for two centuries, Amsterdam's population exceeded 240,000 – the same number as during the heyday of the seventeenth century. The number of people living in the capital more than doubled between 1849 (224,000) and 1899 (510,000). The country's degree of urbanization rose from 29 per cent to 39.7 per cent during the same period. In the traditionally highly built-up west, 65 per cent of people lived in towns and cities in around 1900 (1849: 53.5 per cent).

This move to the towns was also linked to internal migration from the northern, southern and eastern provinces to the west of the Netherlands, where the population grew at the expense of the more agrarian border regions. This trend was most marked during the great agricultural depression of the late 1880s and early 1890s. Interregional resettlement and urbanization also arose from the accelerated population growth that started at this time. The increase was the result of a rising standard of living, healthier nutrition and better hygiene, which between them dramatically reduced mortality. Between 1850 and 1880, the Dutch population grew by 900,000 (from 3.1 million to 4.0 million), and during the following thirty years, this increase doubled to nearly six million in 1910. Growth continued at a rate of about a million more inhabitants per decade, reaching approximately nine million in 1940.

Illustration 2 (see p. 144) gives a clear picture of economic development in the nineteenth century in terms of trends in real wages and industrial output. We can see clearly that after decades of stagnation, there was a virtually continuous increase in real wages from around 1860 to the turn of the century. The more prosperous strata of the population benefitted greatly, and improvement of the middle class's position followed naturally from this. The increase in real wages enabled a rise in investments, which in turn helped productivity to grow and working conditions to improve. This led to the start of an autocatalytic process in which rising incomes, a changing economic structure (and associated jobs matrix), urbanization and internal migration had a positive effect on one another. The farming crisis in the 1880s reinforced the cumulative effect of this process. Falling wages in agriculture stimulated the shift of people to urban areas, where industrialization and house building produced economic growth. Urbanization and population increases led in turn to a revival in demand for agricultural products, while farm productivity rose, thanks to new cultivation methods (machines, chemical fertilizers, etc.) and organizational improvements (cooperatives, agricultural credit unions and so on). This enabled the agrarian sector to emerge from the depression during the 1890s.

Yet while economic growth and modernization were driven to a significant extent by the domestic market, commercial relations with foreign countries and the resulting stimuli were no less important. Economic ties between Germany and the Netherlands were particularly vital. The role of German migrants in the Netherlands, for instance, was very significant in a range of fields. Germans were working as bankers, engineers, ship owners, managers (in Philips and other companies), businessmen and teachers, and had an indisputable impact on Dutch modernization. Many factories were strongly oriented towards Germany for their technology. Be it chemicals, asphalt, tar, cement or beer, numerous manufacturing sectors were dominated by German production methods, introduced and implemented by German entrepreneurs, engineers and technicians. Their number far exceeded the total of other foreigners involved in this area in the Netherlands.[76] German capital also played a significant part. A number of banks in the Netherlands were completely or partially in German hands, including the Amsterdamsche Bank founded in 1871, and so too were many coal mines in southern Limburg. Naturally, German firms also set up shop in Rotterdam. August Thyssen owned Vulkan GmbH, a Rotterdam trading and shipping company. Just before the First World War, he even obtained permission to excavate his own harbour near Vlaardingen – the Vulkaanhaven.[77] And last, the growth of Dutch chain stores would have been unthinkable without well-known German names such as Clemens and August Brenninkmeijer (C&A), Johannes Peek and Heinrich Cloppenburg (P&C), Anton Dreesmann (V&D) and Anton Kreymborg. These merchants, some of whom had crossed the border as simple hawkers and so initially did not belong to the social elite of influential businessmen, bankers and engineers referred to above, went on to build up their empires gradually.

The expansion of the Dutch economy in the late nineteenth century was closely linked to tempestuous economic growth in Germany at the time.[78] Rhine shipping quintupled between 1890 and 1910. In 1913, a third of all German imports, exports and transit goods crossed the Dutch–German border (more than 51 million tonnes out of more than 163 million tonnes of freight). Around 1910, the Dutch share of the transit trade was estimated at between 13 and 18 per cent of national income. During this period, shipping in the Netherlands was increasing faster than world trade and the Dutch merchant fleet expanded by 200 per cent. It was largely the same for employment in shipyards, which grew by over 160 per cent between 1890 and 1910. This development was accompanied by German exports acquiring a dominant position on the Dutch market in the last decades of the nineteenth century (coal, industrial products and machinery). The structure of Dutch–German economic relations that emerged was the same as it is now, namely German exports of manufactures and capital goods matched by Dutch supplies of agricultural produce and services (trade and transport).

The massive increase in the merchant fleet was linked to the blossoming of the Dutch East Indies' economy. The colony's commerce flourished after the end of the Aceh War in 1903 and the arrival of Governor-General J. B. van Heutsz in 1904. Military expeditions were followed by opening up outlying districts to business and government entirely in line with the 'ethical policy' (see p. 170 ff.). Construction and modernization of the infrastructure (roads, communications, ports, etc.), stimulation of economic development, improvement in food supplies and the position of the population created a real economic boom. The upshot was an increase in the value of colonial exports of over 150 per cent between 1900 and 1913. This stupendous trend was also matched by a bigger Dutch East Indies' contribution to national income. The colonial share rose from some 5 per cent in 1890 to about 10 per cent in 1913. The colony thus contributed significantly to Dutch economic vigour.[79]

No matter how impressive these figures are, Dutch industrialization remained modest compared with other countries. The country's manufacturing output in both 1880 and 1913 made it number eleven out of fifteen European nations. The position of the Netherlands in the industrial output ranking on a per capita basis was also towards the lower end, and remained very far behind such countries as Britain, Belgium and Germany.[80] It should be added that the Dutch dynamic was not intermittent, nor was there a rush to innovate. The historian Kossmann points out that social and economic development in the Netherlands was in fact relatively harmonious compared with other European countries.[81] From an international perspective, modern economic growth started from a favourable position, continued gradually and accelerated at the end of the century. Industrialization and urbanization were nevertheless accompanied by dramatic social conditions in the Netherlands too, as Auke van der Woud penetratingly demonstrates, but poverty and serious decline were less widespread than in other countries.[82]

A small neutral power with a big empire

After the end of its United Kingdom in 1830, the Netherlands had to finally accept its position as a minor player. The traditions that had evolved since the seventeenth century could be revived in the renewed quest for a place in international relations and new instruments for pursuing national interests. In the past, the approach had always been to safeguard shipping and trading interests, which was best achieved through an international balance of power. In the international constellation of the second half of the nineteenth century this meant both avoiding any involvement in conflicts between nations, and increasingly emphasizing free trade. After all, the Netherlands profited from the growing liberalization of world trade, as we saw in the preceding section. The importance of good relations with both the British and the Germans contributed to the need for the Dutch to maintain a neutral course. British naval might was the only way to guarantee freedom of the seas and the security of the Dutch East Indies, and this made it essential to remain on good terms with Great Britain. At the same time, one-sided British orientation had to be avoided. The show of strength by Prussia (the German Empire from 1871) and growing economic engagement with Germany created a growing awareness of dependence in the Netherlands, and also the importance of maintaining good relations with the Germans.

During the 1860s, the Netherlands had watched the emergence of Prussian power with concern, and worries as to whether Prime Minister Otto von Bismarck also had surprises in store for the Netherlands were frequently aired. To pursue a consistent policy of neutrality was not easy because, through the province of Limburg and the grand duchy of Luxembourg, the country was part of the German Confederation and – whether it wanted to be or not – was involved in developments in it. The Dutch were pleased when, after British mediation, the institutional ties between Limburg and Luxembourg on the one hand and Germany on the other were cut in 1867. Relief in the Netherlands that Luxembourg and Limburg were now outside the North German Confederation was short-lived, however, as fears of becoming a victim of Prussian power intensified again with the Franco–Prussian War (1870–71). After that war, the Dutch anxiety gradually abated and it became clear that Bismarck had an interest in Dutch neutrality in the light of his policy of maintaining a European balance of power.[83] But of course that did nothing to alter the vulnerability of the Netherlands – in fact, it increased because of the Dutch–German economic involvement discussed above, which took shape during these decades.

The axiom that an equal distance from each of the major European powers had to be maintained appeared to be briefly in danger around 1900. In 1880–81, during the so-called First Boer War, the British tried to settle their scores in South Africa with the two small republics of Transvaal and the Orange Free State and annex them to the British colony there. The Boers, the white inhabitants of these republics, were descendants of primarily Dutch colonists from the heyday of the Republic, and their successful opposition to the British annexation policy was followed in the Netherlands with great sympathy. The accompanying anti-British sentiment intensified significantly when the British made a new attempt to subjugate the Boers in 1899. The background and significance of Dutch sympathy for the Boers is discussed in detail later in this chapter. The point here is that the strong antipathy to the British could represent a threat to the Dutch policy of neutrality. At the end of the Second Boer War (1899–1902), moreover, the Netherlands was governed by Abraham Kuyper (1901–5), who as an anti-revolutionary considered himself to be a kindred spirit to like-minded South Africans and also had pro-German feelings. Nevertheless, Kuyper did not attempt to make sweeping changes to foreign policy, although some contemporaries were concerned that the Netherlands might be entering pro-German waters.[84] Such worries were dispelled with the fall of the Kuyper government in 1905, and the country was to maintain his policy of aloofness until 1940.

The distance the country successfully maintained at the time of German unification, the period of calm that commenced in 1871 and the encouraging economic trends thereafter seemed only to confirm that Dutch foreign policy was right. It was for these reasons that the country was not affected by *fin-de-siècle* feelings of unease and pessimism, but rather by a strong sense of national self-esteem.[85] In foreign policy this found expression in the idea that the Netherlands' successes should serve as an example for the world. The arguments of Leiden professor Cornelis van Vollenhoven (1874–1933), who wanted the Netherlands to play a leading part in the creation of an international legal order, were well known. In the anniversary year of 1913, a century after the defeat of Napoleon and Orange's return from exile, he spoke about a renewed Netherlands 'that wishes to return to the top rank'.[86] Specifically, Van Vollenhoven argued that the country should build on the foundations laid by the seventeenth-century international law scholar Hugo Grotius and take the initiative to establish a peacekeeping force as a military arm of an international legal system. It was no accident that Van Vollenhoven's plea coincided with the opening of the Peace Palace in 1913, which housed the Permanent Court of Arbitration, a body that was to establish The Hague's reputation as the city of international law. The international law professor was hoping that his proposal would make the court of arbitration a powerful institution that could impose sanctions if arbitration could not be invoked or enforced. He believed that, unlike the major powers, the Netherlands as a small and neutral country would not allow itself to be driven by egoism. He also thought that the Netherlands, which hosted two significant international peace conferences in 1899 and 1907, would be ideal for this pioneering role.[87] Moral arguments like this would also be employed repeatedly later in the twentieth century – an ideological policy that justified remaining aloof from international issues and thus compensated for actually having lost international power.

The idea that the Netherlands had a calling in the world was given practical substance around the turn of the century in the 'ethical policy' in the Dutch East Indies. Dutch colonial power in this area had been reinforced and extended in the course of the nineteenth century. Starting in 1830, the Cultivation System discussed earlier had generated huge economic benefits, but was also the subject of growing criticism from liberals. The Cultivation System was not based solely on the Dutch position of power. There were also traditional indigenous elites that had taken up a key position as an 'intermediate level'. This power structure, which was partly modern colonial and partly traditional feudal, had dramatic implications for large sections of the population.

These abuses were described at length in a novel published in 1860 – *Max Havelaar of de koffieveilingen der Nederlandsche Handelmaatschappij* – by Eduard Douwes Dekker, alias Multatuli.[88] Some years earlier, as a young colonial civil servant, the writer had vainly endeavoured to draw attention to the mistreatment and suppression of the Javanese population, and had then resigned. His book, which explained clearly that the colonial administration had shared responsibility for the cruelty, came as a bombshell. Colonial historian Wim van den Doel rightly points out that *Max Havelaar* was not an anti-colonial book nor was its target the Cultivation System.[89] What Multatuli – and the emerging liberal colonial policy – wanted was to create a colonial administration that would bring justice, prosperity and civilization. This was the Netherlands' task. According to Multatuli, it was necessary to increase the number of Dutch officials, modernize the administrative system and weaken the position of indigenous chiefs.

This was the policy that was implemented in the late decades of the nineteenth century – a policy that was accompanied by the expansion of the colony's territory throughout the whole archipelago and made the Dutch East Indies even more of a colonial state than it had been before. At the same time, the abolition of the Cultivation System in 1870 increased the scope for European businessmen and landowners. Even so, the position of large parts of the population did not improve. On the contrary, the cost of modernizing the colonial state had to be borne by the colony itself. Over and above this, the explosive population growth, from some 16 million in Java in 1870 to about 28 million in 1900, had dramatic consequences. Drawing up the balance around the turn of the century, it had to be acknowledged that the progress that had been hoped for in the preceding decades had failed to arrive. This was the backdrop against which the liberal lawyer C. T. van Deventer published an article in 1899 that was to become famous. Entitled *Een eereschuld* (*A Debt of Honour*), it pointed out the obligation on the Netherlands to repay the many millions of guilders that had been earned from exploitation. This money could be used to further the development of the colony.

This historical debt would never be paid off, but Van Deventer's article did contribute to a climate in which an ethical policy could take shape. In the 1901 speech from the throne, Queen Wilhelmina said that the Netherlands, as a 'Christian power' had an 'ethical mission' in respect of the people of the colony. In practice, this aspiration meant increasing the natives' prosperity, improving the infrastructure, providing more and better education, and creating the basis for forms of self-government. Progressive colonial thinkers had a vision of a future colony intimately bound to the Netherlands, with its own image and position, in which western and eastern wisdom would complement one other.

This paternalism in no way excluded harsh action, which in turn was associated with the expansion of colonial authority around 1900. Two military operations played an important part in this – the Lombok expedition (1894) and the military intervention in Aceh, which lasted for decades and reached its gruesome violent nadir around the turn of the century under Lieutenant General Johannes B. van Heutsz. The Lombok expedition was prompted by fighting between native groups, one of which, the Islamic Sasak people, called on the Netherlands for help in their struggle against the old Balinese Radja of Lombok and his district heads. The arrival of Dutch troops appeared to restore peace, but some of the district heads organized surprise attacks on Dutch encampments, leading to about a hundred deaths and some 270 wounded. In the Netherlands there were unprecedented calls for revenge and the large number of dead and wounded was perceived as a national disaster that justified a brutal response. Many volunteered to take part, and the Netherlands stamped its authority on Lombok with considerable violence. Colonial historian Van den Doel described the Lombok expedition as a defining moment in the history of the expansion of Dutch power. After 1894 there was no longer any doubt about the need to permanently establish the colonial authority of the Netherlands beyond Java as well as on it. There was also a strong consensus about the need for ruthless military action to achieve that objective.[90] This, then, was also the blueprint for subsequent operations in Aceh, a region in the north of Sumatra. There had been military confrontations there since 1873 but without the Netherlands actually establishing its authority. Planning to do something about it started in the early 1890s, and in 1898 it was Lieutenant General Van Heutsz who implemented those plans. Unprecedentedly ruthless means were employed to 'pacify' Aceh and bring it under Dutch military rule. Back home, colonial expansion was accompanied by a wave of self-awareness and nationalism. Van Heutsz was hailed as a national hero and his appointment as Governor-General of the Dutch East Indies in 1904 – the highest ranking civilian and military position – was a token of both gratitude and trust. Under his leadership, further peripheral areas of the Dutch East Indies' archipelago were brought under direct colonial rule.[91]

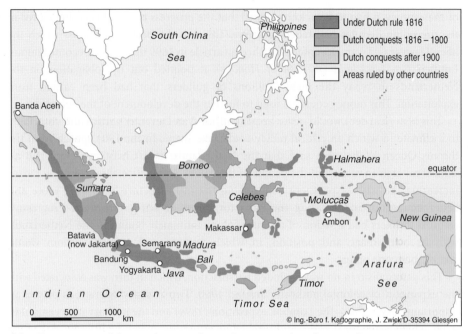

Map 9 Expansion of the Dutch East Indies in the nineteenth and twentieth centuries.

Notwithstanding current perceptions of the contradiction between violent conquest on the one hand and Van Vollenhoven's idealism about the Netherlands as a hub of international law on the other, contemporaries, including Van Vollenhoven himself, thought differently. He shared the pride in Dutch expansion and the consolidation of colonial power. In 1913, he was to say that the victory started in Lombok, referring to the rediscovery of Dutch strength and the associated opportunities to put the Netherlands' moral calling into practice with greater vigour. At the end of the nineteenth century there was thus a fusion of nationalism, colonialism, idealism and the ethical policy that gave shape to the Dutch variant of modern imperialism.

Another change took place in colonial affairs during the 1860s. As we saw earlier, the Netherlands abolished the slave trade in 1814 under pressure from England, but slavery itself had not yet ended. While the concept of a 'debt of honour' was a factor in discussions about colonialism at the end of the nineteenth century, when slavery was abolished in Suriname and the West Indies such slogans were barely heard. The abolition movement in the Netherlands never had more than a few hundred adherents and did not play a significant role in the abolition debate. The factors driving it were developments in other countries, in particular in England, where slavery was abolished in 1833, but also in France and Denmark, which followed suit in 1848. Against this backdrop the Netherlands could not sit on its hands, and by 1863 it was finally the turn of Dutch colonies. On 1 July of that year 33,000 slaves in Suriname and 12,000 on the Antilles were 'freed'. They did not become really free until 1873 however. Until then they had to continue working on Suriname plantations, but they did receive wages and were permitted to change employer.[92] The theme of 'guilt' about Dutch involvement in the history of slavery did not become a political or social factor until the late twentieth century.[93]

State and nation in the nineteenth century

As we saw in the previous chapter, a great deal had been said and written about country and sense of country before the Netherlands became a unitary state in 1795. This continued during the French period, and when Orange returned in 1813, Van Hogendorp sought to merge the concepts of 'country' and 'Orange'. The creation of the United Kingdom of the Netherlands (1815–30) shortly afterwards gave the concept of country a new direction, but the south and north separated before real national solidarity had been able to develop. This jointly shared sentiment had amounted to very little, as emerged from the fact that the secession of the south was accompanied in the north by powerful anti-Belgian feelings, which actually contributed to the growth of North Netherlandish national awareness.

The Dutch unitary state of the 1830s and 1840s was still a long way from being a nation state. Regional differences between provinces and between urban and rural areas were still huge. The separatism in Limburg during the 1840s was certainly an exception, but during the Belgian Revolt politicians in the north began to wonder whether the Catholic province of Brabant might choose the Belgian side. There was a deep dividing line (Catholic–Protestant) between Limburg and Brabant on one side and the northern provinces and Zeeland on the other. Taking the country as a whole, Catholics represented 38 per cent and were thus a minority, but in Limburg and Brabant, the percentages were 98 per cent and 88 per cent, respectively. Protestants made up 60 per cent of the total population – not an overwhelming majority – but they included the members of the political and social elite, who were traditionally concentrated in Holland. In other words, there was essentially no question of any historical solidarity between the southern and northern provinces and there were still major differences between the dominating western part of the country and the other provinces in the centre and the north. 'Holland' considered itself to be superior to the rest of the country, and the tensions this created would still be present in the twentieth century. The very limited engagement with the nation of 'Holland' by the other provinces around 1830 – the year of Belgium's secession – is demonstrated by the fact that in some places the male population refused to obey the royal summons to report for military service. This resistance existed primarily among Catholics and above all in the region, a sign of the distance between 'periphery' and 'centre'.[94]

It is certainly too simplistic to regard the 'periphery' as regionally oriented and the 'centre' as nationally focused. Obviously a lot depended on an individual's social and economic position in nineteenth-century society. Someone who belonged to the small upper crust of the upper middle class or nobility, whose members held all the important positions in government, finance and business, had a different view from someone in the lower middle class (shopkeepers, other self-employed people, teachers) or in the group of labourers or paupers. In rural areas, a distinction has to be made between the aristocracy, independent farmers and labourers. Here too, we can justifiably argue that the higher someone's place on the social ladder, the less regional his focus.

Generally speaking, the established Protestant bourgeoisie, living primarily in the towns and cities of Holland, showed the greatest solidarity with the emerging Dutch nation and expressed these sentiments assertively. A key element in this was the Maatschappij tot Nut van 't Algemeen (the Society for the Public Good, see p. 112), which also had many members in Friesland and Groningen. Since its foundation in 1784 it had taken upon itself the task of educating and training the poorer classes so that they could become citizens. In the nineteenth century this was broadened to include strengthening the awareness of nationhood at the expense of a regional focus. A typical initiative was the publication of the *Nederlandsch Volksliederenboek* – a book of folk songs – in the late nineteenth century. The idea behind it was that distributing folk songs would encourage communal and historical bonding, particularly now that the emergence of pillarization was increasing the distance between different groups in the population.[95] During this period, the Dutch nation also took shape in other areas. Citizens debated, in associations or among themselves, about social, ethical and moral issues. The answers were often different, but a shared awareness of responsibility for solving social problems became evident. Bourgeois men and women became organized, usually without any political ties, in order to improve social conditions, and through such engagement contributed to the process of nation building.[96]

But for many in the provinces, the political and commercial centre of the Netherlands was still far away, both mentally and geographically. Travelling from the northern and southern provinces to Utrecht around 1850, for instance, meant a journey of twelve and a half hours or longer. In the 1860s, travelling times gradually started to decrease as the road and rail networks expanded, so that the Netherlands 'shrank' during the last decades of the nineteenth century. Improved connections also required harmonization of clocks, which, as late as 1909, still ran on different times and time systems across the country.

Starting in 1892, rail services ran according to Western European or Greenwich Mean Time. Amsterdam and many other places used Amsterdam time, while local times were used elsewhere. This chaos did not end until 1909, when Amsterdam time became obligatory for the whole country. In so doing the Netherlands went its own way between British Western European Time and German Central European Time. While this without doubt represented progress, it did not make international embedment any easier.[97] That did not happen until the Second World War. On 16 May 1940, the second day after Dutch capitulation, German occupying forces imposed Central European Time on the Netherlands, and this has not changed since.

The advent of communication networks – telegraph, telephone and post – was also a part of this late nineteenth-century modernization process.[98] In 1852, a law providing for the installation of telegraph lines between the most important towns and cities by authority of the state came into effect. The number of telegrams increased rapidly thanks to expansion of the network, lower prices and increasing prosperity. There were only 200,000 domestic telegrams in 1860, but by 1880, this number had grown to two million, and in 1919 there were six million. On the other hand, telephone usage was still very limited at the end of the nineteenth century. The first private telephone network started up in 1881, with forty-nine subscribers in Amsterdam. After the turn of the century the state was responsible for long-distance and international telephone calls. The government started taking over local networks in 1913, so uniformity was gradually created, and in the 1920s, the volume of telephone traffic rose sharply.[99] The amount of mail also grew substantially from the second half of the nineteenth century. The number of post offices nearly doubled between 1870 and 1900 (from 785 to 1,314), and the number of letters and postcards sent quadrupled (from 27 million in 1870 to 120 million in 1900).

The increase in the number of daily newspapers and weekly magazines – from 92 in 1850, to 357 in 1880 and to 6,760 in 1894 – and the growing size of their circulations reinforced the process of national integration. At the same time, this trend contributed to what the social geographers Hans Knippenberg and Ben de Pater describe as 'mental scaling up'. Many people were exposed to information about a huge number of domestic and foreign subjects that until then they had not been aware of.[100] A dynamic process began in 1870 and continued through the following decades, in which improved infrastructure, growing information and communication options, industrialization, urbanization and the establishment of national political parties went hand in hand, such that the modernization and unification of the Netherlands were significantly advanced.

Starting in the 1880s, this integration process was accompanied by attempts to strengthen the royal house as a symbol of national unity. The liberals were particularly strong supporters of this. In previous decades it had become clear that anniversaries of historical events that related to the sixteenth-century Revolt were not a good platform for fostering national solidarity. This was because such commemorations repeatedly fanned the embers of old political divisions and revealed just how much the history of liberals, Protestants and Catholics differed. The first celebration of Princess's Day on 31 August 1885 laid the foundations for a national holiday that circumvented such problems. Princess Wilhelmina's birthday was a day with no history, a day that summoned up no polarizing historical interpretations, and proved ideal as a symbol of the unity of the people, the country and the royal house. Protestants, Catholics and liberals furthermore discovered that people liked to display their affection for the royal house when they were given the opportunity at House of Orange celebrations. Such festivities also proved very suitable for channelling existing popular amusements into quieter, more dignified activities. Princess's Day thus provided an excellent alternative to anniversaries of historical events. A national holiday like this was conciliatory. The festivities had educational value and reinforced the bond between the people and Orange. At the same time, it seemed to be an effective means of combatting anti-royalist feelings among socialists.[101] The success of this holiday was to be lasting. The tradition of Queen's Day – King's Day since 2014 – has continued for over a hundred years.

The efforts to reinforce national harmony around the House of Orange reached their pinnacle in 1898. After the death of King William III in 1890, Princess Wilhelmina – age ten – formally became queen, but until 1898 her mother Emma of Waldeck and Pyrmont took care of state business as Queen Regent. Princess Wilhelmina turned eighteen that

Figure 17 *Inauguration of Queen Wilhelmina in Amsterdam (1898)*, Otto Eerelman, 1898–1900. Rijksmuseum Amsterdam.

year and could be inaugurated as queen. Naturally the Orange dynasty's roots in Dutch history played an important part in the many national, regional and local festivities. But the organizers deliberately steered clear of any sensitive areas that could revive differences relating to the nation's past. The Revolt was therefore not a central theme, whereas the Golden Age that followed it certainly was. It was presented as the zenith of a glorious past in such a way that it resonated with the entire population. Of course it is impossible to establish with any precision whether there was actually a strengthening of the sense of nation and the bond with the House of Orange. Strikingly, though, the comments about the inauguration were much more enthusiastic than the responses to the two anniversaries of historical events in that same year – fifty years since Thorbecke's constitution (1848) and 250 years since the Peace of Münster (1648). According to historian Jan Bank and literary scholar Maarten van Buuren, the inauguration of Queen Wilhelmina, in a celebratory popular mood, under liberal auspices and with religious support, cemented the monarchy more securely in the Dutch national consciousness.[102]

The social democrats were conspicuously absent from the inauguration ceremonies. As opponents of the monarchy on principle, the SDAP members of the Lower House stayed away, but their protest amounted to little more than that. Apparently the social democrats wanted to remain in the background and not disrupt the royal celebrations, as evidenced by their appeal to their grassroots support not to take part in demonstrations for or against the royal house. The SDAP remained expressly aloof from the national unity that liberal and religious politicians were shaping, but evidently considered themselves too weak to press home this aloofness. They must also have been aware that some of their own rank and file – whose numbers were not yet that big – wanted to join in the festivities. Against this backdrop, a harsh anti-royalist attitude, particularly at a time when a wave of nationalism was sweeping the country, was obviously not appropriate.

The nationalism gripping the population was also linked to events outside Europe, such as the Second Boer War (1899–1902) in South Africa. As we saw above, many Dutch people felt historically related to the Boers. They identified with these 'distant relatives', who supposedly embodied an original purity and strength that appeared to have been lost in their old country. The Boers were seen as a redeeming feature, even a source of hope for a revival of Dutch national vigour. The Beggars of the sixteenth century had created the 'small but plucky' self-image of the Netherlands, and now the Boers were looked on as the Beggars of the nineteenth century. The Netherlands had lost North American territory to England in the seventeenth century, but now, it was believed, the Boers would recapture land from the British and this would herald a new era of Dutch national vitality. Protestants, liberals, Catholics and even social democrats organized innumerable aid committees, collected money and followed the course of the war with intense interest.

The defeat of the Boers – the republics lost their independence – had a profound impact on the development of Dutch nationalism. The limits of belligerently worded nationalism that was powerless in practice had become clear for all to see. There was also greater awareness of the country's position as a minor power that was dependent on the major players, one that could only lose out if international relations were to be determined by war and violence. Unlike Germany, Britain and France, for instance, this meant that militant nationalism had no future in the Netherlands and Dutch nationalism calmed down. Viewed in this light, the Boer War, which had taken place thousands of miles from the Netherlands and was fought with no actual Dutch involvement, had a chastening effect. For a brief period this war had fuelled the dream of a new, large and powerful Netherlands, but when it ended badly for the Boers, people had to face the harsh reality, which was that new ways of expressing Dutch nationalism would have to be found.[103] Whereas other European countries were to plunge into the First World War with deep conviction in 1914 and nationalist sentiments would reach a climax, in the Netherlands this point had already been reached around the turn of the century. Afterwards, the Netherlands kept its distance and concentrated on things that could 'make a small country great' – promoting international law, peace and morals.

The First World War and the Pacification of 1917

As we saw above, Dutch detachment from international tensions and conflicts during the final decades of the nineteenth century also proved to be in German and British interests. Nevertheless the German attitude seemed to change around 1900, and under Kaiser Wilhelm II's *Weltpolitik* it became less self-evident that Dutch neutrality would be respected. In 1905, the German general Alfred von Schlieffen devised a plan of attack, later named after him, for a war in the west. It provided for a military advance through the Dutch province of Limburg, in order to push into France faster and with more troops. Von Schlieffen was counting on weak Dutch resistance and assumed, despite the violation of their neutrality, that the Netherlands would seek to collaborate with Germany.

Helmuth von Moltke the Younger, appointed to succeed Von Schlieffen in 1906, was not so sure and in subsequent years removed the march through the Netherlands from the military plans. Von Moltke feared the military consequences of 'entering a hostile Holland'. In fact, Dutch neutrality was in German interests because the transport of freight to Germany could continue. Moltke's rationale for this change in military strategy was that 'Holland has to remain our airway, so that we can breathe.'[104] This change was to have far-reaching implications for the Netherlands. The German interest in Dutch neutrality is one of two key factors in explaining why the Netherlands stayed out of the First World War.

The second is the attitude of the British. Although initially London was still trying to get the Netherlands on its side in August 1914, Dutch neutrality was actually a better option for Great Britain. Dutch involvement in the war would soon have led to a German occupation of the Netherlands, which would have been strategically unfavourable for the British. The UK's most important objective was to prevent the Netherlands from being an 'airway' for Germany, and London had effective tools for doing this, as was to emerge between 1914 and 1918.

The decision as to whether the Netherlands could remain neutral was thus actually in German and British hands. Obviously, the need for the Dutch to steer a careful neutral course was a condition. And indeed the Netherlands went to great lengths to do exactly that throughout the war. This did not mean there was no sympathy for any of the belligerents. For example, the Dutch prime minister during the war – P. W. A. Cort van der Linden – was pro-German and was consequently referred to in the British embassy as 'Caught unter den Linden'. Nevertheless, he pursued a consistent policy of neutrality based on international law.[105] The Netherlands would not be a beneficiary if either side won the war. In fact, Dutch interests would be served best by the restoration of a European power balance in which the country's independence would be able to thrive.

During the early years of the war, the primary issue was the extent to which the Netherlands could be an 'airway' for Germany. Under international law Britain was entitled to obstruct the supply of goods that directly or indirectly enabled Germany to wage war. From the beginning, the British interpreted these rules such that Dutch imports were severely restricted. In the autumn of 1914 Britain moreover declared the North Sea a war zone and laid extensive mine fields, which made things extremely difficult for free seagoing shipping. This repeatedly led to tensions with London and, after the United States had joined the Allies in 1917, with Washington too. Relations reached rock bottom in March 1918 when approximately 135 Dutch merchant vessels were seized and the Allies subsequently demanded that they be used to transport troops to the continent. By then there had not been any question of an 'airway' for a long time; at most there was extensive smuggling between the Netherlands and Germany. Now the German high command made its own demands on the Netherlands, including military transport through Dutch territory and the supply of construction materials. For a brief period during this crisis in April 1918 it looked as though German troops were going to invade the Netherlands. That had also been the case in April 1917, but then too the danger had receded.[106]

Figure 18 *The Netherlands in 1914: caught in the firing line.*
International Institute of Social History, Amsterdam.

During the war the Netherlands suffered great damage from the Allied blockade policy and the German submarine war. At the beginning of 1915, Germany also declared the North Sea a war zone, after which the Dutch were repeatedly shocked by alarming reports about torpedoed merchantmen. The resulting fierce anti-German sentiments became even stronger when Germany declared unrestricted submarine warfare in 1917. Dutch ships were among the victims. During the course of the war the Netherlands thus increasingly became a football for the belligerent nations because it did not have the means to resist. The warring parties also realized this of course, and so could repeatedly increase the pressure on The Hague.

Economic historian Hein Klemann argues that the economic consequences of the First World War for the Netherlands can broadly speaking be put under two headings.[107] First, international trade came to a virtual standstill because of the war, and the number of vessels calling at Dutch ports had fallen by 90 per cent by the end of hostilities. The ability to meet the needs of the population was not threatened until the beginning of

1917, but the announcement of unlimited submarine warfare and American entry into the war soon changed this situation. Industrial output fell, unemployment rose and food rationing was introduced. Acute food shortages during the summer of 1917 provoked a potato riot in Amsterdam, and people were killed and injured. There were also food disturbances and looting in other towns and cities in 1917 and 1918. At the same time, large profits were being made in agriculture, the black market flourished and other war profiteers also did well. These factors increased the gap between rich and poor during the last years of the war, and large sections of the population became increasingly dissatisfied. During the summer and autumn of 1918 there was consequently little left of the sense of national solidarity that had emerged under the threat of war in August 1914.

On the other hand, the war also had benefits for the Dutch economy in the longer term. Declining trade and the disappearance of most foreign competition stimulated industry, which meant it could both dominate the domestic market and build up a good position for its postwar competitiveness. Large integrated enterprises emerged. The doubling in the number of Dutch companies listed on the Amsterdam stock exchange between 1913 and 1920 is telling. The dramatic fall in imports of coal during the war was a tremendous shot in the arm for the domestic mining industry, and helped enable the Netherlands to meet the lion's share of domestic demand in the 1920s. Food shortages during the last years of the war were also a significant factor in the adoption of the Zuiderzee Act in 1918, in which it was decided to turn large parts of Zuiderzee, the later Lake IJssel, into polders. Eventually, tens of thousands of hectares of agricultural land would be created. More generally, conditions during the war forced the Dutch state to adopt a position as an economic player more than before. It is justified to conclude that the First World War prompted the Netherlands to implement a process of accelerated industrialization and industrial modernization, which laid the foundations for favourable economic trends between the wars.

In 1917, as the war entered its decisive phase and a difficult period began for the Netherlands, in domestic politics a fundamental amendment to the constitution passed with almost universal agreement. It provided a definitive solution for two issues that had been at the top of the political agenda since the late nineteenth century – the school controversy and the suffrage issue. Although the religious parties had made progress in the preceding decades in obtaining equal treatment for private denominational schools, they had still not achieved equal rights with public education. The situation with the suffrage issue was similar. There had been gradual advancement – in 1913, 67 per cent of men over twenty-five were entitled to vote – but still no universal suffrage. Although there was no substantive link between the two questions, they would both be resolved in the Pacification of 1917.

Without a parliamentary majority, the liberal minority government formed in 1913 was theoretically unstable, but it remained firmly in the saddle because the First World War had broken out. In these circumstances the political parties gave national unity high priority, and bringing down an incumbent government was clearly not consistent with this. In addition, Prime Minister Cort van der Linden – who like his distant predecessor Thorbecke was a law professor – soon let it be known he wanted to work towards a historical compromise in the suffrage and school questions that would benefit all parties. Cort van der Linden presented himself not as a great liberal reformer, but as a man who understood the signs of the times and implemented what he deemed politically necessary.[108] Here too he was displaying similarities to Thorbecke, who had said of himself that he did not carry out his role according to political theory, but 'as events dictated'. The reform proposals from Cort van der Linden's government, which had been on the table since 1914, covered universal suffrage, abolition of the constituency system, and proportional representation. Every voter would have one vote, the Lower House would have a hundred members and the electoral threshold would be about 1 per cent. These proposals made clear the outlines of the new suffrage and electoral system that came into effect with the 1917 constitutional amendment.[109]

Working out a system for female suffrage proved more of a challenge. Feminists were campaigning for votes for women and in September 1915 they submitted 150,000 signatures to the prime minister to underline their demands, but there was no parliamentary majority in favour. Many religious delegates were opposed to female suffrage, only a few liberals made a case for it, and social democrats gave priority to the rapid introduction of male suffrage. In the end, the constitutional amendment of 1917 granted women passive suffrage and active female suffrage was made possible in principle, but not yet introduced. This was done in 1919 with straightforward electoral legislation, but it was not until the 1922 Lower House elections that there was actual universal suffrage for the first time.

Although agreement about how to resolve the suffrage issue was reached quite rapidly, it was some time before parliament dealt with it. The religious parties first wanted clarity about the effect of the constitutional amendment with regard to the school controversy. A proposal that could count on substantial acceptance was forthcoming for that too. From now on, public and Christian primary education would be financed equally by the state, provided that the quality requirements applicable to all schools were met. Both issues were debated in the Lower House at the end of 1916. The suffrage change was adopted unanimously, and there was only one vote against adopting the solution to the school issue. This overwhelming majority did not mean there was no uneasiness among a few delegates, but the desire to resolve these issues, which had been dragging on for so long, was stronger. Most of the former differences about both issues between liberal and religious points of view were furthermore defused so that broadly based supra-party agreement was created in the political middle ground.

The 1917 amendment to the constitution has gone down in history as the Pacification, and it had far-reaching consequences for the political culture. First, parliament was definitively no longer *for* the people, but *of* the people (Loots).[110] Under the 1848 constitution, the representative body was sovereign, but now it was the people, represented by political parties. This brings us to the second important change in the political culture. The introduction of proportional representation meant that the tone was now set by national parties, and no longer by individual delegates who were elected in a constituency on the grounds of their special qualities. The political system was now all about parties and, as the historian Piet de Rooy remarks, that made it necessary to professionalize and form parties at a national level.[111] A third significant consequence for the political culture was that cooperation between religious and liberal politicians became possible after the Pacification. Even though there was not to be actual cooperation in government until the 1930s, the obstacles that had existed before 1917 had disappeared.

Now that the controversial issues from the past between liberals and religious delegates had lost their significance, the content of the political concepts of 'left' and 'right' also changed. Until 1917, religious members, who always sat on the right-hand side of the speaker, were on the 'right', whereas liberals and social democrats had their seats on the left-hand side of the speaker and were referred to as being on the 'left'. The 'right' thus had the common feature that its political foundations lay in Christian beliefs, while on the 'left' were members who rejected politics based on faith. The contrasts between left and right were substantially different after 1917 and now indicated where parties stood on the social question.

The Pacification also brought major changes to education. In 1910, 38 per cent of children went to Christian schools, but this percentage skyrocketed after there was financial equality. By 1920, it had already grown to 45 per cent and in 1930, it reached 62 per cent. It increased even more after 1945 and ultimately three-quarters of children would be given instruction in a Christian school. It is remarkable that even after pillarization had lost its impact on politics and society in the 1970s and secularization had advanced, about two-thirds of children were still in Christian schools. The Pacification of 1917 left deep marks on Dutch education that are still visible today.[112]

CHAPTER 6
PILLARIZATION, STABILITY, CRISIS AND WAR (1918–1945)

Introduction

The fact that agreement about the constitution was reached in 1917 does not mean to say there was a generally accepted view about how the Netherlands should be organized. Opinion was too strongly divided for this to be the case. These divisions existed not just between the liberals and the Christian democrats on the one hand and the social democrats on the other. Conflicts between religion-based parties were also not insignificant and were to flare up repeatedly during the 1920s. Although Abraham Kuyper's 'antithesis' (see p. 159) may have grouped the population under the headings of 'believers' and 'unbelievers' and although the need for collaboration between 'believers' may have been stressed, during the interwar years there continued to be virulent anti-popery among Protestants, exacerbated by the Catholics' strong electoral position. The RKSP was, after all, always stronger than the two Protestant parties, the ARP and CHU, combined, with the result that Protestants were permanently on their guard against Roman Catholic 'domination'.

The Pacification of 1917 thus represented more than the end of the political and social conflict about how the Netherlands was to be structured. It also established the framework within which that dispute was continued against a backdrop of a changed balance of political power. Catholics and Protestants had achieved their joint objective of equal financial status for Christian education and together they had attained a comfortable position of power. It was therefore not surprising that their differences would manifest themselves more strongly than before. Catholics, acting with greater self-awareness, envisaged a different country from the one Protestants had in mind with their heritage of Protestant national consciousness. These differences amplified the process of pillarization, described briefly in the previous chapter as a phenomenon of making vertical divisions in Dutch politics and society by creating Protestant, Catholic, social democratic and 'neutral'/liberal pillars, or compartments. The issue now was how the Dutch as a nation should develop and who would be able to achieve their objectives at the same time. Clearly the Protestants and Catholics wanted to strengthen their own bastions in order to maximize their own influence. During this period the social democrats also focused on establishing their pillar. Their isolated position in national politics, internal lurches between a Marxist agenda and a growing realization of the need for reform, and simultaneously the threat of disintegration on the left wing, made it all the more important to reinforce their own 'red family'. The upshot was continuation apace of the process of pillarization, or segmentation, after 1917 – a defining feature of the interwar years. The political and cultural trends that emerged during this period are discussed. The theoretical construct of 'pillarization', which has had such a significant impact on Dutch history and politics is also addressed.

The Dutch economy recovered quickly from the aftermath of the First World War in the 1920s. This period of strong growth and modernization was followed by a sharp decline during the world economic crisis in the 1930s, which lasted longer in the Netherlands than in many other countries. The nadir was not reached until the winter of 1935–36, when the unemployment rate rose to around 20 per cent. This also had implications for faith in parliamentary democracy, but support for anti-democratic movements remained limited. The Netherlands responded to the growing international tensions with a policy of strict neutrality in the hope that the country could once again remain on the sidelines in the event of war. This hope proved baseless when the Germans invaded on 10 May 1940. This was followed by a five-year occupation which, beginning relatively moderately, rapidly descended into repression and terror. Jews soon became victims. The southern part of the country was liberated in the autumn of 1944, but in the rest of the nation liberation did not come until March–May 1945, after a terrible winter famine and thousands of deaths. The concept of pillarization is discussed before the developments during the interwar years and between 1940 and 1945 are addressed.

Pillarization

The Politics of Accommodation: Pluralism and Democracy in the Netherlands, a book by the Dutch-American political scientist Arend Lijphart, was published in 1968. The Dutch edition appeared that same year under the title *Verzuiling, pacificatie en kentering in de Nederlandse politiek*.[1] It soon became a classic and developed into the most influential study of the essence of Dutch politics and political culture in the twentieth century. The concept of 'pillarization', or politico-denominational segregation, makes it possible to create the organizational and ideological sitemap of society and politics at a particular moment in time. Lijphart formulated criteria pertaining to pillarization: one's own ideological beliefs, one's own social organizations/civil society, the presence of formal and informal links between the different organizations in a compartment or pillar, a standoffish attitude to other compartments and actions by the pillar elites to promote the interests of their respective compartments. When translated into everyday life in a pillarized community, this meant that the key facets of life – faith, politics, representation of interests, leisure and social contacts – were played out chiefly in one's own circle, and that the vast majority of the population had barely any contact with members of other pillars. It can be argued on the basis of these criteria that the Catholics were the most segregated group in the Netherlands, followed by the Protestants, with the social democrats a distant third. The compartment containing the liberals was created rather unwillingly since they did not strive for pillarization. Strictly organized segregated networks were at odds with liberal principles, and therefore in a way the liberals were 'left over' after the other groups in the population, organized along ideological lines, had withdrawn inside their own compartments.

Political and social segmentation along philosophical dividing lines is not, of course, a specifically Dutch phenomenon. Comparable examples are to be found in other countries too. The historian Hans Righart, for example, compared pillarization involving Catholics in the Netherlands, Austria, Switzerland and Belgium and identified many similarities and common factors.[2] Until 1933 there were four major 'social milieus' in Germany (Catholic, conservative Protestant, liberal (Protestant) and socialist), which in some ways matched the Dutch pillars. Other countries also had vertical segmentation. Lijphart concluded, however, that in the Netherlands there were deeper dividing lines between the pillars, a more fundamental compartmentalization in political and socioeconomic matters and greater solidarity between parties, pressure groups and publicity media inside the pillars. A typical feature of the Dutch situation was the exceptional stability of the democratic existing order for a lengthy period. According to Lijphart, this combination of rigid vertical segmentation and a stable democracy was specific to the Netherlands. He asked himself how it was possible that, in such a divided country with so many religious and other minorities living alongside one another without meaningful contacts, a durable stable democracy could nevertheless exist. One would after all expect, given the independence of the pillars and the absence of links between them, that the Dutch political establishment would be insufficiently cohesive and would therefore have to be unstable. Lijphart's explanation for why this was not the case was the overarching cooperation between the leadership of the pillars since the Pacification of 1917. Thanks to the elites and their teamwork, the compartments established links at the top. This gave the pillars a common roof, as it were, providing the theoretically shaky structure of the Netherlands with stability. In Lijphart's opinion, this collaboration was governed by specific political rules and it was these rules that propped up the stability of Dutch pacification democracy between 1917 and 1967. Obviously, these were not formally recorded rules, let alone statutorily prescribed ones. Nor was there national consensus, deeply rooted in the different pillars. What it boiled down to is that the elites adopted the same attitude to the basic principles of politics and decision making. Lijphart concluded from the conduct of these elites that they had a responsible and targeted approach (*Rule I: The Business of Politics*) that they accepted the philosophical principles of the other pillars (*Rule II: The Agreement to Disagree*) and that they subjected important issues to joint decision making (*Rule III: Summit Diplomacy*). The rules also included a balanced distribution of finance and appointments across the pillars (*Rule IV: Proportionality*) the reduction of complicated political situations to technical issues (*Rule V: Depoliticization*) and restraint in providing the outside world with information in order to facilitate compromises (*Rule VI: Secrecy*). Finally, the political parties gave the government sufficient leeway to implement pacification politics (*Rule VII: The Government's Right to Govern*). According to Lijphart these rules largely defined the political culture, which created the impression that Dutch politics during the pillarization era was dull and featureless. This was not because there were no disputes or because a general consensus existed. That was impossible given the conflicting ideologies. The reason was that the leaders harmoniously and deliberately ensured that emotions remained contained and tension was defused. These rules worked in practice because the vast majority of the population were politically apathetic and accepted discipline within their own ideological compartments. The tone in which the elites addressed their respective constituencies – and the way they imposed discipline on them – differed radically from the way debates were conducted between leaderships. If the businesslike approach referred to above dominated in these debates, within the pillars the elites dictated directions using highly ideologically tinged pronouncements and they kept a careful watch over the ideological purity of their own compartments. According to Lijphart it was this pillarized structure that provided stability in Dutch politics between 1917 and 1967. This situation ended in Lijphart's view with the results of the 1967 general election, when the losses of the large pillar-based political parties, the electoral breakthrough of new groups and the changing political climate clearly demonstrated that the rules and characteristics of pacification politics had lost their cohesive power.

This is not the place to recount thoroughly the debate about pillarization that went on for decades, but a few key points should be mentioned. Critics rightly pointed out that Lijphart used a segmentation of Dutch society that was much too schematic and took no account of regional differences or of the different degrees of pillarization among Catholics, Protestants, social democrats and liberals. As we have seen, the liberals formed a compartment unwillingly and were by no means homogeneous. The Protestant pillar could similarly not be considered as a unit because it consisted of different denominations and political parties. In many cases there were several places of worship, even in small villages, and the members of these different churches lived partially in separate worlds. If the focus is exclusively on the four major groups, smaller minorities that do not belong to them are lost from view. The communists, for example, who had between about 2 and just under 4 per cent of the vote in elections in the 1920s and 1930s, encapsulated themselves in their own mini-compartment. That was also the case for the no less isolated national socialists in the 1930s. The Jewish minority is also kept out of the picture if an analysis concentrates solely on the four main pillars. Where politics were concerned, there were Jews among the social democrats, liberals and communists, but when it came to religion they created their own mini-pillar. Summarizing, the Netherlands was a country of many minorities. Concentration on the four largest groups blocks the view of that significant diversity.

Lijphart furthermore contended that pacification politics was a deliberate choice by the elites to guarantee political stability. But was it not rather the case that leaders had to cooperate because the Netherlands has traditionally been a nation of many minorities in which majorities only existed through cooperation? The fact that Lijphart only considered pacification politics and the associated rules to be applicable to the 1917–67 period and in so doing also explained the political stability during those decades is similarly open to question. Following this line of reasoning, the years before 1917 and after 1967 should have been characterized by instability, but this was not the case. This appears to demolish a major part of the underpinning of Lijphart's pacification hypothesis, because he believed that pacification politics were a deliberate choice made by the elites to prevent instability. If, however, there was no instability prior to 1917 and there was no threat of it, what are Lijphart's arguments based on? And above all, did he not ignore the historical roots of collaboration between leaders of the pillars?

The Leiden political scientist Hans Daalder was more convincing. In his now famous 1964 lecture he explained the conduct of Dutch elites, the decision-making process and the phenomenon of 'depoliticization' in historical terms. To do this he went back to the era of the Republic of the Seven United Provinces.[3] According to Daalder, the Republic was a 'merchant republic' in which compromises were an obvious necessity. In later publications Daalder also emphasized the legacy of the Republic, which was not a unitary state but a patchwork quilt of provinces, autonomous towns and cities, and manors in which 'diversity was a fact and a norm' in politics, religion and government. Against this backdrop, the leaders developed a tradition of consensus building – a process in which all parties negotiate and compromise in order to achieve an outcome that satisfies everyone. The fundamental principle during the Republic was to seek agreement, not force decisions. This historical tradition is also clearly recognizable in the conduct of the pillar elites in the twentieth century. At the same time this obviously does not mean that political decision making in the Netherlands since the late sixteenth century has always been based on consultation and a search for consensus. There are too many examples in Dutch history of fiercely fought political conflicts for that to be true. It can be asserted, however, that Lijphart's rules of pacification democracy were not devised and introduced by the elites in the early twentieth century. These rules, which can be described as a system for achieving peaceful solutions between opposing groups, have a long history and are part of a historically formed political culture.[4] Although Lijphart later admitted that traditions also had an influence on the creation of the elites' political rules,[5] his approach is remiss from a historical point of view.

Even if criticism is appropriate with regard to the period before 1917, the question arises as to whether his theory is also tenable for the years after 1967. The Netherlands remained a stable democracy after 1967 and, looking ahead to the next chapter, it can be stated here that comparable political rules, which Lijphart characterized as typical features of pillarization and pacification democracy, can be observed in the *depillarized* Dutch political culture of the late twentieth century. Apparently, these rules are more deeply rooted in Dutch political culture than Lijphart realized, and that too undermines his approach.

Although the pillarization debate revolved around Lijphart from 1968 onwards, the academic debate in the 1950s was conducted by sociologists. The sociologist Jacques van Doorn described pillarization as a system of social control in which the pillar-related organizations' primary purpose was to safeguard the group's own ideology and philosophy (*social control theory*). From a comparable perspective one can postulate that pillarization was nothing more than a defensive ecclesiastical strategy to shield the faithful from the influences of industrialization by developing home-grown subcultures (pillars or compartments), thus fending off secularization, materialism and the heathen class struggle (*protection theory*). From the point of view of political history, one can assert that pillarization was not just an instrument to safeguard a particular constituency from undesirable external influences. It was also intended to facilitate moving with the times while maintaining group identity. According to this approach, pillarization played a role in the national integration of the different groups in the population, which in the Netherlands was conducted on a segmented basis (*modernization theory*). It should be pointed out in this regard that the creation of modern political parties and pillarization were simultaneous phenomena that were also interlinked. Continuing this line of reasoning, pillarization can also be categorized as an instrument for and result of the emancipation of minorities. This approach therefore considers pillarization as a phenomenon that provided the opportunity, from the late nineteenth century onwards, for Catholics, Protestants and social democrats to get organized with like-minded people and then become emancipated in political and social arenas (*emancipation theory*).

The number of theories about the phenomenon of pillarization is therefore considerable and the value of the different approaches depends very much on the research questions, the period investigated, the pillarized organizations, the region etc. being addressed. Whether one's analysis of pillarization is from the point of view of social control, protection, modernization, emancipation or Lijphart's pacification theory, no single approach provides conclusive answers to the many questions associated with the phenomenon. It is also important to be continually aware of the historical context in which, and analytical coherence with which, 'pillarization' is being addressed. It furthermore emerges that the different approaches, some of them contradictory, are not necessarily mutually exclusive. Pillarization contributed to the emancipation of groups in the population, but was also an instrument for social control and disciplining. It provided protection from external influences and conserved a group's social environment, yet at the same time was a vehicle for modernization. And despite all the criticism that can be aimed at Lijphart, his pacification theory continues to make a significant contribution to political and historical discussions about the Netherlands in the twentieth century.

Standing back and viewing the debate about the concept of pillarization from a distance, it is fair to say it is impossible to give an unambiguous scholarly definition.[6] The historian Blom offers a pragmatic solution. According to Blom, if one uses the concept of 'pillarization' as a metaphor, something emerges clearly without complicated descriptions. Pillarization as a metaphor is 'an indication of four-way segmentation in Dutch society that manifested itself in very diverse ways and that resulted from a number of different but intimately entwined processes'. Blom adds that if one wants to analyse those processes in detail, the concept is of less help and additional terminology, appropriate to the phrasing of the question, needs to be developed.[7] In other words, even though the concept of 'pillarization' cannot be given a sufficiently precise scholarly definition, it has a useful function as a metaphor that illuminates – an approach that deserves to be followed up.

Politics and the economy between the wars (1918–40)

The first elections under the suffrage rules laid down in the 1917 constitution were held in July 1918. All men aged twenty-five or over could vote under a proportional representation system. The outcome was a fundamental departure from all previous results. At the same time, a party-political landscape emerged that was to have a high degree of stability and continuity until the 1960s. Dutch politics were dominated during these decades by a pillarized spectrum, and religious parties virtually always had a parliamentary majority. Their position of power was unassailable between the wars. They ruled alone until 1933, then jointly with liberals until 1937. A coalition government that included social democrats alongside Christian democrats and left-wing liberals did not form until 1939.

The strong position of Catholics was a striking feature of the 1918 election results. They benefitted most from the introduction of proportional representation. As we have seen, they had a huge majority in Limburg and North Brabant. Under the constituency system, this meant that many Catholic votes were always 'lost'. After 1917, the Catholics were able to convert their position as a large minority (35 per cent of the population) into political coinage. Almost without interruption, their party was to acquire the biggest share of electoral support (some 30 per cent) and remain permanently in government until the 1970s, when they joined with the ARP and the CHU in the broad-based Christian Democratic Party, the CDA. The Protestants, on the other hand, were divided into a number of parties, of which the ARP and CHU were the most important. For many years at a stretch their joint share of the vote was between 20 and approximately 30 per cent (see illustration 3, p. 190–2).

This comfortable Christian democrat electoral position contrasted with the decline of the liberals. They had dominated politics in the nineteenth century, but the achievement of citizenship for the male population led to dwindling political liberalism.[8] While between them the various liberal parties had just about 20 per cent of the votes in 1918, this percentage soon decreased to between 10 and 15, and sank into single figures in the 1930s. Yet the long-lasting reinforcement of the Christian democrat camp and the weakening of the liberal parties did not mean that the role of liberal ideas was played out. Christian democrat dominated governments in the 1920s and 1930s continued to build on existing liberal national and economic foundations. The historian Woltjer tellingly describes politics between 1918 and 1940 as 'a liberal legacy under Christian democrat management'.[9]

The 1918 electoral results were particularly disappointing for the SDAP. The party got no more than 22 per cent of the votes, and that percentage was to remain more or less constant in the 1920s and 1930s. Social democrats had to conclude bitterly that they – who had fought the hardest for universal suffrage – reaped almost none of the rewards, while Christian democrats walked off with all the prizes. They had failed to detach Catholic and Protestant workers from their pillars. The presence of three small radical left-wing parties was another problem for the SDAP. Although they had no more than 4 per cent of the votes between them, they were a constant electoral threat. If the SDAP were to be unable to cover the left wing of the labour movement sufficiently, there was a danger it would lose voters to the small left-wing parties.

A striking result of the 1918 election was that a large number of splinter parties succeeded in winning parliamentary seats – a phenomenon we still see today. This arises

Party	1918	1922	1925	1929	1933	1937	1946	1948	1952	1956	1959	1963	1967	1971	1972	1977	1981	1982	1986	1989	1994	1998	2002	2003	2006	2010	2012	2017
RELIGIOUS PARTIES																												
RKSP/KVP	30.0	29.9	28.6	29.6	27.9	28.8	30.8	31.0	28.7	31.7	31.6	31.9	28.5	21.9	17.7	-	-	-	-	-	-	-	-	-	-	-	-	-
ARP	13.4	13.7	12.2	11.6	13.4	16.4	12.9	13.2	11.3	9.9	9.4	8.7	9.9	8.6	8.8	-	-	-	-	-	-	-	-	-	-	-	-	-
CHU	6.6	10.9	9.9	10.5	9.1	7.5	7.8	9.2	8.9	8.4	8.1	8.5	8.1	6.3	4.8	-	-	-	-	-	-	-	-	-	-	-	-	-
CDA	-	-	-	-	-	-	-	-	-	-	-	-	-	-	-	31.9	30.8	29.4	34.6	35.3	22.2	18.4	27.9	28.6	26.5	13.6	8.5	12.4
Orth. prot. parties	-	0.9	2.0	2.3	2.5	1.9	2.1	2.4	3.1	3.0	2.9	3.0	2.9	4.0	4.0	3.7	4.1	4.2	3.6	4.1	4.8	5.1	3.7	4.2	5.6	5.0	5.2	5.5
LEFT-WING PARTIES																												
SDAP/PvdA	22.0	19.4	22.9	23.8	21.5	22.0	28.3	25.6	29.0	32.7	30.4	28.0	23.6	24.6	27.3	33.8	28.3	30.4	33.3	31.9	24.0	29.0	15.1	27.3	21.2	19.6	24.7	5.7
Green Left	-	-	-	-	-	-	-	-	-	-	-	-	-	-	-	-	-	-	-	4.1	3.5	7.3	7.0	5.1	4.6	6.6	2.3	9.1
SP	-	-	-	-	-	-	-	-	-	-	-	-	-	-	-	-	-	-	-	-	1.3	3.5	5.9	6.3	16.6	9.9	9.6	9.1
Small left-wing parties	2.3	1.8	1.2	2.0	3.2	3.4	10.6	7.7	6.2	4.8	4.2	5.8	6.5	7.1	10.8	4.2	6.2	5.8	3.1	-	-	-	-	-	-	-	-	-
LIBERAL PARTIES																												
LSP/PvdV/VVD	14.0	9.3	8.7	7.4	7.0	4.0	6.4	8.0	8.8	8.8	12.2	10.3	10.8	10.3	14.5	18.0	13.3	23.1	17.4	14.6	20.0	24.7	15.4	18.0	14.7	20.4	26.5	21.3
D66	-	-	-	-	-	-	-	-	-	-	-	-	4.5	6.8	4.2	5.4	11.1	4.3	6.1	7.9	15.5	9.0	5.1	4.1	2.0	6.9	7.9	12.2
VDB	5.3	4.6	6.1	6.2	5.1	5.9	-	-	-	-	-	-	-	-	-	-	-	-	-	-	-	-	-	-	-	-	-	-
OTHERS																												
LPF	-	-	-	-	-	-	-	-	-	-	-	-	-	-	-	-	-	-	-	-	-	-	17.1	5.7	-	-	-	-
PVV	-	-	-	-	-	-	-	-	-	-	-	-	-	-	-	-	-	-	-	-	-	-	-	-	5.9	15.5	10.1	13.1

Continued

Illustration 3 Lower House election results 1918–2017.

Party	Name	Political category
RELIGIOUS PARTIES		
RKSP/KVP	Rooms-Katholieke Staatspartij/Katholieke Volkspartij	Roman Catholic, KVP succeeded the RKSP in 1946
ARP	Anti-Revolutionaire Partij	Protestant
CHU	Christelijke-Historische Unie	Protestant
CDA	Christen-Democratisch Appèl	Christian democrat
	KVP, ARP and CHU worked together as CDA from 1977	
ORTHODOX PROTESTANT PARTIES		
GPV	Gereformeerd Politiek Verbond	Orthodox Protestant
SGP	Staatkundig Gereformeerde Party	Orthodox Protestant
RPF	Reformatorische Politieke Federatie	Orthodox Protestant
CU	GPV and RPF merged in 2001 under the name ChristenUnie	Orthodox Protestant
LEFT-WING PARTIES		
SDAP/PvdA	Sociaal-Democratische Arbeiderspartij/Party van de Arbeid	Social democrat
GL	Groen Links	'Green', progressive
SP	Socialistische Partij	Socialist

SMALL LEFT-WING PARTIES

CPN	Communistische Partij van Nederland	Communist
PPR	Politieke Partij Radicalen	Splinter party of the KVP, progressive
PSP	Pacifistisch Socialistische Partij	Pacifist, socialist
CPN, PPR and PSP merged in 1989/90 under the name Groen Links (see p. 191)		

LIBERAL PARTIES

LSP/PvdV/VVD	Liberale Staatspartij/Partij van Vrijheid/Volkspartij voor Vrijheid en Democratie	Conservative liberal, LSP until 1946, PvdV until 1948, since then VVD
D66	Democraten 66	Left wing-liberal
VDB	Vrijzinnig Democratische Bond	Left wing-liberal

OTHERS

LPF	Lijst Pim Fortuyn	Right wing-populist
PVV	Partij voor de Vrijheid	Right wing-populist, anti-Islam

from the combination of proportional representation and a very low electoral threshold. In 1918, the Lower House had seventeen parties, of which nearly half – eight – had only one seat. Although it was made somewhat more difficult for small parties to enter the Lower House from 1922, between ten and fourteen would always be represented in it until 1940. During these years only three of them – the RKSP, SDAP and ARP – received over 10 per cent in all Lower House elections.[10] This system had the democratic advantage of being relatively simple for new political movements to be given a voice. But this multiplicity of parties also gave rise to dissatisfaction and unease. This was very much the case in the 1930s, when the democratic establishment proved ineffective and unsuccessful in tackling the economic crisis.

There was nevertheless a high degree of electoral stability between 1918 and 1940, as emerges from illustration 4. Given this political equation, it is not surprising that governments between the wars were virtually completely under the control of the Christian political parties: they governed for seventeen of the twenty-two years without liberals and/or social democrats and there were only three prime ministers between 1918 and 1940 (see Illustration 5). Upon closer examination, though, it is clear that the religion-based parties had their differences. None of the governments between the wars survived to the end of their four-year term, and the three prime ministers presided over a total of ten cabinets, which had an average lifetime of just over two years. The bonds between the three Christian democrat parties depended very largely on their common distaste for the secular parties, which they could keep out in the cold thanks to their joint majority. But their agreement on political, economic and social matters was limited, as

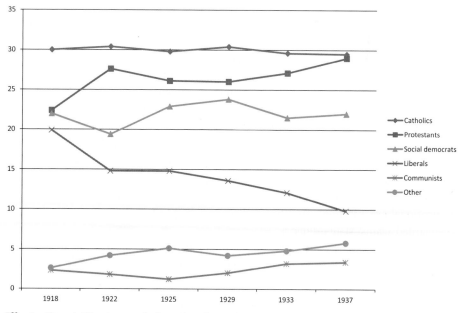

Illustration 4 Election results by political movement 1918–1937 (in per cent).

Cabinets

Christian democrats   Conservative liberals   Social democrats   Left-wing liberals   Other

1918-1922 Ruys de Beerenbrouck (ARP, CHU, RKSP)
1922-1925 Ruys de Beerenbrouck (ARP, CHU, RKSP)
1925-1926 Colijn (ARP, CHU, RKSP)
1926-1929 De Geer (ARP, CHU, RKSP)
1929-1933 Ruys de Beerenbrouck (ARP, CHU, RKSP)
1933-1935 Colijn (ARP, CHU, RKSP, VDB, LSP)
1935-1937 Colijn (ARP, CHU, RKSP, VDB, LSP)
1937-1939 Colijn (ARP, CHU, RKSP)
1939 Colijn (ARP, CHU, LSP)
1939-1940 De Geer (ARP, RKSP, CHU, VDB, SDAP)
1940-1945 Gerbrandy (Government in exile with many changes of ministers)

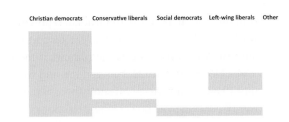

Illustration 5 Coalition governments 1918–1940.

was their willingness to resolve their differences. According to the historian Jac Bosmans, the result was 'a network of political compromises', and governments usually stumbled from one crisis to the next.[11]

There were several reasons for this lack of harmony. Firstly, while Catholics and Protestants achieved a major common objective through the Pacification of 1917 (equal rights and position for denominational education), they had no joint answers as to how Dutch politics, economics and society should be shaped. Viewed in this light, the Pacification of 1917 was not so much the end of a political and social dispute about suffrage and the financing of education, but rather a framework in which the conflict about the structure and organization of the Netherlands could continue with a changed balance of political power. It was therefore inevitable that the differences between Catholics and Protestants would come to the fore more prominently than before. The Catholics, whose actions now reflected their greater self-assurance, had more seats than the Protestant ARP and CHU combined and were continually faced with Protestant 'vigilance' with regard to this 'dominance'. In some cases there was blatant anti-popery. In 1926, for example, some of the Protestants wanted to withdraw Dutch diplomatic representation from the Vatican, after which the Catholics left the government. Collaboration at government level often remained difficult in later years too.

There were also fundamental differences in views about the best relationship between state and society. Protestants resolutely maintained Kuyper's 'sovereignty in your own circle' and so built a protective shield against a ubiquitous and controlling state. As we saw in the previous chapter, the anti-revolutionaries based their politics on the 'organic society' predating the French Revolution, in which different groups with organic links worked together and had not yet been driven apart by industrial capitalism and Enlightenment ideas – or so they believed. To approach this old, idealized situation as closely as was practicable, the independence of groups and bonds in society – the family, occupational organizations, societies and so on – had to be as strong as possible and safeguarded against state influence.

Under the subsidiarity principle, the Catholics also turned against the all-powerful centralized state, but the principle of decentralizing functions was not opposed to the fundamental concept of state influence. In social and economic matters, for instance, the government should play an organizing role, where employers and employees in an industry would make agreements about wages, production, innovation, training and so on under its supervision. Central government was thus assigned a major responsibility in this Catholic organizational thinking. Collaboration between Catholics and social democrats on manifesto matters would consequently prove easier, although it was the mid-1930s before the Catholics were prepared for this. In turn, many Protestants were closer to liberal views about state restraint. These interdenominational differences were still manageable during the economic prosperity of the 1920s, but in the depression years they put cooperation between Catholics and Protestants in government under immense pressure.

Looking at the performance of the political system during this period, and asking to what extent Lijphart's rules of pacification democracy (see p. 185) apply, it is necessary to once again point out that a subtle interpretation of Lijphart's approach is appropriate. Firstly, it emerged that even cooperation between denominations was often not a matter of businesslike politics and dissemination of pragmatic tolerance. The many cabinet crises, the difficult government formation negotiations and fierce anti-popery among Protestants emphasize how narrow the joint basis usually was. The elites did not display adroitness, and although the political system was stable, as a rule it came across as powerless. Secondly, it is striking that throughout the interwar years the social democrats remained outside political debate at the top level, and were thus not a part of the political elite in the sense that Lijphart used the term. During these years the liberals were often also not involved in political consultation between the pillar elites. From this perspective, political relationships at that time were dominated more by the antithesis between Christian and non-Christian than by the rules of Lijphart's pacification democracy.

In parallel with the often laborious collaboration within the cabinet, there was a process of ongoing pillarization in society during the interwar years. Even before 1918, as we have seen, every pillar had its own party or parties, union and press, but after the war the pillars expanded to cover virtually everything in the life of the community. It went without saying that a new and modern phenomenon like broadcasting (radio) would be organized along pillarized lines, with the result that pillar-based broadcasting organizations were created in the 1920s, for example, the Catholic Radio Broadcasting System (KRO), the Dutch Christian Radio Association (NCRV) and the social democratic Workers' Association of Radio Amateurs (VARA). Pillarization also extended into fields not directly associated with specific religious objectives (sport, leisure, general cultural activities and the like), leading to further subcultural segmentation of the Netherlands. Led by clergy, the Catholics in particular developed a strong monolithic pillar that slowly but surely encompassed virtually all facets of life. This included the foundation of the Catholic University of Nijmegen (1923), an important breeding ground for the Catholic political and social elite in subsequent decades.

Like the Protestants and Catholics, the social democrats also vigorously continued the pillarization process between the wars. Their initial position in 1918 could hardly have been worse. The disappointment of the July election results was followed in November by a half-hearted attempt at revolution by SDAP leader Pieter Jelles Troelstra, which landed the party in political isolation. We saw in the last chapter that social and economic conditions in the Netherlands deteriorated dramatically during the last year of the war.

The social democrats' poor showing at the ballot box, agitation by small left-wing groups, food riots and unrest in the army and among the population had caused confusion and divisions about the party's future course. A revolution broke out in Germany on 9 November 1918, and in a turbulent Rotterdam on 11 November, Troelstra told demonstrators that the bourgeoisie was on the brink of handing over power to the workers' movement. The following day, during a speech in the Lower House that went on for hours, he demanded transfer of power and told the government it could no longer count on the support of the army and police. He argued that it was also in the interests of the bourgeois parties to get out of the driving seat because social democracy was the only force that could still halt the impending anarchy.[12]

But there was no anarchy, nor was there a revolutionary mood. The impulsive Troelstra consequently received no significant support for instigating a revolution from his own party. The government simply stayed in office, but security measures were tightened. The demonstrations that had taken place were not revolutionary but expressions of affection for Queen Wilhelmina and the monarchy.[13] Troelstra soon had to admit that he had made a mistake. The implications of the 'revolution that never was' were far-reaching. The positions of the royal house and the bourgeois parties were strengthened by it, while the integration of social democracy in the Netherlands suffered a major setback. Although Troelstra's party had given him almost no support, the stigma of unreliability would cling to it throughout the 1920s and 1930s.

During the interwar years, its election results hovered around the outcome in 1918 (22 per cent). Nevertheless social democratic organizations were growing hand over fist.[14] The number of party members nearly doubled between 1918 and 1930, rising from 37,000 to 70,000. The party was allied to the Dutch Association of Trade Unions (NVV), which expanded from 200,000 in 1919 to 300,000 in 1932. In 1929, the SDAP and NVV jointly established the publishers NV De Arbeiderspers. This was a shot in the arm for the social democratic press – the circulation of the national party newspaper, *Het Volk*, nearly trebled between 1927 and 1931 to almost 200,000 – and the movement now published its own books and magazines. Organizations like the Dutch Workers' Sports Association (NASB) and the Federation of Workers' Dramatic, Musical and Choral Associations added further dimensions to life in the 'red family'. There was the Federation of Social Democratic Women's Clubs for female party members. Its membership was about 12,000 and it was concerned primarily with education and training for women. The Workers' Youth Movement (AJC) led by Koos Vorrink – later to be party chairman – also became very well known. Members were aged between twelve and twenty-one.

From a political point of view, the Netherlands was thus divided into four movements during the 1920s and 1930s. Social life was permanently partitioned into 'moral communities' with their own identities, codes of conduct and customs.[15] According to the historian Ivo Schöffer, this impacted upon a person's style, use of language and behaviour to such an extent that 'it only took a minute of conversation with someone to know whether that individual was a Protestant, Catholic, liberal or socialist'.[16] This remained the case until long after the Second World War. It was not until the late 1960s that the intuitive sense described by Schöffer, and possessed by many Dutch people, gradually disappeared.

In terms of economics, the Christian democrat governments of the 1920s had a following wind. The Dutch economy suffered severely during the First World War, but, unlike many other European countries, the Netherlands sustained no actual war damage. The problems related primarily to international transport routes (blockades, submarine warfare, confiscation of shipping and so forth), and as soon as sea routes were free again in November 1918, a commercial boom – one of the most spectacular in the history of Dutch business – got under way.[17] Growth in manufacturing and services topped 10 per cent and the economy developed such a head of steam that the recession in the world economy that started at the end of 1920 had little impact in the Netherlands. Gross domestic product (GDP) continued to grow, even during the worst of the downturn between 1921 and 1923. From 1923 to 1929, there was annual growth of close to 7 per cent in exports, 8 per cent in private investments and nearly 3 per cent in consumption. The increase in international services was even more spectacular. Between 1920 and 1929 (except in 1923 and 1928) the annual rise in goods transhipped in Dutch ports increased by 16 per cent, largely thanks to transit trade with Germany. The Netherlands had never seen such growth – the figures actually exceeded those of the 1950s and 1960s, which are generally described in the history books as the greatest boom years.[18]

Even so, the global economic reverses of the early 1920s also took their toll on the Dutch. There was a serious banking crisis and government finances were in a wretched state at the time. High deficits compelled drastic spending cuts, which included reductions in salaries, welfare benefits and countless other government expenditures.

For many years, the interbellum era in the Netherlands has been associated with stagnation and conservatism. As we have seen, this is not inaccurate where political developments were concerned, but things were different in the business world. The 1920s saw strong economic modernization and dynamic development. During the last years of the decade, major established companies like Philips and the Anglo-Dutch Royal Dutch Shell group were joined by new multinationals such as the Anglo-Dutch Unilever and the Dutch-German Algemene Kunstzijde Unie (AKU). The Netherlands also developed its own steel industry. KLM Royal Dutch Airlines was founded in 1919 and soon thrived. Anthony H. G. Fokker's aircraft factory was one of the most successful of the era.

This modernization also included a major rationalization of farming, which resulted in significant productivity growth. Technology, research and development were important elements in this Second Industrial Revolution. It became a matter of course for major companies to set up and expand research institutes. The United States set the tone for a modern dynamic cultural pattern that was developing in the Netherlands and other Western countries, based on rationality, progressive thinking and a positive attitude to change. Irrespective of how great the political differences were between liberals, social democrats and Christian democrats, everyone put their shoulder to the wheel to increase output further for the general good through rationalization and the use of new technology.[19]

Companies, laboratories and higher education modernized, and, as everyone could see, the infrastructure did too. The rail network was largely completed around the turn of the century, but growth in passenger and freight transport did not really take off until after the First World War. Sections of track were electrified and timetables were improved. Road transport also increased. Long-distance buses gradually began to eclipse tram lines. Private cars were still rare, but traffic grew so quickly that both road and rail bridges were built across the major rivers. The construction of the Lake IJssel Dam between North Holland and Friesland and the reclamation of new polders in Lake IJssel, which started in the 1920s, were sensational. The primary objectives of these projects were a shorter coastline, better protection from water, less salinification of the surrounding areas and more agricultural land (see Map 10).

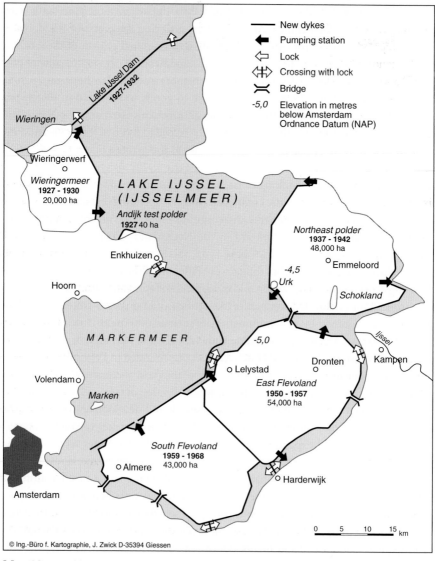

Map 10 Impoldering in the Zuiderzee/Lake IJssel 1927–1968.

Better transport links and technological innovation had 'shrunk' the Netherlands during the nineteenth century. This process of expanding internal communications accelerated in the 1920s. The number of telephone calls rocketed, thanks to new technology and reduced charges, although the number of telephone subscribers was still limited. For instance, in 1930 only 5–10 per cent of rural homes had a telephone, as opposed to 15–20 per cent in urban areas. Radio also contributed to breaking the mould of conventional ways to communicate. The wireless developed within the pillarized system, of course, and programme content was subject to strict government rules, but nevertheless it brought information into the nation's living rooms in a modern way. It developed into a mass medium in the 1930s. Compared with the yardsticks of the decades after 1945, modernization was certainly still limited and life continued to be far from dynamic, but from the perspective of contemporaries the Dutch were in a process of renewal that was bringing rapid changes in the workplace, homes, mobility and communication.[20]

The economic good times came to an end in 1929 when the Netherlands, too, fell victim to the Great Depression. At first the consequences were not too severe, but in 1931, when Britain abandoned the gold standard and devalued sterling and Germany introduced foreign exchange restrictions, the Dutch were also dragged down into the global slump. While the crisis made itself felt somewhat later in the Netherlands, it also lasted longer. In most European countries the nadir was reached in 1932 and recovery started in 1933, but the Dutch economy lagged behind. It was not until 1936, when the Netherlands also went off the gold standard and devalued the guilder that the country joined in the international recovery, although there was a brief interruption in 1938. The increase in unemployment followed the same trajectory. About 100,000 people were out of work in the Netherlands as 1930 ended. This figure rose to 300,000 by 1933, but the peak of nearly 590,000 jobless (about 20 per cent of the workforce) was not reached until the winter of 1935–36. The number of job seekers remained high despite the arrival of a resurgence in business. There were still 400,000 unemployed in the summer of 1937.

The Christian democrat and Christian democrat/liberal governments responded to the economic crisis with a policy of deflation and a dogged adherence to the gold standard. Their argument was that the economy would recover from the slump not by devaluing, but by lowering labour costs and reducing prices, and the Netherlands would be able to improve its international competitiveness. The government also had to play its part in cutting costs by spending less, for example by reducing civil servants' salaries and endeavouring to eliminate budget deficits. According to government parties, this policy of adapting to international economic conditions would lead to recovery as a matter of course. The alternative – following the British example of abandoning the gold standard and devaluation – was rejected because it would damage confidence in the Dutch financial sector and could furthermore lead to capital flight, inflation and undermining balanced budgets.

Retaining the gold standard consequently remained the guiding principle of the policy, but it came at a high price. The guilder was relatively expensive compared with the devalued pound, Dutch exports fell sharply, many business sectors sustained heavy losses and unemployment grew rapidly. After France and Switzerland also went off the gold standard in September 1936 and the Netherlands was left as the only surviving member of the gold bloc, The Hague turned its back on monetary orthodoxy and relinquished gold parity for the guilder. Its exchange rate fell by some 20 per cent, which brought it in line with the other devalued currencies (the British pound, Belgian, French and Swiss francs) and the economy turned around. Economic historian Van Zanden uses an international comparison to show that countries which devalued sooner performed better economically than those that clung to the gold standard. According to Van Zanden, Dutch unemployment would have been nearly 50 per cent lower in 1935 if the country had abandoned the gold standard in 1931 as the British had done.[21]

Meanwhile, there is consensus among historians that the Netherlands would have emerged from the depression more quickly had it implemented a different crisis policy, but people thought otherwise at the time. Alternative scenarios did not play an important part until the end of 1935, and the principle of economic and monetary orthodoxy was initially supported by the leading political parties, employers and trade unions. In the spring of

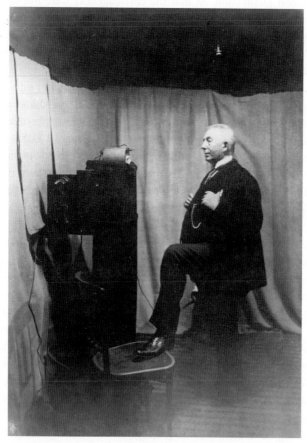

Figure 19 Hendrikus Colijn (1869–1944), prime minister 1925–6, 1933–9. Historical Documentation Centre for Dutch Protestantism (1800 to the Present Day), Amsterdam.

1935, not one of the parties in the Lower House spoke out in favour of devaluing the guilder. People knew about the counter-cyclical demand management policy formulated at that time by the British economist John Maynard Keynes, but it produced a sceptical response among a majority. The prime minister during the depression, Hendrikus Colijn (ARP), is said to have remarked: 'Among the detective stories on my bedside table there are also Keynes's publications. I'm fascinated by fantasy theories, but I don't put my trust in them.'[22]

The economic crisis and the social consequences put the SDAP in a particularly awkward position. It lost many votes to small radical left-wing parties in the 1933 Lower House elections. A year later, protests in working class neighbourhoods in Amsterdam against a reduction in unemployment benefit turned into serious battles with the police and even the army. Six people were killed and two hundred were injured. But this brief spontaneous outburst of popular fury was not the start of a larger protest. The SDAP immediately distanced itself from the aggression and blamed revolutionary socialists and communists for the violent escalation, but of course such accusations were not enough to convince its own supporters. The party was supposed to formulate its own programme as an alternative to Colijn's crisis policy.

And indeed such a programme – Plan for Labour – was forthcoming in September 1935. The basis was provided by the economist Jan Tinbergen and Hein Vos, an engineer and a university friend of his. Inspired by Keynes and informed by experience that had meanwhile been acquired in Sweden, they advocated a policy of counter-cyclical demand management. Government should create jobs by investing in public works and industry. The message was to invest and not cut spending. A temporary increase in the national debt in order to finance the programme would be acceptable. As employment increased, purchasing power would rise too, which would give the economy a further stimulus and boost tax revenues. The core of the social democratic plan was that once the economy picked up again, the national debt that had accumulated could be reduced. Six hundred million guilders would have to be invested over three years to tackle the crisis. This was a substantial sum, given that the government's annual budget was 900 million, and this contributed to the cool reception the plan was given by the other parties.

Although it had little effect, it was a clear signal that the SDAP was changing the direction of its thinking. The struggle against capitalism made way for arguments in favour of a mixed economy, which would provide the population with ample social security. In so doing the party took a step towards becoming a popular movement that aimed to reach out to more groups than the workers alone. A second step followed two years later in 1937, when the party adopted a new manifesto from which the old dogmas had been removed. By abandoning the demand for disarmament, the SDAP accepted the need for national defence for the first time.[23] The rejection of the monarchy also disappeared from the manifesto. This fulfilled an important condition for the further integration of social democracy in the nation.

Nevertheless, this new look programme did not lead to inclusion in government. Although Colijn's Christian democrat/liberal government fell in 1935 because of its handling of the crisis, and there were discussions with the SDAP about possible involvement in a coalition government for the first time since 1913, the door remained shut. The moment did not come until 1939. The Colijn government fell again, this time after a dispute with the Roman Catholic State Party about economic policy. A great deal of irritation had meanwhile built up on the Catholic side because Colijn had repeatedly blocked RKSP proposals for a more proactive approach to unemployment, which was still high. As a result the RKSP became more inclined to cooperate with the SDAP. In the summer of 1939, scope was thus created for the SDAP's first involvement in government. It had two ministers in a government coalition with the RKSP, CHU and the left-wing liberal VDB, and Dirk Jan de Geer (CHU) as prime minister.

Becoming part of government was a historic moment for the SDAP. The social democratic pillar was accepted at national level as a fully fledged partner, which also enabled it to participate completely in the pillarized system. This put an end to a long period of isolation that was partly self-sought and partly imposed by the religious parties and the liberals. The Netherlands was the last of the democratic countries in this regard because elsewhere social democrats had become involved in national governments much earlier.

Although the depression in the Netherlands was long and the policy pursued by government and parliament failed, the democratic system was not endangered during these years. Democracy did come under pressure, though, and people's dissatisfaction with the performance of the parliamentary system increased. As in other European countries, there was also a growing desire in the Netherlands for strong leadership that did not sit despondently by and wait, but promised effective policies. In regard to the threat to European democracies between the wars, the historian A. A. de Jonge makes the simple and useful distinction between a 'minor crisis' and a 'major crisis' of democracy. His category of minor crisis includes uneasiness about slow decision making, the laborious formation of coalitions and the lack of an effective economic policy. This minor crisis is therefore primarily about the performance of state institutions, but does not relate to the system's fundamental ideals. So in the event of a minor crisis of democracy, the democratic system is put on the defensive but there is no descent into a left-wing or right-wing dictatorship. During a minor crisis, however, the desire for a 'strong man' can become very real and there can be calls for changes to the system that damage democracy.

This is why the transition to a major crisis is a seamless one. This sort of crisis has its anti-liberal and anti-democratic roots in the nineteenth century and manifests itself in mass movements longing for national unity under a charismatic leader. According to de Jonge, the principles of freedom and equality of citizens are swept aside in a major crisis, the ideological foundations of democracy meet a violent end, and there is a very real switch to a fascist or national socialist system.[24]

The Netherlands was spared a major crisis of democracy, but displayed many features of a minor one. Since the early 1920s, some people had become disappointed with and turned their backs on the newly completed democratic system. The historian Koen Vossen demonstrated this convincingly in his study of small parties during the 1920s and 1930s.[25] There was no mass movement, just a motley group of left-wing and right-wing political adventurers who, along with their parties, often disappeared from the scene as quickly as they arrived. They had no serious political significance, but they did function as a seismograph for unrest in the population. Uneasiness about the performance of the democratic system resulted in a jumble of small anti-democratic clubs and parties, but there was also discontent inside the big parties.

While the largest party, the RKSP, without doubt remained within the boundaries of parliamentary democracy, there was a certain degree of sympathy among Catholics for authoritarian right-wing ideas, and corporative thinking was highly regarded. In 1934, there were positive comments about Austria's corporatist constitution in the official party organ and at the beginning of 1940 it was reported that the form of government in Portugal, which had an authoritarian regime, was the purest reflection of Dutch Catholics' ideals. The position of C. P. M. Romme, then a young political talent who would become party leader after the war, is typical. According to Romme, Catholic policy should be aimed at an organically structured corporative society in which political parties and parliament would no longer play a leading role. But the path leading there must be followed democratically, and the RKSP should play an important part in this.[26] During the 1930s, Romme also repeatedly advocated a system with a stronger monarchy in which the monarch needed to have a real leadership role and – if necessary – could impose his will on parliament.

There were also authoritarian ideas in orthodox Protestant circles, and it was primarily Hendrikus Colijn (1869–1944) who embodied such thinking. Colijn became leader of the ARP in the early 1920s. He served as minister of finance (1923–5) and prime minister (1925–6) before dominating Dutch politics once again during the 1930s as prime minister (1933–9) and 'strong man'. As his biographer Herman Langeveld reveals, Colijn had an equivocal attitude to parliamentary democracy.[27] He expressed clear sympathy for anti-democratic thinking and was convinced that popular influence should be reduced. But this had to be implemented – and here there was agreement with the thinking in Catholic circles – through the existing political parties using the apparatus of the current political system. He rejected German national socialism more explicitly than Italian fascism. He approved of eliminating communists and socialists, but unambiguously and fundamentally rejected anti-Semitism.

A conservative mentality thus dominated the political culture between the wars in which concepts like 'order', 'enforcing power' and 'authority' had important places as a matter of course. This type of attitude became more prominent at the beginning of the 1930s than it had been during the 1920s – a phenomenon that can be explained by the economic crisis and fear of left-wing radicalism. In those uncertain times the self-assured Colijn was a source of solidity and comfort, both inside and outside his own ARP. Leading liberal and neutral newspapers like the *Algemeen Handelsblad*, *Nieuwe Rotterdamsche Courant* and *De Telegraaf* also propagated an image of Colijn as the strong helmsman who steered the Dutch ship of state with a firm hand into safer waters.[28]

But there were also groups and parties that actively waged war against democracy, and the National Socialist Movement (NSB), founded in 1931, was without doubt the most important. Mussolini was the shining example for co-founder and party leader Anton Adriaan Mussert (1894–1946). The NSB's political profile was not fully crystallized to begin with, which explains the relative success of Mussert's faction between 1931 and 1935.[29] Mussert based his movement's manifesto on the National Socialist German Workers' Party

(NSDAP), but during that period the NSB was not yet anti-Semitic and the *Führerprinzip* (leader principle) had not been adopted either. Above all, Mussert's NSB was an organization that wanted to convert frustration about the political and social discord into a revived powerful national identity, with the royal house, the national flag and the national coat of arms as 'inviolable symbols of the nation's unity'.[30] He made himself a mouthpiece for criticism of political 'bickering' among the parties and the existing parliamentary system's lack of perspective. In so doing, he gave direction to the malaise that is described above as a minor crisis of democracy, without employing vulgar, violent or revolutionary language.

Mussert played on the realization that the crisis in the Netherlands was more than just political and economic – it was mental too. Not that he had a solution for getting out of the crisis, but the NSB's style and organization – uniforms, flag parades, processions, carefully orchestrated conventions with thousands of attendees, and great flamboyance – made an impression and conveyed a sense of power, whereas the existing establishment seemed to project only weakness and indecision. It was actually Mussert's respectable, lower middle class image – combined with a vague political profile on the one hand and good organizational talent on the other – that initially enabled the NSB to grow quickly and attract wide-ranging public support.

The NSB's major success came in 1935 when it gained almost 8 per cent of the vote in provincial elections. In the balloting for the Lower House two years later, this percentage was nearly halved (4.2 per cent) and the NSB had already passed its peak. During those two years, the decent bourgeois element faded and the party became more militant and radical. In October 1935, the NSB supported Mussolini's invasion of Abyssinia (now Ethiopia) and in 1936 it also started to openly embrace the national socialist racial doctrine. The more emphatically the NSB expressed its support for Italy and Germany, the greater the opposition it encountered in the Netherlands.

As early as 1933, the SDAP and NVV set up a bureau to combat communism and fascism, which published its own mass circulation newspaper – Freedom, Work, Food (*Vrijheid, Arbeid, Brood*). The NSB was one of the subjects of its fierce attacks. That same year the government put the NSB on the list of organizations civil servants were banned from joining. The party was targeted even more savagely after its electoral success in 1935. In June, the politically unattached Dutch Movement for Unity through Democracy (EDD) was established. It consisted mainly of liberals with a range of views and social democrats. This organization grew to about 30,000 members and conducted campaigns (mass demonstrations, exhortations to participate in elections such as 'vote for democrats') against fascism, national socialism and communism (see Figure 20, p. 205). The disciplining messages from the top of the Catholic and Protestant pillars also helped weaken the NSB. In May 1936, a pastoral letter was read out in all Catholic churches rejecting national socialism in unmistakable terms. It also announced that anyone who supported the NSB would be excluded from the sacraments. A number of Protestant churches made similar declarations a few months later.

There was thus resistance from different sides to the radicalizing NSB, which was put on the defensive and responded vindictively and aggressively. What followed was a spiral of mutual denunciation that subsequently pushed the NSB into even greater isolation. In

Figure 20 *The Dutch People. Vote for Democrats. Unity Through Democracy.* Dutch Political Parties Documentation Centre, Groningen.

the final analysis, the limited power of the NSB can also be explained by the actions of Prime Minister Colijn who, while not averse to authoritarian political views, dissuaded many people in Protestant and liberal circles from voting for Mussert's party.

Independent and neutral: Foreign policy up to 1940

The Netherlands did not take sides during the First World War and so it did not take part in the Paris Peace Conference or sign the Treaty of Versailles in 1919. Nevertheless the Dutch were more than neutral observers during the peace negotiations. The Hague had to defend itself against Allied accusations that, despite its professed neutrality during the war, it had in fact adopted a pro-German stance. One of the arguments underpinning these allegations was that at the end of war the Netherlands had given permission for 70,000 unarmed German soldiers to pass through Dutch territory (Limburg) on their way home. Allied fury was even greater when the Netherlands granted Kaiser Wilhelm II asylum and refused to hand him over to the victors for trial.[31]

It was important for the country to conduct active diplomacy after the First World War, if only to defend itself against such recriminations, and this was all the more necessary because Belgium tried to take advantage of the weakened Dutch position to take over parts of Limburg and Zeeland, so it could better defend itself against aggression in the future. In the end, the Belgians did not succeed, not least because the French and

British wanted to avoid driving the Netherlands into the pro-German camp by forcing the country to cede territory. However, Belgo–Dutch relations remained tense for many years afterwards.

The friction between the Netherlands and the Entente powers about the extradition of Wilhelm II decreased significantly at the beginning of 1920. Although the Treaty of Versailles stipulated that the former Kaiser should appear before an international criminal court and the Netherlands received two official extradition requests, behind the scenes London and Paris let it be known that they could accept Wilhelm II staying in the country provided that the ex-Kaiser did not get involved in politics. The Dutch also wanted to impose a similar ban on him, and in March 1920 Wilhelm II signed a solemn declaration accepting this demand. He led a secluded life near Utrecht until his death in 1941. He was buried in the grounds of his modest residence, Doorn Manor, and to this day this small country house contains a museum dedicated to the last German Kaiser.[32]

Even after the tensions about extraditing the Kaiser and Belgium's annexation ambitions had eased, criticism of the Treaty of Versailles dominated the political scene in the Netherlands. According to most reactions, Germany had been humiliated by the treaty. This, it was argued, would disrupt the European balance of power in favour of France, and the continuation of international tensions would be inevitable. It had already become clear during the war that the Netherlands had no interest in victory for one side or the other – an attitude that was in step with traditional Dutch foreign policy. It now became apparent once more, as the postwar international order took shape, that the Netherlands would be best served by the restoration of equilibrium between major European powers, and a politically and economically stable Germany was an essential part of this. Thanks to the Treaty of Versailles, there was a danger that exactly the opposite would happen, but as a minor power with a bad image among the Allies, the Netherlands essentially had no means of contributing to the recreation of this stability.

The Dutch consequently had little latitude in their foreign policy, but the international situation gave The Hague no choice but to be more active than before. Under foreign minister Herman Adriaan van Karnebeek (1918–27) the Netherlands departed from its strict neutrality, and by joining the League of Nations The Hague demonstrated its willingness to contribute to international stability.[33] Van Karnebeek even lobbied for the headquarters of the organization to be located in the Netherlands, using the presence of the Peace Palace in The Hague as one of his arguments. But his efforts came to nothing because of the anti-Dutch mood in Allied circles. The Dutch lobby to get the Permanent Court of International Justice to set up shop in The Hague was more successful. Its goal was achieved in 1922 and these efforts were crowned with the appointment of a Dutch lawyer, Bernard Loder, as the first president.

The tense European relations that had arisen because of the war gave way in the second half of the 1920s to détente and optimism. The Netherlands also benefitted from the international climate, expressed most clearly in the Locarno Treaties (1925), Germany joining the League of Nations (1926) and the Kellogg–Briand Pact (1928), which branded all wars as unlawful. This period came to an end when the economic world crisis struck in 1929. During the 1930s, Dutch foreign policy was once again dominated by clashes of interests in trade and security policy that fuelled rising tensions in Europe.[34] Many countries raised the height of their tariff walls and introduced other trade barriers to protect their national economies. The upshot was that Dutch exports – which were already expensive because the country was still adhering to the gold standard – fell sharply; shrinking export volumes to Germany and the UK were a particularly heavy blow. Attempts to coordinate trade policy and save free trade as much as possible through collaboration with Belgium, Luxembourg and the Scandinavian countries (the Oslo States) had little effect.[35] The endeavour to strengthen economic ties with the British also failed, and this, among other things, led the Netherlands to concentrate above all on safeguarding trade relations with Germany during the 1930s. The dramatic drop in agricultural exports to the Netherlands' eastern neighbour reveals just how difficult that was. In 1934, about 31.5 per cent of total Dutch exports of farm products were still going to Germany, but a year later this had dropped to only 24.2 per cent, and by 1936 the volume had fallen further to 19.4 per cent. In 1930, the Netherlands accounted for 9 per cent of German agricultural imports, but only 5 per cent in 1938.

On the one hand, the Third Reich was seeking to be economically self-sufficient, and on the other it was focusing on south eastern European states. All that was left for the Netherlands was 'the position of a stopgap'.[36] Given this vulnerable situation, The Hague sought to establish a depoliticized relationship with Nazi Germany so as to avoid giving Berlin reason to reduce the volume of trade still further. It was important to tread very carefully in order to keep on good terms with this neighbour and not damage commercial interests. There was a great deal of overlap between politics and economics, but they had to remain strictly separated from each other, and Dutch trade policy would suffer if there was open criticism of Nazi Germany in the Netherlands. So the Dutch response to rising international tensions during the 1930s was to resort to putting their own neutrality back at the top of the agenda. To begin with, the primary concern was safeguarding economic interests, but later in the decade aspects of security policy also emerged.

Initially, the League of Nations played a meaningful role in regard to Dutch reactions to the increasingly grim international climate. When Italy invaded Ethiopia in the autumn of 1935, the League of Nations responded by imposing economic sanctions. The Netherlands scrupulously obeyed, with the result that Dutch exports to Italy came to a virtually complete standstill. But the League's actions had no effect, and after Italy annexed Ethiopia it had to be recognized that the League of Nations had failed utterly. There were soon calls in the Netherlands and elsewhere to end the punitive measures against Italy, and in the summer of 1936 the Dutch voted in the League of Nations Assembly in favour of lifting the sanctions.[37] During this period, the failure of the League of Nations also came closer to home. In March 1936, the German remilitarization of the Rhineland was criticized in the League of Nations Assembly, but this did not lead to sanctions. The Netherlands would not have participated in them anyway. The German action was condemned behind the scenes, but the government expressed no opinion in public. The cabinet were fearful of the economic and political consequences of opposing Germany.

Many people thought that Hitler only wanted to bury the 'humiliating' Treaty of Versailles. As long as Germany believed it had legitimate reasons to feel discriminated against – so went the argument – it would remain a turbulent factor in international politics. This assumption made the Dutch government a strong supporter of the British appeasement policy, even when German demands went beyond amending the Versailles treaty. Prime Minister Colijn was a great admirer of his British counterpart Neville Chamberlain. He was jubilant at the results of the Munich conference in September 1938, when the UK and France capitulated to Hitler's Czechoslovakia demands. Colijn's position in 1938 and 1939 was that the Netherlands would be in no danger because Germany's primary ambitions were in Eastern Europe, and as long as Germany could achieve these ambitions peacefully, it should be given the latitude to do so.[38]

The failure of the League of Nations and the growing international tensions had two immediate implications for Dutch foreign and security policy. First, on 1 July 1936, the Netherlands, together with other states that had been neutral during the First World War (including the Oslo States), declared it no longer considered itself bound by sanctions under the Covenant of the League of Nations (article 16). This ushered in the return to absolute neutrality, which was completed in 1938.[39] Second, after the army had been neglected for years on end, defence spending was increased and the defence budget grew substantially every year until 1940. But the consequences of many years of spending cuts could not be undone overnight, and the problem was compounded by the fact that the country no longer had an armaments industry of any consequence. The upshot was that the Dutch had virtually no modern weapons by the spring of 1940. Some of the military equipment actually dated from the 1870s and 1880s.[40]

Using these two instruments – a return to strict neutrality and strengthening defence – in the second half of the 1930s the Netherlands tried to minimize the risks it faced. People were hoping that if a new war broke out in Europe, the Netherlands would be able to keep out of the conflict as it had during the First World War. But in 1938 Hitler had already included Dutch territory in his strategic plans. In 1938 and 1939 he repeatedly referred in public to 'befriedeten Grenzen' – pacified borders – between Germany and the Netherlands (and Belgium). But in May 1939, he decided that the Netherlands and Belgium would have to be occupied by Germany in the event of war with the British and French. After the German invasion of Poland and the start of the Second World War on 1 September 1939, on Hitler's instructions, the attack on the Netherlands was due to begin on 19 October. The invasion was postponed seventeen times until early May 1940, when the time was ripe for the Germans to swoop on the Netherlands, Belgium, Luxembourg and France under the code name Operation Fall Gelb.

This came as no surprise to the Dutch army and government. The Hague had been told repeatedly about the planned attacks, for example by Hans Oster of the *Auslands-Abwehr des Oberkommandos der Wehrmacht* (Foreign Defence of the High Command of the Wehrmacht). Oster had been involved in preparations for a coup against Hitler in 1938 and was put to death in April 1945 for his resistance to national socialism. He had good contacts with staff in a number of embassies in Berlin and was friendly with the military attaché at the Dutch embassy, Major G. J. Sas. The Hague also received warnings from British sources during these months. Information about these specific threats did not, however, reach the Dutch population, and the government did everything it could to avoid disquiet. Without doubt, a large part of the political elite and people preferred to turn a blind eye to the danger, and many gratefully accepted the government's reassuring words.

The Hague had few options for putting up a satisfactory defence because France and the UK were also constrained by their appeasement of Germany. Tension rose at the beginning of May 1940. Reports of troop movements along the German border, new warnings via Hans Oster in Berlin and other intelligence led, in 9 May 1940, to the expectation at Dutch headquarters that a German attack was imminent. That evening, the last telephone warning from the Dutch military attaché in Berlin reached the Ministry of Defence in The Hague. 'I have just one thing to tell you. Tomorrow at daybreak. Never say die!'[41] The Second World War started for the Netherlands in the small hours of 10 May 1940. The country was occupied by foreign troops for the first time since the Napoleonic era.

War and occupation (1940–5)

No other period in Dutch history has been studied as intensively as the occupation. For many years the moral perspective of 'right' and 'wrong' dominated – the contrast between Dutch people who were 'right' since they had resisted German occupying forces and those who were 'wrong' because they had collaborated. This overlooks the fact that most of the population had not belonged to either group, but had adapted to living under a national socialist dictatorship. This moralist approach to historiography meant that many important questions about the 1940–45 period were not addressed. How did the mood of the population shift during the changing circumstances between 1940 and 1945? What mechanisms developed that altered behaviour seamlessly from collaborating to adapting to resisting? What differences and similarities were there between the occupied Netherlands and other countries under German rule? Why, for example, were so many more of the Jews living in the Netherlands deported than Jews from Belgium and France? Because of the focus on the war years, without embedment in the history before and after them, the question as to whether this period represented a watershed in Dutch history has also remained unanswered. After 1945, people soon started talking about 'before' and 'after' the war, as though the war itself had been a fundamental dividing line. But did the restoration of the pillarized political landscape after the liberation not in fact indicate continuity? These questions have been asked with increasing frequency since the 1980s, primarily thanks to the influence of historian Blom, later to be director of the NIOD Institute for War, Holocaust and Genocide Studies. Blom thus contributed to initiating the historicization of the occupation.

Not surprisingly, oppression, terror, the deportation and murder of Jews, starvation and forced labour for hundreds of thousands occupy very prominent places in the Dutch history of the 1940–45 period. Many also associate the occupation with the Dutch famine or 'hunger winter' of 1944–45, when living conditions in the west of the country severely deteriorated and thousands died from cold and lack of food. But concentrating on these dramatic nadirs does not do justice to the development and cohesion between various aspects of the occupation that took place after the capitulation on 14 May 1940. This period can be divided into four phases. They are discussed below, and in each phase we consider occupation politics, living conditions and the attitude of the Dutch in their interactive dynamic.[42]

The first phase lasted from 10 May 1940 to the end of February 1941, and bears the stamp of defeat, acceptance and adaptation. The hope that the Netherlands could stand up to a German invasion for a few weeks soon proved illusory. The German bombing of Rotterdam on 14 May, which destroyed virtually the entire city centre and killed between seven and eight hundred people, made it clear that further resistance was pointless. This rapid defeat was entirely in accordance with expectations from a German perspective, although they did not succeed in arresting Queen Wilhelmina and her ministers, who fled on 13 May, just in time, to London, where they remained in exile during the war.

A few days after the capitulation, Hitler signed a decree declaring that the Netherlands would have a civilian administration headed by Reich Commissioner of the Occupied Dutch Territories, the Austrian Arthur Seyss-Inquart (1892–1946). After the Anschluss (annexation) of Austria in 1938, Seyss-Inquart had been appointed Reich Governor for Ostmark (the former independent Federal State of Austria). Later, he was Reich Minister without portfolio and, after the invasion of Poland, he became Hans Frank's deputy in the General Government in Poland. Seyss-Inquart was a national socialist who could come across as moderate and was consequently considered able to win the Dutch population over to the occupying forces through tactful and calm behaviour. He did not have his own power base in the party, Protection Squad (SS) or army. He owed his position to Hitler, to whom he reported directly.[43] Under him were four General Commissioners, responsible for the different administrative areas. General Commissioner Hanns Albin Rauter – also Austrian – had a powerful position and was responsible for public order and security. He was SS and Police Leader and so he represented Reichsführer-SS (national leader of the Protection Squad) Heinrich Himmler in the Netherlands. Fritz Schmidt, General Commissioner for Political Affairs and Propaganda, represented the NSDAP and would deal with public opinion and non-business associations. The two other General Commissioners, the Austrians Friedrich Wimmer and Hans Fischböck, the former responsible for administration and justice and the latter for economic affairs and finance, stayed rather more in the background. The Supreme Commander of the Wehrmacht in the Netherlands was F. C. Christiansen, however his position soon became less important. The German Foreign Office was represented by Otto Bene, who held a rank equal to a General Commissioner and also attended the weekly meetings chaired by Seyss-Inquart.[44]

Formally, the General Commissioners reported to Seyss-Inquart, but in fact they were agents of their respective departments in Germany. The result was that the various occupation departments had to cooperate yet also compete with one another, while at the same time they often had different interests, intentions and methods. The competition between them and mutual distrust were consequently often significant. Although it sometimes assumed the character of a free-for-all, this structure was not fortuitous. It reflected the polycratic power structure in Germany itself, where Hitler's policy of divide and rule fuelled competition between different power blocks (SS, party, army, etc.) and these power bases often worked alongside but also against one another.[45]

The Reich Commissioner did not take office with the objective of administering the Netherlands, but of directing the country using the intact Dutch governmental system.[46] After the government's departure on 13 May, it was the permanent secretaries of the ministries who were left at the top of that system. They were the central link in the new administration, which formed relatively quickly and without much friction. While a few permanent secretaries refused to cooperate with the Reich Commissioner and resigned or were dismissed, most saw it as their duty to ensure continuity of government, prevent unrest and search for a *modus vivendi* with the German authorities. The permanent secretaries were prepared to reconcile themselves to the new power structure in the hope they could retain their own freedom of action and prevent the appointment of NSB members to key positions. And what applied to the senior level at the ministries was also true of the majority of the queen's commissioners in the eleven provinces and the mayors. Their motto was: 'Stay calm, do not provoke, cooperate loyally, and wait and see how the situation develops.'[47]

This attitude was in line with the behaviour of the occupying forces, which saw avoiding conflicts as being very much in their interests during this first phase. As a rule they conducted themselves properly, which was consistent with the two key objectives they had in mind for the Netherlands. As 'a fellow Germanic people' the Dutch should first and foremost be won over to national socialism. The sympathy that the Germans were hoping to earn also served the second objective – making the Dutch economy subservient to the German war effort. Under the umbrella of the moderate policy during this initial phase, behind the scenes, the Germans still did not have any clear-cut plans for the future constitutional position of the Netherlands, and it was not yet time to decide on the exact form of integration into the Greater Germanic Reich.

It was not immediately clear in the first phase of the occupation that these two objectives – gaining sympathy and economic exploitation – were mutually incompatible. The initially moderate policy of the occupying forces made it easy for the overwhelming majority of people to follow their own instinctive reaction – to adapt to the new situation while retaining their former way of life as far as possible, and trying to make the best of it. To many, adapting also appeared to be the most realistic option because German dominance in Europe seemed unassailable. The success of the Dutch Union (*Nederlandse Unie*), a political movement established in July 1940 with German permission, was typical of the attitude of the majority of the population. The Union distanced itself from the pre-war party democracy and saw the new circumstances as an opportunity to build up an organically structured society in which, under strong central authority, it would be possible to do greater justice to national unity and national community.[48] That called for a loyal attitude towards the occupying forces, in the hope that there would later be scope for maintaining the Dutch 'national character' and a certain degree of national independence. The Union was soon hundreds of thousands strong. No Dutch organization had ever acquired so many members as the Union did in the first year of the war. The Union could not be considered as 'anti-German', but it was certainly 'pro-Dutch', and so people demonstrated their willingness to adapt by joining it. On the other hand, because of the emphasis on Dutch individuality, membership was also a signal of distance to the German occupiers. The Union also clearly dissociated itself from the NSB, which most people considered to be an 'un-Dutch' German tool.

As far as the occupying forces were concerned, the Union was a mass movement that could be used to make it easier to bring the Netherlands into line and integrate it into the Greater Germanic Reich. This was the only reason they had allowed the Union to be established. This apparent openness was therefore subject to clear limits. The Union had not been allowed to express any loyalty to the House of Orange in its programme and Seyss-Inquart soon started demanding support for his executive measures and German war aims. Conflicts with the Union were inevitable. The movement lost more and more members in the course of 1941 and it was finally banned in December 1941. From then on the NSB was the only political group that was allowed.

Despite the relatively restrained actions of the Germans during the first phase of the war, the importance of the changes that occurred in politics and society should not be underestimated. Censorship was imposed on the media, parliament was suspended and political parties disappeared. Seyss-Inquart furthermore made it clear from the outset that resistance or support for the Allies would incur the death penalty. The first anti-Jewish measures were taken in the summer of 1940, and it soon became clear that there was systematic coherence between them. Starting in August 1940, Jewish civil servants could not be promoted and Jews were no longer allowed to become government officials. In October 1940, all Dutch nationals working for government had to sign a declaration that they were either 'Aryan' or 'wholly or partially Jewish'. After this measure it was a small step to dismiss all Jews in government jobs. This purge went ahead in November 1940, and the Germans cracked down hard where there were protests.

The start of the second phase of the occupation coincided with the increasing severity of the anti-Jewish policy. This phase lasted from February 1941 to the summer of 1943, during which there was increasing oppression of the population and persecution of the Jews. The systematic registration of Jews living in the Netherlands started in January 1941. Physical intimidation of Jews also grew worse and took the form of provocations, destruction of Jewish property and induced fights. Jewish gangs formed in Amsterdam to protect themselves from this violence and there was a large-scale brawl in February 1941, which the Germans seized upon as an excuse for tougher tactics. During a two-day period some four hundred male Jews aged between twenty and thirty-five were rounded up in a very violent fashion, and shortly afterwards they were deported to Buchenwald concentration camp and then to Mauthausen. These raids were the background to a brief protest against the occupying forces on 25 February 1941, which has gone down in Dutch history as the February Strike. It was centred in Amsterdam, but people stopped work in some other towns and cities too, including Zaandam, Haarlem and Utrecht. This action took the Germans completely by surprise, and they reacted brutally. There were deaths and injuries, and also many arrests. The strike came to a rapid end.

Figure 21 Isolation of Jews in Amsterdam. NIOD Institute for War, Holocaust and Genocide Studies, Amsterdam.

The 1941 February Strike was the first act of resistance that received widespread support from different levels of the community. It was an indication that adapting to the occupation regime in the first phase had its limits, and had certainly not resulted in sympathy for the occupying Germans. This does not mean that the February Strike heralded a phase of broadly backed resistance or that the accommodation from the first phase had come to an end. Adapting to the circumstances remained the motto for the majority of people after February 1941. Yet something had changed. The Germans had not previously acted so savagely, nor had the differences between them and a large part of the nation become so blatantly obvious.

The result was that the occupiers increasingly had to turn to the NSB as a prop. But Mussert's party was not a mass movement. Its membership at the end of 1941 was some 85,000, which corresponded to about 1.5 per cent of the Dutch adult population. The party was a reservoir of people from which the Germans could draw when they were looking for reliable personnel to work in ministries, regional and local government and the police. Increasing numbers of government posts were held by NSB members, particularly at more senior levels, for example mayors, provincial commissioners (the former queen's commissioners) and permanent secretaries, but the NSB did not develop into an independent power base. It remained an instrument in German hands.

The second phase of the occupation featured the enforced organizational and ideological conformity (Gleichschaltung) of societies, foundations and institutions, which was increasingly accompanied by pressure and repression. No end of new organizations sprang up to replace the former pillarized institutions, but there was no ideological permeation. Some organizations lost their members, while others only attracted people seeking to avoid sanctions. It is even fair to say that this attempted

Gleichschaltung actually had the reverse effect. It is true that the pre-war pillarized structure was demolished, as everyone could see and feel. But in fact this compulsory destruction reinforced the existing solidarity inside the pillars and resistance to national socialism.[49] The occupying forces' unpopular measures furthermore overcame long-standing opposition to cooperation that transcended pillars, so national cohesion increased too. And yet only a few abandoned their accommodating behaviour. Provided that people's lives continued more or less 'normally', which was the case for very many until well into 1942, there was a degree of pragmatism in the daily routine. Obviously, the occupation had many unpleasant consequences and anti-German feeling became stronger, but sense of duty, lack of alternatives, responsibility for family and children or just plain fear were some of the many reasons for continuing to cling as much as possible to the familiar way of life.

Starting in 1942, the population was increasingly exposed to the economic implications of occupation. When the Germans realized they had not succeeded in winning the Netherlands over to national socialism, there was less need to take account of people's criticism or sense of unease. Berlin took greater control of coordinating the economic exploitation of occupied areas and demanded more functional involvement in the German war machine. The upshot was that more had to be sent to Germany and so less remained for the Dutch market. Companies and services that were not deemed to be relevant to Nazi Germany were shut down. People were not yet starving, but the range of available food dwindled significantly and the population's supply of such products as fuel, textiles and soap dropped far below the levels of 1940.

During the second phase of the occupation, the volume of Dutch products going to Germany and the number of workers being put to work there grew substantially. In the first phase, some people still went to work in Germany on a voluntary basis, but now the coercion increased. While an estimated 227,000 Dutch nationals were working in Germany in the spring of 1942, by April 1943 a further 163,000 people had been compelled to go. The increasingly harsh living conditions and more severe sanctions meant growing numbers of people were personally affected by the problems of war and occupation, so it is not surprising that anti-German sentiment grew sharply in 1942 and 1943. Strikingly, though, the deportations of Jews that took place in this period were a very minor factor in this reaction.

The occupying authorities had decided in May 1941 that eventually all Jews had to vanish from the Netherlands. In the following months, a large number of anti-Jewish measures were introduced, with the result that by the summer of 1942 Jews had been deprived of any mobility. Most of them lived in Amsterdam and virtually all were transported to the Westerbork transit camp in Drenthe, from where they were taken to death camps to be murdered. Between July 1942 and September 1943, the deportation trains were so frequent that some 80,000 people were taken away.

Altogether 102,000 Jews from the Netherlands were murdered – 75 per cent of the Jewish population in the country in 1940 (140,000). Despite considerable research, it is difficult to give a conclusive answer to the question as to why this percentage was so much higher than it was, for example, in Belgium (40 per cent) or France (25 per cent).[50]

Without doubt there were expressions of sympathy for the Jews and there was resistance to the persecution. Some 24,000 Jews are estimated to have gone into hiding, and non-Jewish Dutch people were prepared to put their lives on the line to help them. There were also policemen who refused to collect Jews from their homes, but there were many more police and other civil servants who obediently carried out the German orders. It was also more difficult for Jews than for non-Jews to find a safe house. This compliance by the Dutch government organization was based not so much on strong anti-Semitism, as on traditional docility and respect for power and authority in general. As we have noted before, the default response of most Dutch people was to adapt and accommodate. Offering help to Jews moreover brought personal risks that only a few were prepared to take. The obedience of many Dutch people was also linked to pillarization, under which the elites traditionally had great authority.

Pillarization and the position of Jews in pre-war Dutch society are also factors that help to explain the large number of Jewish victims. On the one hand, the assimilation of Jews in the Netherlands was relatively comprehensive and until 1940 Jews had been able to feel safe there. On the other hand, there was also anti-Semitic prejudice in the country and most Jews were outside the pillarized structure of Dutch political and social systems. When the persecution started, Jews were consequently left to their own devices to a greater extent than might have been expected given their assimilation.[51] Finally – while it is not conclusive – a major factor in explaining the large percentage of Dutch Jews who perished is that the Netherlands, unlike Belgium and France, for example, had a civilian rather than a military occupying administration that persecuted the Jews with greater thoroughness and unanimity. There was also what Blom calls the 'Austrian connection'. There were many Austrians in the Reich Commissioner's organization in the Netherlands who were strongly anti-Semitic and had short lines of communication with Adolf Eichmann and Ernst Kaltenbrunner – also Austrians – who played a key role at the Reich Security Head Office in organizing and planning the mass murder of Jews.[52]

It was not the persecution of the Jews but growing pressure on the non-Jewish population that fuelled opposition to the occupying forces. That happened during the third phase, which lasted from the summer of 1943 to September 1944, a period of increasing exploitation and growing resistance. This was prompted by German plans to transport a further 300,000 Dutch people to Germany as forced labourers. At the end of April 1943, for instance, former Dutch soldiers were summoned to report. A wave of protest swept across the country and strikes broke out in many places. Later they would be called the April/May strikes. The unrest was brutally suppressed. Nearly two hundred people were killed, over four hundred were seriously wounded, and hundreds more were arrested and sacked. The target of 300,000 extra Dutch forced labourers was not met, but many tens of thousands had to go, and tens of thousands more went into hiding. This, coupled with further deterioration in living conditions, meant that the occupation became a permanent state of emergency in all sorts of areas during this phase, and anti-German feelings became increasingly intense. The daily routine that it had been possible to maintain to a degree during the early war years disappeared and people increasingly had to decide where they stood.

The rise in the number of people in hiding in 1943 was both an indication of the growing anti-German sentiment and a shot in the arm for the resistance. This was because people in hiding needed addresses, false identity papers, ration books and so on, and that required organization, coordination and contacts. Alongside the organizations that helped people to find safe houses to hide, there were assault groups that raided municipal employment offices, population registers, rationing offices and sometimes arms depots. As arrests of resistance fighters increased, so too did the number of rescue actions to get them out of prison.

In 1943, the illegal press also started to become more important. The number of publications grew and illegal newspapers that had existed for some time, such as *Vrij Nederland*, *Trouw*, *De Waarheid* and *Het Parool*, professionalized. By December 1943, the combined circulation of the underground press had reached about 450,000. A feature of the illegal printed media – and of the resistance in general – was that the pre-war pillarized structure remained clearly visible. Although many publications had articles about the need to get away from the former pigeon-hole mentality, and despite the fact that the war had reinforced the sense of national solidarity under the House of Orange, every paper had its own clear profile.

Another important element of the resistance's work was maintaining contacts with the Dutch government in London. Numerous messages went to London via Switzerland and, starting in the autumn of 1943, a lot of information came back. Growing resistance was met with savage reprisals. One such was the reaction of the Wehrmacht after an attack on a German military vehicle on 30 September 1944 in Putten. Virtually the entire male population of the village was transported to Neuengamme concentration camp. Only forty-nine of the 660 deported men survived the war. After 1945, Putten became the Dutch symbol of the German army's crimes during the war.[53]

Despite the growing antagonism between the German occupiers and the Dutch people, there was a glimmer of hope in the summer of 1944. German armies were being pushed back on all fronts and the rapid advance of the Allies after the successful invasion of Normandy in June 1944 seemed to point to a swift collapse of the German Reich. Paris was liberated in August, and when Brussels fell into Allied hands on Monday 4 September 1944 the days of the German occupation of the Netherlands appeared to be numbered. But the hope and joy that these events inspired proved premature. The Allied Market Garden operation in 1944 failed and that autumn the country was split into a liberated southern part (North Brabant, Limburg to the west of the Meuse and the area around Nijmegen) and the north, which was still occupied.

September 1944 was thus the start of the fourth phase of the occupation. The important concepts during this period were 'front', 'Dutch famine' and 'total upheaval'. By the autumn of 1944, over 850,000 people had been evacuated and the number of people in hiding had grown to some 350,000; 107,000 Jews had been deported, a further 20,000 people were political prisoners and there were about 300,000 Dutch forced labourers in Germany. After September 1944, some 140,000 additional men were forcibly put to work, and many of them were transferred to Germany. There was a notorious round-up in Rotterdam on 10 and 11 November 1944 when approximately 50,000 men were taken away. Compounding the misery, the supply of food and energy in the major cities in the west collapsed completely during the autumn of 1944. Never before had the war been so total.

One reason for the dire living conditions was the German response to the rail strike in September 1944, which brought rail traffic to a standstill. At the request of the Allied supreme command, the Dutch government in London had called the strike in order to support the expected rapid advance of Allied troops. Initially, the stoppage hit the occupiers where it hurt, but after a brief period German train drivers were brought in and rail transport started again. In reprisal the Reich Commissioner banned trains from carrying food and fuel. This caused severe shortages during the bitter winter of 1944–5 and an estimated 22,000 people died from starvation and cold. The famine continued until just before the liberation when, after long and difficult negotiations, the German authorities permitted the Allies to make food drops.

During the last phase of the war the number of resistance operations increased sharply, one reason being that liberation was now on the horizon. There was also professionalization of countless areas (including courier services, forgeries, spying, underground press, telephone communication and financing of the resistance movement). But the influx of new resistance fighters was also responsible for a degree of dilution because their numbers included people with opportunistic motives who went about things in a much more amateur way.[54] The biggest problem now that liberation was in sight was the increase in competition and tensions between the different resistance organizations and their leaders, which impacted on their effectiveness.

Some people in the resistance thought their task would end with the liberation of the Netherlands. Others, though, considered the struggle against the German occupiers and the creation of a new Netherlands as two sides of the same coin, and demanded a political role after the liberation. A divergence between left and right soon emerged. Those on the left pointed to the need for fundamental modernization of society, the economy and politics to lead to the strengthening of democracy, social justice and a new relationship between the Netherlands and its colonies based on equal rights. On the other side of the political spectrum, the conservative Protestant newspaper *Trouw* feared that 'the resistance as a whole could be serving as a cloak for the ambition of turning the Netherlands in a radical left-wing direction after the war'.[55] This underground publication advocated a return to the antithesis, which went back to Abraham Kuyper, between the Christian and non-Christian sections of the population.

The Allied advance, which had been brought to a standstill in the autumn of 1944, started again in March 1945. The eastern and northern provinces were liberated in April by Canadian troops, supported by one British and one Polish division. During this last part of the war there were still 120,000 German troops in the west of the country. They had put large areas under water and could have made life difficult for the advancing Allies through further flooding and destruction. But it never came to a military confrontation because all Wehrmacht forces in northwestern Europe capitulated on 4 May 1945. On 5 May in the Hotel de Wereld in Wageningen, a German general accepted the capitulation instrument for the troops in the Netherlands.

That marked the end of five years of occupation, which would leave deep scars in many areas – in the collective Dutch historical consciousness, in the political and cultural thinking about 'right' and 'wrong', in the focus of foreign policy, in literature and cinema, to name just a few. A number of these subjects will be addressed below. The key issue in 1945, though, was much more practical and was about political and socioeconomic reconstruction. Would the liberation herald the end of the pre-war pillarized order and thus be the dawn of political renewal, as many were hoping? Or would the old structures prove to be firmly embedded and would the political reconstruction come down to a return to the former relationships?

CHAPTER 7

THE NETHERLANDS AFTER 1945: RECONSTRUCTION, CHANGES IN FOREIGN POLICY AND IN POLITICAL CULTURE, THE POLDER MODEL AND THE CHALLENGE OF POPULISM

Introduction

For years, splitting contemporary national history into 'before the war' and 'after the war' was an obvious classification in the perception of many Dutch people. The period before 1940 was one of economic malaise, social differences, political stagnation in the domestic arena, and keeping a low profile in the major foreign policy issues. According to this image, the Netherlands had had substantial colonial and maritime interests, but at the same time had been very inward looking, and this had fostered its conservative individuality and frugality. After 1945 things were very different, with openness, unprecedented growth in prosperity and political and economic modernization. The Netherlands lost Indonesia, its most important colony, in the immediate postwar years, but in contrast to the situation before 1940 it had a presence on the international stage. Pre-war neutrality made way for an active foreign policy. Transatlantic cooperation and European integration became the cornerstones of Dutch activities in the international arena. The Netherlands was swept up in the Pax Americana, which was one of the factors in the development, from the late 1940s, of an unstoppable drive to modernize. It is therefore not surprising that there is a fundamental distinction in the historical awareness of many contemporaries between the pre-war and postwar years.

Yet it would not be appropriate to analyse the postwar period solely from the perspective of renewal. Essentially all the pre-war political parties returned, there was a high degree of party-political continuity, and the 1950s are seen for good reason as the pinnacle of pillarized Dutch politics and society. Against this backdrop, some historians therefore refer to post-1945 politics as a 'failed renewal' and point out that new political and cultural patterns did not emerge until the 1960s.[1] Viewed in this light, the first postwar phase was about renewal and recovery. It ended in 1958 with the fall of the fourth Drees government, which typified the reconstruction period because of its pragmatic policies founded on broadly based cooperation.

The period that followed bore the stamp of depillarization, the advent of protest movements and polarization, increased prosperity and a desire for political and social change. The epicentre of these developments was during the second half of the 1960s. The 1958–65 period was an overture, while the period after 1970 saw the definitive breakthrough of these changes. The historian Duco Hellema pointed out that these movements, which are often associated with the 1960s, were created primarily during the 1970s or reached a peak then. To take a few examples: university students organized massive demonstrations, protests about the role of America in Vietnam grew rapidly, the Dolle Mina feminist pressure group was founded in 1970 and national servicemen also made their voices heard primarily at that time.[2] The Den Uyl government (1973–77), which had an ambitious programme of reforms, had a team of young cabinet ministers with a political style that represented a clear break with the past. This means that the1960s and 1970s should be discussed as being one and the same era.

The 'long 1960s' ended when the Den Uyl government fell in 1977. This heralded a new phase in Dutch politics in which soberness, realism and pragmatism took over from enthusiasm and reforming zeal. The upshot of large wage increases in the 1960s and 1970s, higher public sector expenditure and the 1973 and 1979 oil crises, was the need to cut spending. Unemployment rose and the growing confidence in the controllability of the economy that had developed during the 1960s evaporated. The Netherlands was not alone. Other Western Europe countries also embarked on a period of conservative dominance, free market forces and smaller government. Having been on the offensive for many years, the left wing was now on the defensive, and initially vociferously opposed the policy of retrenchment pursued during the 1980s. It proved to be a rear-guard action. Social democrats had to learn that the way to regain power was not by clinging to the ideas of the 1960s and 1970s, but by adapting to the direction set by the Christian democrats and liberals of reducing public spending and government involvement. This process was neither fast nor painless. To begin with, the polarization of the late 1960s and the 1970s persisted. This struggle between the Christian democrats and liberals on the one hand and the left-wing parties on the other became fiercer as a result of foreign policy differences. While most Christian democrats and liberals supported the 1979 NATO double-track decision and wanted a new generation of NATO nuclear weapons if the Soviet Union did not remove its SS-20 ballistic missiles, many social democrats joined the peace movement, which organized huge protests against the deployment of new nuclear weapons in the West. The split was not resolved until 1987, when the Intermediate-Range Nuclear Forces Treaty was signed by the United States and the Soviet Union. Under the treaty, Moscow would destroy its SS-20 missiles and NATO would reverse the deployment of cruise missiles, which had already started.

In socioeconomic terms, the policy of austerity during the 1980s resulted in economic recovery, and the PvdA, which was now becoming more pragmatic, became a partner in government again in 1989. The former trade union leader and new party leader Wim Kok was prepared to work with both the Christian democrats and the liberals, and so social democracy returned to the centre of politics. This approach reached a peak between 1994 and 2002, when Wim Kok led a government made up of the social democrats, the VVD and D66, referred to as the 'purple' governments because that was the colour obtained by mixing the red of the social democrats and the blue of the liberals. A government was formed without Christian democrats for the first time since 1918. It was furthermore the first occasion since 1952 that social democrats and the VVD cooperated in a coalition. Meanwhile, the differences between the political parties had become very slight and talk of the 'polder model' concept became widespread as a description of the broadly based pragmatic cooperation between 'left' and 'right', which also included unions and employers. As a consequence, the political centre ground became so overcrowded that scope was created for the colourful populist Pim Fortuyn, who terminated years of consensus politics at the 2002 general election at a single stroke.

That heralded a new political phase for the Netherlands, in which national populism was a permanent element in the ever more volatile political spectrum. Pim Fortuyn was murdered in May 2002. Since 2006, Geert Wilders and his Party for Freedom (PVV) was primarily responsible for an anti-Islamic and anti-European trend in the political agenda. Political stability declined and, with the exception of the second Rutte government (2012–17), all governments since 1998 fell prematurely. In this increasingly turbulent political climate, the Netherlands was looking primarily for a new source of certainty and stability – a difficult quest in a more troubled international financial and political context.

These four periods are discussed in this chapter: the reconstruction years of renewal and recovery (1945–58), the 'long 1960s' of depillarization, protest, and political-cultural change (1958–77), heralding an era of spending cuts and smaller government, resulting in the 'polder model' of the 1990s, and finally the turbulent phase from 2002 to the present day in which newly arisen national populism, economic and international financial problems as well as European and international political friction produced new challenges.

Between political renewal and continuity (1945–58)

Much had already been written and said during the war years in the underground press, government circles in London and the Sint-Michielsgestel internment camp near Den Bosch about political renewal in the Netherlands after the liberation. Although opinions about the substance of this modernization varied, many were united in their hope that the divisions of a pillarized country would come to an end. The debates in Sint-Michielsgestel were particularly important.[3] The occupying forces had turned a school there into an internment camp for hostages in 1942 and until September 1944 a significant proportion of the political, economic and cultural elite had been incarcerated for varying lengths of time. Apart from the threat of executions during the initial phase, the hostages' lives were privileged compared with those of detainees in other camps. Altogether there were 1,900 prisoners, although there were never that many interned at the same time. The 'spirit of Gestel' reflected the views of the many who wanted to purge the former pillarized, pigeon-hole mentality and were searching for a new basis for political and social relationships. There was a growing conviction that the postwar formation of parties should take place on a new basis and that the multiplicity of political and social dividing lines and the resulting jumble of pillarized organizations should disappear. It would also strengthen national solidarity in the postwar Netherlands. It is not surprising that such reinforcement of the community nationwide was a significant element of the 'spirit of Gestel'. The extraordinary circumstances during the occupation had brought the Netherlands closer together as a nation. The sense of national unity that was now perceived so strongly contrasted vividly with the traditional segmented divisions, which were in fact seen as a cause of the pre-war crisis phenomena. The key words emerging from the deliberations of the elite internees were national unity, a renewed frame of mind and – with regard to social and economic issues – cooperation between capital, labour and government. This thinking laid the foundations for the Dutch People's Movement (NVB), which was established on 24 May 1945 and was intended to be a mass movement for the purposes of disseminating this renewal.[4]

After the external pressure of war conditions had disappeared, the old patterns returned faster than many, in their modernizing optimism, had been hoping. Apparently the 'spirit of Gestel' had produced above all a sense of national solidarity, but no basis for practical and coherent politics. The social democrats and Catholics who should have had a meeting of minds in a progressive new political party were too divided internally and had too many differences with each other to get that far, and so one pre-war party after another reappeared on the scene in 1945 and 1946. All the same, the foundation of the Labour Party (PvdA) in February 1946 seemed to suggest that a breakthrough in the old structure was possible. It inherited the legacy of the pre-war SDAP and, as a 'breakthrough party', also integrated left-wing liberals and progressive Protestants and Catholics. Tried and trusted social democratic symbols like 'The Internationale' and the red flag disappeared into the background to facilitate the change for newcomers. During the first postwar elections, though, the party got only just over 28 per cent of the votes, a result that indicated a carry-over from the 1930s, not renewal.

However, as discussed above, renewal dominated. First and foremost, the parties developed principles into manifestos. Ideological and religious principles remained important starting points for the political parties, of course, but they were much less prominent in the initial positions for political haggling than before the war. This made political dealings more businesslike and modern. Another important factor was the absence of the sense of malaise of the 1930s, when many had doubted whether parliamentary democracy had the right tools for tackling the big political, social and economic issues. By 1945 the 'minor crisis' of democracy (see chapter 6) was already a thing of the past and people's experience with war and occupation had discredited any shred of sympathy for authoritarian thinking. After the liberation there was therefore general political consensus about parliamentary democracy, and this aroused a great deal of hope and confidence.

Secondly, the changed position of social democrats in the political system was of great significance. The SDAP had been isolated for a long time before the war and did not become part of the government until 1939. After 1945, social democracy finally attained the centre of political power and would bear government responsibilities until 1958. The hoped-for breakthrough had not happened, but the inevitability of social democratic participation in government was a new phenomenon in Dutch politics. Between 1948 and 1958, the PvdA even provided the prime minister in the person of Willem Drees. His calm 'paternal' leadership embodied the non-party political reconstruction thinking with everyone putting their shoulders to the wheel and where

Figure 22 *Drees Asks You to Put Your Trust in List 2*. PvdA election poster 1952. Dutch Political Parties Documentation Centre, Groningen.

job security for all, safety, common sense and reliability were at the top of the agenda.[5] The fact that a social democrat could play such a role clearly showed the changes that had taken place since the 1930s.

A third new aspect was the broad agreement between all parties, except for the Communist Party of the Netherlands (CPN), about the main points of domestic and foreign policy. Until 1958, the Catholic People's Party (KVP) and the PvdA were the key players in the broad-based governments, in which initially (1948–52) the liberals (People's Party for Freedom and Democracy, VVD) and the CHU participated. Then, until 1958, the two big hitters were joined by the ARP and the CHU (see Illustration 9, p. 262). In those days, governments could on average count on the support of about 80 per cent of Lower House members. Cooperation in government between social democrats, Christian democrats and liberals was certainly not stress free, but nevertheless the reconstruction years are looked on as a period of pragmatism and seeking agreement.[6]

It was the same story with employers and employees, the fourth major change after the Second World War. In stark contrast to the polarized social climate during the 1930s, after 1945 there was usually harmonious cooperation. During the war, employers' and employees' organizations had decided to found a joint organization after the liberation, and the Labour Foundation (STAR) duly came into being in 1945. The Foundation developed into a major government advisory body on social policy and industrial relations. There was also cooperation between employers and unions, referred to as the social partners, in the Social and Economic Council (SER), which was established in

1950 and also had independent members appointed by the government. The government had given itself a statutory obligation to ask the SER for advice on every major socioeconomic issue. Later, in the 1990s, the Netherlands would create an international stir with its 'polder model'. During that period, the impression was often given that its characteristic social and political harmony was a new phenomenon. Yet the STAR and the SER, both set up in the immediate postwar years, embodied exactly the same cooperative political and social climate that was later to be called the polder model. That model was certainly not without contradictions and differences of opinion, but they were normally depoliticized and channelled into a compromise-building process.

Finally there was also a distinct contrast with the 1930s in social policy. During the 1930s the state was still adopting a cautious stance in this area, but after the war there was general agreement that everyone was entitled to social security, and that the state could not remain passive. One of the factors that gave rise to this objective was the work of the British economist Sir William Beveridge, who published his famous report *Social Insurance and Allied Services* in 1942. In it he advocated a universal system of social insurance. This report made a significant impression on the Dutch government in exile, which had it amended in London to suit the Dutch situation. There was consequently a report tailored to the Netherlands on which a social insurance system could be based, on the table when liberation arrived in 1945. In a moral sense it was a weapon to fight poverty, from an economic point of view it stimulated purchasing power, and in politics it legitimized the Western political and economic system of democracy and consultation. The introduction of social provisions was another important internal Western weapon in the Cold War. During the years of reconstruction, the foundations were thus laid for an extensive social welfare system that was not actually completed until the prosperous 1960s. This Dutch trend was part of a broader Western European context, in which every country developed its own version of what was later called the welfare state.

There were no major differences of opinion about the government's objective and responsibility, but there was controversy about the implementation of social security. The social democrats continued to stress the state's central position, while the Christian democrats championed implementation in the private sector through industrial and occupational associations. Yet such differences did not stand in the way of a harmonious policy under which decision making took place on the basis of close consultation between the social partners (employees' and employers' organizations) and government. First of all, each participant prepared a report about the issue concerned (for example provisions for old age, disability insurance or child allowances). In that context, social democrat, Catholic and Protestant parties, unions and employers formulated their opinions, and in so doing prepared the issue for discussion in the SER referred to above. This last body then advised the minister, after which a government bill might be submitted. It should not come as a surprise that the broader the agreement in the SER, the faster the legislative process. Some subjects were soon backed by a parliamentary majority, while others languished for years.[7] Willem Drees, the PvdA Minister of Social Affairs and later Prime Minister, was inextricably linked to the Dutch welfare state. In 1947 he introduced emergency legislation, named after him, that guaranteed the elderly a minimum income.

At the beginning of 1957, while he was Prime Minister, the definitive General Old Age Pensions Act (AOW) came into effect. It was a compulsory insurance for a universal state retirement pension, which to this day remains part of the Dutch provisions for old age. During the years of reconstruction, the foundations were thus laid for an extensive social welfare system that was not actually completed until the prosperous 1960s.

Only the communist party (CPN) had a political and economic vision that differed from the one described above. The prestige that the communists had acquired thanks to their role in the resistance, and which contributed to their historic 1946 election result (10.6 per cent), soon evaporated during the Cold War. The CPN became isolated as a result of the increase in tensions between East and West and its unconditional agreement with the communist conformity imposed in Eastern Europe. Opinion about it soon changed from a respected resistance group to a Soviet Russian 'fifth column' that needed to be rigorously opposed. Pre-war anti-communist sentiment returned at heightened levels and reached a peak in 1948 (the communist seizure of power in Prague). In 1956 (the suppression of the Hungarian uprising) it even led to violence in a few towns and cities. CPN premises, for example Felix Meritis in Amsterdam, suffered.[8] The CPN's growing isolation was also evident in their consistently declining share of the vote in every general election in this period. By 1959 only 2.4 per cent remained of the 10.6 per cent of votes achieved in 1946. Another factor in this decline was the attitude of the communist trade union EVC (United Trade Union), which was influenced by the CPN. Unlike the social democratic, Catholic and Protestant unions, it resisted the social climate of pragmatic cooperation with employers and government. Apart from the stance of the CPN and EVC, there was therefore a substantial degree of harmony during the years of reconstruction between government, political parties, employers and employees. The number of strikes in the Netherlands was lower than in virtually any other Western European country.

What typified the 1950s climate was that political and social debate took place within pillarized frameworks. This period is consequently considered, not without reason, to have been the pinnacle of pillarization. The implications of the rapid pace of modernization (urbanization, industrialization, secularization) for families and society (the role of women, leisure, education, sexuality) were discussed primarily in people's own circles. Inside the pillars, the elites delivered their disciplining messages. From this perspective, the pillarized world was indeed still completely intact. Yet after the war, movements developed below the surface which, in hindsight, presaged the major shifts and depillarization of the 1960s. Viewed from this perspective, the 1950s can be considered as more innovative in this regard than the clichéd image of political and social restoration suggests.

Immediately after the liberation an attempt was made to get young people involved in the re-established traditional pillar-related youth organizations, but without success, and in fact the number of members started to fall rapidly from the early 1950s. Being young at this time was fundamentally different from during the 1930s. A large proportion of young people remained 'young' for longer because participation in education grew spectacularly. In 1950, only 27 per cent of people in the twelve to twenty-five age group were in education, but by 1960 this had risen to 41 per cent. Many boys and girls reached a higher educational level than their parents, remained in peer groups longer and consequently developed a more independent awareness of youth and their own stronger youth culture. Thanks to the gradually growing prosperity, young employees could afford greater economic autonomy and decide for themselves how to spend their free time. Youth wages began to shoot up in the second half of the 1950s and rose by 150 per cent between 1955 and 1965, and at weekends recreation could be found in cinemas, bars and dance halls. This increased liberty, free of the old pillarized ties, also came from greater mobility. Sales figures for young people's preferred means of transport in the Netherlands – mopeds – were tremendous. In 1949, there were 4,000 in the Netherlands; by 1955 there were 500,000, 1 million by 1960 and 1.5 million five years after that.[9]

The Catholic pillar also lurched to and fro between old and new. In May 1954, the Dutch bishops published a charge forbidding Catholics from joining social democratic associations and trade unions, listening regularly to radio programmes broadcast by VARA and frequently reading newspapers with a social democratic bias. If Catholics did not obey these prohibitions, they would be refused the Holy Sacraments and a religious funeral. Membership of the PvdA was not banned – the bishops did not want to go that far – but was described as 'irresponsible'. Evidently, the bishops had watched in dismay as the KVP was overtaken by the PvdA as the biggest party in the 1952 elections and feared further crumbling of Catholic unity and power. There was also a threat of collapse on the right. In 1948, the former minister C. J. I. M. Welter left the KVP and won one seat at the elections. The Catholic National Party (KNP) he set up won two seats in 1952. The charge also served to bring KNP supporters back to the apron strings of the KVP.

The bishops' message was tailor-made for the pillarized structure. While the elites at the top worked together – the KVP and PvdA were after all the most important members of the coalition government – big guns were used to ban the lowly in the Catholic pillar from getting involved with the ideas of others. The bishops' intervention had two effects. On the one hand, the KVP acquired many new members. Its share of the vote in the 1956 Lower House elections rose from 28.7 per cent to 31.7 per cent. This indicates that the elite of the Catholic pillar still had its supporters largely under control and disciplinary pillar mechanisms were still working. On the other hand, some of the Catholic intelligentsia distanced themselves from the pastoral letter and criticized the outdated authoritarian mentality of such admonitions. Catholics in the PvdA also rejected the charge, which tells us that pillar-related disciplining was no longer a matter of course and that its days were numbered.

This was the political background to economic reconstruction, which started slowly after 1945, but built up a head of steam after 1948. Although the economic historian Hein Klemann calculates that the war damage was less than what was believed for many years, the Dutch economy was in dire straits in 1945.[10] The occupying forces had taken a huge amount of capital goods and other valuable items to Germany, particularly during the last year of the occupation, and large areas of arable land had become unusable as a result of the hostilities, as had many ports, bridges, locks and sluices. The national debt had rocketed, as had the amount of money, so monetary reform was urgently needed. There was a dramatic trade gap because imports hugely exceeded exports, and there was a shortage of capital for investments – something for which, of course, there was a pressing need in order to put an end to the import–export imbalance. There would have been no escape from this vicious circle without economic aid from outside.

The situation was furthermore exacerbated by the loss of income from Indonesia, which prior to 1940 had amounted to about 14 per cent of gross national product. Instead of generating money, after 1945 it was a major burden on the national budget because of the high cost of the colonial war that the Netherlands waged against the Republic of Indonesia between 1945 and 1949. The Dutch naturally responded eagerly to the American offer in June 1947 to support European economic reconstruction. The Marshall Plan aid that started to flow to Europe in 1948 played an important role in the breakthrough to economic recovery that began at the end of 1940s, and would make the Netherlands a rapidly modernizing country in the 1950s.[11]

Marshall Plan aid was more than an economic support programme – it brought with it an Americanization of thinking about production and consumption. American ideas about free trade dovetailed perfectly with Dutch traditions and interests, so the Netherlands modernized along American lines, not so much in the form of imitation or colonization but, as the sociologist Kees Schuyt and the literary historian Ed Taverne observe, through adaptation, interpretation and diffusion.[12] This did not just apply to business. Universities and the scientific community also abandoned their pre-war focus on Germany and looked to the United States.[13]

This trend was in line with the infusion of science into political and economic thinking, of which Jan Tinbergen – later to win a Nobel Prize – was a key initiator. He had been one of the driving forces behind the Social Democratic Party's Plan for Labour in the 1930s. Tinbergen was searching for economic and political instruments that could manage the issues of economic growth, inflation, employment and stability. In 1945, the Dutch government decided to establish the Netherlands Bureau for Economic Policy Analysis (CPB) and Jan Tinbergen became its first director. Although the CPB's task did not extend beyond preparing socioeconomic forecasts and advising the government, its creation was nevertheless an important sign that political and economic thinking was changing.

In their study of the postwar Netherlands, Schuyt and Taverne talk about the advent of a 'mathematizing view of reality' in the 1950s.[14] The impact of mathematicians, and their scientific, model-based approach to facts, was increasing in many areas. Whether it was economic policy, calculating the height of dikes, urban planning, land consolidation, developing the road network, recreation or consumption, the advance of experts and their calculations was unstoppable. The country rose again, prosperity grew – in dribs and drabs, but everyone felt it – the welfare state was established and education expanded. Everyone became a partner in a dynamic modernization process that seemed to work according to rational principles and in which there appeared to be no losers. The conflict between capital and labour looked as though it had been superseded and concepts like 'consumers', 'producers' and the 'general interest' had replaced it.[15] At the same time, belief in the ability of science and technology to solve problems rose to unprecedented heights. Of course this feeling did not suddenly appear after 1945, it had its roots in the pre-war years, but what was new was that the grounds for this optimism were now constantly confirmed and reinforced by ongoing economic growth and modernization.[16]

Economic reconstruction thus went ahead with a different mind-set from that in the 1930s. In 1950, the budget was back in balance and per capita GDP surpassed the 1929 level. After twenty years of stagnation, according to the economic historian Van Zanden, the Netherlands now stood at the beginning of a long period of economic growth that continued until 1973.[17] During this era, the Dutch economy expanded at the high annual average rate of 5 per cent. Unemployment fell to less than 2 per cent, and even dipped below 1 per cent in the 1960s. This extremely favourable economic trend is in line with the international growth pattern of the 1950s and 1960s, but it also had some specifically Dutch traits. For example, the government pursued a policy of wage restraint and kept prices low, so Dutch products were relatively cheap on the world market and exports grew strongly. In 1948, exports accounted for less than a third of GDP, but the figure had risen to over 50 per cent by 1954. The engines driving economic growth in the 1950s were manufacturing and trade.

Industrialization and the increasing urbanization associated with it changed the Dutch self-image. Before the Second World War, people had looked on the Netherlands primarily as a country of trade, agriculture and stock breeding, which governed a large colonial empire, including the Dutch East Indies. Little of that picture remained after 1945. The Netherlands lost its colonial possessions in Asia in the immediate postwar years, and during this phase reconstruction and industrialization in fact provided a goal that helped in finding a new identity. The government encouraged this trend with what it called a 'proactive industrialization policy'. The awareness of living in a country that was modernizing rapidly was boosted by the annual publication of industrialization news, which documented this successful progress. For many people in the 1950s, the years after the war were fundamentally different from those before the war.

Cracks started to appear in the broad-based political and social harmony in the late 1950s. The broadly supported governments led by Willem Drees came to an end in 1958 and the social democrats ended up in opposition until 1973 – except for a short break in 1965–66 – while Christian democrats and conservative liberals ran the country. Relations between employers and employees also became more difficult. In 1960, the Dutch Association of Trade Unions (NVV), the Dutch Federation of Catholic Trade Unions (NKV) and the National Federation of Christian Trade Unions in the Netherlands (CNV) staged their first strikes since 1945. This was an early portent of the 1960s and 1970s, when the political and social harmony of the reconstruction years gave way to polarization.

Watershed in foreign policy and the decolonization of the Dutch East Indies

While the war was still going on, the Dutch government in London made it clear that it did not wish to return to the pre-war policy of aloofness after liberation but wanted to pursue a more active foreign policy. In practice, this proved to be little more than a declaration of intent during the first postwar years, and the Netherlands adopted a cautious stance. Until quite late in 1947, The Hague clung to the hope that the United States, United Kingdom and Soviet Union would reach an agreement about a common policy on Germany and that economic reconstruction would take place in an undivided Europe.[18]

In other words, there was no actual break with pre-war policy in the years immediately after 1945. On the contrary, it is the continuity that is most striking. In fact, the Netherlands had precious few alternatives to a wait-and-see attitude. The uncertainty about future relations in Europe was too great and the opportunity to exert any influence on them too small. The Netherlands furthermore had no tradition of a proactive foreign policy to fall back on, and attention was focused primarily on national reconstruction, internal political renewal and, increasingly, the Indonesia issue as well. However, the split between east and west in 1947 created a situation that gave the Dutch the opportunity to get on to the international stage with more success than before.

This development started when the Soviet Union and the Eastern European countries rejected the Marshall Plan. This made the economic division of Europe in the summer of 1947 inevitable and also increased the opportunities for the Benelux countries (Belgium, the Netherlands and Luxembourg) to give their own input into the substance of this American plan. They seized this chance to act jointly to strengthen their position during that summer.[19] At the Paris conference on the Marshall Plan, these three small nations also projected themselves as a potential engine for driving Western European integration. A year later, the Netherlands was one of the signatories of the Treaty of Brussels, together with the United Kingdom, France, Belgium and Luxembourg, which established the Western Union. It was clear, however, that without American support this Western European security organization would not be able to build up much strength in the impending Cold War. It was therefore essential that the United States should be prepared to guarantee the security of Europe. Washington gave that assurance in April 1949 with the foundation of NATO. The Netherlands was a loyal member from the beginning and in subsequent decades the watchword of Dutch foreign policy was: 'What's good for NATO and American engagement in Europe is also good for the Netherlands.'[20]

As far as The Hague was concerned, this meant that during this era European integration was subordinate to Atlantic cooperation. French plans in the early 1950s for establishing a European Defence Community (EDC) were initially rejected by the Dutch government in no uncertain terms. The Hague was concerned that as a result American and British involvement in European security would be endangered. The Dutch were also opposed to security cooperation in continental Europe because the country would be pulled 'inland', would come under French influence and and – as soon as the Federal Republic of Germany developed enough strength – would become dependent on the Germans. The Netherlands would then have precious little latitude left in its foreign policy, and no less importantly there would be insufficient counterweight to German power. The risk that a 'restive' Germany would set out to restore unity within its 1937 borders could only be minimized by the Americans and NATO.[21]

This did not mean that the Netherlands pursued an anti-Germany policy during that period. On the contrary, The Hague was a strong advocate of controlled reconstruction of the German economy and the aim was the complete integration of the Federal Republic of Germany into the western alliance, including in a military sense. As early as the signing of the Treaty of Brussels in March 1948 referred to above, the Dutch Minister of Foreign Affairs, C. W. H. G. van Boetzelaer, had argued behind the scenes that the West German state, which had not yet been founded, should be a future member of the Union. Over two

Figure 23 1948 Liberty Ship. The Netherlands will come out on top. Marshall Plan propaganda poster. National Archives of the Netherlands, The Hague/RVD/photographer unknown.

years later, after the war in Korea (1950–53) had broken out, the Netherlands advocated prompt German rearmament and German membership of NATO. The Cold War and the perceived Soviet Russian threat thus made the Netherlands an obvious and active partner in the western alliance. In this context, 'active' means that The Hague routinely intervened at moments when it saw its interests embedded in the West coming under threat.

It is also striking that as far as the Federal Republic of Germany was concerned, the Netherlands pursued a policy of positive integration. Starting in 1949–50, the Dutch urged a fully fledged position for West Germany in the western alliance, and in so doing also a reduction in the authority powers of the occupying powers. The underlying idea was that only then could the Federal Republic become a reliable partner of the West, in other words when it had the same rights and duties as the other Western European countries. This goal was attained through the ratification of the Paris Agreements in May 1955. West Germany became a member of NATO and acquired virtually complete sovereignty. The fact that The Hague did not play a significant part in the creation of the agreements and treaties did not diminish the satisfaction of the Dutch with the result. The United States and the United Kingdom guaranteed European security and the Federal Republic of Germany became firmly embedded in the Atlantic block.[22]

For many years this Atlantic priority led The Hague to resist European political cooperation. It was in this area that the Dutch were particularly concerned about continental pull and the risk of a future Franco–German alliance. Economically, on the other hand, as a trading nation the Netherlands had a substantial interest in integration and the removal of trade barriers. This is why the Dutch were always in favour of openness and the expansion of European economic cooperation and – for commercial reasons, too – rejected a continental European bloc. Initially, the Netherlands directed its efforts at the Organisation for European Economic Co-operation (OEEC), which was formed to administer the Marshall Plan and foster trade liberalization. In so doing, the Dutch opted at first for intergovernmental cooperation. They responded cautiously to proposals for supranational integration, for example, the 1950 Schuman Declaration that would lead to the foundation a year later of the European Coal and Steel Community (ECSC).[23] During the negotiations, the Netherlands safeguarded its national powers as much as possible through the intergovernmental Special Council of Ministers, which set limits to the powers of the supranational High Authority.

There was a U-turn in 1952 after the creation of the ECSC. The new foreign minister, J. W. Beyen (1952–56), opted for a supranational approach based on the view that the interests of small European countries would be better safeguarded by transferring national powers to European institutions.[24] This would be the most effective way to prevent the danger of dominance by the major European powers. Broadly speaking, the Netherlands would continue to pursue this policy in subsequent decades. It was also from this perspective that Beyen was involved in the inception of the Benelux memorandum of May 1955, on the basis of which the European Economic Community (EEC) would emerge two years later.

The pro-European reputation that the Netherlands has always had in other countries is largely due to this important contribution to the creation of the EEC by the Benelux countries. That picture is correct, provided one is aware that the pro-European Dutch attitude did not extend to political integration or the threat of supranational European Community institutions being undermined by intergovernmental structures. At such moments the Netherlands blocked institutional changes and sometimes collided head on with Bonn and Paris. For example, in the early 1960s, the Dutch, together with the Belgians, obstructed the creation of a European Political Union advocated by Konrad Adenauer and Charles de Gaulle.[25]

Comparison of the international positions of the Netherlands in the years before 1940 and after 1945 reveals there had been a fundamental change. After a brief transition phase in the immediate postwar years, when the Dutch had little choice but to wait and see, foreign policy took a new direction as European blocs emerged. The new foreign policy cornerstones became security through the Atlantic alliance and economic cooperation in Europe. This represented an irreversible departure in 1948–49 from the former Dutch stance of neutrality and abstention.

During this period there was a second foreign policy watershed. In December 1949, the Republic of Indonesia became independent and the Dutch lost their most important colony. The Netherlands was still a colonial power, thanks to overseas territories in the Caribbean (Suriname and the Antilles) and New Guinea, which stayed outside the Republic of Indonesia, but what remained was of only marginal importance. So whereas the Netherlands had been a small country with a large empire in Asia, after the difficult and partially violent decolonization process between 1945 and 1949 it was only a minor European power. In view of the great importance of this development, it makes sense to interrupt this chronological discussion of events to briefly address the history of postwar decolonization.

In common with other colonial powers, the Netherlands was faced with nationalist movements and the desire for independence in colonies for several decades before the Second World War. The foundation of Boedi Oetomo (Noble Endeavour) in 1908 is generally considered to have been the birth of the Indonesian nationalist movement. It was a native organization based on a Western model with the declared objective of developing Javanese culture. Boedi Oetomo was not a mass movement. It recruited its supporters primarily from the indigenous elite who had enjoyed a Dutch education. Sarekat Islam (Islamic Union), established in 1911, developed into a much more powerful player. Initially, it projected itself primarily as an organization that represented the economic and cultural interests of the Muslim population, but Sarekat Islam soon grew into a mass movement demanding democratization of the colonial administration. People in progressive Dutch colonial circles at the time were not hostile to such aspirations and they considered the advent of such movements as evidence of the success of the 'ethical policy' (see p. 170). The Volksraad (People's Council) was set up in the Dutch East Indies in 1918. It included representatives of the native population and it was permitted to discuss the colonial government's policy. It was not given any actual influence, but its foundation as such was an expression of enlightened colonial thinking. Ultimately, it proved to be insufficient to prevent escalation.

The optimism projected by the 'ethical policy' and the platform for discussion that the Volksraad should have provided disappeared in the 1920s. The tide turned on the Dutch side after the First World War and the progressive colonial thinkers and politicians lost influence, while there was radicalization on the Indonesian side. A small revolutionary group from Sarekat Islam sought armed confrontation, and plans were developed in 1925–26 in the small Partai Kommunis Indonesia (Communist Party of Indonesia, PKI) to demolish Dutch power. And indeed in January 1927 there was an armed uprising in Sumatra. While it was possible to suppress it easily, it resulted in further hardening of the Dutch position. During the same period, a new generation of nationalist leaders emerged, of whom Sukarno, Mohammed Hatta and Sutan Sjahrir were the most important. It was no coincidence that on 4 July 1927 – American Independence Day – they founded the Perserikatan Nasional Indonesia (Indonesian National Party, PNI), which rejected collaboration with the colonial regime and wanted to achieve Indonesian independence through mass mobilization. According to the Leiden historian Van den Doel, an unbridgeable gulf had developed between colonial power and the colonized.[26] And during the 1930s, this gulf became bigger and bigger.

During the decade, tensions in internal relations became increasingly numerous, while the Dutch colonial regime was subjected to ever-growing external pressure too. It was recognized on the Dutch side that the Dutch East Indies could not keep going for long against any Japanese aggression, particularly after war broke out in Europe. The Indonesian Archipelago became easy meat after the Netherlands had also been trampled underfoot in May 1940. The Dutch troops in Java capitulated on 8 March 1942, a week after the Japanese had invaded it. Initially, the indigenous population welcomed the Japanese as liberators from the rule of the Netherlands, but it soon became apparent that the situation under the Japanese was even worse than under the Dutch. An estimated ten million Javanese were forced to become slave labourers, of whom hundreds of thousands died. The total number of native victims of the Japanese occupation in the Indonesian Archipelago as a whole was about 2.5 million. The Dutch colonial administration was dismantled and the Dutch population disappeared into internment camps, where many thousands, particularly during the last year of the war, expired in wretched circumstances.

Japan professed support for Indonesian nationalism to the outside world for propaganda reasons, but in fact the country's intent was to make the potential of Indonesia subservient to Japanese war aims. Sukarno, assuming there would be an extended period of Japanese domination in Asia, was prepared to cooperate with the new rulers in the hope that it would bring Indonesian independence closer. Yet the Japanese did not make many concessions. They went no further than making vague promises about independence in the future. Sukarno continued to hope in vain for support from Japan for Indonesian independence until Japanese capitulation on 15 August 1945. But radical young people (referred to as pemuda), who for some time had perceived Sukarno's strategy as humiliating, wanted action. After Sukarno and Hatta had persuaded themselves that the Japanese authorities that were still present would take no action against a unilateral declaration of independence, they proclaimed the independent Republic of Indonesia on 17 August 1945 – a date on which the creation of the Republic is celebrated to this day. It soon emerged after August 1945 that conflicts between the Netherlands and the Republic were inevitable.

Restoration of Dutch authority was out of the question because there were virtually no Dutch troops. Initially, British and Australian forces acted on behalf of the Netherlands, and Dutch troops did not take over from them until July 1946. But even then it was clear that it would be impossible to return to the pre-war situation. Firstly, the Republic of Indonesia had meanwhile become a fait accompli, and secondly, in December 1942 Queen Wilhelmina had given a startling radio talk from London in which she announced that after the war the relationship with the Dutch East Indies should continue on a different, more equal basis. Yet the Netherlands did not have many options for implementing such plans after Japanese capitulation. Sukarno and Hatta had not only gone far further than what the Dutch had in mind when they proclaimed the Republic.

Sukarno, as a 'Japanese puppet', was also unacceptable to the Dutch government as a negotiating partner. As a result, the violence soon escalated.

In the power vacuum created after the Japanese defeat, groups of radical pemuda turned to violence throughout the whole archipelago to impede the return of the Dutch. They also took revenge on those who had profited from the Japanese occupation at the expense of the population. In order to save their own lives, many Dutch people ensconced themselves in the internment camps and had themselves protected by the Japanese troops still present. An estimated 3,500 Dutch people lost their lives during this explosion of violence. In November 1945, British troops conquered the major Javanese port of Surabaya by defeating Sukarno's Republican Army and several tens of thousands of unorganized pemuda. This bloody battle gave the British cause to withdraw from Indonesia as quickly as possible, which was confirmation for the Netherlands that Sukarno's Republic was a significant power factor. The departure of the British and Australians from Indonesia and the handover of power to the Dutch in July 1946 consolidated that power.

Governor-General H. J. van Mook, the top representative of the Netherlands in the Dutch East Indies and the man behind Queen Wilhelmina's enlightened 1942 speech, was able to persuade the government in The Hague of the need to engage in serious negotiations with the Republic, and to take as a starting point Indonesian independence in a new alliance with the Netherlands. In November 1946, the Netherlands and the Republic of Indonesia signed a draft agreement in Linggadjati on Java, in which the Dutch recognized the Republic's de facto power over Java, Sumatra and Madura and in which it was stated that before 1 January 1949 the United States of Indonesia would be formed from three states: the Republic (Java, Sumatra, Madura), Borneo and the Great East (the islands east and northeast of Java). As a federal nation, this United States of Indonesia, together with the Netherlands, would create the Netherlands–Indonesian Union, with the Dutch queen as its head.

This draft agreement had attractive features for both sides. There was de facto recognition of the Republic, with sovereignty on the horizon. The establishment of two further states had strengthened the hand of the Netherlands and restricted the Republic's. The links with Indonesia would furthermore remain through the Union. On the conservative side, however, 'Linggadjati' provoked a storm of protest in the Netherlands. The PvdA/KVP government was even faced with the prospect of falling as a result of the KVP's resistance to it. This was avoided, however, by putting a spin on 'Linggadjati' as being disadvantageous for the Republic and no longer talking about a sovereign Indonesian federation, but only a sovereign Netherlands–Indonesian Union. This weakening of the Republic's position, decided unilaterally by the Netherlands, made conflict inevitable. This was not unwelcome to many on the Indonesian side because they were dissatisfied with 'Linggadjati' and actually wanted to continue the armed struggle. The Linggadjati Agreement was nevertheless officially signed in March 1947. It was not really a positive signal because both parties made it clear they interpreted the agreement differently.

Given this background, it is not surprising that discussions between the Netherlands and the Republic of Indonesia about the detailed substance of 'Linggadjati' soon stalled.

In the spring of 1947 there were stronger and stronger calls on the Dutch side to settle things with the Republic militarily. In addition to the political and prestige-related motives, economic considerations also played a role. In 1947, the Netherlands faced dire financial and economic problems. This situation was made even worse by the huge costs associated with attempts to restore Dutch authority in Indonesia (an army of 100,000 men had already been mobilized). American and British pressure on the Dutch-Indonesian negotiations prevented a military escalation on a number of occasions, but in July 1947 the Netherlands launched Operation Product with the dual objective of forcing the Republic into moderation and safeguarding Dutch commercial interests. Oil fields and coal mines on Sumatra and over a thousand plantations and businesses on Java were soon brought under Dutch control.

From a military point of view the operation was a success, but it was a pyrrhic victory. The Dutch actions actually gave the Republic momentum and cost the Netherlands a substantial amount of international support. The United Nations Security Council called unanimously for a ceasefire. The UN established the Security Council Committee of Good Offices on the Indonesian Question to intermediate. It consisted of representatives from the United States, Belgium and Australia, who developed more sympathy for the position of the Republic than that of the Netherlands. Meanwhile, hardliners in the Dutch camp acquired progressively greater control of policy. The first Drees government took over in the summer of 1948 and a supporter of the hard line, E. M. J. A. Sassen (KVP), became Minister of Overseas Territories. Soon afterwards, Governor-General Van Mook was replaced by former prime minister Beel (KVP), who began to work on the military elimination of the Republic. This operation commenced in December 1948 and resulted, among other things, in the imprisonment of the members of the Republic's government in Yogyakarta. The Security Council acted once more by expressing a wish for the military action to end and the Republic's government to be released. It also demanded that the United States of Indonesia be granted sovereignty by 1 January 1950 at the latest. Under this international pressure, which was increased still further by the American threat to exclude the Netherlands from aid under the Marshall Plan, Dutch freedom of action decreased even more.

In May 1949 the Netherlands and the Republic agreed a ceasefire and the outline of a political settlement, which was fleshed out during the subsequent Round Table Conference. The Netherlands transferred sovereignty to the United States of Indonesia on 27 December 1949. Viewed in the light of Dutch efforts during the preceding years, the Indonesians could be well pleased. The Republic was completely independent and the Union with the Netherlands was granted no binding powers. It was nothing more than a weak cooperative alliance between two independent nation states and looked very much like what had been agreed in 1946 in Linggadjati, which the Netherlands subsequently rejected.

The Netherlands nevertheless appeared to have been successful in two areas. Firstly, Indonesia had become a federal state, and secondly, New Guinea remained outside the United States of Indonesia. The federal character of Indonesia did not last for long, however, because in 1950 Sukarno put a stop to it and Indonesia became a unitary state.

Figure 24 Transfer of sovereignty to the Republic of Indonesia (1949). National Archives of the Netherlands, The Hague/Anefo/photographer unknown.

The retention of New Guinea was nothing more than a sticking plaster on a gaping colonial wound, but it gave the Netherlands the feeling that not everything had been lost and persuaded doubters in the Lower House to get off the fence and agree to the transfer of sovereignty to Indonesia.

Soon, however, the New Guinea question developed into a new controversy. During the 1950s, the Netherlands kept hold of this remnant of colonial possession, primarily for psychological reasons, while Sukarno was aiming at annexation by Indonesia. The indignation that arose when this did not succeed resulted in Jakarta terminating the Netherlands–Indonesian Union in 1956 and, a year later, expropriating virtually all the Dutch companies in Indonesia. That same year, all Dutch people and many Indo-Europeans were forced to leave the country. This resulted in the breakdown of diplomatic relations in 1960. Military skirmishes, with fatalities on both sides, even threatened to escalate into an actual war between the Netherlands and its former colony. Ultimately, after renewed international pressure on the obstinate Dutch, New Guinea was transferred to the UN in 1962 and to Indonesia on 1 May 1963. In 1969, Indonesia definitively annexed New Guinea after a plebiscite – manipulated by the Indonesians – among the Papuans.[27]

The transfer of sovereignty to the United States of Indonesia at the end of December 1949 marked the end of a difficult decolonization process. Looking back, one has to conclude that after 1945 the Netherlands was faced with the consequences of its pre-war policy of confrontation with the nationalist movement. According to Van den Doel, in view of Dutch colonial policy after 1920 it was 'inevitable that Indonesian independence would be brought about by a revolution.'[28] On top of that, Indonesian nationalism had developed a strength during the Second World War that many Dutch people failed to recognize. As far as they were concerned, the colonial era had stood still during the

German occupation and they wanted to pick up the threads with the old colony where they thought the outbreak of war had left them. In so doing, they failed to realize that their recollection of the situation did not even reflect the realities of Indonesia before the war.

This misperception of the situation in the colony betrayed a deep-rooted paternalistic attitude according to which the Netherlands had a 'moral duty', in fact even an entitlement, to develop the Dutch East Indies. 'The East Indies were our pride and joy,' said Minister of Overseas Territories H. J. van Maarseveen in 1949 in the debate in the Lower House about transferring sovereignty. He continued, 'To be sure, we had undertaken to grant the East Indies independence ... but the Dutch people nevertheless believed in their hearts that this would only happen in the long term and even then only hand in glove with us, perhaps even under our ultimate leadership.'[29] This was far from reality, but only a few were able to fully realize it. Even the moderates in the Netherlands, who advocated a new relationship with greater input from the Indonesians, continued to think along such paternalistic colonial lines. For the Indonesians thirsting for independence – who also included moderates – that was not enough. Even the moderates on both sides did not have enough to offer one another, and so the hardliners in both the Dutch and Indonesian camps gained more and more ground, and the conflict became increasingly acute in both political and military terms.

The military interventions in the summer of 1947 and at the end of 1948 became known in the Netherlands as the first and second police actions. By using these terms the Dutch were trying to imply that it was a domestic matter. It was furthermore suggested that the operations were of limited extent and duration. That was euphemistic because in fact it was a colonial war that went on for several years. A notorious example was the action of the special forces unit Korps Speciale Troepen (Corps Special Troops) that at the end of 1946 was unleashed on Celebes, now known as Sulawesi, and under the command of Raymond Westerling killed thousands in targeted reprisals. In his comprehensive study of the Dutch colonial past, Joop de Jong describes the period between the summer of 1947 and August 1949 as a 'continuous, small-scale war that was only interrupted by short-lived truces'.[30] The spiral of terrorism and counter-terrorism reached a grisly peak in 1949 with many victims. Dutch troops, who had been forced on to the defensive, resorted to measures that were not much different from those taken by German forces in the occupied Netherlands. For example, there were summary executions, innocent people were murdered 'to set an example', prisoners were tortured, and homes, or even entire villages, were burned to the ground. According to a rough estimate, some 100,000 Indonesians and about 5,000 Dutch troops lost their lives.[31] The conduct of the hostilities on both sides was more complicated than the conflict between the Netherlands and the Republic would suggest. In some cases, the fighting also had the character of a civil war because in its ranks the Royal Netherlands East Indies Army (KNIL) had Moluccans and members of the large Indo-European community (offspring of mixed marriages), who had loyalties to both sides.

It was to take years before the war crimes in Indonesia could be discussed openly in the Netherlands. In 1969 there was much public and political commotion when

Indonesian veteran Joop Hueting talked candidly about Dutch 'war crimes' in Indonesia during an edition, which subsequently became famous, of the VARA television current affairs programme *Achter het Nieuws*.[32] The government response was to launch an official investigation, which resulted in a report containing an admission that there had been some excesses, but the term 'war crime' was carefully avoided.[33] At the end of the 1980s, however, when Loe de Jong did not shrink from denouncing Dutch war crimes in Indonesia in draft passages for the last volume of his standard work about the Netherlands in the Second World War, there was a storm of protest from veterans. The upshot was that De Jong removed the expression 'war crimes' in the final text and referred only to excesses.[34]

The emotions that the term 'war crimes' provoked for decades are an indication of the lengthy aftermath of the decolonization of Indonesia.[35] That also emerged during the preparations for Queen Beatrix's state visit to Indonesia in 1995. A great deal of effort went into the appropriate form of words the queen would use when referring to Dutch violence in her speech. In the end, however, she remained cautious and, by saying 'it deeply saddens us that so many died in that struggle or have had to bear the scars for the rest of their lives', she carefully recognized the suffering on both sides. During the planning for the state visit the queen's presence on Independence Day (17 August) was furthermore expressly avoided.[36] It was not until 2005 that a Dutch minister attended the annual independence celebrations in Indonesia for the first time. Since then, there has now and again been a call for a large-scale investigation into the armed conflict during the 1945–49 decolonization period. In December 2016, referring to this 'black page in Dutch history' (Minister of Foreign Affairs Bert Koenders), the Dutch government finally decided to launch such an enquiry. During the years leading up to it, compensation was also paid for the first time, pursuant to court judgments, to descendants of victims of crimes committed by Dutch troops. Rémy Limpach's study *De brandende kampongs van Generaal Spoor*, published in 2016, played a significant role in the recent debate about Dutch conduct during the 1945–49 period. It proved convincingly that Dutch troops acted with extreme violence on a large scale in this colonial war. Never before had there been such a detailed and comprehensive description of Dutch war crimes.[37]

'The East Indies are lost, disaster is born': that sort of slogan dating from the immediate postwar years indicates how fearful the Netherlands was about the implications of losing the Dutch East Indies. Economic ramifications were not the only concern. The country's self-image as a colonial power was also cherished. Indonesia separate from the Netherlands – in the late 1940s this concept was still unimaginable for many people. When Indonesian independence became a fact in 1949, however, there was no economic disaster. As we saw earlier, after 1950 the Netherlands enjoyed a lengthy period of substantial economic growth and it soon found its feet in Atlantic-European cooperation. Integration of some 300,000 people from Indonesia (about 100,000 'real' Dutch subjects and approximately 200,000 East Indies Dutch), who arrived in the Netherlands in a number of waves, did not, with the exception of the Moluccans (see p. 256 ff.), cause any problems.[38] So there was no catastrophe, but the end of the Dutch East Indies was a watershed in Dutch history that was to leave its mark for decades.

Crisis at Soestdijk: The Greet Hofmans affair

During the 1950s, shielded from public view, another struggle was raging. It even brought the country to the verge of a crisis of monarchy – a crisis that also spoke volumes about the political culture at that time. At the beginning of June 1956, the German weekly magazine *Der Spiegel* published a controversial article about the influence the faith healer Greet Hofmans was said to have over Queen Juliana. Akin to the way the monk Rasputin promised the Czar of Russia in the early twentieth century to cure the heir to the throne and became *en passant* an influential political schemer, according to *Der Spiegel*, Greet Hofmans had acquired a position of trust with Queen Juliana. She did that by promising to restore complete vision to the partially sighted Princess Marijke (later called Christina). 'As was the name of Rasputin in Czarist Russia,' continued the Hamburg magazine, 'the role of this sorceress is completely unknown to the Dutch people and even senior civil servants. At the same time a few insiders at court and in the cabinet are divided into two opposing camps, and the risk of a government crisis is not fanciful.'[39] The article was written in sensational style and *Der Spiegel* greatly exaggerated, but many of the facts were completely correct.

What was going on? The deeply religious Hofmans had appointed herself as a link between sufferers and God, and allegedly had the gift of healing. Her first meeting with Queen Juliana was in November 1948 and afterwards Hofmans rapidly became a confidant and stayed at Soestdijk Palace regularly. Prince Bernhard soon lost confidence in Hofmans after the cure of Princess Marijke failed to materialize. He put a stop to her stays at the palace in 1950, but the intensive contacts with the queen continued. In later years Hofmans appears to have had a significant influence on Juliana's views and conduct. For a considerable length of time, for instance, Juliana's refusal in 1952 to agree to the enforcement of the death sentence passed on the German war criminal Willy Lages was linked to the intensive contacts between the monarch and Hofmans. The government stuck to its guns about wanting to carry out the execution while Juliana threatened to abdicate if it went ahead. The Netherlands found itself on the brink of a constitutional crisis, which was only avoided because the cabinet changed its mind and Lages's death sentence was commuted to life imprisonment. The question of whether Hofmans actually exerted her influence in this matter has meanwhile been downplayed. In his comprehensive study of the Hofmans affair, the historian Cees Fasseur doubted that the faith healer played a part in it. Fasseur pointed out, however, that Prime Minister Drees, who was obviously closely involved in the Lages issue, explicitly observed Hofmans's influence.

In the year of Lages's commutation, tensions also arose between the government and the queen about speeches that Juliana wanted to give during a visit to the United States (including to Congress and the United Nations General Assembly). The cabinet bears political responsibility for the queen's speeches and some ministers had serious misgivings about the woolly pacifist sentiments the queen wanted to express. To advocate disarmament and display 'Third Way' (i.e. neither the communist East nor the capitalist West) sympathies in the United States – the most important guarantor of Dutch security – during the Cold War was, to put it mildly, politically highly explosive and imprudent.

Dirk Uipko Stikker, Foreign Minister from 1948 to 1952, threatened to resign unless the Queen amended her speeches. A compromise eventually emerged. Juliana's trip was a success, but the small political circle of insiders were very concerned about the close relationship between the monarch and the faith healer. The situation also became increasingly incomprehensible to Prince Bernhard. Slowly but surely, Soestdijk Palace divided into a 'Juliana camp' and a 'Bernhard camp'. The queen was surrounded by advisors and friends from Hofmans's clique. Dutch journalists who caught wind of rumours about the mystical religious influences on Juliana were given to understand by bigwigs that publications on the subject were undesirable. It emerged that they convinced themselves it was in their best interests to follow such instructions. Foreign journalists were told in no uncertain terms that their work in the Netherlands would become extremely difficult if they were to make disclosures. In 1952 it was still possible to stop the American magazine *Life* from publishing anything about the situation in Soestdijk, but in 1956 the lid was blown off. After publications appeared in Germany, information also started to seep into the Netherlands. The Dutch press remained very cautious, however, and editors checked the outline of their intended newspaper reports with Prime Minister Drees. Dutch people who wanted to read about the affair found more

Figure 25 Cover of the 13 June 1956 issue of the German weekly magazine *Der Spiegel*: 'Between Queen and Rasputin – Secrets in the House of Orange.'

information in foreign newspapers than in domestic ones. There was no censorship, but there was voluntary self-restraint by the Dutch media.[40]

The affair continued to fester behind the scenes in the Netherlands to such an extent that even Juliana's abdication or the divorce of the royal couple could not be ruled out. In order to calm things down at court, Juliana and Bernhard took the initiative – seconded by the Minister of the Interior and former Prime Minister (from 1946 to 1948) L. J. M. Beel – to appoint a committee of three wise men, with Beel as chairman. The committee submitted its recommendations to the queen and prince at the beginning of August 1956. The most important conclusion was that any impression of Hofmans and her followers influencing the queen should be avoided, which was only possible if the ties with Hofmans and her circle were to be severed. The queen proved not to be prepared to do so without a struggle, so the issue dragged on for another few months. In the end she relented, broke her ties with Hofmans and also removed her advisors from Greet Hofmans's entourage. As far as the outside world was concerned the royal marriage remained intact and Juliana's reign left the crisis behind it. And so, after seven years in which the country had been left in the dark, but during which Soestdijk and a few insiders remained in a state of uproar, this queen's drama finally came to an end.[41]

But what was the significance of this episode? It was not, as *Der Spiegel* suggested – and greatly exaggerated – the influence of 'the Dutch Rasputin' in political matters. The importance of the affair lies elsewhere. To begin with, it demonstrated that a constitutional monarchy, where the head of state is part of the government and at the same time 'can do no wrong', is not immune to conflicts that can seriously disrupt the system's equilibrium. Personal convictions of the queen and some of her advisors, the court's internal organization and Juliana's and Bernhard's marital problems resulted in entanglement of private and state issues, which repeatedly brought the monarchy perilously close to a real crisis.

Secondly, it is striking that the seriousness of the situation was completely unknown to the Dutch people. This came about through the skilful crisis management of Prime Minister Drees and the other cabinet ministers, and also the high degree of trust in the powers that be that the Dutch media had during the 1950s. News stories that could have harmed the Royal House or the monarchy were deliberately suppressed. The consensus about this in the small circle of insiders was so robust that the press was silenced without pressure being exerted from on high. Cabinet members and editors were of the same opinion and largely determined what the Dutch population read about the affair. When, in due course, information nevertheless leaked out, the public proved to accept this policy uncomplainingly. The population, like the media, was still very submissive and trusting in authority.

The long 1960s: protest, depillarization, participation (1958–1977)

Even before the party-political landscape changed radically in the second half of the 1960s, it had already become clear from a political and cultural point of view that the era of pillarization was coming to an end. The typical characteristics of the traditional pillars had been to retain one's own principles, remain steadfast and fend off external influences. That cohesion had already diminished by the mid-1950s, and by about 1960 the former certainty ('*we* are the true believers') was no longer present in either Protestant or Catholic circles. The pillar elites moreover realized that their former moral, disciplinary and – in Christian compartments – theological leadership was no longer automatic during this period of increasing individualization and secularization. This was particularly evident in the Catholic Church in the early 1960s. The liberal message of the second Vatican Council in 1962 was given a more positive reception in the Netherlands than in other countries. Wilhelmus Bekkers, Bishop of Den Bosch, was an important representative of the modernizing Catholic Church in the Netherlands. His frankness and openness made him popular outside the Catholic Church too. When asked what the attitude of the Catholic Church was to the contraceptive pill, which had just appeared on the market, he answered on television in 1963 that married couples had to decide for themselves about using it. The explanation for this remarkable response does not lie in Bekkers's progressiveness. In fact, until the end of the 1950s he was known as a conservative. Bekkers had become convinced that the Catholic Church could only continue to have pulling power if it developed into an open, critical and liberal institution. If the church were to oppose the advance of modernization, Bekkers was concerned that the faithful would turn their backs on it. In so doing he, together with other leading Catholics, was not so much in the vanguard of the drive to innovate – it was more a case of a certain lack of resistance, as the historian Kennedy wrote in his influential study of the Netherlands in the 1960s. The upshot was that the door to more far-reaching renewal continued to open and eventually the church was being spurred on more and more without being in the driving seat. According to Kennedy, this attitude was also typical of the way the elites of the other pillars responded to change during the 1960s. This resulted in cultural, religious and political changes that happened quickly and were also more sweeping than many people had envisaged when they went along with them.[42]

Because of such a compliant stance, the churches proved powerless to stop the secularization process. At this time the Catholic Church in particular lost members. According to calculations published by the Netherlands Institute for Social Research (SCP), between 1958 and 1980 the Catholic part of the population dropped from 42 to 25 per cent. During the same period the share of people with no church more than doubled. It grew from 24 per cent to 50 per cent of the population. The Dutch Reformed Church (*Nederlandse Hervormde Kerk*) also lost many members. In 1979, 23 per cent of non-churchgoers had a Dutch Reformed background and 28 per cent a Catholic background. The phenomenon of 'non-practising' – referring to church members who never or only rarely went to church – increased dramatically. In 1960 this percentage for Catholics was only 10. By 1966 it had risen slightly to 14 per cent and by 1979 it had shot up to 40 per cent. On the other hand, the number of members of the Reformed churches (*gereformeerde kerken*) was remarkably stable. One of the reasons was the relatively high birth rate in this group over an extended period.[43] The data in Illustration 6 (p. 243) show that the rate of secularization dropped after 1980.[44]

Year	None	Roman Catholic	Dutch Reformed Church	Reformed Churches in the Netherlands	Other
1958	24	42	23	8	3
1966	36	30	17	14	3
1970	39	34	16	8	3
1975	42	30	16	10	3
1979	42	30	17	8	3
1980	50	25	14	8	2
1981	49	27	14	7	3
1983	50	28	12	6	3
1985	52	26	12	8	3
1986	52	26	12	7	3
1987	54	24	11	7	4
1991	57	22	11	7	4
1992	57	23	10	6	4
1993	60	20	10	6	4
1994	58	21	9	7	5
1995	62	19	9	6	4
1996	62	18	9	6	5
1997	60	20	9	7	4
1998	60	19	9	7	5
1999	63	18	8	7	4
2000	65	17	9	6	4
2002	66	18	7	5	4
2004	64	17	6	4	8

Illustration 6 Membership of denominations 1958–2004 (in per cent).

Another typical feature of the fundamental changes in the pillars was the debates initiated about the future of their own political parties or their own pillarized identities. In 1966, a year before the KVP (see p. 247) sustained its first major electoral defeat, an internal report about the party's cornerstones concluded there were no longer any fundamental reasons to justify a separate Catholic party. Emancipation of Catholics had after all been completed, and the old ideological differences with the liberals and socialists had been largely eroded. The report did not advocate winding up the KVP – which was described as 'irresponsible' – but it did clearly state that the old natural sense of self had disappeared.[45] A new era had arrived – there was a difficult quest for a new identity. This ultimately resulted in the 1970s in the merger of the KVP, ARP and CHU to form the Christian democratic party (CDA).[46] Although the ARP was initially less affected by depillarization and was spared a serious identity crisis, in 1966 the Reformed theologian Harry Kuitert asserted that the traditional protected and isolated Reformed world no longer existed. According to Kuitert, there was only 'one world, in which being a member of the Reformed Churches in the Netherlands or otherwise was irrelevant'.[47] These were not the words of an elite that was clinging to old patterns, but of people who wanted to actively shape renewal. The upshot was that the 1960s protest movement did not run into a brick wall of incomprehension.

The best-known Dutch protest group, Provo, was set up in May 1965. The hard core members added up to no more than a few dozen and the movement dissolved itself in

1967. It was not a political protest movement with a real manifesto, and it did not want to be. Nor did it seek reform of the political system, 'socialism' or the overthrow of capitalism or the monarchy. Its goal was to provoke the authorities and make them nervous through anarchist slogans and stunts. Members called themselves anarchists, and without doubt a few Provos had read one or more anarchist or Marxist classics, but their activities had little to do with political theory or profound criticism of capitalism. As historian Niek Pas describes in detail, Provo was concerned as much as anything with enjoying their refusal to conform.[48]

Provo's high point coincided with the agitation about the engagement and marriage of Princess Beatrix and the German diplomat Claus von Amsberg in 1965 and 1966. It gave the Provos great satisfaction to note that the police and security service took seriously their threats to drug the horses in the royal retinue at the wedding in Amsterdam using sugar lumps laced with LSD, and then causing them to bolt using a horde of white mice. A Provo announcement that time bombs would be placed under bridges and on quays along the route of the wedding procession resulted in inspections by navy frogmen. The only bombs these anarchists used, though, produced smoke as the royal cavalcade passed, and the resulting television pictures attracted a great deal of attention, and not just in the Netherlands. In addition to 'playful' provocation, Provo took practical action to improve the quality of life in Amsterdam through its 'white plans'. The best known of these was the 'white bicycle plan' of the summer of 1965. To combat Amsterdam's air pollution problem, cars were to be banned from the city and white-painted bicycles were to be made available free of charge as an alternative means of transport. This plan was anything but realistic, but in their concern for the environment the Provos were ahead of their time. Although the vast majority of people disapproved of Provo's methods, the movement also generated support because it brought up themes that resonated in wider circles.

Compared with confrontations between protest movements and the establishment in other countries, there was not much violence in the Netherlands. This does not, however, mean there were no serious irregularities. In June 1966, for instance, there was a riot in Amsterdam after the death of a construction worker at a protest meeting. Dozens were injured and the damage ran into millions of guilders. The committee that investigated police actions concluded that the Amsterdam authorities lacked modern conflict management methods.[49] The result was a change in strategy by politicians and police. In future, the approach had to be one of de-escalation with a friendly image, not enforcement of public order using violence.

It cannot be proved, but it is highly likely that protests in later years would have been more serious but for the consequences of the events of 1966. Such protests were increasingly tolerated provided that civil disobedience was not accompanied by violence or serious breaches of the peace. In 1969, the government and parliament responded similarly when protesting students occupied university buildings in Tilburg, Amsterdam and elsewhere and demanded democratization. The University Administration Reform Act, which fundamentally changed the balance of power in universities, came into effect in 1970. Professors had to cede a great deal of influence to students, lecturers, researchers and other employees.

Figure 26 The Provo's smoke bomb at the wedding of Princess Beatrix and Claus von Amsberg in Amsterdam, 10 March 1966.

The pillar elites now accepted that openness, not rigidity, had to be the order of the day, and in consequence the split between protest movements and the establishment was not as deep in the Netherlands as it was in the Federal Republic of Germany and elsewhere.[50] The protest movements themselves contributed to this because they did not hold inflexible ideological world views and remained pragmatic in their radicalism. All these factors meant that changes in the Netherlands took place quickly and relatively quietly, with major consequences for the pillarized system. In their futile attempt to steer the renewal process by adapting their views, the elites eroded the pillarized system from within.

Furthermore, far-reaching changes in views about sexuality, marriage and family began to emerge. The introduction of the contraceptive pill in 1963 – referred to above – enabled family planning and also provided scope for more liberal sexual morality. By the mid-1960s the number of children per family had dropped, particularly among Catholics. More and more women were putting their existing disadvantaged position on the agenda. A number of legal relics, apparently from bygone days, were still in force or had just been repealed. It was not until 1957, for instance, that a married woman was deemed to be 'legally competent', but from a legal point of view the man would remain head of the family until 1970. The rule that the husband had the decisive vote in the event of a difference of opinion about education or where the family lived was not abolished until 1984. The position of women on the labour market was no less discriminatory. Until 1958 it was a statutory requirement that female civil servants who got married had to be dismissed. In 1969 the Social and Economic Council (SER) recommended that women should not be dismissed on the grounds of marriage or pregnancy, but such a prohibition did not become part of the law until 1976. It is therefore not surprising that in the early 1960s the Netherlands had relatively few women in the workplace. In 1960 only 16 per cent of Dutch women received an income from employment, which was about half the average in comparable European countries. While this percentage had grown to 23 by 1966, only 19 per cent of these working women were married.

It was in this climate that the pressure group Man Woman Society (MVM) was founded in 1968.[51] While the MVM was a moderate feminist organization, it was followed in 1970 by the creation of the more radical Dolle Mina, named after Wilhelmina (Mina) Drucker, a Dutch feminist famous around the turn of the century. The MVM concentrated primarily on influencing political decision making in a conventional fashion (petitions, contacts with political parties and the like). Dolle Mina regarded this as 'soft' and tried to get publicity by staging a varied range of actions (for example, burning bras, wolf-whistling at men in the street, and occupying Nijenrode – a private university that did not admit women). Many Dolle Mina members were convinced that real change could only happen in a socialist society. It became famous in 1970 with its 'boss in your own belly' campaign, which signalled the start of a long battle about a woman's right to abortion.

There was no one feminist movement as such – too many different groups started to emerge in the early 1970s and they were too ideologically diverse. Their activities ranged from discussion groups, establishing refuges for female victims of male violence, and debates about sexuality, feminism and socialism to practical campaigns to foster the positive discrimination of women on the labour market. The 'second feminist wave', which started in 1968, brought changes to the complexion of the Netherlands in many areas. As with other Dutch protest movements, one is struck by the relative ease with which many feminist groups' demands found their way on to the political agenda – this is not, however, to say that these demands were tackled with any degree of urgency. All the same, the government did take feminist aspirations seriously; they gave women's groups financial support and facilitated their further development, particularly during Den Uyl's government (1973–77). Pressure from the MVM was one of the factors behind the government's decision to set up the Equal Rights Commission in 1974 and the national committee for International Women's Year 1975, which was tasked with preparing appropriate Dutch activities. As organizations, the MVM and Dolle Mina were not large, but during this period their political and social influence certainly was.

Against this backdrop, it is understandable that the stable political landscape that had been so familiar since 1918 rapidly imploded in the second half of the 1960s. The KVP came off particularly badly. Its share of the vote in 1963 had been nearly 32 per cent, but this dropped to just over 18 per cent in 1972. The Christian democrats lost the majority they had enjoyed for decades. This was one reason why the KVP, ARP and CHU came together during this period and formed one combined Christian democratic party. In 1977, they contested the elections to the Lower House for the first time as the democratic CDA. They gained the same share of the vote as the KVP had achieved on its own in 1963 (almost 32 per cent). To begin with, the PvdA also lost out through depillarization, but it recovered in the early 1970s. Echoing the withdrawal of the pillar elites described above, the PvdA provided plenty of scope for the internal New Left movement, which attacked the 'grandees' in its own party. It moved the party significantly to the left, and this restored its fortunes at the ballot box.

The biggest winners of depillarization were new parties on both sides of the political spectrum, and a number of them won seats in the Lower House. The left-wing liberal Democrats 66 party (D66) was particularly successful. D66 set out to get the pillarized political system to 'explode', after which a modern, transparent two-party system along the lines of the Anglo–American model, with a directly elected prime minister, should be created. They wanted to replace the secretive backroom politics, where the pillar elites made all the decisions, with political clarity, democratic control and participation by the population. D66 entered the Lower House in 1967 with 4.5 per cent of the votes, which at the time was considered to be a sensationally high figure for a new party. The following year, the Political Party of Radicals (PPR) was established. It sprang from the KVP and in 1971 it too entered the Lower House, with a 1.8 per cent share. In response to the PvdA's shift to the left, the moderate Democratic Socialists '70 (DS'70) broke away and got 5.3 per cent of the votes in 1971. On the right, the Farmers' Party led by Hendrik 'Farmer' Koekoek was advancing, and it attracted a 4.7 per cent share of the votes in 1967. The party-political landscape became more varied, on both the left and the right, and the political system proved able to integrate and channel the political uneasiness.

Traditionally, it had been easy for small parties to win seats in parliament because of the low electoral threshold (0.67 per cent). It is, however, striking that since the introduction of universal suffrage and the system of proportional representation in 1917, on average small parties had acquired only 10 per cent of the votes between them, and during the second half of the 1950s this share dropped to between 7 and 8 per cent. The opposite was true for the big parties, which at that time accounted for over 91 per cent of the votes and were assured of loyal, pillar-related grass roots support. A typical feature of the political landscape in the 1960s was a decline in this traditionally high percentage of votes for the established parties. By 1967 it had dropped to barely 79 per cent and fell further in 1971–72 to about 72 per cent. Never before in the country's parliamentary history had the large established parties won so few votes as they did between 1967 and 1972. The other side of the coin was that small new parties had never been so successful.

In 1972 almost 20 per cent of the electorate voted for new parties such as D66, PPR, DS'70 and the Farmers' Party (*Boerenpartij*), and between them small parties acquired over 28 per cent of the votes. After the 1956 general election, seven parties were represented in the Lower House, whereas after 1971 and 1972 there were fourteen. As was the case in the 1930s, when small parties were also relatively successful, these gains were a sign of political dissatisfaction. During the 1930s there were doubts about whether the democratic system was able to solve the economic and social problems decisively. This 'minor crisis' of democracy did not lead to a 'major crisis' (see p. 202), one reason being that the pillars had a strong hold on people, and this reduced the opportunities for extreme right-wing or left-wing groups. During the 1960s there were no doubts about democracy as a system, but there was criticism of the rigid pillarized elite democracy and the associated power relationships, and the desire for greater participation by ordinary people. In this regard, the protest movements of the 1960s dovetailed well with developments in party politics.

In this new political climate, the political conventions that had characterized the pillarized Netherlands since 1945 disappeared. The search for agreement was displaced by an emphasis on differences. In the late 1960s, the left opted for a strategy of polarization that was designed to produce a political dichotomy, with progressive and conservative blocs. This polarization was targeted primarily at the Christian democrats and was intended to further weaken their declining electoral performance and force their supporters to make a choice between 'left' and 'right'. The long-term objective was to form a left-wing majority. In the short term, this strategy appeared to achieve success because 1973 saw the formation of a new government dominated by left-wing parties and led by Joop den Uyl (PvdA).[52] Under the slogan 'spreading knowledge, income and power', an ambitious programme of reforms was drawn up; its goal was to level incomes, cream off high company profits for the benefit of the employees (sharing out capital growth), increase government influence on investments, promote employee participation in businesses and so on. There was a single-minded drive to reduce social inequality and emancipate the weaker members in the community.

The results of the politics of reform were limited to only a few minor changes. The excuse given by Joop den Uyl years later was that his government came to power when the social support base for reforms had already started shrinking and he furthermore had to combat the strong economic headwinds of the 1973 oil crisis. Den Uyl's excuses are not entirely incorrect, but a more important explanation is to be found in the overestimate at the time of the state's power to guide economic, social and political processes. The existing structures were both tougher and much less controversial, and consequently much more difficult to change than many had suspected in their zeal for reforms. The Den Uyl government's plans to bring changes to corporate structure, ownership structure and employee participation got nowhere, thanks to resistance from the Catholic and Protestant coalition partners and businessmen. Den Uyl antagonized this last group in 1974 in a speech to Christian employers in which he lambasted capitalist industrial methods and announced he wanted to curtail them through 'democratically reviewed communal decisions'. In the years that followed there were many complaints

Figure 27 Prime Minister Joop den Uyl at a demonstration protesting against death sentences in Spain (1975). National Archives of the Netherlands, The Hague/Anefo/Bert Verhoeff, 2.24.01.05, 928.1747, CC-BY-SA.

from the business community about the 'hostile climate' they were confronted with by the prime minister and his party. So the private sector resisted additional government involvement, and the opportunities for the government to direct the economy proved to be limited in other areas too. The Keynesian tools that the cabinet wanted to use to combat the economic problems of the 1970s turned out to be no longer effective.

Expectations in another field were not realized either – the polarization strategy in regard to the Christian democrats failed. It had indeed contributed to electoral gains in the early 1970s, and the historic PvdA result in 1977 (from 27.3 per cent in 1972 to 33.8 per cent) could also be seen in that light. As a strategy for the longer term, however, it did not succeed. The intended left-wing majority was not achieved and the decline in the Christian democrat vote ended after 1972. In fact, the polarization strategy generated strong anti-PvdA sentiment in the political centre ground. It drove the Christian parties together and as a result contributed to the formation of the CDA in the 1970s. Officially the KVP, ARP and CHU merged to form the CDA in 1980, but they had successfully campaigned under this name in the 1977 general election. The decline in the Christian democrat vote stopped. With 31.9 per cent of the votes, the CDA did slightly better than the combined results of the three parties in 1971 (31.3 per cent). The conservative-liberal VVD also profited. The young party leader, Hans Wiegel, successfully pursued a hard liberal confrontational campaign, which displayed several populist features and was the right wing's response to the left-wing polarization strategy. During the 1960s the VVD consistently attracted over 10 per cent of the votes. By 1977 the figure reached 18 per cent and continued growing to over 23 per cent in 1982. In 1977 the upshot was once again a small parliamentary majority for a Christian democrat–liberal coalition government. Despite its good electoral showing, the PvdA found itself on the sidelines for an extended period. Between 1977 and 1989 – with the exception of a brief interruption in 1981 and 1982 – the CDA and VVD ran the country between them.

Despite the very modest results of the reforming policies of the Den Uyl government, there were nevertheless relevant changes during these years. Concepts such as 'openness', 'involvement', 'looser conventions', 'engagement' and 'zeal' were key words in the political and cultural evolution during this period, and the governing style reflected the climate of participative democracy, which had been an indelible political and social element since the 1960s. Under pillarization, democracy was characterized by realism, pragmatism, compromise, consultation among elites, secrecy and depoliticization. Depillarization brought ideologization, participation, polarization, openness and politicization. This legacy of the 1960s reached its apex during the Den Uyl government which was the primary significance of this period. The man in the street was becoming more vocal, was searching for answers and no longer wanted to be patronized by ecclesiastical and political elites. Conventions in general also became more casual and informal, as the permissive society was ushered in. The political scientist Herman de Liagre Böhl rightly concludes that the exercise of power was no longer self-evident, and persuasiveness and negotiating skills became increasingly required.[53]

There was fundamental change in the economy during the long 1960s. During the years of reconstruction, there was tripartite consultation between government, employers and employees where the outlines of social and economic policy were always staked out in an atmosphere of broad agreement. Cracks began to appear in this system in the late 1950s. Wages in Belgium and West Germany were higher than in the Netherlands and dissatisfaction among employees increased in the border regions and beyond. They wanted a bigger share in the increased affluence and a tougher stance by union leaders when dealing with government and employers. This resulted in gradual erosion of the foundations of the harmony model dating from the 1940s and 1950s, and a period of growing social tensions dawned. In 1960 there was the first strike since 1945, supported by the three large trade unions, the NVV, KAB and CNV. This put the strike weapon back on the agenda in social relationships and, contrary to the situation during the era of reconstruction, it is fair to say there was a rift between capital and labour during the 1960s and 1970s. Relationships polarized during these decades in politics and in society. After the fall of the Drees government in December 1958, the low wage policy was phased out and there was explosive growth in wages during the first half of the 1960s. Pay increased by 9 per cent in 1963, 15 per cent in 1964 and a further 10.7 per cent in 1965. Wages went up by nearly 6 per cent a year in real terms during the 1960s as a whole. The social security system was also significantly expanded. The major new social insurances and benefits introduced included the General Child Benefit Act (1963), the Social Assistance Act (1965) and the Invalidity Insurance Act (1967). Benefits paid out under existing schemes were increased and admission critera were relaxed. As a result, between 1960 and 1975 the number of people receiving support nearly doubled from 1.3 to 2.6 million. These figures exclude recipients of child benefit. During the same period the percentage of GDP spent on social security rose from just under 10 per cent to over 28 per cent. This brought the Netherlands from lagging behind the rest of Europe in this respect to becoming one of the leaders, slightly below the level of the Scandinavian countries.[54] The associated cost increases could be covered thanks to income from natural gas, which started to flow after the discovery of huge gas fields in the north of the country in around 1960.

Increasing prosperity made daily life more comfortable for many people. To give some examples, in 1957 3 per cent of the population had a fridge, whereas 88 per cent did in 1972, and the corresponding figures for washing machines were 31 per cent and 86 per cent. Mobility also grew substantially as the number of cars increased by a factor of five between 1960 and 1970. It was the same story with audio-visual equipment. In 1957 there were eight televisions per 100 families. By 1970 that had increased to ninety, while the number of record players rose from forty-six to 103.[55] Foreign holidays during the 1950s were only possible for a relatively small group. This option became available for an ever-growing part of the population during the 1960s. Between 1965 and 1970, higher levels of comfort spread particularly quickly throughout the population. This was so marked that it gave rise to growing criticism of the 'consumer society' and the associated neglect of intangible values.

The lengthy period of economic growth that started in around 1950 came to an end in the early 1970s. Inflation increased and reached record levels of around 10 per cent a year in 1974 and 1975. Unemployment rose (2.5 per cent in 1973, 6.2 per cent in 1976) and corporate profits fell. One of the reasons was the high level of social insurance premiums, which in turn was the result of the more comprehensive social insurance system. Falling profits led to more joblessness, which put further strain on the social welfare system. The need for spending cuts gradually dawned on more and more people and in the 1980s and 1990s resulted in a painful adjustment process accompanied by many social conflicts. The 1973 oil crisis – when crude oil prices jumped by 400 per cent – caused a recession in all industrialized nations. The Netherlands had additional problems thanks to an oil boycott imposed by Arab countries because of its pro-Israel stance during the 1973 Arab–Israeli war.

Economic vulnerability was also linked to the collapse of the Bretton Woods system, which had brought international monetary stability since the Second World War. Under this system, there had been fixed exchange rates between many currencies and the dollar, the value of which was in turn, linked to gold. In 1971 the United States was no longer able to sustain the dollar's burdensome role, which heralded a period of major shifts in exchange rates. This made the guilder a relatively expensive currency. The income from natural gas exports, which created a positive balance of payments, was another factor. Dutch exports, which were already expensive, became even more costly as a result of a rise in the guilder's value. This brought about the loss of many jobs, primarily in industry. At the same time, the unions continued to demand high wage increases to compensate, at least in part, for inflation. During the 1950s, the Netherlands had been a 'low wage country', whereas in the 1970s it was a nation with very high labour costs.[56]

Summarizing, the economic history of the 'long 1960s', the years of reconstruction and the tempestuous surge in affluence in the 1960s were followed, precisely at the moment when the Den Uyl government took office, by an economic downturn with increasing joblessness, rising inflation, growing government borrowing and declining economic growth. We saw earlier that the disappointing results of the Den Uyl government's policy of reform had primarily political causes, and that the left wing had overestimated the guiding power of the state. It is also clear, however, that the mounting economic problems constrained the freedom of action of Den Uyl and his ministers.

The Den Uyl government's term in office was not solely typified by reforming zeal, polarization, a changing political culture and economic setbacks. It was also a period in which a serious crisis involving the Royal House was on the cards. Twenty years after the Greet Hofmans affair was at its peak (see p. 239 ff.), the Netherlands was once again subjected to a controversy relating to the monarchy. A major difference between the 1950s and the 1970s, however, was that the Hofmans affair was largely kept out of the public eye, whereas the crisis in the 1970s played out in the open and was accompanied by intensive public debate. At the beginning of 1976, American rumours about the aircraft manufacturer Lockheed that had been circulating for some time were confirmed. Since the early 1960s the company had repeatedly tried – by paying bribes to Prince Bernhard – to persuade the Dutch government to buy Lockheed aircraft. This prompted the Den Uyl government to set up a committee of inquiry, which in August 1976 arrived at a critical judgement of the prince's conduct. According to the committee's conclusion he supposedly got involved 'much too rashly' in 'transactions that inevitably created the impression that he was susceptible to favours'. He also allegedly demonstrated that he was amenable to 'improper wishes and offers'. Even though Prince Bernhard never had any influence on government procurement policy, his conduct was deemed to be 'completely unacceptable'. Tension in the country was palpable when the Prime Minister went to the Lower House at the end of August 1976 to announce the government's position on the issue. The proceedings in the chamber, which was full to overflowing, were televised live. There was extra suspense as a result of the Prime Minister's clothing. Completely contrary to his normal practice, he appeared in a sober dark suit. The head of the government told the Lower House of its conclusion that 'the prince's conduct has damaged the interests of the state'.[57]

Consequences were therefore inevitable. The Den Uyl government, which had to steer a middle course between a conservative pro-Bernhard camp in public opinion and a left-wing anti-Bernhard one, decided that the prince should step down from his posts in the private sector. The most difficult thing for the prince and his followers to accept was his honourable discharge as Inspector General of the Armed Forces. The government also expressed a wish for the prince to no longer appear in public in a military uniform. This unofficial uniform ban was lifted in 1991 on the occasion of Queen Beatrix and Prince Claus's silver wedding. Prime Minister Ruud Lubbers (CDA) then let it be known that the government would in fact appreciate it if Prince Bernhard were to wear uniform again on ceremonial occasions, for example the annual remembrance on 5 May of the liberation in 1945. The fifteen-year uniform ban may have been very painful for the prince, but he was spared the humiliation of a criminal investigation and a trial. The decision not to take such steps was not uncontroversial. There was a highly charged atmosphere during cabinet deliberations about the continued existence of the government, but above all about the future of the monarchy. Den Uyl made it clear during cabinet meetings that there was a threat of an uncontrollable monarchical crisis. Without spelling out in concrete terms what the crisis would precipitate, all those involved realized that Queen Juliana would abdicate if the government resorted to criminal prosecution. It could furthermore be assumed that Princess Beatrix would not succeed her mother in such circumstances, which would have made the constitutional crisis a perfect storm. Through cautious manoeuvring, Den Uyl managed to get the cabinet ministers to sing from the same hymn sheet – sanctions, but no criminal prosecution.[58] A crisis could furthermore be averted by a declaration from the prince in which he expressed his regret about his conduct and stated his acceptance of the measures taken by the government. How social democrat Den Uyl guided the monarchy through the Lockheed affair unscathed rose above party politics, and even his political opponents saw a statesman in him, albeit for only a brief period.

According to Den Uyl's biographer, Anet Bleich, the Prime Minister went a step further in preventing a constitutional crisis. During its investigation into the payment of bribes by Lockheed to Prince Bernhard, the committee of inquiry unearthed a second flow of money and concluded that the aircraft manufacturer Northrop had paid money to the prince between 1968 and 1973.[59] Den Uyl kept silent about this information and gave evasive answers to questions on the subject, prompted by rumours, asked in the Lower House. Bleich suspected that if it had become known that Bernhard had accepted money from *two* aircraft companies, a criminal prosecution could not have been avoided and the dreaded royal crisis would have happened. Did Den Uyl indeed save the monarchy by keeping the prince's links with Northrop under his hat, as Bleich contended? The biographers of Dries van Agt, Minister of Justice (1973–1977) and Prime Minister from 1977 to 1982, took a more balanced view. Firstly, they pointed out that other ministers (including Van Agt) were also involved in the decision making. Secondly, they confirmed that these ministers jointly decided to have *no further* investigation conducted into the Northrop issue because they were concerned that it *could* have revealed facts that would have made a criminal prosecution unavoidable. The Northrop file was used, however, to put pressure on Bernhard and get him to accept the Lockheed committee of inquiry's recommendations.[60] If we compare the two points of view, Van Agt's biographers appear to have the sources on their side. Yet more important than that is the conclusion that under Den Uyl's leadership the ministers concerned deliberately shrank from taking steps that could have pushed the monarchy into a profound crisis. Sweeping the Northrop file under the carpet served that purpose.

Dealing with the colonial past: Suriname's independence in 1975 and the violent actions of young South Moluccans in the Netherlands

Looking back, Prime Minister Joop den Uyl described the way he and his cabinet led Suriname's path to independence as 'the biggest success' of his term in office.[61] And indeed, if we are mindful of the drama of Indonesia's journey to independence between

1945 and 1949, the transfer of sovereignty to Suriname in 1975 does seem to have been a model of decolonization. Den Uyl (who was among the critics of Dutch Indonesia policy in the postwar years) and the others involved believed that the Netherlands should adopt an accommodating stance with regard to Suriname.

The relationship between the Netherlands, Suriname and the Netherlands Antilles was defined in the 1954 Royal Charter. Under it, the three countries were autonomous and equal parts of the Kingdom of the Netherlands. The Charter provided for a joint administration for the non-internal matters of the separate countries. These 'Kingdom affairs' included foreign policy, defence and preservation of the same legal norms throughout the Kingdom (civil rights, legal certainty, proper administration, etc.). Until the end of the 1960s, this Charter provided a stable basis for relationships between the countries and was only seriously challenged once – by Suriname – in around 1960. Political instability in Suriname in 1969 underlined awareness in the Netherlands that it could become involved against its will in internal conflicts in the Caribbean region. At the end of May 1969, the Netherlands was even compelled to intervene militarily on Curaçao because a labour dispute got out of hand. A few hundred marines, some of whom were flown in from the Netherlands, soon restored order on the island, which had been ravaged by arson and plundering. These events resulted in a fundamental discussion in the Netherlands about the Royal Charter. Photographs of Dutch marines who restored order on Curaçao were published all over the world and generated concern about the image of the Netherlands. This concern was amplified by the debate that flared up at this precise moment about Dutch war crimes in Indonesia in the 1945–49 period. 'No more excesses, no more colonial intervention, ever', was the motto as formulated by Gert Oostindie and Inge Klinkers in their three-volume standard work about Dutch decolonization policy in the Caribbean.[62] The upshot was that in the Netherlands, initially primarily in the left-wing parties, the word 'independence' was heard with increasing frequency. When members of the Parliamentary Standing Committees on Suriname and the Netherlands Antilles visited both parts of the kingdom in 1971, they spoke out frankly for speedy independence for Suriname and the Antilles. Later that year a large majority of the Lower House did exactly the same. This message provoked cautious responses in Suriname and the Antilles. There were fears in multi-ethnic Suriname that the Creoles would dominate the rest of the population, and on the Antilles a majority wanted to remain part of the Kingdom anyhow. It was therefore not surprising that the tripartite consultations about the future relationships inside the Kingdom, which had been taking place since 1970 and were continued formally from the beginning of 1972 in the Kingdom Commission, did not bring transfer of sovereignty any closer. On the contrary, inside the Dutch government under Barend Biesheuvel (1971–72) people appeared to be assuming to an increasing degree that the Charter would remain in force for some time.

That changed when the Den Uyl government came into office in 1973. In the government policy statement at the end of May, the Prime Minister declared he wanted to begin discussions with Suriname and the Antilles about independence. Yet for the government, which with its progressive zeal wanted to move with the times, decolonization remained wishful thinking as long as the parts of the Kingdom concerned had not expressed a desire to that end. There was a breakthrough in the deadlock over Suriname in February 1974 when a new government led by Henck Arron stated the country wanted to become independent before 1976. Oostindie and Klinkers pointed out that pressure from the Netherlands on Suriname to express this intention would not have been surprising. The Dutch had repeatedly made it clear during the preceding years that, 'as far as the mother country was concerned the sooner the political ties were broken the better'.[63] It soon emerged that the Netherlands Antilles were indeed not interested in independence, so the discussions were limited to Suriname.

During various rounds of negotiations, which alternated between The Hague and Paramaribo, there were discussions about finance, future development cooperation, nationality and migration, build-up of a Suriname army etc. The slightness of Arron's majority in the Suriname parliament was a problem. In fact, in the late summer of 1975 there was a stalemate between supporters and opponents of independence. The leader of the opposition, Jagernath Lachmon, who represented the Hindu part of the population, was against the hasty implementation of independence. He feared ethnic discord and was afraid that a young Suriname democracy would not be able to withstand it. He therefore advocated a transitional period of ten years and a referendum about independence.

This gave rise to the unique situation in which The Hague increasingly negotiated with the government of Suriname and also acted as an intermediary between the government and the opposition in Paramaribo in order to canvass as much support as possible for independence and to minimize ethnic tensions in Suriname. If one also takes into account the fact that the Dutch objective to achieve Suriname independence quickly was given additional impetus by the desire to contain the flow of migrants from Suriname that had developed, it is not surprising that under this pressure The Hague repeatedly made more concessions than it had intended to. It was only with political acrobatics – Suriname reopened the negotiations the night before sovereignty was transferred – that the ceremonial transfer of sovereignty took place on 25 November 1975 in the presence of Queen Juliana. The Netherlands provided the country with 3.7 billion guilders in the form of gifts, cancellation of debts and guarantees. This was substantially more than the sum The Hague originally had in mind (1 billion), but also considerably less than what Suriname had wanted (10 billion). Agreements were also made about Dutch involvement in spending development aid funding. As regards nationality and migration, until the transfer of sovereignty, Suriname people were automatically Dutch and were therefore free to settle in the Netherlands. From 25 November 1975, in principle those living in Suriname received Suriname nationality and those living in the Netherlands received Dutch nationality (the country of residence criterion) and thus the principle of freedom of movement ended. However, in order to accommodate the Suriname opposition – which, as we have seen, opposed independence being implemented too quickly – a five-year transitional arrangement was agreed, with the result that after 1975 several tens of thousands more Suriname people could move to the Netherlands without hindrance.

There was great satisfaction on the Dutch side after transfer of sovereignty, but since then opinion has become more nuanced. On the positive side of the equation The Hague involved the Suriname opposition in the process and decolonization took place without violence, and in the end it was actually relatively harmonious. Other positive aspects were that The Hague helped in the drafting of a Suriname constitution; it conducted the discussion with great flexibility and expressly set out to have a 'decent' handover of power. This does not mean that the Dutch concessions were ultimately also in the interests of Suriname. The transitional migration arrangement and the departure of many people from Suriname for the Netherlands without doubt damaged the young republic. It also emerged that the guarantees to monitor development funding were by no means watertight and there is said to have been widespread corruption. Oostindie and Klinkers criticized the excessive haste and eagerness with which the Den Uyl government pushed through independence and the fact that the process took place in 'a timeframe that was far too short'. They also took the view that The Hague paid too little attention to the resistance there was in Suriname to rapid implementation of independence. Looking back at the process as a whole, they summarized by concluding that it 'failed to comply with the basic criteria of sound public administration'.[64] At the same time, however, the authors pointed out that the Den Uyl government had no real alternatives. Putting the brakes on the transfer of sovereignty was not acceptable in the political climate of the 1970s and would have been rejected by a majority of Dutch people. After Paramaribo had proposed a date for proclaiming independence, there was furthermore little that The Hague could do except cooperate in implementing it. If the Netherlands had adopted an inhibitive or reluctant attitude, it would without doubt have provoked a storm of protest from Suriname, and the Netherlands would certainly have been pilloried internationally. In this light one can agree with Anet Bleich's conclusion that, given the circumstances, the Netherlands probably did as well as possible.[65]

A completely different colonial legacy surfaced during the 1975–78 period. Young South Moluccans took violent action, such as hijacking trains and taking hostages, to underline their political demands for an independent Republic of South Maluku (RMS). The historical background is rooted in the early 1950s and the more distant colonial past. In April 1950 a number of South Moluccans, also known as Ambonese, proclaimed the RMS in response to, among other things, the abolition of the Indonesian federal state of East Indonesia by Sukarno. Later that year the Indonesian army wiped this republic off the map, but the problem was more complex than just a desire by the Ambonese population for independence. During Dutch rule, many Ambonese had served in the Royal Netherlands East Indies Army (KNIL) and had consequently fought on the Dutch side. That was also the case after 1945 in the struggle against Sukarno's Republic. After Indonesian independence, some 4,000 Ambonese soldiers stationed on Java, resisted inclusion in the new Indonesian army. Instead they wanted to relocate to their own newly proclaimed RMS, but this was turned down by the Indonesian government. The 4,000 troops then took the matter to court in the Netherlands. This resulted in an agreement between The Hague and Jakarta that the Netherlands would take in the men concerned and their families for a transitional period. And so, approximately 13,000

Moluccans came to the Netherlands in 1951, where they were put in the former Vught and Westerbork concentration and transit camps and elsewhere. These Moluccans assumed, as did the Dutch government, that they would return to the Maluku Islands, also known as the Moluccas, after a cooling-off period, and their provisional accommodation in camps only appeared to confirm that. The Moluccans soon felt betrayed by the Dutch government. The former KNIL soldiers were demobilized when they arrived in the Netherlands and support for the RMS aspiration failed to materialize. The care provided for the Moluccans was minimal, and for the first few years they were not allowed to work.

The deteriorating relations between the Netherlands and Indonesia and the Moluccans' desire for their own republic made the probability of returning smaller and smaller. The temporary stay in the Netherlands acquired an ever more permanent character. By the end of the 1960s, radical young Moluccans, brought up with the perspective of an independent RMS, were no longer prepared to accept idealized promises and tried to bring about the creation of their own republic through protest. This group also opposed the Dutch government, which meanwhile had started to implement a policy of integration. The radicalization of these young people was also a response to the repression of the RMS in Indonesia itself. Earlier protests included occupying the official residence of the Indonesian ambassador in Wassenaar in 1970. Between 1975 and 1978 hostage taking and occupations also attracted attention from outside the Netherlands. In December 1975 a train was hijacked for ten days in the province of Drenthe in the northeast of the country. Occupation of the Indonesian consulate in Amsterdam started at about the same time and lasted nearly three weeks. Five people died during these protests. In May 1977 another train was hijacked in Drenthe – the province where the majority of Moluccans lived, in their own neighbourhoods. A primary school in the Drenthe village of Bovensmilde was occupied at the same time. The hijacking was terminated with violence almost three weeks later. Two passengers and six of the nine hijackers were killed. There were no fatalities when the school, from which the children had meanwhile been released, was stormed. Finally, in March 1978 a few Moluccans occupied the Drenthe provincial offices in Assen, and two people died. The building was stormed and the occupation ended the following day.[66]

If one looks back at these five acts of terrorism, which led to fifteen deaths in the 1975–1978 period, one has to conclude first and foremost that the hijackers and the occupiers did not achieve their political objective. Their attempts to get the Netherlands to advocate the creation of a free RMS to Indonesia and the United Nations failed completely. Despite the absence of any Dutch political support for the RMS ideal, after 1978 there was no hardening of attitudes and radicalization among the Moluccans. The Dutch government established a committee to investigate the different aspects of the Moluccan question (including the circumstances in which the Moluccans came to the Netherlands in 1951 and their treatment by the Dutch government since then). The committee's report published in 1978 criticized the policy pursued by the Dutch government since 1951 and provided the basis for a new integration policy.[67] The key part of the report was the requirement for moral and financial redress for past errors, support for developing the Moluccan cultural identity and at the same time improvement in the position of Moluccans in education and the labour market. Tensions eased in the Moluccan community from the 1980s. The ideal of the RMS lived on, but more and more Moluccans realized that their future was in the Netherlands. So in fact the Moluccan protests and violence achieved the opposite of what had been intended. The Dutch government did not respond by supporting the establishment of a Moluccan republic, but by formulating a modern integration policy under which maintaining the Moluccan identity was to go hand in hand with having equal rights in society. During the 1980s the integration policies for other ethnic minorities were to be developed along the same lines – an approach that earned the Netherlands a reputation in other countries for many years as being liberal, tolerant and progressive in its treatment of its minorities.

From Christian democrat dominance to polder model: 1977–2002

The formation of a CDA–VVD government in 1977 soon resulted in an attitude to social and economic matters that differed from the situation when Den Uyl's centre-left government was in office. The new Prime Minister, Dries van Agt (CDA), and his conservative-liberal coalition partner distanced themselves radically from the policy of the preceding years. He presented an ambitious programme of spending cuts that was intended to significantly slim down the public sector, to restore profits and investments in the private sector and – through this – to contain the rapidly climbing unemployment. Civil service salaries and social security benefits would furthermore no longer be automatically linked to wages paid in the private sector because that would be too costly for the public purse.

The PvdA, now in opposition, and the labour movement, headed by the later Prime Minister Wim Kok, joined forces to oppose the policy of austerity launched by the new government, which had a majority of only two seats in parliament and repeatedly had to fine-tune its plans. Consequently, only meagre results were achieved. The malaise was made even worse by the second oil crisis in 1979, which sparked off inflation and a downward economic spiral. In 1982 this resulted in joblessness of 13.5 per cent. A further 13 per cent or so of the workforce was unfit for work, so approximately a quarter of the working population was not in work. The budget deficit rose substantially, from 3.8 per cent of national income in 1977 to 8.2 per cent in 1981. The Dutch economy was in dire straits.[68] Initially the government and parliament were powerless to turn the tide. A divided government that relied on a shaky parliamentary majority, a social climate that was becoming bleak and a strongly polarizing PvdA were not the preferred ingredients for success of the course as mapped out.

The situation did not change until 1982, when a Christian democrat-liberal government was formed with Ruud Lubbers (CDA) as Prime Minister. This government implemented the policy of spending cuts that had been announced in previous years, but had not been carried out. Civil servants' salaries were slashed and drastic cuts were also made in the social welfare system (lower benefits paid for shorter periods). The state withdrew from a number of traditional public sector services (including Postbank and the PTT (Post Telegraph Telefone)) through privatization, and sold large parts of its shareholdings in such companies as KLM, DSM (Dutch State Mines) and Hoogovens. In 1982 changes were also made in the relationship between employers and employees. A decisive step in the direction of economic recovery was made on the basis of the Wassenaar Agreement. Employers and employees had both recognized that continuation of trench warfare between capital and labour would not be able to stop the downward spiral. By then unemployment was increasing by about 15,000 a month. Against this backdrop, the chairman of the FNV union (Dutch Trade Union Confederation) Wim Kok was willing to accept wage restraint and Chris van Veen, the head of the VNO (Association of Dutch Enterprises), promised a proactive policy to combat the loss of jobs. Together with other unions and employers' organizations, they gave top priority to jobs rather than income. This meant that discussions about recovery of profits, a more flexible labour market, reducing working hours, creating part-time jobs and so on could take place in an atmosphere of 'ideological pacification'.[69] This did not mean, incidentally, that tensions between employers and employees immediately evaporated in 1982, and to begin with the speed and scope of the austerity policy were very much at odds with what trade unions considered acceptable.

At the same time, the policy bore fruit. The budget deficit, which was more than 10 per cent in 1982, was reduced to just over 6 per cent by 1986, and profits and investments

Figure 28 'Let Lubbers Finish The Job'. 1986 CDA election poster. Dutch Political Parties Documentation Centre, Groningen.

gradually recovered. Although unemployment remained high and many Dutch people had had to accept a drop in wages in real terms since 1982, Lubbers was rewarded in the 1986 elections for managing to turn things around (from 29.4 per cent in 1982 to 34.6 per cent). The 1980s were thus dominated politically, socially and economically by Lubbers and the CDA. Lubbers became the undisputed leader of the new Christian democrat alliance, which when he took over still needed to be forged into a real unified organization. Despite unpopular measures, Lubbers was respected as a successful mover and shaker. It was also Lubbers who brought the CDA back to the almost natural position of power that the Christian democrats had enjoyed since 1918 and which appeared to have been lost during the 1970s. The CDA's success can be explained by Lubbers's pragmatism and the low religious profile he gave the party. The CDA evolved into a catch-all party in the centre ground of politics.[70] Putting it another way, under Lubbers the CDA executed a 'reverse breakthrough'. Instead of a shift of voters from the religious to other parties, as had been the intention of the postwar breakthrough and the later policy of polarization, there was a reverse shift and the CDA actually succeeded in attracting non-Christian voters. In 1989 he teamed up with the PvdA as coalition partner instead of the VVD and in so doing confirmed the image of a CDA that called the shots in Dutch politics and decided whether to govern with the 'left' or the 'right' depending on the political landscape.

This was not a recipe for long-term success, however. The last government led by Lubbers (1989–94) was faced with new economic headwinds, which generated problems for the social democrat coalition partners in particular. The PvdA was punished severely at the 1994 general election for the socioeconomic policy (from nearly 32 per cent in 1989 to 24 per cent), but the CDA lost a lot of ground too (from over 35 per cent in 1989 to approximately 22 per cent), which was due primarily to the lack of political direction when Lubbers's departure was announced. The CDA's apparently automatic position of power, which Lubbers had regained for the Christian democrats in the 1980s, thus disappeared at a stroke. Unfortunately for the Christian democrats, during the chaotic run-up to the 1994 election thought was also being given out loud inside the CDA to the need to cut the state retirement pension enjoyed by all Dutch people (General Old Age Pensions Act, AOW). The upshot was a haemorrhage of votes among older voters and brief success for two seniors' parties: Union 55+ and the General Elderly Alliance (AOV). Between them they attracted about 4.5 per cent of the votes. The big winners were the liberals. During the pillarization era, the VVD's share of the vote was around 10 per cent. As a result of depillarization and the establishment of the left-wing liberal D66, the liberal potential grew to between 15 and 20 per cent in the 1970s and between 25 and 30 per cent in the 1980s. In 1994 the two liberal parties reached a historic zenith with over 35 per cent of the votes between them. Never before in Dutch political history had the voters been so 'disloyal'. Half of the Dutch voting population voted for a different party than at the previous election.

The political earthquake of 1994 heralded a period of major electoral fluctuations, and this has remained the case up to the present day (see Illustration 7, p. 261). During the years of pillarization, social democrats and Christian democrats attracted about 80 per cent of the votes between them. After the depillarization of the 1960s this dropped to approximately 60–65 per cent, and in 1994 they lost the absolute majority with a joint

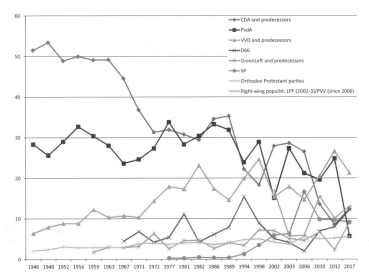

Illustration 7 Election results by political movement 1946–2017.

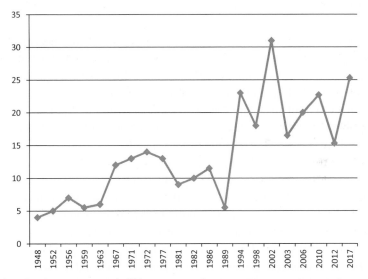

Illustration 8 Changes in seats held by parties in the Lower House 1948–2017 (in per cent).

share of the vote of around 45 per cent. At the end of the 1950s, fewer than ten seats (of the 150) changed hands after elections, whereas in 1994 there were nearly four times as many and in 2002 a record was set at nearly five times (see illustration 8).

In 1994 Wim Kok and the PvdA found themselves in the paradoxical situation that while the party had sustained a significant defeat, they nevertheless 'won' and came out of the election battle as the biggest party because the CDA had sustained even greater losses. The defeat had no political consequences for Wim Kok, who capitalized on the 'profit' from the CDA by becoming Prime Minister, thereby crowning his political career.

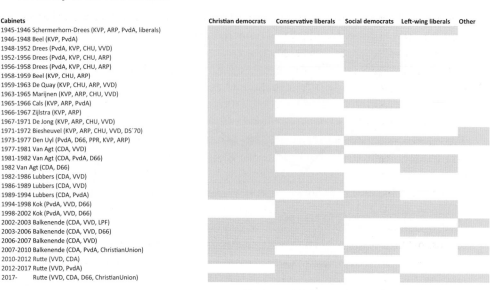

Illustration 9 Coalition governments since 1945.

What happened to the PvdA in 1994 was the opposite of the events in 1977. In 1977 the party had a historic victory but nevertheless started a long period in opposition whereas in 1994 a historic defeat was followed by successful years in government. The PvdA teamed up with the VVD and D66 to form the first of two 'purple' governments that were to remain in office until 2002. These were exceptional coalitions. They were not just the first governments since 1918 without Christian democrats – fifty years had passed since the PvdA and VVD last served together in government.

During these years the Netherlands was in the international headlines because of a form of policy that became known as the 'polder model'. Unemployment dropped, the budget deficit shrank, affluence increased, there was smaller government amid free market forces, the public had more responsibility and there were economies in social security expenditure. This approach was buttressed by substantial political and social agreement. Even the PvdA and the VVD (which had been at daggers drawn during the polarization years) worked together without major feuds. Beyond the borders, Wim Kok in particular was important to the image of this harmony in the Dutch polder, and when social democrats in other countries discovered the 'third way' in the mid-1990s, Kok was seen as an important representative of this movement. 'You were the first, Wim,' was how American President Bill Clinton complimented Kok at a meeting of like-minded heads of government. Anthony Giddens, the British sociologist and advisor to Labour leader Tony Blair, referred to the Dutch purple coalition in the same breath as the 'third way', and the Dutch translation of Giddens's famous *The Third Way* was *Paars. De Derde Weg* (*Purple: The Third Way*).[71]

Although the policies of Wim Kok in the Netherlands, Tony Blair in the United Kingdom (from 1997) and Gerhard Schröder in Germany (from 1998) displayed similarities, there was no joint programme, let alone a 'model'. This was not just because the national backgrounds and courses were too different. The term the 'third way' also suggests, incorrectly, that it is based on a well-considered concept or a grand design. In the Netherlands, in any event, this was not the case.[72] There was agreement at a political level about the need to put public finances in order, to cut spending on the social welfare system and to create more scope for free enterprise. At the same time the core objective was employment. 'Jobs, jobs, jobs,' was the motto of the first Kok government. The different objectives were achieved by a substantial margin, but that success had nothing to do with a 'model'. Joblessness fell faster than expected because of a thriving economy. The huge increase in part-time working, particularly among women, was similarly not the result of political helmsmanship. Economic expansion meant that some of the agreed spending cuts were not necessary. Consequently, no tough measures needed to be taken in the social field, while the budget deficit could be reduced. Thanks to this, potential conflicts between the PvdA and VVD could be nipped in the bud because both parties were able to point out successes to their respective grassroots supporters.

For a few years the Netherlands enjoyed an exceptional degree of political and social harmony, high levels of satisfaction and also pride in the international spotlight on the polder model. At the 1998 elections the voters rewarded the PvdA (up from 24 to 29 per cent) and the VVD (up from 20.0 to 24.7 per cent) with significant gains and, despite the loss of votes sustained by D66 (down from 15.5 to 9 per cent), Wim Kok's purple government was able to carry on in office with an increased majority. The decline of the CDA continued and it became clear that the Christian democrats had no alternative policies to offer. Their share of the vote sagged from 22.2 to 18.4 per cent, which meant that they had lost almost half of the support they had enjoyed during the successful years under Lubbers. Kok's

Figure 29 1998 PvdA election poster featuring Wim Kok, Strong and Fair. Dutch Political Parties Documentation Centre, Groningen.

strength lay in his caution and his keen intuition for sensing a feasible compromise. He had a wait-and-see political style. He would let the others talk, listen and then bring the strands together to produce a balanced view. He was a pragmatic leader. In 1995, in one of his rare speeches about programmes, he said the following. 'For a political party such as ours, casting off our ideological principles is not entirely problematic. In some respects it can also be a liberating experience.'[73] In other words, he was sweeping aside the few remaining ideological dogmas. His reliable and at the same time caring image was reminiscent of his social democrat predecessor from the 1950s, Willem Drees, but he also continued the policies of the man he took over from, Ruud Lubbers.

Looking back at the political history since the war, we see that the three longest-serving and most successful prime ministers – Drees (1948–58), Lubbers (1982–94) and Kok (1994–2002) – were pragmatic and sober politicians who focused on obtaining compromises. Drees's period in office, when the country was still pillarized, was of course completely different in many respects from the depillarized 1980s and 1990s under Lubbers and Kok, but the political styles of these government leaders displayed clear similarities. They built bridges between the parties and were in governments of differing compositions. All three embodied the image of a Dutch political culture that was, and still is, primarily concerned with achieving agreement and cooperation. No matter how striking these parallels between the 1950s on the one hand and the 1980s and 1990s on the other may be, the political and cultural differences between the pillarized Netherlands and the depillarized one are substantial. Political and social authority in the 1980s and 1990s was no longer a matter of course and had to be legitimized repeatedly. In this context the political philosopher Gabriël van den Brink referred to the 'assertive citizen', being the average Dutch person who meanwhile had changed. They had become individualized, with little respect for the authorities, no strong links with party, church or movement, but politically aware.[74] The political and mental environment of the Dutch had evolved so much since the 1950s that it was unrecognizable.

All the same, the heyday of political and social harmony under Wim Kok also had its drawbacks. Discussion of issues about which social democrats and primarily conservative liberals could not reach agreement was postponed. For example, the number of people claiming disability benefit had started to grow again and how could this trend be reversed? Other issues, such as immigration and integration, were largely ignored. Another part of the great harmony's downside was the growing malaise about the overcrowded political centre. Had politics not become bland now that there appeared to be virtually no differences between political parties? Was there still any sort of real choice? And what had happened to the flair of the first purple government, which took office promising to rejuvenate politics?

During the second Kok government (1998–2002), the new zeal and political openness seemed to have been replaced by ever more exclusive political decision making by a small select group comprising the prime minister, ministers and state secretaries and chairs of parties in the Lower House. The concept of 'backroom politics' – a term used back in the 1960s as critique of the political dealings of the pillar elites – made a comeback. Another factor was that by about 1998 the political, social and economic programme of the purple coalition had been essentially implemented. The first Kok government had chosen the motto 'jobs, jobs, jobs' and had also achieved a great deal in that regard, but there was no new political message and objective to follow it. This fact was recognized in the cabinet, and comments were made repeatedly about the need to formulate a social democrat-liberal agenda for the future. Most such discussions remained behind the scenes, however, without the emergence of a recognizable political profile.[75] The upshot of all this was that by around 2000 there was discomfort about a government that appeared to be spent and seemed to be doing little more than pragmatically 'minding the store'. There was also dissatisfaction because the purple government had not got on top of a number of persistent problems, such as long hospital waiting lists, impending gridlock on continually congested roads, trains that did not run on time, and a growing feeling of insecurity in major cities.

The way the second Kok government fell, shortly before the May 2002 general election, reinforced the malaise. On 10 April 2002 the NIOD Institute for War, Holocaust and Genocide Studies presented a report, some 3,400 pages long, about the fall of the Srebrenica safe area in Bosnia in the summer of 1995.[76] Dutch soldiers in the United Nations Protection Force (UNPROFOR) had been assigned the task of protecting the Muslim population in this enclave from any advancing Bosnian Serb forces. This assignment ended in tragedy for the Muslims, who had imagined themselves to be safe and sound. Some 8,000 males were murdered by Bosnian Serb troops under the command of General Ratko Mladic in what was the worst war crime in Europe since the end of the Second World War. During the years that followed, questions were asked in the Netherlands and other countries about whether the Dutch soldiers could and should have defended the enclave and whether, because they had failed to do so, they were also guilty of mass murder. Photographs of the Dutch commander, Colonel Thom Karremans, having a drink with General Mladic only appeared to confirm the validity of the domestic and foreign criticism. There were even rumours that the Dutch had looked on as the mass murder took place.

'Srebrenica' was soon treated in Dutch politics and media as a national disgrace. It was against this backdrop that the NIOD was instructed in 1996 to reconstruct and analyse the fall of the Muslim enclave in an independent investigation. The report presented in April 2002 criticized the Dutch government for the fact that the Dutch troops had been sent to Bosnia with an ambiguous mandate and after insufficient preparation. According to the NIOD, with half-hearted support from UNPROFOR and the international community, the Dutch soldiers were powerless when Mladic decided to wipe the enclave off the map. This conclusion did not rehabilitate Dutchbat, as the Dutch unit was known, but it did make it clear that the genocide did not take place as the Dutch looked on. It was also pointed out, among all the criticism of the Dutch government, that it was not The Hague that had responsibility for the operational actions of Dutchbat but the UN and UNPROFOR. All in all, the report presented by the NIOD was very balanced, sensible and detailed.

Anyone looking for a black and white description of guilt and innocence was disappointed, since the report did not contain any moral or ethical judgments. Someone who did draw political and moral conclusions was Prime Minister Kok. A few days after the publication of the NIOD report he announced the resignation of his cabinet. In so doing Kok did not assume the burden of the nation's political guilt. He wanted to show he shared moral responsibility. That gesture, no matter how sincere and honest, missed the target. Some people criticized his action as an attempt, with a moral gesture, to make a good impression during the election campaign. Others were disappointed that through his premature departure, Kok had already drawn political conclusions before the debate about the report had really got going. Yet others thought Kok should have shown that moral responsibility seven years before, in the summer of 1995, and that stepping down at the end of his political career was nothing more than an empty gesture. So, by resigning, Kok achieved the opposite of what he had intended, which was to contribute to political purity and morality. That was a tragedy for Kok personally and it did no good at all to the already shattered trust in 'politics'.

These developments and the uneasiness in society that had surfaced since the start of the new century did not, however, mean that there was widespread dissatisfaction or that the Kok government was unpopular. When Wim Kok announced in August 2001 that he wanted to retire from front line politics after the 2002 elections, his party's biggest worry was what impact the popular Prime Minister's departure would have on the PvdA's electoral results. In December 2001 – shortly before Pim Fortuyn launched his campaign – 70 per cent of voters still had confidence in the incumbent Kok government. At this time the Netherlands Institute for Social Research similarly reported that the Dutch were by and large satisfied. So as the New Year approached, there were precious few indications of the political earthquake that was to come just a few months later.

Foreign policy in a changed international context

As has clearly emerged, NATO became the cornerstone of Dutch foreign policy in 1949. While consensus about this on the left wing began to crumble in the second half of the 1960s, no change was made to the policy actually pursued in The Hague, even under the Den Uyl government, which had not questioned Atlantic loyalty at all. During the 1970s the Netherlands was still regarded as a loyal ally. This image came under pressure when a mass peace movement sprang up in opposition to NATO's December 1979 double-track decision. This included the announcement that the Atlantic alliance would deploy 108 Pershing II missiles and 464 cruise missiles in Western Europe in response to the Warsaw Pact's SS20 missiles. At the same time, however, it proposed negotiations about the mutual reduction of such weapons systems. The Netherlands insisted on a separate position with regard to this decision. On the one hand, the Dries van Agt government (1977–81), consisting of the CDA and VVD, let there be no doubt about the fact that loyalty to NATO had to remain the cornerstone of security policy. On the other hand, there were divisions inside the CDA in the Lower House and so there was no majority for the implementation of the NATO double-track decision. On top of that, Christian organizations – the Protestant Interchurch Peace Council and the Catholic Pax

Christi – were the pacesetters behind the mass peace movement.[77] In November 1981, 400,000 people demonstrated in Amsterdam against nuclear weapons and in November 1983 a demonstration in The Hague was attended by a throng of 550,000. Never before had there been such huge protests in the Netherlands, and the political and social divide between supporters and opponents of deploying cruise missiles appeared to be unbridgeable.

This damaged the country's reputation as an exemplary NATO ally. By manoeuvring between loyalty to the alliance and domestic political opposition, Prime Ministers Van Agt and Lubbers (after 1982) repeatedly managed to defer the final decision, but in 1985 Lubbers saw no other alternative and the cabinet decided to deploy. The peace movement mobilized once again and collected 3.75 million signatures against the government, which could no longer reverse its decision because it would lose international credibility. In the end, deployment was not necessary because before things got to that point Washington and Moscow reached an agreement in December 1987 to eliminate all intermediate-range missiles. This treaty between the United States and the Soviet Union wiped the differences of opinion about foreign policy from the Dutch political agenda. In fact, the traditional pro-Atlantic consensus was resurrected after the fall of the Berlin Wall in 1989 and the end of the Cold War. Gratifying as the end of the Cold War may have been, The Hague nevertheless saw risks for European security associated with it. According to the government, these could best be parried by retaining the American security guarantee. While Dutch confidence in the Atlantic alliance may have appeared to weaken during the 1980s as a result of the cruise missile issue, from the 1990s it was clearly visible again, and in international crises the Netherlands expressly demonstrated it was a NATO partner fully behind American policy (Iraq, 1991; Yugoslavia, 1991–99; Afghanistan, 2001–10; Iraq, 2003–5).

The Netherlands also remained in familiar territory when it came to Europe. Faced with the choice of whether, in the newly emerging Europe, the European Community should intensify integration between the existing member states (deepening) or strive to increase the number of member states (expansion), initially The Hague opted for intensification of the prevailing cooperation. Dutch foreign policy in the early 1990s was therefore based on maintaining the primacy of Atlanticism and cooperation in the European Community. Nevertheless, the coordinates gradually shifted during the years thereafter. It became clear that the traditional approach of putting the brakes on intergovernmentalism and promoting communitarianism was no longer satisfactory when it came to safeguarding Dutch influence on European decision making. Starting in the mid-1990s, it was decided to pursue a more flexible policy, under which it was not the form of integration that was determining but – depending on the issue – a pragmatic review of how Dutch interests could best be served. That also meant a re-evaluation of bilateralism and intergovernmentalism in European relations. Policy cooperation and coordination with one or more large partners could be a worthwhile alternative to the earlier adherence to supranational decision making.

This shift in Dutch European policy took place primarily during the second Kok government (1998–2002) and Europe was seen more as a 'negotiating arena' than as an ever-developing supranational union. With the completion of the single market and the advent of an economic and monetary union, the Netherlands had achieved the central objectives of its postwar Europe policy. The historians Anjo Harrivan and Jan van der Harst describe the result of these developments as 'a degree of saturation' of Dutch goals in Europe.[78] A characteristic feature of the new wind that started to blow in the Netherlands in the late 1990s was the rejection by Foreign Minister Jozias van Aartsen and the State Secretary of European Affairs Dick Benschop of the plea made by German Foreign Affairs Minister Joschka Fischer in 2000 for a future federal Europe. 'Fantasizing' and 'absurd' were the unfriendly comments emanating from these politicians responsible for Dutch foreign policy.

The new businesslike Dutch attitude was also reflected in The Hague's success in reducing the net amount paid to Brussels, and in 2000 in a tough struggle during the European debate in the Council of Ministers about a new weighting of votes in order to get more votes than other small countries such as Belgium. The measure of success was modest (the Netherlands acquired one vote more than Belgium), and in the process the Dutch generated surprise and irritation among their European partners. Finally, that changed attitude also manifested itself in the more frequent appearance of the concept of 'subsidiarity' in the positions adopted by The Hague about European cooperation. According to political scientist Jan Rood, in the context of European cooperation the Netherlands evolved into a 'dissatisfied nation' with a minimalist integration model.[79]

In the quest for an explanation for the new businesslike Netherlands, we have to look first at the aforementioned 'saturation' that developed in The Hague with regard to the European agenda. There is no doubt that the decreased keenness on European integration was due in part to the marginalization of the Dutch position in the EU. When the ECSC was created in 1951, followed six years later by the EEC, the Netherlands was still one of the six member states and could at some moments exert decisive influence. During the 1990s this number rose to fifteen and the Netherlands became one of many small nations with correspondingly little sway. This trend reinforced the inclination to keep power to make decisions in the country's own hands.[80] As we shall see below, this trend became more marked as time passed.

The populist revolt and the quest for a new equilibrium since 2002

A major shock in 2002 made it clear for all to see that the years of the 'polder model' under the Kok governments (1994–2002) were over. The parties in the coalition government (PvdA, VVD and D66) commanded nearly 63 per cent of the vote in 1998, but in 2002 this slumped to barely 36 per cent. Never before in Dutch history had government parties been so soundly beaten in an election. The cause of this political earthquake was Pim Fortuyn. He found the Achilles heel of the second purple government and acted as a catalyst for the different strata of negative sentiment. As a colourful anti-politician on the right, he gave people the feeling that there was more to choose from than one of the parties in the overfull political centre. Through his populist manner, he created a contrast between the 'political caste' in The Hague, which no longer listened to voters, and himself, who 'wanted to give the Netherlands back to the Dutch'. He could unerringly sense dissatisfaction. He spoke in plain terms about the failed integration of migrants, he took concerns that people had about safety seriously, and he confronted self-satisfied politicians with unsolved problems in health care, in education and on the roads. He had neither a consistent political message nor any solutions, but he nevertheless succeeded because he gave many people the feeling he was talking on their behalf. In particular, his positions with regard to migration and integration were radical and broke taboos. He openly described Islam as a 'backward culture' and advocated scrapping the anti-discrimination article in the Dutch constitution. He did not, though, adopt right-wing extremist points of view, such as those of Jean-Marie le Pen in France or Jörg Haider in Austria. However, he did call for a halt to immigration ('the Netherlands is full') and a tougher integration policy under which migrants not only had to learn Dutch but also internalize Dutch legislation and codes of conduct.

Fortuyn's big breakthrough came on 6 March 2002, when his list of candidates in Rotterdam's council elections came out of nowhere to win 35 per cent of the votes and become the biggest party in the city. Two months later, shortly before Lower House elections, he was murdered by a radical environmental activist. Even after his death the Netherlands remained under his spell. In the elections on 15 May 2002, the Pim Fortuyn List (LPF) won over 17 per cent of the votes and became the second biggest party in the Lower House.[81]

The established parties' response to this electoral success was to adopt the same pattern as the reaction to the protest movements since the 1960s – integration with the goal of assimilation. In the summer of 2002, the CDA and VVD included the LPF in the government headed by Jan Peter Balkenende (CDA) as prime minister. During the months that followed it soon became clear that the LPF without Fortuyn was rudderless and amateurish. The LPF members of parliament were mostly inexperienced political adventurers who argued with one another virtually continuously and had little interest in their actual parliamentary tasks. In no time the turmoil spread to the cabinet and even the LPF ministers started to let fly at one another. In October 2002, the CDA and VVD announced they no longer had confidence in cooperation with LPF, so in January 2003 it was back to the ballot box for the second time in a year.

At first glance these elections restored the political landscape to what it had usually been before the Fortuyn whirlwind, with the CDA as the centre party, and an equally large PvdA to the left and a slightly weaker VVD on the right. In that former environment, the Christian democrats had always been able to decide whether to form a centre-left or a centre-right government. As had usually been the case in the past, the CDA elected to work with the VVD. Yet this return to the old ways was only a pretence because the 2003 election results were a reflection of a democracy with many floating voters.

The new Balkenende government (2003–6) did not create the calm and stability that many wanted after the turbulence of 2002. Deteriorating economic circumstances contributed to this failure. Unemployment climbed to over 6 per cent in 2005. The budget deficit rose too and for a brief period was actually higher than the 3 per cent tolerated

Figure 30 2002 Pim Fortuyn election poster for Lower House elections. Dutch Political Parties Documentation Centre, Groningen.

under the EU fiscal compact. Once again social security spending was cut, prompting large trade union demonstrations. Such conflicts were still part of a normal and regularly recurring pattern, but things changed in November 2004 when the film director Theo van Gogh was murdered by a Dutch Muslim of Moroccan descent. Fortuyn's murder had caused great division and polarization among the indigenous Dutch population, but the shooting and stabbing of Van Gogh led to a hardening of relations between home-grown Dutch nationals and immigrants. Emotions escalated at the end of 2004 when a few mosques and Islamic schools were torched by indigenous Dutch people and there was comparable retaliation against Christian institutions.

Although further escalation did not happen, by then many agreed with the publicist Paul Scheffer's diagnosis. In a now famous article in the *NRC Handelsblad* in 2000 he had written about 'a multicultural drama'. He did not mince his words when he asserted that the integration of migrants had largely failed. In his view, home-grown and immigrant communities did not live together but on the contrary had no real contact, and the highly praised Dutch tolerance was not much more than mutual lack of interest. The realization there was a crisis in integration policy was amplified at the end of 2004 when more details about Van Gogh's murderer were published. Born in Morocco, he had emigrated to the Netherlands as a child and had completed his education in the Netherlands. His command of Dutch was good, as were his prospects on the Dutch labour market. In other words, the ingredients for successful integration were present, but the young man of Moroccan descent nevertheless fell under the influence of radical Muslims. These facts prompted the conclusion that even those who meet the basic requirements for integration – language skills, diploma and opportunities on the labour market – are not protected from the risk of radicalization. There were already major concerns about the best integration policy to pursue, and this conclusion made them even greater. On top of that, Van Gogh's murderer appeared to have operated in an Islamic fundamentalist network. This was the period of 9/11 in the United States and the attacks in Madrid (2004) and London (2005). Fears of Islamic terrorist atrocities grew throughout the Western world, and the Netherlands was no exception. These concerns were understandable, particularly given Dutch political support for the Anglo–American invasion of Iraq (2003) and later the presence of Dutch troops there, not forgetting the military engagement in Afghanistan.

This was the backdrop to the tightening of Dutch immigration and integration policy that has taken place since 2002. In 2006, the polarizing actions of the minister responsible, Rita Verdonk of the VVD, resulted in the premature end of the second Balkenende government, and once again the calling of early elections. Now, too, it was the floating voters who made the difference, and the shifts between parties were substantial. A remarkable outcome was that all established parties lost votes – something that had never happened before (see Illustration 3, pp. 190–2). The PvdA, VVD and D66 lost many votes, the CDA and GreenLeft a few. The big winner was the Socialist Party (SP), which increased its share of the vote by 10 per cent and became the second largest party in the Lower House. On the right wing, Geert Wilders's aggressive anti-Islamic PVV captured part of Fortuyn's legacy and in its first showing won just under 6 per cent of the vote. The Christian Union (CU) was also a winner, doubling its votes to 4 per cent. No matter how divergent the politics of the three victorious parties may have been, they also shared common features. In 2005 all of them had called for people to vote against the European Constitution (see below) in the referendum and they each stressed in their own way the importance of retaining Dutch identity. The SP advocated greater national historical awareness, the PVV wanted to drive back Islam and the CU supported the traditional values of an orthodox Protestant Netherlands. A second feature shared by the victors was that none of the leaders had a political track record in office. They had not borne any political responsibility and therefore also certainly got the benefit of the doubt. In marked contrast to this, the losses by the established parties clearly demonstrated that their leaders no longer had the confidence of many voters.

The formation of a government has traditionally been a complicated business in the Netherlands, and usually takes several months. This was exacerbated after the 2006 elections because none of the conventional combinations commanded a majority. Even a coalition of Christian and social democrats could not govern without support from others, and thus in the end a government was formed by the CDA, PvdA and CU. At first blush this was a curious cocktail because the CU was a fundamental opponent on religious grounds to what had been standard practice for many years in the Netherlands, in part thanks to the PvdA, with regard to euthanasia, abortion, same-sex marriage etc. Amazement about it soon died down and this coalition government came across as not being significantly different from past traditional combinations. The political landscape had changed, however. On the left wing the SP presented itself as the 'conscience of the left' and in so doing put the PvdA on the defensive, while on the right wing Geert Wilders's PVV continued its campaign against Islamic migrants. For a brief period, former minister Rita Verdonk also operated on the right wing, not without success, with her populist Proud of the Netherlands (TON) movement. She was soon eclipsed by Geert Wilders, however, and according to the polls for a few months in 2009 his PVV had the greatest number of supporters. Wilders was also repeatedly in the news outside the Netherlands too. In 2008, for instance, with his film *Fitna*, in which he made much of his warnings about the 'threatening Islamization' of the Netherlands and Europe and suggested that hate and terrorism would automatically result from Islam.[82]

Balkenende's new government also had to navigate choppy waters. This was due to the poor personal relationship between the Prime Minister on the one hand and the PvdA leader and Minister of Finance Wouter Bos on the other, and also to friction about foreign policy (see below) and social and economic issues. There was concerted joint action to deal with the international financial crisis that broke out in 2008, and billions were injected into the system to preserve Dutch banks from insolvency. When it came to addressing the subsequent budget deficit, however, things were different. Nobody doubted the need to reduce spending, also incidentally because of structural economic and social causes. But there was disagreement about how much and how quickly to cut and about the political choices that had to be made. The result was that decisions were not taken and were postponed.

Figure 31 Prime Minister Jan Peter Balkenende in a group with the Deputy Prime Ministers Wouter Bos (PvdA) and André Rouvoet (CU). Photo: Michiel Sablerolle.

The conclusions of the Davids Committee brought about a substantial deterioration in the atmosphere around the cabinet table in January 2010. This committee was set up by the government in 2009 and asked to investigate the internal Dutch decision making concerning the political support for the United States when Iraq was invaded in 2003. The politically sensitive aspect of this assignment was that the cabinet at the time, under Balkenende's leadership, had backed the American invasion, while the PvdA had criticized it on the grounds of international law. When the Davids Committee concluded in January 2010 in a substantial report that there had not been a 'sufficient mandate under international law' for the invasion of Iraq, that in 2003 Prime Minister Balkenende had given insufficient leadership to Dutch decision making and that the Lower House had furthermore repeatedly not been given enough information, relations between the CDA and the PvdA were put on a knife edge.[83] Although it was possible to avoid a cabinet crisis, it was clear that the basis for trust had shrunk dramatically. Against this backdrop it was not going to take much to bring the coalition government down. During that same period very profound differences of opinion about a possible extension of the Dutch military presence in Afghanistan (PvdA against, CDA for) were the cause of the fall of Balkenende's last cabinet in February 2010.

The June 2010 elections made necessary by the fall of the government created a completely new political situation. The CDA sustained a historic defeat (a drop from 26.5 per cent in 2006 to 13.6 per cent), the VVD became the biggest party for the first time (up from 14.7 per cent in 2006 to 20.4 per cent) and the PVV was very successful, achieving 15.5 per cent (2006: 5.9 per cent), which made it the second largest party. Wilders did not receive this high percentage solely because of his positions on migration, integration and safety on the streets. An important factor was his stance on socioeconomic issues, which tended to lean towards the 'left'. He did not support cuts in social security spending and in this way attracted many politically disaffected and socially vulnerable voters. Electors who vote for nationalist-populist groups are indeed more dissatisfied than average with Dutch democracy and their representatives. They also feel threatened and uncertain as a result of the loss of traditional social and cultural certainties. People like Fortuyn and Wilders were able to profit from this uneasiness and contributed during the first decade of the twenty-first century to making 15 to 20 per cent of the electorate receptive to nationalist-populist policies.

The 2010 election results revealed further fragmentation of the political landscape. There has been no increase in the number of parties in the Lower House, where the normal pattern is for there to be a dozen or so. The fragmentation that has been taking place since 1994 has resulted in weakening the 'big' parties. Never before did a party with just over 20 per cent of the votes emerge from the elections as the biggest. Similarly, the joint vote attracted by the former major people's parties CDA, PvdA and VVD slumped for the first time to not much more than half. It goes without saying that this ongoing fragmentation makes it more difficult to put a stable government together. The apparent erosion of the political 'centre ground', which is consequently no longer able to play its traditional stabilizing role, exacerbates the problem. Another factor is that the long-standing generally accepted differences between 'left' and 'right' have lost their traditional

Figure 32 Geert Wilders, Lower House (2010).
Photo: Michiel Sablerolle.

significance. Election research has shown that more than before Dutch voters have 'left-wing' views about socioeconomic policy and intangible issues (for example euthanasia) while at the same time the vast majority of electors have 'right-wing' ideas about migration and integration. These last views are increasingly linked to a Eurosceptic attitude.[84] The upshot of these trends is that for years the electorate has found itself in two minds: usually left leaning in social, economic and immaterial matters and generally right leaning on migration and integration issues. These new political dividing lines made it particularly difficult to define the positions of social and Christian democrats, which enlarged electoral mobility even more. The success of Geert Wilders, who in fact combines these 'left' and 'right' stances in his political one-liners, has to be viewed against this background.

Notwithstanding his electoral success in 2010, Wilders did not become part of the government, but his group helped the cabinet of right-wing liberals and Christian democrats to get a majority by being a 'tolerance partner'. This gave him a comfortable position of power with substantial influence on government policy but without having to bear any responsibility. The tolerance experiment came to an end in the spring of 2012 when Wilders refused to support the austerity plans of the two government parties (VVD and CDA). The fifth Lower House elections in ten years were a neck-and-neck race between the VVD and PvdA and their candidates Mark Rutte and Diederik Samsom. The VVD won by a slim margin, and agreement with the PvdA was soon reached about forming a coalition government. It would be hasty, though, to conclude from this that the political centre emerged stronger from the 2012 elections and that the population had chosen stability. It appears more likely that people voted strategically for a candidate who stood a chance of becoming prime minister. The PvdA won the support of many potential SP voters and the VVD took many votes away from the PVV. The new government of liberals and social democrats did not make a stable and energetic

Figure 33 Prime Minister Mark Rutte, Press Centre 'Nieuwpoort', The Hague (2016). Picture Alliance/ANP, Photo: Jerry Lampen.

impression from the outset, in part because it had no majority in the Upper House. Nevertheless, the VVD and PvdA government led by Prime Minister Mark Rutte until the 2017 election remained in the driving seat. This made it the first government since 1998 not to fall prematurely.

The 2017 election made the VVD the biggest party with 21.3 per cent, followed by a group of medium-sized parties with some 9 to 13 per cent each. The former people's parties CDA, PvdA and VVD, which between them still accounted for 80 to 85 per cent of the votes in the 1980s, had a combined vote in 2017 of below 40 per cent, while the other parties made big gains. The PvdA's slump, from just under 25 per cent in 2012 to 5.7 per cent in 2017, was historic (see Illustration 3, pp. 190–2 and Illustration 7, p. 261). Against this backdrop the formation of a coalition government, a traditional but nevertheless difficult and time-consuming process in the Netherlands, became even more burdensome. It took 225 days after the March 2017 general election to form a new government, consisting of four parties (VVD, CDA, D66 and CU). Never before in Dutch history had the formation of a government taken so long.[85]

International comparison shows that the trends in the Netherlands are not unique. In other countries, too, traditional people's parties are losing support, the number of floating voters has grown and it has become more difficult to form coalitions. However, the political uncertainty in the Netherlands is greater than elsewhere in Europe. In 2008 the Leiden political scientist Peter Mair found that on three occasions between 1950 and 2006 the Netherlands was in the 'top ten' of countries in Western Europe with elections resulting in the biggest electoral shifts (1994, 2002, 2006).[86] If Mair had been able to include election results from later years, they would also have achieved high scores. It is striking that this high level of voter disloyalty was not (and is not) found in an exceptional period of political reordering, such as in France in the 1950s (demise of the Fourth Republic) or in Italy in the 1990s (downfall of Italian Christian democracy). The situation in the Netherlands since 1994 appeared to be one of continual reordering, with many seats changing hands in the Lower House (see Illustration 8, p. 261) without a new equilibrium emerging. Mair examined trends in the Dutch party system in search of an explanation.

He identified the lingering effect of former depillarization processes, the proportional representation electoral system with an extremely low electoral threshold and the associated open structure of party-political competition. In many countries voting behaviour is determined strategically because choosing a particular party also implies a choice of a particular government or government coalition. In the open Dutch structure, on the other hand, the selection of a party is the prime issue. That was also the case during the pillarization era, but then the electorate was still relatively set in its ways in a stable political landscape with a clear overview of coalition combinations. Dutch voters were cast completely adrift by the disappearance of the established link between voter and party without its being replaced by the option to express a preference for a specific government coalition. This trend that Mair identified is made more emphatic by the fact that voter preference is being determined much more strongly than before by *people* and less by *parties*. This is not just the case for the personal success of Pim Fortuyn in 2002 and Geert Wilders since 2010. It also applies to the traditional parties. A good example of this was the significant advance of the PvdA in March 2010 after Job Cohen became its new figurehead. It soon emerged that Cohen could not fulfil the high expectations and the PvdA fell out of favour with the electorate. At the beginning of 2012 he handed over to Diederik Samsom, who had a marked personal electoral success that took the social democrats into government that same year. Five years later, a few months before the elections, he was replaced by Lodewijk Asscher, the Minister of Social Affairs and Employment, in the hope that the latter would be able to attract more votes. The opposite happened and the change of leadership contributed to a shattering defeat for the PvdA (from 24.7 per cent in 2012 to 5.7 per cent in 2017). Of course, political personalization is not a new phenomenon, but outward appearances and effectiveness, and thus the impressions and feelings created in the voter, have meanwhile become much more important to voting behaviour than in the past. Politicians and parties can consequently gain favour with voters much quicker, but they can also lose out dramatically just as rapidly. It has become clear since 2002 that populism can really flourish in such a context.[87]

All parties have been faced with large fluctuations during elections since 1994. The modern, uncommitted citizen has become a floating voter. These fluctuations have resulted in political instability and unpredictability since 2002, and the end is not yet in sight. It is therefore not surprising that the calls for political reforms, including changes to the electoral system, have become more insistent. Such pleas are not new, incidentally, and since the 1970s many committees and advisory bodies have published reports with a variety of proposals and plans for reform, none of which have been ever been implemented because a political majority was lacking. Even if that were to change in the future, political reforms cannot be expected to produce more than systemic solutions for reducing political instability. Substantive answers to key questions about the future of social security in an ageing society, about migration and integration, about national identity and political culture, about the Netherlands in Europe and the world etc. are separate issues. Increased social and cultural differences have indeed made it more difficult to find answers that have a broad support base in the community. On top of that there is also growing uncertainty about European and international cooperation.

We saw earlier that during the 1990s the Dutch position in the EU changed and that achieving economic and monetary objectives resulted in a more businesslike and even cautious approach to further European integration. It emerged in June 2005 that the general public's reservations went much further than in political circles. In a referendum, a substantial majority of 63 per cent rejected the European Constitution, which was intended to provide a framework for cooperation and decision making in a much enlarged EU. This repudiation by the Netherlands – and France, where the constitution was also given the thumbs down in a plebiscite – drove the EU into a profound crisis. At a time when politicians were trying to learn lessons from the Fortuyn revolt and to listen 'better' to the public, the referendum results came across as a kick in the teeth for the political elite in The Hague, which in a paternalistic campaign had repeatedly primed voters to say 'yes' to the constitution. The resounding 'no' should therefore not be interpreted as an actual rejection of European cooperation by the Dutch population. Polls have invariably confirmed widespread support for Dutch membership of the EU. Yet, the result was a clear signal that many Dutch people considered that the number of EU member states was growing too rapidly and were sceptical about further enlargement. As far as the Dutch government was concerned, this could only mean ongoing reservation about the European integration process.[88]

Nothing has changed in that regard since 2005. The results of the 2009 European Parliament elections once again confirmed the way the electorate was going. Eurosceptic parties such as the PVV and SP received nearly 25 per cent of the votes between them, and Wilders's group, with 17 per cent, came in second behind the CDA, which with 20.1 per cent of the votes came out on top. The combined percentage achieved by D66 and GreenLeft (20.2 per cent), which explicitly advocate further European integration, did not match up. There was a slight shift in the 2014 European elections in favour of pro-European D66 and GreenLeft, but reservations about further European integration remained dominant. Dutch scepticism at government level about European cooperation peaked for the time being between 2010 and 2012. During this period the minority VVD and CDA government, which was tolerated by the PVV, only got support from parliamentary opposition parties for those EU measures that were aimed at keeping the joint European currency afloat. Even when the tone of the language used by The Hague when communicating with 'Brussels' during the VVD and PvdA government (2012–17) became slightly more positive again, it is telling that when Frans Timmermans (PvdA), known as a pro-European, became Minister of Foreign Affairs in 2012, Dutch government vocabulary changed and 'European integration' disappeared to be replaced by the much less ambitious sounding 'European cooperation'.

The growing unease about European integration also surfaced in 2016 in the referendum about the EU association agreement with Ukraine. This agreement created the basis for a more intensive relationship between the EU and Ukraine and had to be ratified by all EU member states. The Dutch population was asked to approve this agreement in a referendum, but it was rejected by 61 per cent of those voting. While the turnout was very low, at 32.2 per cent, and the government was not bound by the result (it was an advisory referendum and not binding), the message was clear. Even though most voters were probably not familiar with the content of the agreement, their 'no' vote was intended as an indication of mistrust of 'Brussels' and a signal of opposition to greater influence for the European Union.

So, Euroscepticism has grown in the Netherlands, but not many people support 'Nexit'. This is because political and social circles are profoundly aware of the sober reality that, as a trading nation, the Netherlands would sustain very serious economic damage without the benefits of the internal European market. The vast majority of the Dutch also deeply regret the departure of the United Kingdom from the European Union – and not solely because of the expected negative economic impact. There are also political implications. As far as The Hague is concerned, London has always been a welcome counterweight to the Franco–German axis, which is sometimes considered as too strong. That counterweight will now disappear and there is a justified expectation that The Hague will respond with restraint to Franco–German initiatives aimed at more far-reaching European cooperation. European federal visions are not to be expected from The Hague. A more likely approach will be under the motto of 'subsidiarity' meaning 'as much Europe as necessary' and 'as much national power of control as possible'.

Since the 1990s there have been clear shifts in Dutch policy on Europe, but The Hague's security policy has remained focused on Atlantic cooperation. As we saw above, as far as The Hague was concerned the end of the Cold War and German reunification only confirmed the importance of NATO and Atlantic security relationships. In the rapidly changing field of international relations, NATO proved to be one of the few stabilizing organizations, while neither the Organization for Security and Co-operation in Europe (OSCE) nor the UN were able to play such a role. The Netherlands has therefore been a constant loyal ally of the United States since the end of the Cold War (Iraq, 1991; Yugoslavia, 1991–99; Afghanistan, 2001). As referred to briefly above, the Netherlands also supported the Anglo–American invasion of Iraq in 2003, which provoked considerable disunity in the EU. The Hague even sent troops to Iraq after the defeat of Saddam Hussein. The appointment of the Dutchman Jaap de Hoop Scheffer, Minister of Foreign Affairs since 2002, as Secretary-General of NATO in 2004 cannot be considered in isolation from The Hague's resolute loyalty to the United States. After the early 1980s, when strong opposition arose in the Netherlands to deployment of new American nuclear weapons and the country temporarily lost its reputation as a loyal NATO partner, Dutch security policy returned completely to the tradition of the postwar era. The departure of Dutch troops from Afghanistan in 2010 was not a material violation of this and did not herald a change of course in this regard. This became clear in 2013, for instance, when The Hague decided to contribute Dutch troops to the UN peace mission in Mali in West Africa. In 2018 it was announced that the Netherlands will leave Mali in 2020, but at the same time it will resume its engagement in Afghanistan.

CHAPTER 8
EPILOGUE

The history of the Netherlands since the sixteenth century is often considered by the Dutch and others as a continuous, gradual and largely peaceful process. In this oversimplified and clichéd picture, the country is portrayed as a Calvinist nation, tolerant of religious minorities and with relatively generous spiritual freedom. The political decision making in this nation, with its many minorities and long-established federal structure, involved an ongoing quest for broadly supported compromises. According to this elementary model, the search for unity in decision making remained a quintessential feature, even after the Netherlands became a unitary state in the late eighteenth century.

The pillarization of politics and society since the end of the nineteenth century reflects this culture of gradualness and moderation. The compartmentalized structure controlled the emerging conflicts between groups in the population with religious and philosophical differences, and created national unity despite all the diversity. Another ingredient of that harmony was the traditional decision-making culture, which involved the pragmatic pursuit of agreement. The national political culture this created survived the depillarization and individualization of the 1960s. In the 1990s, the term 'polder model' was coined for this climate, in which differences of opinion were always talked through and settled in a sober and rational way to produce an end result that was acceptable to everyone. According to this picture of moderation and gradualness, making compromises was not associated in the Netherlands with cowardice or weakness, but on the contrary was appreciated as a way to create win-win situations.

In a nutshell, the course of political history was determined not by violence, revolution or civil war, but by peaceableness, moderation and tolerance. How widespread this image of the country was in the recent past emerged from the reactions to the rise of right-wing populism and the associated coarsening of political interaction since 2002. Many domestic and foreign commentators referred to an 'un-Dutch' phenomenon, without roots in the history of the nation's political culture.

Just as any simplification contains a grain of truth, so the picture outlined above is not completely inaccurate, but it certainly needs to be corrected. It is the same story with the characterization of the Netherlands as having been small-but-brave, as Blom ironically phrases it.[1] This myth, which harks back to the 'courageous forefathers', the Batavians, who had resisted the Romans, emerged as far back as the Revolt. In later centuries it was stoked primarily by the illustrious Eighty Years' War (1568–1648), during which the suppressed Protestants under the inspiring leadership of William of Orange, the Father of his Country, put an end to the 'occupation' by world power Spain. After that the small, peaceable Republic defied powers like England and France for decades, and was not brought to its knees until the eighteenth century, when it had to gradually accept that it had become a minor league player. Yet it could remain proud of its colonial empire in Asia, which was many times larger and had a much greater population than the modest mother country. Finally, the German occupation (1940–45) resulted in strengthening the small-but-brave self-image. Was this not another case of a small, peaceful and freedom-loving nation pluckily taking a stand against the injustice and violence of an apparently dominant occupier?

This cliché of peaceableness and courage is just as inaccurate as the idealized picture of centuries of consensus-based decision making, gradualness and tolerance when it comes to the reality of Dutch history since the sixteenth century. As this book has repeatedly shown, the internal goings-on were far from quiet and peaceful, and the small-but-brave self-image is a retrospective nationalistic construct. A feature of self-images is their function in historical and current debates about national identity. Depending on the period one is in, the theme one is concerned with, and the people speaking in the debate, it is easy to transform the 'essence of our history' or 'nature of our country' into certain 'historical roots'. This makes history a lucky dip, where everyone can take what they want according to their needs. The purpose of these final comments is to identify a few historical lines running from the sixteenth century to the present day that do greater justice to the country's history.

It is first and foremost important to put the image of consensus and gradualness into perspective.[2] Compared with other countries, there have certainly been fewer splits, violent internal conflicts, revolutions and sudden regime changes in Dutch history, but they have not been absent. The Revolt contained aspects of a civil war, and the conflict between Stadholder Maurice and Advocate of Holland Oldenbarnevelt threatened to become one. Before it got that far, however, in 1618 Maurice pushed Oldenbarnevelt aside in a coup d'état. In 1650 his nephew, Stadholder William II, also attempted a coup, but his early death stopped it in its tracks. The next regime change, to the 'true freedom' of the First Stadholderless Period, came about without fighting. Things were different when this period ended in 1672 with the violent death of Grand Pensionary Johan de Witt and his brother Cornelis in The Hague.

The way Stadholder William III then took hold of the reins of power similarly had no trace of consensual decision making and gradualness. It was no different after his death in 1702, which was followed by the Old Crew/New Crew dispute, leading to serious conflicts here and there. The Patriot era and the quasi-civil war situation in the mid-1780s are other clear examples. William V was only able to return to The Hague as stadholder, thanks to Prussian military intervention. He conducted an unprecedented purge and thousands of Patriots fled the country. There was a fundamental regime change in 1795, when the Republic fell during the advance of French troops and Stadholder William V took refuge in England. Power changed hands many times during the years thereafter, always after a coup d'état engineered by the French, although their involvement varied from case to case.

It is striking that domestic conflicts, which had dominated the Republic since the Patriot era, became less significant at the beginning of the nineteenth century. Important crossroads such as return of Orange in 1813, the birth of the United Kingdom of the

Netherlands (1815–30) and the constitutional amendments of 1848 and 1917 all took place without noteworthy internal consternation, violence or revolution. The only exception was the secession of Belgium in 1830, but this involved a revolt by the *Southern* Netherlands, so it can be left out of this overview. Yet it would be wrong to conclude from the absence of violent domestic watersheds in politics since 1813 that political and ideological differences disappeared in the Netherlands of the nineteenth and twentieth centuries, or that there was broad political consensus in the country.

Bitter disputes between the monarch and parliament flared up repeatedly during the reign of William I (1815–40) and also in the aimless years without clear political direction under William II (1840–49). In 1853, the emergence of the April Movement was further evidence of the deep divide between the dominant Protestant majority and the large Catholic minority. This antithesis was to remain evident until far into the twentieth century. There were also substantial differences of opinion about the structuring of the Netherlands after the constitutional amendments of 1848 and 1917, as became clear in previous chapters. It was no different behind the scenes of the pillarized political and social system that took shape at the end of the nineteenth century. As a rule, there were profound contrasts between the pillars, which were furthermore far from the ideal monolithic units they were often said to have been. Finally, there were also countless groups that did not fit into any of the four pillars and went their own way.

Looking more closely at Dutch political history, it is clear that the gradualness and moderation were less significant than would appear from a superficial examination. One is also struck by the fact that really deep-seated political conflicts were taking place beneath the veneer of quiet times. The fact that this struggle did not give rise to abrupt turning points and radicalism in the nineteenth and twentieth centuries may consequently not be interpreted as evidence of a broad-based consensus in Dutch politics. To the extent there was general agreement, it usually did not go much further than a shared realization that in a country with so many minorities, progress could only be made on the basis of consultation. That is certainly a key feature of the Dutch political culture, but it does not indicate general consensus about political substance. The key word here is pragmatism.

The Dutch version of pragmatism is closely tied to tolerance – a concept that has without doubt played a major role in both the national self-image and international perceptions of the Netherlands. In this context, many people draw a simple continuous line from the freedom of conscience and relative religious liberty of the sixteenth and seventeenth centuries, by way of the rationalistic eighteenth-century thinking about tolerance and the nineteenth-century political emancipation ambitions, to the broadmindedness of the permissive society that has been developing since the 1960s. Sociologist Schuyt rightly points out that forbearance in these different periods should be seen against the specific historical backdrop of the era concerned, and that the concept's substance, form and legitimacy have undergone significant changes.[3] He makes a distinction, for example, between the seventeenth-century pragmatic 'ecumenical dealings in the public domain' (Frijhoff/Spies) of the various churches and religious movements on the one hand, and tolerance as a positively perceived virtue based on philosophical theories on the other.

It should also be borne in mind that it was very difficult to impose policies and beliefs top down in the Republic because of its decentralized organization, its highly fragmented system of government and the many different religious groups it housed. Peaceful co-existence among Christian persuasions based on pragmatism was the primary reason why, in the seventeenth-century Republic, the Netherlands was a safe haven for victims of persecution elsewhere. The newcomers duly contributed to the economic and cultural vigour, which justified the course that had been chosen. Yet it should be noted that tolerance in the Republic often meant no more than turning a blind eye, and those who were not members of the Dutch Reformed Church were disadvantaged in many ways. It is clear that tolerance in the Netherlands had very clear limits and, not unimportantly, was a *relative* phenomenon: the repression of dissidents outside the Republic was substantially more vigorous.

Summarizing, if the political situation, legitimacy and international context are considered, it makes little sense to compare the relative freedom of religion in those days with the permissiveness of Amsterdam in the late twentieth century. Even so, bearing Schuyt's insights in mind, it is possible to identify some correspondence between then and now. In the pluriform Netherlands, tolerance arose and arises primarily from changing pragmatic considerations and much less from the dissemination of in-depth philosophical reflections.

As well as being tolerant, the Netherlands is said to have been an orthodox Calvinist country. According to Schutte, in contemporary parlance the Calvinist Netherlands is associated with 'straightforwardness, moralism, pedantry, narrow-mindedness, frugality and the inability to make a grand gesture'. This caricature has many aspects: the Netherlands as a country of clergymen, where there is little laughter, where wealth is an embarrassment, and where – thanks to a Calvinist work ethic – people work hard. These clichés speak volumes about how Calvinism is perceived, but says very little about its historical reality.[4] In addition, religious forbearance – which was so typical of the Republic – in fact often had to be persisted with and defended to constrain Calvinism. William of Orange's calls for religious tolerance during the Revolt frequently led to clashes with Calvinists, and the wrangling between Oldenbarnevelt and Maurice about the official church also reflected the differences between intolerant strictly orthodox Calvinists (Gomarists) and more open-minded moderates (Arminians). The victory of the Gomarists linked with Maurice was only temporary, however, and different voices were soon heard again inside the official church. Comparable tensions arose between the Voetians and Coccejans in the middle of the seventeenth century. An important feature of the Republic was thus not a dominant orthodox Calvinism, but an official Dutch reformed church in which strict Calvinists were also represented. So there were always different movements inside the Republic's official church and later, in the Kingdom of the Netherlands, Protestantism was also much too diverse and divided to be able to talk about overriding orthodox Calvinism. In the late nineteenth century, Abraham Kuyper was not able to attract more than 10 per cent of the population to his Dutch Reformed Church, and this figure is an accurate reflection of the numerical strength of orthodox Calvinism at that time.

Finally, it should be pointed out again that the Netherlands has always had many simultaneously functioning churches, among which the Catholic Church has always represented a large minority of between about 35 and 45 per cent of the people. To describe the Netherlands as 'Calvinist' furthermore completely ignores one part of the country – the history of the Generality Lands with their essentially homogeneous Catholic population. Yet this qualification of the significance of orthodox Calvinism obviously does not deny the fact that it has played an important role in Dutch history since the sixteenth century. It was one of the major factors behind the Revolt and also always occupied a key position in the debates and wrangling about the place of the Christian faith in politics and society, but it was never strong enough to justify describing the Netherlands as a Calvinist country. It is, though, correct to label Protestantism, with its multiplicity of movements, as a dominant religious factor.

Bearing in mind the regional differences between the Protestant controlled north and the Catholic south, it is important to warn against taking a too strongly Holland-centric approach to the history of the Netherlands. Of course, the province of Holland was the economic, political and cultural centre during the Republic and remained so afterwards. What was true of Holland was not necessarily the case for other provinces. The historians Wijnand Mijnhardt and Paul Brusse observe the existence of two worlds in the Republic at the end of the seventeenth century – one in the west and one in the other parts of the country. The aristocracy and major landowners remained important in the rural provinces, and the political and economic weight of the nobility actually increased in the second half of the eighteenth century.[5] Holland, by contrast, was much more extensively urbanized, and largely determined the Republic's bourgeois character. Looking at the current Netherlands, the differences between the major conurbation in the west and the rest of the nation are still important – in political traditions, cultural tastes and, not least, the reciprocal perceptions of being the 'centre' and the 'periphery'. Historical simplification thus threatens once again if regional historical differences are not taken into account.

Despite these contrasts between Holland and the other provinces, the country as a whole can be classified as bourgeois compared with other European nations. First and foremost this is understandable if one bears in mind that the nobility in the Northern Netherlands had a relatively modest place as early as the Revolt, although its position and prestige varied from province to province. Another important factor is the urban character of the Republic, particularly dominant in Holland. There were many towns and cities in a relatively small territory and also, compared with other countries, a large population from an early stage. Around 1700, nearly half the Republic's people lived in a built-up environment, which – save for the Southern Netherlands – was unique in the world. That led to a society dominated by the bourgeoisie, and thanks to the Republic's federal structure it acquired a typical Dutch character. Prak points out that the special position of Dutch citizens lies in the connection between their roles at local and national levels. In the towns, cities, provinces and States General, the burghers dominated political decision making even though only a small segment of the population was involved and the influence of the aristocracy in the eastern provinces should not be underestimated.[6] The dominant position of the burghers in the Republic made it very different from countries like France and England and central European states, where power was concentrated in the aristocracy's hands.

The bourgeois nature of the Netherlands during the Republic would suggest that the Dutch were relatively early in treating each other as equals. After all, in principle, civil rights imply equality. And indeed, the idea of equality was given more substance in the Republic than elsewhere. Here again, the absence of monarchy could be an explanatory factor. A warning about oversimplification is appropriate here, too, however. First, a significant part of the population did not belong to the group of privileged individuals who could be considered citizens in a legal sense. Besides, being a citizen of a town or city did not automatically mean a say in politics. Power was reserved for a small group of regents, and without wealth, access to that small upper crust of the population was unthinkable. It was not until the 1780s, during the Patriot era, that this oligarchical system was seriously challenged for the first time, so it would be going too far to draw conclusions about a highly developed democratic content from the Republic's bourgeois character.[7]

A number of values and standards did develop in the seventeenth-century metropolitan community, however, which Aerts describes as the core of the concept of citizenship – a pragmatic cocktail of self-interest and a collective sense of responsibility, with an express willingness to contribute to the prosperity, safety and development of urban society. This was elaborated in the eighteenth and nineteenth centuries, during which the citizenship ethos of politeness, diligence, responsibility and moderation gradually acquired a national character and was propagated as part of a sought-after Dutch identity. Finally, if one compares Dutch citizens with those in other European countries such as France, Germany or England, it can be asserted that greater homogeneity could be seen in the Netherlands in terms of prosperity, social conventions and political behaviour.[8] Associated with this, there were also fewer social and ideological conflicts among the Dutch citizenry, which in turn has contributed to the relatively measured and gradual course of political developments in the Netherlands since the nineteenth century.

If there was one area to which gradualness applies, it is the evolution of a parliamentary and democratic system in the nineteenth and early twentieth centuries. Here too, though, it cannot be claimed that this process took place without differences of opinion and tensions. Following the restoration regime of William I and the transformation into a parliamentary system in 1848, by around 1870 parliament had established its position as a controlling and corrective body. Political parties were created in the decades thereafter and suffrage was extended in a gradual process to become universal for men in 1917 and women in 1919. Under the pillarized umbrella, Dutch political history then followed a stable course and it remained possible to channel internal tensions.

As in other countries, uneasiness about the effectiveness of parliamentary democracy grew in the Netherlands between the wars, and although anti-democratic thinking was more widespread than has been assumed for many years, the Dutch democratic system was never in danger. The 'unrest' of the 1960s and 1970s similarly remained manageable and protest movements could be integrated with relative ease. Once again the instrument of pragmatic tolerance proved to be extremely effective in overcoming conflicts and tensions. A key feature of these years was that the elite were prepared to compromise and, according to Kennedy, opened everything up to discussion, seeking above all a clear understanding of the signs of the times.[9] The Netherlands depillarized rapidly and the result of this process was a more vocal public which, individualized and secularized, went its own way.

By the end of the twentieth century, the number of floating voters had risen to an unprecedented level and the numbers of Lower House seats lost and won by the various parties have been consistently very large since the 1994 elections. The emergence of Pim Fortuyn in 2002 and Geert Wilders's success in 2006 and 2010 signified a breakdown of confidence between the political elites and a section of the population. Part of this voter dissatisfaction was channelled into support for the leftist SP which, a few weeks before the 2012 Lower House elections, actually appeared to be becoming the biggest party. Yet the results produced a completely different picture, with large gains by VVD and PvdA. In other words, voter volatility remained substantial in 2012 too. It was no different in 2017, as was evident, for instance, in the historic defeat of the PvdA (from 24.7 to 5.7 per cent). In 2002, many people thought or hoped that the former 'normality' would return after a turbulent intermezzo. Now, though, one could say that electoral turmoil has become part of a new norm.

A final key factor in Dutch history that needs to be considered is the country's geographical position and interactions with other nations. It goes without saying that the location, size and international embedment of a state have a crucial influence on its past. The course of Dutch history as presented in this book would be unthinkable without the North Sea, the Zuiderzee – the later IJsselmeer – and the basins of the Scheldt, Rhine and Meuse. Since the early sixteenth century the most important international trade routes intersected here, greatly to the benefit of the Southern Netherlands initially and the Northern Netherlands afterwards. This paved the way for the spectacular development of the north during and after the Revolt. Later, too, long after the Netherlands had become a minor power, its strategic location on the North Sea remained a determining factor for trade and defence. The nature of the goods changed, but the volume of freight continued to grow. For many years Rotterdam has been the biggest port in Europe and one of the largest in the world.

Geographical position was also a contributory factor in determining the power and security policy interests that the Netherlands sought to safeguard. These usually lay in maintaining an international balance of power, which boosted Dutch trade and gave the country the greatest possible freedom of action in international politics. In the heyday of the seventeenth century, the Republic was powerful enough as a rule to be a key player in the global political equation. Its ability to be in that position was linked to the relative weakness of the other powers. The Republic was relegated to the second division after potentially stronger countries like France and England had overcome their own weaknesses – as far as the latter is concerned thanks not least to King-Stadholder William III – or joined forces, for example as they did in the 'Disaster Year' of 1672. The weakened Republic's interests in international equilibrium between the great powers remained during the eighteenth century. It was usually about a balance between England

and the major continental nations. The Dutch needed a good relationship with England to retain its colonial position, while they also had to remain friends with stronger continental countries as trading partners or competitors. The upshot was that the Netherlands developed a tendency to stay out of international conflicts.

A fortuitous side effect was that the major powers had an interest in a relatively independent Dutch position and that they begrudged one another possession of the Rhine delta.[10] The neutrality of the Netherlands during the First World War was also a consequence of German and British calculations, and so the country emerged from it virtually unscathed. Nazi Germany's plans for conquest, however, had no place for Dutch neutrality.

After 1945, the Netherlands exchanged its former aloofness for an active role in Atlantic-European cooperation, and once again it profited from its strategic location. For its size, the country had a relatively influential position in Western collaboration during the Cold War, which compensated to an extent for the painful loss of the Dutch East Indies in 1949. For many years, the Netherlands considered itself – not without overestimating its own powers – as the biggest tiddler in Europe. The validity of that self-image decreased further with the end of the Cold War and the substantial enlargement of the European Union, and the Netherlands became one of many small nations.

At different times over the centuries, the country played a larger role on the international stage than could have been expected on the grounds of its relatively modest size. This was clearly the case first and foremost in the seventeenth century, when the Republic was a leading economic, cultural and scientific power. To this day its traces can be seen in every continent. As a colonial power, the Netherlands was later to become a small European country with a large empire. For a long time that may have fuelled the small-but-brave self-image, but finally it is more realistic to point out the Netherlands' vulnerability.

Obviously, all countries feel the consequences of international developments and events in neighbouring nations. If one looks at Dutch history, though, one is struck by how external influences always very largely determined internal developments. The favourable outcome of the Revolt for the Northern Netherlands was due in part to the course of the fighting that Spain was engaged in on other fronts. The return of the Oranges to the political stage in 1672 and 1747 was directly linked to foreign military interventions. The Patriot era of the 1780s would have been unthinkable without the disastrous outcome of the Fourth Anglo–Dutch War, and likewise the stadholder regime in 1787 was saved by Prussian involvement, while the Republic disappeared in 1795 as a result of the French advance. Even the creation of the 1848 amended constitution is difficult to explain without King William II's fears that the revolutions in other European countries would spread to the Netherlands. Conversely, the country's neutrality during the First World War is an explanatory factor for the peaceful domestic political scene in the 1920s and 1930s.

Vulnerability and sensitivity to international developments have thus been permanent features in Dutch political history, but the decisive element has been how the Netherlands responded to these external impulses against the backdrop of its own traditions. The regime changes during the Republic (1672, 1747 and 1795) cannot be considered in isolation from the arrival of foreign troops, but their nature was a domestic matter. The constitutional debates after 1795 did not simply imitate French patterns, but had their own specific character.[11] With the exception of the Second World War, things were no different in the nineteenth and twentieth centuries, as exemplified by the country's inclusion in the Pax Americana after 1945. It was Dutch tradition to be receptive to foreign influences, and the cosmopolitanism associated with that tradition also often played a positive part in the national self-image and foreign perceptions. Some Dutch people linked this positive self-image to the idea that their nation had a calling in the world as a 'model country'. The moral self-overestimation that was part and parcel of this was certainly unwarranted and often bore witness to a lack of insight into international relations, but in the twentieth century it regularly resulted in a characteristic Dutch voice.

Meanwhile, the Dutch reaction to international developments appears to be moving in a different direction. Uncertainty about the future in an era of globalization, increased concern about the European Union's great influence on national policy, and dissatisfaction about the integration of immigrants have turned attention inwards and the issue of national identity is higher up the agenda than before. This increasingly national focus in politics and society is happening in other European countries too and is certainly not just a Dutch phenomenon. It is more striking in the Netherlands, though, because in the past the country often referred to an international focus, openness and tolerance.

CHAPTER 9
AFTERWORD

This history of the Netherlands was published previously in German (*Geschichte der Niederlande*, Stuttgart 2012) and in Dutch (*Geschiedenis van Nederland. Van de Opstand tot heden*, Amsterdam 2012, second edition 2013, third edition 2014). I was supported by many people during the course of my work and I would like to thank them in the afterword of this English edition too. First and foremost, Professor Maarten Prak, who commented on large parts of the manuscript. His expertise in the early modern era was an indispensable support for me and his stimulating recommendations were always very valuable. The same can be said for remarks by Professor Gerrit J. Schutte and Dr Hans Peterse, who also read a number of draft chapters. I derived great benefit from their knowledge of the early modern period. I want to express my heartfelt gratitude to Professor Remieg Aerts for his comments on the chapter addressing the nineteenth century and the final comments. My thanks furthermore extend to Frans Becker, who also provided feedback on a part of the text. The chapter about the twentieth century is an updated summary of my earlier publication *Nederland in de twintigste eeuw* (Amsterdam, third edition 2013). At the time the comments of Professor Jac Bosmans and Professor Jan Bank were very important, and hence I also want to thank them in this afterword.

Contributions from the Dutch Foundation for Literature and the M. A. O. C. Gravin van Bylandt Stichting helped to make this English edition possible. Finally, I thank Marie Wolf-Eichbaum for making the indexes and Lynne Richards for her outstanding and meticulous translation of the Dutch into English.

Friso Wielenga
Münster, Autumn 2014

Afterword to the second edition

The first edition, published in 2015, was reprinted a number of times. This second edition incorporates recently published literature, and the text has been substantially extended, primarily covering history since 1918. In this edition, the theme of pillarization is discussed as part and parcel of factual political history and also against a backdrop of political theory. More detailed attention is paid to the decolonization of Indonesia and Suriname and to the debates about and consequences of colonial history. In addition, a new and detailed periodization of the era since the Second World War is presented in a new chapter about the years after 1945. This chapter addresses economic trends, foreign policy and changes in the political culture. New themes, such as the crises surrounding the Royal House in the 1950s and 1970s and the after-effects of Dutch involvement in Srebrenica in 1995, are also discussed. Finally, the passages about populism since 2002 and its consequences have been expanded. This new edition therefore describes the last hundred years of Dutch history in more depth and greater detail. The additions have been translated from Dutch into English by Lynne Richards, whom I thank wholeheartedly, as I did in the first edition, for her excellent translation. Finally, I thank Janine Martschinske for compiling the indexes.

Münster, Summer 2019.

NOTES

Chapter One

1. Anton van der Lem, *De Opstand in de Nederlanden (1555–1609)*, Utrecht/Antwerp, 1995, p. 13. See also, Anton van der Lem, *Die Entstehung der Niederlande aus der Revolte. Staatenbildung in Westen Europas*, Berlin, 2016.

2. Ernst H. Kossmann, 'De Nederlanden in Coornherts tijd', *Naoogst*, Amsterdam, 2007, p. 126.

3. Van der Lem, *De Opstand* (1995), p. 141.

4. For William of Orange, see Olaf Mörke, *Willem van Oranje (1533–1584). Vorst en 'vader' van de Republiek*, Amsterdam, 2010; Arie T. van Deursen, *Willem van Oranje. Een biografisch portret*, Amsterdam, 1995.

5. Simon Groenveld and Huib L. Ph. Leeuwenberg, *De Tachtigjarige Oorlog. Opstand en consolidatie in de Nederlanden (ca. 1560–1650)*, Zutphen, 2008, p. 9.

6. Jonathan I. Israel, *The Dutch Republic. Its Rise, Greatness and Fall, 1477–1806*, Oxford, 1995, p. 2 ff.

7. Arie T. van Deursen, *De last van veel geluk. De geschiedenis van Nederland 1555–1702*, Amsterdam, 2004, p. 28.

8. Horst Lademacher, *Die Niederlande. Politische Kultur zwischen Individualität und Anpassung*, Berlin, 1993; published in Dutch as *Geschiedenis van Nederland*, Utrecht, 1993, originally published as *Geschichte der Niederlande. Politik – Verfassung – Wirtschaft*, Darmstadt, 1983.

9. For the prehistory, see W. P. Blockmans, *Metropolen aan de Noordzee. Nederlandse Geschiedenis 1100–1560*, Amsterdam, 2010.

10. Ernst H. Kossmann, *The Low Countries 1780–1940*, Oxford, 1978. The Dutch version was published in two volumes and covered the period up to 1980: *De Lage Landen 1780–1980: Twee eeuwen Nederland en België*, volume I 1780–1914 and volume II 1914–1980, Amsterdam/Brussels, 1986; Piet de Rooy, *Republiek van rivaliteiten. Nederland sinds 1813*, 4th edition, Amsterdam, 2010; Piet de Rooy, *Ons stipje op de waereldkaart. De politieke cultuur van Nederland in de negentiende en twintigste eeuw*, Amsterdam, 2014.

11. Maarten Prak and Jan Luiten van Zanden, *Nederland en het poldermodel. Sociaal-economische geschiedenis van Nederland, 1000–2000*, Amsterdam, 2013.

12. István Bejczy, *Een kennismaking met de Nederlandse Geschiedenis*, Bussum, 2010.

13. Christoph de Voogd, *Geschiedenis van Nederland. Vanaf de prehistorie tot heden*, 2nd edition, Amsterdam, 2000.

14. Han van der Horst, *Nederland. De vaderlandse geschiedenis van de preshistorie tot nu*, 7th edition, Amsterdam, 2009.

15. James Kennedy, *A Concise History of the Netherlands*, Cambridge, 2017.

16. Paul Arblaster, *A History of the Low Countries*, Basingstoke, 2006; Michael North, *Geschichte der Niederlande*, 3rd edition, Munich, 2008; Paul State, *A Brief History of the Netherlands*, New York, 2008.

Notes

17. Michael Erbe, *Belgien, Niederlande, Luxemburg. Geschichte des niederländischen Raumes*, Stuttgart, 1993.

18. P. D. Blok et al. (eds), *Algemene Geschiedenis der Nederlanden*, Bussum, 1982. This series is also referred to as the 'new' version to differentiate it from the series published with the same name in the 1950s.

19. Dick E. H. Boer and M. H. Boon, *Nederlands verleden in vogelvlucht. De middeleeuwen: 300 tot 1500* (delta 1), Leiden/Antwerp, 1992; Simon Groenveld and Gerrit Jan Schutte, *De nieuwe tijd: 1500 tot 1813* (delta 2), Groningen, 1992; Jan T. M. Bank, J. J. Huizinga and J. T. Minderaa, *De nieuwste tijd: 1813 tot heden* (delta 3), Groningen, 1993.

20. J. C. H. Blom and E. Lamberts (eds), *Geschiedenis van de Nederlanden*, 4th edition, Amsterdam, 2006. Also published in English as *History of the Low Countries*, 2nd edition, New York, 2006.

21. Geert Mak, Jan Bank, Gijsbert van Es, Piet de Rooy and René van Stipriaan, *Verleden van Nederland*, Amsterdam/Antwerp, 2008.

Chapter Two

1. Van der Lem, *De Opstand* (1995), p. 26.

2. W. P. Blockmans, 'De vorming van een politieke unie (veertiende-zestiende eeuw)' in Blom and Lamberts (eds), *Geschiedenis van de Nederlanden*, p. 95. For more detail, see Blockmans, *Metropolen aan de Noordzee*.

3. For this period, see J. J. Woltjer, *Op weg naar tachtig jaar oorlog. Het verhaal over de eeuw waarin ons land ontstond*, Amsterdam, 2011.

4. Groenveld and Leeuwenberg, *De Tachtigjarige Oorlog*, p. 25.

5. Guido de Bruin, 'De Nederlandse Opstand (1555–1588)' in *Spiegel Historiael* 29 (1994), p. 442.

6. Groenveld and Leeuwenberg, *De Tachtigjarige Oorlog*, p. 34.

7. Israel, *The Dutch Republic*, p. 40.

8. Groenveld and Leeuwenberg, *De Tachtigjarige Oorlog*, p. 13 ff.

9. Groenveld and Leeuwenberg, *De Tachtigjarige Oorlog*, p. 24.

10. Israel, *The Dutch Republic*, p. 40.

11. Van Deursen, *De last van veel geluk*, p. 21.

12. Woltjer, *Op weg naar tachtig jaar oorlog*, p. 77 ff.

13. Israel, *The Dutch Republic*, p. 80.

14. Israel, *The Dutch Republic*, p. 85.

15. Woltjer, *Op weg naar tachtig jaar oorlog*, p. 113. See also p. 179 ff.

16. Groenveld and Schutte, *De nieuwe tijd*, p. 59. For more detail, see Woltjer, *Op weg naar tachtig jaar oorlog*, p. 179 ff.

17. Israel, *The Dutch Republic*, pp. 103–5.

18. For William of Orange, see Mörke, *Willem van Oranje (1533–1584)*, passim, and van Deursen, *Willem van Oranje*, passim.

19. Mörke, *Willem van Oranje*, p. 62.

20. Van Deursen, *De last van veel geluk*, p. 36. For Granvelle in detail, see Woltjer, *Op weg naar tachtig jaar oorlog*, p. 337 ff.

21. Van Deursen, *Willem van Oranje*, p. 27.

22. Woltjer, *Op weg naar tachtig jaar oorlog*, p. 375 ff.

23. Groenveld and Leeuwenberg, *De Tachtigjarige Oorlog*, p. 76 ff.

24. Mörke, *Willem van Oranje*, p. 105. There are no unambiguous written sources with regard to this.

25. Van der Lem, *De Opstand* (1995), p. 54.

26. Israel, *The Dutch Republic*, p. 147.

27. Lademacher, *Geschiedenis van Nederland*, p. 81 ff; Geoffrey Parker, *Van Beeldenstorm tot Bestand*, Haarlem, 1978, p. 62 ff.

28. Groenveld and Leeuwenberg, *De Tachtigjarige Oorlog*, p. 82 ff.

29. Groenveld and Leeuwenberg, *De Tachtigjarige Oorlog*, p. 85.

30. De Bruin, *De Nederlandse Opstand*, p. 447.

31. Parker, *Van Beeldenstorm tot Bestand*, p. 97 ff.

32. Mörke, *Willem van Oranje*, pp. 143–4.

33. Mörke, *Willem van Oranje*, p. 169.

34. Parker, *Van Beeldenstorm tot Bestand*, p. 171 ff; Woltjer, *Op weg naar tachtig jaar oorlog*, p. 421 ff; Lademacher, *Geschiedenis van Nederland*, p. 97 ff.

35. De Bruin, *De Nederlandse Opstand*, p. 449.

36. Groenveld and Leeuwenberg, *De Tachtigjarige Oorlog*, p. 108 ff.

37. Maarten Prak, *Gouden Eeuw. Het raadsel van de Republiek*, Nijmegen, 2002, p. 28.

38. Van Deursen, *Willem van Oranje*, p. 83.

39. Lademacher, *Geschiedenis van Nederland*, p. 123 ff.

40. For Oldenbarnevelt, see Ben Knapen, *De man en zijn staat. Johan van Oldenbarnevelt 1547–1619*, Amsterdam, 2005

41. Groenveld and Leeuwenberg, *De Tachtigjarige Oorlog*, pp. 132–3.

42. Knapen, *De man en zijn staat*, p. 97.

43. Van Deursen, *De last van veel geluk*, p. 137 ff.

44. For Maurice, see Arie T. van Deursen, *Maurits van Nassau 1567–1625. De winnaar die faalde*, Amsterdam, 2000.

45. Groenveld and Leeuwenberg, *De Tachtigjarige Oorlog*, p. 135; van Deursen, *Maurits van Nassau*, p. 77 ff

46. Van Deursen, *De last van veel geluk*, p. 123; cf. Parker, *Van Beeldenstorm tot Bestand*, p. 217 ff.

47. Van Deursen, *Maurits van Nassau*, pp. 180–1; Knapen, *De man en zijn staat*, p. 179 ff.

48. Groenveld and Leeuwenberg, *De Tachtigjarige Oorlog*, p. 143 ff; Israel, *The Dutch Republic*, p. 437 ff.

49. What follows is mainly based on Jan de Vries and Ad van der Woude, *Nederland 1500–1815. De eerste ronde van moderne economische groei*, 3rd edition, Amsterdam, 2005; W. M. Zappey, 'Het economisch leven in de Nederlanden vanaf het midden der 16de eeuw'; 'Het economisch leven in de Republiek tot het begin der 17de eeuw' in Groenveld and

Notes

Leeuwenberg, *De Tachtigjarige Oorlog*, pp. 25 ff, 160 ff; Prak, *Gouden Eeuw*, p. 99 ff; Groenveld and Schutte, *De nieuwe tijd*, p. 8 ff.

50. De Vries and van der Woude, *Nederland 1500–1815*, p. 198 ff.

51. De Vries and van der Woude, *Nederland 1500–1815*, p. 345.

52. Van Deursen, *De last van veel geluk*, p. 129.

53. Israel, *The Dutch Republic*, p. 306 ff.

54. De Vries and van der Woude, *Nederland 1500–1815*, p. 767.

55. Femme S. Gaastra, *Geschiedenis van de VOC. Opkomst, bloei en ondergang*, Zutphen, 2009, p. 11 ff.

Chapter Three

1. Israel, *The Dutch Republic*, p. 465 ff; Knapen, *De man en zijn staat*, p. 234 ff.

2. For the differences of opinion between Remonstrants and Calvinists, see Arie T. van Deursen, *Bavianen en Slijkgeuzen. Kerk en kerkvolk ten tijde van Maurits en Oldenbarnevelt*, Assen, 1974; cf. *Mensen van klein vermogen. Het 'kopergeld' van de Gouden Eeuw*, Amsterdam, 1999, p. 304 ff.

3. Knapen, *De man en zijn staat*, p. 266 ff.

4. H. Gerlach, 'Het bestand in de Noordelijke Nederlanden 1609–1621' in *Algemene Geschiedenis der Nederlanden*, volume 6, Bussum, 1979, p. 307.

5. Van Deursen, *De last van veel geluk*, p. 201.

6. Israel, *The Dutch Republic*, p. 487 ff.

7. Groenveld and Leeuwenberg, *De Tachtigjarige Oorlog*, p. 199 ff.

8. Van Deursen, *Maurits van Nassau*, p. 279.

9. Israel, *The Dutch Republic*, p. 460.

10. Israel, *The Dutch Republic*, p. 489.

11. For Frederick Henry, see J. J. Poelhekke, *Frederik Hendrik. Prins van Oranje. Een biografisch drieluik*, Zutphen, 1978.

12. Prak, *Gouden Eeuw*, p. 48.

13. For the extensive literature on this topic, see the handy overview by Gerd Dethlefs (ed), *Der Frieden von Münster – De vrede van Münster 1648*, Münster, 1998.

14. Simon Groenveld, *Unie – Bestand – Vrede. Drie fundamentele wetten van de Republiek der Verenigde Nederlanden*, Hilversum, 2009, p. 153 ff.

15. For the stadholdership of William II, see Israel, *The Dutch Republic*, p. 598 ff; van Deursen, *De last van veel geluk*, p. 248 ff; Groenveld and Leeuwenberg, *De Tachtigjarige Oorlog*, p. 294 ff.

16. Willem Frijhoff and Marijke Spies, *Nederlandse cultuur in Europese context. 1650. Bevochten eendracht*, The Hague, 1999, p. 106; published in English under the title: *Dutch Culture in a European Perspective, I: 1650: Hard-Won Unity*, Palgrave Macmillan, 2004; Prak, *Gouden Eeuw*, p. 54.

17. Luc Panhuysen, *De Ware Vrijheid. De levens van Johan en Cornelis de Witt*, 2nd edition, Amsterdam, 2005.

18. Israel, *The Dutch Republic*, p. 700 ff; Prak, *Gouden Eeuw*, pp. 54 ff, 275; cf. also Groenveld and Schutte, *De nieuwe tijd*, p. 226 ff.

19. De Vries and van der Woude, *Nederland 1500–1815*, p. 71.

20. Prak, *Gouden Eeuw*, p. 157; Frijhoff and Spies, *Nederlandse cultuur in Europese context*, p. 160 ff; see also Leo Lucassen and Jan Lucassen, *Winnaars en verliezers. Een nuchtere balans van vijfhonderd jaar immigratie*, Amsterdam, 2011, p. 189 ff.

21. Y. Kaplan, 'De joden in de Republiek tot omstreeks 1750. Religieus, cultureel en sociaal leven' in J. C. H. Blom, R. G. Fuks-Mansfeld and I. Schöffer (eds), *Geschiedenis van de Joden in Nederland*, 2nd edition, Amsterdam, 2004, p. 129 ff.

22. Groenveld and Leeuwenberg, *De Tachtigjarige Oorlog*, p. 332 ff.

23. Prak, *Gouden Eeuw*, p. 166; for the position of regents in the seventeenth and eighteenth centuries, see Joop de Jong, *Een deftig bestaan. Het dagelijks leven van regenten in de 17e en 18e eeuw*, Utrecht, 1987.

24. Joop de Jong, *Een deftig bestaan*, p. 39.

25. Joop de Jong, *Een deftig bestaan*, p. 56.

26. Frijhoff and Spies, *Nederlandse cultuur in Europese context*, pp. 50–1.

27. Frijhoff and Spies, *Nederlandse cultuur in Europese context*, p. 101; see also Olaf Mörke, 'Stadtholder' oder 'Staetholder'? *Die Funktion des Hauses Oranien und seines Hofes in der politischen Kultur der Republik der Vereinigten Niederlande im 17. Jahrhundert*, Münster, 1997.

28. Wout Troost, *Stadhouder-koning Willem III. Een politieke biografie*, Hilversum, 2001, p. 51 ff.

29. Prak, *Gouden Eeuw*, p. 10.

30. Prak, *Gouden Eeuw*, pp. 202–3, 216–17.

31. Frijhoff and Spies, *Nederlandse cultuur in Europese context*, pp. 126–7.

32. Frijhoff and Spies, *Nederlandse cultuur in Europese context*, p. 221.

33. For this, see the standard work by van Deursen, *Bavianen en Slijkgeuzen*, passim; see also van Deursen, *Mensen van klein vermogen*, p. 263 ff. For religious differences, see Hans Knippenberg, *De religieuze kaart van Nederland. Omvang en geografische spreiding van de godsdienstige gezindten vanaf de Reformatie tot heden*, Assen/Maastricht, 1992; Peter van Rooden, *Religieuze regimes. Over godsdienst en maatschappij in Nederland, 1570–1990*, Amsterdam, 1996; Joris van Eijnatten and Fred van Lieburg, *Nederlandse religiegeschiedenis*, Hilversum, 2006.

34. Groenveld and Leeuwenberg, *De Tachtigjarige Oorlog*, p. 368.

35. Frijhoff and Spies, *Nederlandse cultuur in Europese context*, p. 358.

36. Frijhoff and Spies, *Nederlandse cultuur in Europese context*, p. 128.

37. Gerrit J. Schutte, *Het Calvinistisch Nederland*, Utrecht, 1988, p. 13.

38. Frijhoff and Spies, *Nederlandse cultuur in Europese context*, pp. 68–9.

39. Panhuysen, *De Ware Vrijheid*, p. 275.

40. For foreign observation of the Republic, see Horst Lademacher, *Phönix aus der Asche? Politik und Kultur der niederländischen Republik im Europa des 17. Jahrhunderts*, Münster, 2007, p. 77 ff.

41. The subtitle of his 2002 study, *Gouden Eeuw*.

42. Jaap R. Bruijn, *Varend verleden, De Nederlandse oorlogsvloot in de zeventiende en achttiende eeuw*, Amsterdam, 1998, p. 91 ff.

43. Panhuysen, *De Ware Vrijheid*, p. 150 ff; van Deursen, *De last van veel geluk*, p. 285 ff.

44. Bruijn, *Varend verleden*, p. 95 ff.

45. Cf. Troost, *Stadhouder-koning Willem III*, pp. 56–7; Israel, *The Dutch Republic*, p. 749 ff.

46. Van Deursen, *De last van veel geluk*, p. 292.

47. Panhuysen, *De Ware Vrijheid*, p. 317 ff.

48. Troost, *Stadhouder-koning Willem III*, p. 37 ff; Panhuysen, *De Ware Vrijheid*, p. 264 ff.

49. Michel Reinders, *Gedrukte chaos. Populisme en moord in het Rampjaar 1672*, Amsterdam, 2010, p. 172 ff.

50. Reinders, *Gedrukte chaos*, pp. 214 ff, 272 ff.

51. Panhuysen, *De Ware Vrijheid*, p. 466.

52. Israel, *The Dutch Republic*, p. 877.

53. Arie T. van Deursen, 'De Republiek der Zeven Verenigde Nederlanden (1588–1780)' in Blom and Lambert (eds), *Geschiedenis van de Nederlanden*, p. 159; for William III, see Troost, *Stadhouder-koning Willem III*, passim.

54. For Michiel de Ruyter, see Arie T. van Deursen, Jaap R. Bruijn and Johanna Elisabeth Korteweg, *De Admiraal. De wereld van Michiel Adriaenszoon de Ruyter*, Franeker, 2007.

55. Israel, *The Dutch Republic*, p. 813.

56. Van Deursen, *De last van veel geluk*, p. 320; Israel, *The Dutch Republic*, p. 826.

57. Troost, *Stadhouder-koning Willem III*, p. 115.

58. Troost, *Stadhouder-koning Willem III*, p. 111.

59. Israel, *The Dutch Republic*, pp. 992–3.

60. Israel, *The Dutch Republic*, p. 850.

61. For William III as king of England, see Troost, *Stadhouder-koning Willem III*, p. 213 ff.

62. Van Deursen, *De last van veel geluk*, p. 320 ff.

63. Troost, *Stadhouder-koning Willem III*, p. 293.

64. For an overview of economic development in the seventeenth century and the different economic sectors, see Karel Davids and Leo Noordegraaf (eds), *The Dutch Economy in the Golden Age. Nine Studies*, Amsterdam, 1993.

65. De Vries and van der Woude, *Nederland 1500–1815*, p. 45 ff.

66. Frijhoff and Spies, *Nederlandse cultuur in Europese context*, p. 169 ff.

67. De Vries and van der Woude, *Nederland 1500–1815*, p. 320.

68. Prak, *Gouden Eeuw*, pp. 114–15, 120 ff.

69. Groenveld and Leeuwenberg, *De Tachtigjarige Oorlog*, p. 325.

70. Gaastra, *Geschiedenis van de VOC*, passim.

71. Jur van Goor, *Jan Pieterszoon Coen 1587–1629. Koop-koning in Azië*, Amsterdam, 2015, p. 513 ff.

72. Piet Emmer and Jos Gommans, *Rijk aan de rand van de wereld. De geschiedenis van Nederland overzee 1600–1800,* Amsterdam, 2012, p. 13.

73. Prak, *Gouden Eeuw*, p. 135.

74. De Vries and van der Woude, *Nederland 1500–1815*, p. 529 ff.

75. For the WIC, see Henk den Heijer, *De geschiedenis van de WIC*, 3rd edition, Zutphen, 2012.

76. Prak, *Gouden Eeuw*, pp. 130–1.

77. Piet Emmer, *De Nederlandse slavenhandel 1500–1850*, 3rd edition, Amsterdam, 2007.

78. De Vries and van der Woude, *Nederland 1500–1815*, p. 767 ff.

79. Jan Luiten van Zanden, 'De economie van Holland in de periode 1650–1805: groei of achteruitgang? Een overzicht van bronnen, problemen en resultaten' in *BMGN* 102 (1987), number 4, p. 608.

80. Frijhoff and Spies, *Nederlandse cultuur in Europese context*, p. 498.

81. Prak, *Gouden Eeuw*, p. 252.

82. P. J. Rietbergen, *Geschiedenis van Nederland in vogelvlucht. Van prehistorie tot heden*, Amersfoort, 2007, p. 104.

83. Prak, *Gouden Eeuw*, p. 247.

84. Israel, *The Dutch Republic*, p. 623.

85. Frijhoff and Spies, *Nederlandse cultuur in Europese context*, p. 495.

86. What follows is based on Frijhoff and Spies, *Nederlandse cultuur in Europese context*, p. 237 ff.

87. Israel, *The Dutch Republic*, p. 920 ff; Bejczy, *Een kennismaking met de Nederlandse geschiedenis*, p. 142.

88. Frijhoff and Spies, *Nederlandse cultuur in Europese context*, p. 264 ff.

89. Frijhoff and Spies, *Nederlandse cultuur in Europese context*, p. 258 ff.

90. Groenveld and Schutte, *De nieuwe tijd*, p. 151.

Chapter Four

1. Israel, *The Dutch Republic*, p. 972 ff.

2. Joost Kloek and Wijnand Mijnhardt, *Nederlandse cultuur in Europese context. 1800 Blauwdrukken voor een samenleving*, The Hague, 2001, p. 26.

3. Duco Hellema, *Nederland in de wereld. De buitenlandse politiek van Nederland*, 4th edition, Utrecht, 2010, p. 31.

4. Kloek and Mijnhardt, *Nederlandse cultuur in Europese context*, p. 27.

5. Israel, *The Dutch Republic*, p. 964 ff; Lademacher, *Geschiedenis van Nederland*, p. 197 ff.

6. Israel, *The Dutch Republic*, p. 1065 ff.

7. Van Deursen, 'De Republiek der Zeven Verenigde Nederlanden (1588–1780)' in Blom and Lamberts (eds), *Geschiedenis van de Nederlanden*, p. 168.

8. Gerrit J. Schutte, *Oranje in de achttiende eeuw*, Amsterdam 1999, p. 39 ff; for William IV and William V in detail, see A. J. C. M. Gabriëls, *De heren als dienaren en de dienaar als heer. Het stadhouderlijk stelsel in de tweede helft van de achttiende eeuw*, The Hague, 1989.

9. Jan A. F. de Jongste, 'The Restoration of the Orangist Regime in 1747' in M. C. Jacob and W. W. Mijnhardt (eds), *The Dutch Republic in the Eighteenth Century. Decline, Enlightenment, and Revolution*, Ithaca/London, 1992, p. 57.

10. Quoted in Schutte, *Oranje in de achttiende eeuw*, p. 43.

11. Van Deursen, 'De Republiek der Zeven Verenigde Nederlanden (1588–1780)' in Blom and Lamberts (eds), *Geschiedenis van de Nederlanden*, p. 169.

12. Schutte, *Oranje in de achttiende eeuw*, p. 90; Erwin van Meerkerk, *Willem V en Wilhelmina van Pruisen. De laatste stadhouders*, Amsterdam/Antwerp, 2009, p. 74 ff.

13. Maarten Prak, *Republikeinse veelheid, democratisch enkelvoud. Sociale verandering in het Revolutietijdvak, 's-Hertogenbosch 1770–1820*, Nijmegen, 1999, p. 191.

14. N. C. F. van Sas, *De metamorfose van Nederland. Van oude orde naar moderniteit, 1750–1900*, Amsterdam, 2004, p. 175 ff; see also J. Roegiers and N. C. F. van Sas, 'Revolutie in Noord en Zuid (1780–1830)' in Blom and Lamberts (eds), *Geschiedenis van de Nederlanden*, p. 225. For an accessible overview of the political and socioeconomic history of the 1780–1830 period, see Wantje Fritschy and Joop Toebes (eds), *Het ontstaan van het moderne Nederland. Staats- en natievorming tussen 1780 en 1830*, Nijmegen *s.a.* (1996).

15. Kloek and Mijnhardt, *Nederlandse cultuur in Europese context*, p. 78.

16. Kloek and Mijnhardt, *Nederlandse cultuur in Europese context*, p. 169 ff; Wijnand W. Mijnhardt, 'The Dutch Enlightenment' in Jacob and Mijnhardt (eds), *The Dutch Republic in the Eighteenth Century*, p. 212.

17. Kloek and Mijnhardt, *Nederlandse cultuur in Europese context*, p. 63.

18. Remieg Aerts, 'Een staat in verbouwing. Van Republiek naar constitutioneel Koninkrijk, 1780–1848' in Remieg Aerts, Herman de Liagre Böhl, Piet de Rooy and Henk te Velde, *Land van kleine gebaren. Een politieke geschiedenis van Nederland 1780–1990*, 5th edition, Nijmegen, 2007, p. 23.

19. Van Sas, *Metamorfose*, p. 97 ff.

20. Prak, *Republikeinse veelheid*, p. 190 ff.

21. Prak, *Republikeinse veelheid*, p. 23.

22. Prak, *Republikeinse veelheid*, p. 321.

23. Van Sas, *Metamorfose*, p. 192; see also Joost Rosendaal, *De Nederlandse Revolutie. Vrijheid, volk en vaderland 1783–99*, Nijmegen, 2005, p. 21 ff.

24. Van Meerkerk, *Willem V en Wilhelmina van Pruisen*, p. 133 ff.

25. Joost Rosendaal, *De Nederlandse Revolutie*, p. 70.

26. Jan Luiten van Zanden, 'De economie van Holland in de periode 1650–1805: groei of achteruitgang? Een overzicht van bronnen, problemen en resultaten' in *Bijdragen en Mededelingen betreffende de Geschiedenis der Nederlanden* 102 (1987), number 4, p. 562.

27. Jan Luiten van Zanden and Arthur van Riel, *Nederland 1780–1914. Staat, Instituties en Economische Ontwikkeling*, Amsterdam, 2000, p. 27 ff.

28. Jan Luiten van Zanden and Arthur van Riel, *Nederland 1780–1914*, p. 43 ff.

29. Prak, *Republikeinse Veelheid*, pp. 22 ff, 319 ff.

30. J. Hovy, 'Institutioneel onvermogen in de 18e eeuw' in *Algemene Geschiedenis der Nederlanden*, volume 9, Bussum, 1980, p. 126 ff.

31. De Vries and van der Woude, *Nederland 1500–1815*, p. 174 ff.

32. Joop de Jong, *De waaier van het fortuin. Van Handelscompagnie tot Koloniaal Imperium. De Nederlanders in Azië en de Indonesische Archipel*, 3rd edition, The Hague, 2009, p. 141 ff; De Vries and van der Woude, *Nederland 1500–1815*, p. 520 ff.

33. For the internal development of the VOC, see Gerrit J. Schutte, *De Nederlandse Patriotten en de koloniën. Een onderzoek naar hun denkbeelden en optreden 1770–1800*, Groningen, 1974, p. 23 ff.

34. Emmer and Gommans, *Rijk aan de rand van de wereld*, p. 129.

35. Emmer, *De Nederlandse slavenhandel 1500–1850*, p. 157, 168 ff.

36. De Vries and van der Woude, *Nederland 1500–1815*, p. 553.

37. Emmer, *De Nederlandse slavenhandel 1500–1850*, p. 188.

38. Wim van den Doel, *Zo ver de wereld strekt. De geschiedenis van Nederland overzee*, Amsterdam, 2011, p. 29.

39. Paul Brusse and Wijnand W. Mijnhardt, *Towards a New Template for Dutch History. De-urbanisation and the Balance between City and Countryside*, Zwolle, 2011, p. 29. This study provides a very stimulating analysis of the relationship between town and country in the 1750–1850 period.

40. Van Zanden and van Riel, *Nederland 1780–1914*, p. 40.

41. Aerts, 'Een staat in verbouwing. Van Republiek naar constitutioneel Koninkrijk, 1780–1848' in Aerts, Liagre Böhl, de Rooy and te Velde, *Land van kleine gebaren*, p. 38.

42. J. T. J. van den Berg and J. J. Vis, *De eerste honderdvijftig jaar. Parlementaire geschiedenis van Nederland 1796–1946*, Amsterdam, 2013.

43. Prak, *Republikeinse veelheid*, p. 225.

44. Martijn van der Burg, *Nederland onder Franse invloed. Culturele overdracht en staatsvorming in de napoleontische tijd 1799–1813*, Amsterdam, 2009, p. 36 ff.

45. Israel, *The Dutch Republic*, p. 1125.

46. Kloek and Mijnhardt, *Nederlandse cultuur in Europese context*, p. 583.

47. For financial issues during the Batavian Republic, see Wantje Fritschy, *De patriotten en de financiën van de Bataafse Republiek. Hollands krediet en de smalle marges van een nieuw beleid (1795–1801)*, Amsterdam, 1988.

48. Van Sas, *Metamorfose*, p. 122 ff; Kloek and Mijnhardt, *Nederlandse cultuur in Europese context*, p. 230 ff.

49. Van Sas, *Metamorfose*, p. 128.

50. Van der Burg, *Nederland onder Franse invloed*, p. 77 ff.

51. Van der Burg, *Nederland onder Franse invloed*, pp. 270–1.

52. Van Sas, *Metamorfose*, pp. 94–5; see also J. Roegiers and N. C. F. van Sas, 'Revolutie in Noord en Zuid' in Blom and Lamberts (eds), *Geschiedenis van de Nederlanden*, p. 233.

53. Prak, *Republikeinse veelheid*, p. 323.

Chapter Five

1. Henk te Velde, *Van regentenmentaliteit tot populisme. Politieke tradities in Nederland*, Amsterdam, 2010, p. 17.

2. Jeroen van Zanten, *Schielijk, Winzucht, Zwaarhoofd en Bedaard. Politieke discussie en oppositievorming 1813–1840*, Amsterdam, 2004, p. 32.

3. Jeroen van Zanten, *Schielijk, Winzucht, Zwaarhoofd en Bedaard*, p. 35; for the constitution, see also I. J. H. Worst, 'Koning Willem I. Het begin van "ons grondwettig volksbestaan"' in C. A. Tamse and E. Witte (eds), *Staats- en natievorming in Willem I's koninkrijk (1815–1830)*, Brussels, 1992, p. 56 ff; N. C. F. van Sas, 'Onder waarborging eener wijze consitutie. Grondwet en politiek, 1813–1848' in N. C. F. van Sas and Henk te Velde (eds), *De eeuw van de grondwet. Grondwet en politiek in Nederland 1798–1917*, The Hague, *s.a.* 1998, p. 114 ff.

4. Piet de Rooy, *Republiek van Rivaliteiten*. p. 23.

5. Aerts, 'Een staat in verbouwing. Van Republiek naar constitutioneel koninkrijk, 1780–1848' in Aerts, Liagre Böhl, de Rooy and te Velde, *Land van kleine gebaren*, p. 68.

6. For an overview of historical writings, see J. P. de Valk, 'Landsvader en landspaus? Achtergronden van de visie op kerk en school bij koning Willem I (1815–1830)' in Tamse and Witte (eds), *Staats- en natievorming in Willem I's koninkrijk*, p. 76 ff.

7. Aerts, 'Een staat in verbouwing. Van Republiek naar constitutioneel koninkrijk, 1780–1848' in Aerts, Liagre Böhl, de Rooy and te Velde, *Land van kleine gebaren*, p. 75.

8. For William I's governing style, see van Sas, *Metamorfose*, p. 413 ff; Van Zanten, *Schielijk, Winzucht, Zwaarhoofd en Bedaard*, pp. 73 ff, 335 ff.

9. Van Zanten, *Schielijk, Winzucht, Zwaarhoofd en Bedaard*, p. 158 ff.

10. Jeroen Koch, *Koning Willem I, 1772–1843*, Amsterdam, 2013, pp. 247, 369.

11. Van Sas, *Metamorfose*, p. 417.

12. Van Zanden and van Riel, *Nederland 1780–1914*, p. 128.

13. A. van der Woud, 'De Kanalenkoning en zijn reputatie' in Tamse and Witte (eds), *Staats- en natievorming in Willem I's koninkrijk*, p. 237 ff.

14. Van Zanden and van Riel, *Nederland 1780–1914*, pp. 142–8, 152–62, 185–94.

15. Van den Doel, *Zo ver de wereld strekt*, p. 52 ff.

16. Van den Doel, *Zo ver de wereld strekt*, p. 73 ff; Van Zanden and van Riel, *Nederland 1780–1914*, pp. 144, 220 ff.

17. Van Zanden and van Riel, *Nederland 1780–1914*, p. 203 ff.

18. Van Zanten, *Schielijk, Winzucht, Zwaarhoofd en Bedaard*, p. 279.

19. For the role of the crown prince during the Belgian uprising, see Jeroen van Zanten, *Koning Willem II, 1792–1849*, Amsterdam, 2013, p. 301 ff. For the role of King William I, Koch, *Koning Willem I*, p. 445 ff.

20. Ernst H. Kossmann, *De lage landen 1780–1940. Anderhalve eeuw Nederland en België*, Amsterdam, 1976, p. 103 ff.

21. Niek van Sas, *Onze Natuurlijkste Bondgenoot. Nederland, Engeland en Europa, 1813–1831*, Groningen, 1985, p. 299 ff.

22. Van Zanten, *Schielijk, Winzucht, Zwaarhoofd en Bedaard*, p. 291 ff.

23. Van Zanten, *Schielijk, Winzucht, Zwaarhoofd en Bedaard*, p. 401 ff.

24. Aerts, 'Een staat in verbouwing. Van Republiek naar constitutioneel koninkrijk, 1780–1848' in Aerts, Liagre Böhl, de Rooy and te Velde, *Land van kleine gebaren*, p. 92.

25. J. C. Boogman, 'De politieke ontwikkeling in Nederland 1840–1862' in J. C. Boogman et al. (eds), *Geschiedenis van het moderne Nederland. Politieke, economische en sociale ontwikkelingen*, Houten, 1988, p. 66 ff.

26. For a biography of Thorbecke, see Remieg Aerts, *Thorbecke wil het. Biografie van een staatsman*, Amsterdam, 2018; see also Jan Drentje, *Thorbecke. Een filosoof in de politiek*, Amsterdam, 2004.

27. For De Gids, see Remieg Aerts, *De letterheren. Liberale cultuur in de negentiende eeuw: het tijdschrift De Gids*, Amsterdam, 1997.

28. De Rooy, *Republiek*, p. 51.

29. Jan Bank, J. J. Huizinga and J. T. Minderaa, *Nederlandse verleden in vogelvlucht. De nieuwste tijd: 1813 tot heden*, Gronigen, 1993, p. 30.

30. Hellema, *Nederland in de wereld*, p. 41.

31. Van Zanten, *Schielijk, Winzucht, Zwaarhoofd en Bedaard*, p. 443.

32. Boogman, 'De politieke ontwikkeling in Nederland 1840–1862' in Boogman et al., *Geschiedenis van het moderne Nederland*, p. 62.

33. Van Zanten, *Schielijk, Winzucht, Zwaarhoofd en Bedaard*, p. 441.

34. Van Zanten, *Schielijk, Winzucht, Zwaarhoofd en Bedaard*, p. 545 ff.

35. Siep Stuurman, *Wacht op onze daden. Het liberalisme en de vernieuwing van de Nederlandse staat*, Amsterdam, 1992, p. 160.

36. Henk te Velde, *Stijlen van leiderschap. Persoon en politiek van Thorbecke tot Den Uyl*, Amsterdam, 2002, p. 25 ff.

37. For the constitution, see Henk te Velde, 'Constitutionele politiek. De parlementair politieke praktijk en de Grondwet van 1848' in van Sas and te Velde (eds), *De eeuw van de grondwet. Grondwet en politiek in Nederland 1798–1917*, p. 146 ff; Aerts, *Thorbecke wil het*, p. 317 ff; Stuurman, *Wacht op onze daden*, p. 135 ff.

38. This percentage is valid for the Lower House and Provincial States elections. It was barely 19 per cent in local authority elections.

39. For the electoral system, see Ron de Jong, *Van standspolitiek naar partijloyaliteit. Verkiezingen voor de Tweede Kamer 1848–1887*, Hilversum, 1999, p. 12 ff; De Rooy, *Republiek*, p. 55.

40. Te Velde, *Van Regentenmentaliteit tot populisme*, p. 59.

41. For more detail, see Jouke Turpijn, *Mannen van gezag. De uitvinding van de Tweede Kamer 1848–1888*, Amsterdam, 2008, passim; for the period since the 1860s, see Erie Tanja, *Goede politiek. De parlementaire cultuur van de Tweede Kamer, 1866–1940*, Amsterdam, 2010.

42. Turpijn, *Mannen van gezag*, p. 33.

43. Dik van der Meulen, *Willem III, 1817–1890*, Amsterdam, 2013, p. 203.

44. Ronald van Raak, *In naam van het volmaakte. Conservatisme in Nederland in de negentiende eeuw*, Amsterdam, 2001, p. 76 ff; Ido de Haan, *Het beginsel van leven en wasdom. De constitutie van de Nederlandse politiek in de negentiende eeuw*, Amsterdam, 2003, p. 62 ff. Annemarie Houkes, *Christelijke Vaderlanders. Godsdienst, burgerschap en de Nederlandse natie (1850–1900)*, Amsterdam, 2009, p. 25 ff.

45. Van Raak, *In naam van het volmaakte*, p. 102 ff.

46. Van der Meulen, *Willem III*, p. 628.

47. Turpijn, *Mannen van gezag*, p. 123 ff; Te Velde, *Stijlen van leiderschap*, p. 50.

48. De Jong, *Van standspolitiek naar partijpolitiek*, p. 35; Tanja, *Goede politiek*, p. 56 ff.

49. Maartje Janse, *De afschaffers. Publieke opinie, organisatie en politiek in Nederland 1840–1880*, Amsterdam, 2007, p. 301.

50. Maartje Janse, *De afschaffers*, p. 251 ff.

51. Jaap van Rijn, *De eeuw van het debat. De ontwikkeling van het publieke debat in Nederland en Engeland 1800–1920*, Amsterdam, 2010, p. 168 ff.

52. For Abraham Kuyper, see Jeroen Koch, *Abraham Kuyper. Een biografie*, Amsterdam, 2006; for the history of the ARP, see Roel Harinck, Roel Kuiper and Peter Baks (eds), *De Antirevolutionaire Partij 1826–1980*, Utrecht, 2001. For a detailed overview of the rise of political parties, see Gert van Klinken, *Actieve burgers. Nederlanders en hun politieke partijen*, Amsterdam, 2003.

53. Kossmann, *De lage landen*, p. 211.

54. Houkes, *Christelijke Vaderlanders*, p. 203.

Notes

55. De Haan, *Het beginsel van leven en wasdom*, p. 175 ff; van Klinken *Actieve burgers*, p. 111 ff.

56. Koch, *Abraham Kuyper*, p. 178 ff.

57. De Rooy, *Republiek*, p. 94.

58. Henk te Velde, 'Van grondwet tot grondwet. Oefenen met parlement, partij en schaalvergroting 1848–1917' in Aerts, Liagre Böhl, de Rooy and te Velde, *Land van kleine gebaren*, p. 125.

59. De Rooy, *Republiek*, p. 98.

60. Houkes, *Christelijke Vaderlanders*, p. 231 ff.

61. For the CHU, see Marcel ten Hooven and Ron de Jong, *Geschiedenis van de Christelijk-Historische Unie 1908–1980*, Amsterdam, 2008.

62. J. A. Bornewasser, *Katholieke Volkspartij 1945–1980. Volume 1: Herkomst en groei (tot 1963)*, Nijmegen, 1995, pp. 7–60.

63. For Christian democrat governments since then, see Paul Luykx and Hans Righar (eds), *Van de pastorie naar het torentje. Een eeuw confessionele politiek*, The Hague, 1991.

64. Jan Willem Stutje, *Ferdinand Domela Nieuwenhuis. Een romantische revolutionair*, Amsterdam, 2012.

65. For programmatic development of social democracy, see Bart Tromp, *Het sociaal-democratisch programma. De beginselprogramma's van SDB, SDAP en PvdA 1878–1977*, Amsterdam, 2002, p. 83 ff; for the history of the SDAP, see Madelon de Keizer, Jos Perry, Maarten van Rossem, Louis Zweers and Maarten Brinkman (eds), *Honderd jaar sociaal-democratie in Nederland 1894–1994*, Amsterdam, 1994; Piet de Rooy, *De rode droom. Een eeuw sociaal-democratie in Nederland*, Nijmegen, 1995.

66. Dirk Jan Wolffram, *Vrij van wat neerdrukt en beklemt. Staat, gemeenschap en sociale politiek, 1870–1919*, Amsterdam, 2003, p. 61 ff.

67. Wolffram, *Vrij van wat neerdrukt en beklemt*, p. 65.

68. For social policy at this time, see also Bert Wartena, *H. Goeman Borgesius (1847–1917). Vader van de verzorgingsstaat. Een halve eeuw economische en sociale politiek in Nederland*, Amsterdam, 2003.

69. Jasper Loots, *Voor het volk, van het volk. Van districtenstelsel naar evenredige vertegenwoordiging*, Amsterdam, 2004.

70. C. A. Tamse, 'De politieke ontwikkeling in Nederland 1874–1887' in J. C. Boogman et al., *Geschiedenis van het moderne Nederland*, p. 232 ff.

71. Van Klinken, *Actieve burgers*, p. 190 ff; De Haan, *Het beginsel van leven en wasdom*, p. 114 ff.

72. For the liberal parties, see Patrick van Schie, *Vrijheidsstreven in verdrukking. Liberale partijpolitiek in Nederland 1901–1940*, Amsterdam, 2005.

73. Van Klinken, *Actieve burgers*, p. 265 ff.

74. What follows is based on van Zanden and van Riel, *Nederland 1780–1914*, p. 237 ff.

75. Van Zanden and van Riel, *Nederland 1780–1914*, p. 343.

76. Marc Frey, *Der Erste Weltkrieg und die Niederlande. Ein neutrales Land im politischen Kalkül der Kriegsgegner*, Cologne, 1996, pp. 46–7.

77. André Beening, *Onder de vleugels van de adelaar. De Duitse buitenlandse politiek ten aanzien van Nederland in de periode 1890–1914*, Thesis University of Amsterdam, 1994, p. 110 ff.

78. See also Hein Klemann, *Waarom bestaat Nederland eigenlijk nog? Nederland-Duitsland: Economische integratie en politieke consequenties 1860–2000*, Rotterdam, 2006.

79. De Jong, *De waaier van het fortuin*, p. 345.

80. Beening, *Onder de vleugels van de adelaar*, p. 138.

81. Kossmann, *De lage landen*, p. 312.

82. Te Velde, 'Van grondwet tot grondwet' in Aerts, Liagre Böhl, de Rooy and te Velde, *Land van kleine gebaren*, p. 129. For poverty, see Auke van der Woud, *Koninkrijk vol sloppen. Achterbuurten en vuil in de negentiende eeuw*, Amsterdam, 2010, passim.

83. For relations with Prussia around 1870, see Pieter de Coninck, *Een les uit Pruisen. Nederland en de Kulturkampf, 1870–1880*, Hilversum, 2005, p. 161 ff.

84. Koch, *Abraham Kuyper*, p. 461.

85. Jan Bank and Maarten van Buuren, *1900: The Age of Bourgeois Culture*, Basingstoke, 2004, p. 16; for the Netherlands around 1900, see also Frits Boterman and Piet de Rooy, *Op de grens van twee culturen. Nederland en Duitsland in het Fin de Siècle*, Amsterdam, 1999.

86. Quoted in Bank and van Buuren, *1900: The Age of Bourgeois Culture*, p. 80.

87. For van Vollenhoven, see Michael Riemens, *De passie voor vrede. De evolutie van de internationale politieke cultuur in de jaren 1880–1940 en het recipiëren door Nederland*, Amsterdam, 2005, p. 82 ff.

88. Published in English in 1868 as *Max Havelaar: Or the Coffee Auctions of the Dutch Trading Company*.

89. Van den Doel, *Zo ver de wereld strekt*, p. 141 ff.

90. Van den Doel, *Zo ver de wereld strekt*, p. 122.

91. For colonial expansion, see van den Doel, *Zo ver de wereld strekt*, p. 95 ff; Maarten Kuitenbrouwer, *Nederland en de opkomst van het moderne imperialisme. Koloniën en buitenlandse politiek, 1870–1902*, Amsterdam, 1985; De Jong, *De waaier van fortuin*, p. 319 ff.

92. Emmer, *De Nederlandse slavenhandel 1500–1850*, p. 202 ff.; Van den Doel, *Zo ver de wereld strekt*, p. 81 ff.

93. Emmer, *De Nederlandse slavenhandel 1500–1850*, p. 257 ff.

94. Hans Knippenberg and Ben de Pater, *De eenwording van Nederland. Schaalvergroting en integratie sinds 1800*, Nijmegen, 1988, pp. 30–1; De Rooy, *Republiek*, p. 24.

95. Knippenberg and De Pater, *De eenwording van Nederland*, p. 35.

96. Hanneke Hoekstra, *Het hart van de natie. Morele verontwaardiging en politieke verandering in Nederland 1870–1919*, Amsterdam, 2005, p. 179 ff.

97. Knippenberg and De Pater, *De eenwording van Nederland*, p. 77 ff; Auke van der Woud, *Een nieuwe wereld. Het ontstaan van het moderne Nederland*, Amsterdam, 2006, p. 157 ff.

98. Van der Woud, *Een nieuwe wereld*, p. 337 ff.

99. Knippenberg and De Pater, *De eenwording van Nederland*, p. 60 ff.

100. Knippenberg and De Pater, *De eenwording van Nederland*, p. 70.

101. Henk te Velde, *Gemeenschapszin en plichtsbesef. Liberalisme en Nationalisme in Nederland, 1870–1918*, The Hague, 1992, p. 123 ff.

102. Bank and van Buuren, *1900: The Age of Bourgeois Culture*, p. 30; Te Velde, *Gemeenschapszin en plichtsbesef*, p. 148 ff.

Notes

103. For the Boer War in detail, see te Velde, *Gemeenschapszin en plichtsbesef*, p. 163 ff; Bank and van Buuren, *1900: The Age of Bourgeois Culture*, p. 91 ff.

104. Quoted in Beening, *Onder de vleugels van de adelaar*, p. 280.

105. Johan den Hertog, *Cort van der Linden (1846–1935). Minister-president in oorlogstijd. Een politieke biografie*, Amsterdam, 2007, p. 675 ff.

106. For the international position of the Netherlands during the First World War, see Frey, *Der Erste Weltkrieg und die Niederlande*, passim; Maartje M. Abbenhuis, *The Art of Staying Neutral. The Netherlands in the First World War*, Amsterdam, 2006 and Hubertus P. Tuyll van Serooskerken, *The Netherlands and World War I. Espionage, Diplomacy and Survival*, Leiden, 2001; for the Netherlands between 1914 and 1918 in general, see Paul Moeyes, *Buiten schot. Nederland tijdens de Eerste Wereldoorlog 1914–1918*, Amsterdam/Antwerp, 2001; Martin Kraaijestein and Paul Schulten (eds), *Wankel evenwicht. Neutraal Nederland en de Eerste Wereldoorlog*, Soesterberg, 2007.

107. Hein A. M. Klemann, 'Ontwikkeling door isolement. De Nederlandse economie 1914–1918' in Kraaijestein and Schulten (eds), *Wankel evenwicht*, p. 271 ff. See also Jan Luiten van Zanden, *Een klein land in de twintigste eeuw. Economische geschiedenis van Nederland 1914–1995*, Utrecht, 1997, p. 128 ff.

108. Den Hertog, *Cort van der Linden*, p. 311 ff.

109. Van Klinken, *Actieve burgers*, p. 510 ff.

110. In Dutch (Voor het volk, van het volk) this is the title of his book about the development of the electoral system and the consequences for the 1917 amended constitution.

111. Piet de Rooy, 'De Pacificatie van 1917' in *Historisch Nieuwsblad* (2005), number 3; for more detail, see Jasper Loots, *Voor het volk, van het volk*, p. 145 ff.

112. De Haan, *Het beginsel van leven en wasdom*, p. 207.

Chapter Six

1. The source here was Arend Lijphart, *Verzuiling, pacificatie en kentering in de Nederlandse politiek*, Amsterdam, third completely revised edition, 1979. Lijphart updated a few passages in later editions (up to the ninth edition in 1992), but the text remained broadly speaking the same. The ninth edition was reprinted in 2007.

2. Hans Righart, *De katholieke zuil in Europa. Een vergelijkend onderzoek naar het ontstaan van verzuiling onder katholieken in Oostenrijk, Zwitserland, België en Nederland*, Amsterdam 1986.

3. Hans Daalder, 'Leiding en lijdelijkheid in de Nederlandse politiek' in Hans Daalder, *Van oude en nieuwe regenten. Politiek in Nederland*, Amsterdam 1994, p. 11–39.

4. Hans Daalder, 'De erfenis van de Republiek' in Hans Daalder, *Van oude en nieuwe regenten*, p. 146–151; for decision making and discussion culture in the seventeenth century see Willem Frijhoff and Marijke Spies, *1650. Bevochten eendracht*, The Hague 1999, p. 21 ff, p. 105, p. 218 ff.

5. Arend Lijphart, 'Time politics of accommodation. Reflections – Fifteen years later' in *Acta Politica* 19 (1984), number 1, p. 12.

6. For a critical analysis of the concept of 'pillarization' see Peter van Dam, *Staat van verzuiling. Over een Nederlandse mythe*, Amsterdam 2011.

7. J. C. H. Blom, 'Vernietigende kracht en nieuwe vergezichten. Het onderzoeksproject verzuiling op lokaal niveau geëvalueerd' in: J. C. H. Blom and J. Talsma (eds), *Verzuiling voorbij. Godsdienst, stand en natie in de lange egentiende eeuw*, Amsterdam 2000, p. 36.

8. Van Schie, *Vrijheidsstreven in verdrukking*, p. 169 ff.

9. J. J. Woltjer, *Recent verleden. De geschiedenis van Nederland in de twintigste eeuw*, Amsterdam, 1992, p. 59.

10. For small parties between the wars, see Koen Vossen, *Vrij vissen in het Vondelpark. Kleine politieke partijen in Nederland 1918–1940*, Amsterdam, 2003; see also Jasper Loots, *Voor het volk, van het volk*, pp. 146 ff, 215 ff.

11. Jac Bosmans, 'Het maatschappelijke leven in Nederland 1918–1940' in J. C. Boogman et al., *Geschiedenis van het moderne Nederland*, p. 411; for a detailed overview of the political events, see P. J. Oud and J. Bosmans, *Staatkundige vormgeving in Nederland*, p. 224 ff.

12. Bas van Dongen, *Revolutie of integratie. De Sociaal-Democratische Arbeiderspartij in Nederland (SDAP) tijdens de Eerste Wereldoorlog*, Amsterdam, 1992, p. 691 ff; Piet Hagen, *Politicus uit hartstocht. Biografie van Pieter Jelles Troelstra*, Amsterdam, 2010, p. 638 ff.

13. Cees Fasseur, *Wilhelmina. De jonge koningin*, Amsterdam, 1998, p. 559 ff.

14. Peter Jan Knegtmans, 'De jaren 1919–1946' in Keizer, Perry, Rossem, Zweers and Brinkman (eds), *Honderd jaar sociaal-democratie in Nederland*, p. 64 ff; Piet de Rooy, *De rode droom. Een eeuw sociaal-democratie in Nederland*, Nijmegen, 1995, p. 34 ff.

15. Piet de Rooy, 'Een zoekende tijd. De ongemakkelijke democratie 1913–1949' in Aerts, Liagre Böhl, de Rooy and te Velde, *Land van kleine gebaren*, p. 199.

16. Quoted in J. C. H. Blom, 'Nederland in de jaren dertig: een "burgerlijk-verzuilde" maatschappij in een crisis-periode' in J. C. H. Blom, *Crisis, bezetting en herstel. Tien studies over Nederland 1930–1950*, The Hague, 1989, p. 10.

17. Van Zanden, *Een klein land*, p. 113 ff.

18. Van Zanden, *Een klein land*, pp. 144–5.

19. J. de Vries, 'Het economische leven in Nederland 1918–1940' in Boogman et al., *Geschiedenis van het moderne Nederland*, pp. 375–7.

20. De Rooy, *Republiek*, p. 171.

21. Jan Luiten van Zanden, *De dans om de gouden standaard. Economisch beleid in de depressie van de jaren dertig*, Amsterdam, 1988; for Colijn's crisis policy, see Herman Langeveld, *Schipper naast God. Hendrikus Colijn 1869–1944*, volume 2, *1933–1944*, Amsterdam, 2004, p. 69 ff.

22. Quoted in Langeveld, *Colijn*, volume 2, p. 149.

23. For the 1937 manifesto, see Tromp, *Het sociaal-democratisch programma*, p. 187 ff.

24. A. A. de Jonge, *Crisis en critiek der democratie. Anti-democratische stromingen en de daarin levende denkbeelden over de staat in Nederland tussen de wereldoorlogen*, Utrecht, 1982 (1st edition, Assen 1968), p. 6 ff. De Jonge's twin concepts are still being used in recent literature.

25. Koen Vossen, *Vrij vissen in het Vondelpark*, passim.

26. For Romme in detail, see Jac Bosmans, *Romme. Biografie 1896–1946*, Utrecht, 1991; for corporatism, see p. 243 ff.

27. Langeveld, *Colijn*, volume 2, p. 13 ff.

28. Langeveld, *Colijn*, volume 2, p. 600.

Notes

29. For the early years of the NSB in great detail, see Robin te Slaa and Edwin Klijn, *De NSB. Ontstaan en opkomst van de Nationaal-Socialistische Beweging, 1931–1935*, Amsterdam, 2009.

30. L. de Jong, *Het Koninkrijk der Nederlanden in de Tweede Wereldoorlog*, volume 1, The Hague, 1969, p. 260. For Mussert, see Jan Meyers, *Mussert, een politiek leven*, Soesterberg, 2005; Tessel Pollmann, *Mussert & Co. De NSB-Leider en zijn vertrouwelingen*, Amsterdam, 2012.

31. Ries Roowaan, *Im Schatten der Großen Politik. Deutsch-niederländische Beziehungen zur Zeit der Weimarer Republik 1918–1933*, Münster, 2006, p. 58 ff.

32. Sigurd von Ilsemann, *Wilhelm II in Nederland 1918–1941. Dagboekfragmenten bezorgd door Jacco Pekelder en Wendy Landewé*, Soesterberg, 2015.

33. Remco van Diepen, *Voor Volkenbond en vrede. Nederland en het streven naar een nieuwe wereldorde 1919–1946*, Amsterdam, 1999, p. 42 ff.

34. Rolf Schuursma, *Vergeefs onzijdig. Nederlands neutraliteit 1919–1940*, Utrecht, 2005, p. 89 ff.

35. For the Oslo States in detail, see Ger van Roon, *Kleine Landen in crisistijd. Van Oslostaten tot Benelux 1930–1940*, Amsterdam, 1985.

36. Gerhard Hirschfeld, 'Hans Max Hirschfeld und die deutsch-niederländischen Wirtschaftsbeziehungen, 1931–1945' in Walter Mühlhausen, Bert Altena, Friedhelm Boll, Loek Geeraedts and Friso Wielenga (eds), *Grenzgänger. Persönlichkeiten des deutsch-niederländischen Verhältnisses. Horst Lademacher zum 65. Geburtstag*, Münster, 1998, p. 193.

37. Van Diepen, *Voor Volkenbond en vrede*, p. 229.

38. Langeveld, *Colijn*, volume 2, p. 464.

39. Hellema, *Nederland in de wereld*, p. 87 ff.

40. For Dutch defence in the 1920s and 1930s, see C. M. Schulten and P. M. J. de Koster, 'Tussen hoop en vrees. De Nederlandse krijgsmacht in het Interbellum' in Herman Amersfoort and Piet Kamphuis (eds), *Mei 1940. De strijd op Nederlands grondgebied*, Amsterdam, 2005, p. 61 ff.

41. Quoted in Teo van Middelkoop, *Een soldaat doet zijn plicht. Generaal H.G. Winkelman, zijn leven en betekenis als militair (1876–1952)*, The Hague, 2002, p. 164.

42. This periodization is based on J. C. H. Blom, 'Nederland onder Duitse bezetting 10 mei 1940 –5 mei 1945' in J. C. H.Blom, *Crisis, bezetting en herstel. Tien studies over Nederland 1930–1950*, Rotterdam, 1989, p. 97. This layout can also be derived from the historical work by Loe de Jong, *Het Koninkrijk der Nederlanden in de Tweede Wereldoorlog*. For the important contribution of Hans Blom in the historiography of the 1940–5 period, see also his *In de ban van goed en fout. Geschiedschrijving over de bezettingstijd in Nederland*, Amsterdam, 2007.

43. Cf. in extenso the biography by Johannes Koll: *Arthur Seyß-Inquart und die deutsche Besatzungspolitik in den Niederlanden 1940–1945*, Vienna, 2015.

44. For the structure of the resistance organization, see L. de Jong, *Het Koninkrijk*, volume 4, p. 44 ff; Gerhard Hirschfeld, *Bezetting en collaboratie. Nederland tijdens de oorlogsjaren 1940–1945*, Haarlem, 1991, p. 24 ff.

45. Hirschfeld, *Bezetting en collaboratie*, p. 29.

46. For the Dutch governmental system under German occupation, see the standard work by Peter Romijn, *Burgemeesters in oorlogstijd. Besturen onder Duitse bezetting*, Amsterdam, 2006.

47. Romijn, *Burgemeesters*, p. 116 ff; see also Chris van der Heijden, *Grijs verleden. Nederland en de Tweede Wereldoorlog*, Amsterdam, 2001, p. 129 ff.

48. See the standard work by Wichert ten Have, *De Nederlandse Unie. Aanpassing, vernieuwing en confrontatie in bezettingstijd 1940–1941*, Amsterdam, 1999.

49. J. C. H. Blom, 'Nederland onder Duitse bezetting 1940–1945' in Blom, *Crisis*, p. 76.

50. For greater detail, see Pim Griffioen and Ron Zeller, *Jodenvervolging in Nederland, Frankrijk en België, 1940–1945. Overeenkomsten, verschillen, oorzaken*, Amsterdam, 2011; see also Bob Moore, *Slachtoffers en overlevenden. De nazi-vervolging van de Joden in Nederland*, Amsterdam, 1998, p. 230 ff.

51. Dienke Hondius, *Terugkeer. Antisemitisme in Nederland rond de bevrijding*, The Hague, 1998, p. 52 ff; for the position of Jews in the Netherlands before 1940, see various contributions in Blom, Fuks-Mansfeld and Schöffer (eds), *Geschiedenis van de Joden in Nederland*.

52. J. C. H. Blom, 'De vervolging van de Joden in Nederland in internationaal vergelijkend perspectief' in Blom, *Geschiedenis van de Joden in Nederland*, Crisis, p. 139.

53. For greater detail, see Madelon de Keizer, *Putten. De razzia en de herinnering*, Amsterdam, 1998.

54. De Jong, *Het Koninkrijk*, volume 10b, p. 552 ff.

55. Quoted in De Jong, *Het Koninkrijk*, p. 944; see also p. 453.

Chapter Seven

1. Jan Bank, 'Die unvollendete Neuordnung. Das niederländische Grundgesetz und die Folgen des Zweiten Weltkrieges' and Doeko Bosscher, 'Die Rekonstruktion des Parteiensystems in den Niederlanden zwischen 1945 und 1952' in Horst Lademacher and Jac Bosmans (eds), *Tradition und Neugestaltung. Zu Fragen des Wiederaufbaus in Deutschland und den Niederlanden in der frühen Nachkriegszeit*, Münster, 1991, pp. 60, 103; J. C. H. Blom, 'De Tweede Wereldoorlog en de Nederlandse samenleving: continuïteit en verandering' in Blom, *Crisis, bezetting en herstel. Tien studies over Nederland 1930–1950*, The Hague, 1989, p. 180.

2. Duco Hellema, 'Das Ende des Fortschritts. Die Niederlande und die siebziger Jahre' in Friso Wielenga and Loek Geeraedts (eds), *Jahrbuch Zentrum für Niederlande-Studien* 18 (2007), p. 87 ff.

3. Madelon de Keizer, *De gijzelaars van Sint Michielsgestel. Een eliteberaad in oorlogstijd*, Alphen aan den Rijn, 1979.

4. Jan Bank, *Opkomst en ondergang van de Nederlandse Volksbeweging (NVB)*, Deventer, 1978, p. 54 ff.

5. For Drees's leadership, see te Velde, *Stijlen van leiderschap*, p. 155 ff.

6. Cooperation in government after 1945 is described in Jac Bosmans and Alexander van Kessel, *Parlementaire geschiedenis van Nederland*, Amsterdam, 2011.

7. Kees Schuyt and Ed Taverne, *1950. Welvaart in zwart-wit*, The Hague, 2000, p. 294.

8. Ger Verrips, *Dwars, duivels en dromend. De geschiedenis van de CPN 1938–1991*, Amsterdam, 1991, p. 328 ff.

9. Hans Righart, *De eindeloze jaren zestig. Geschiedenis van een generatieconflict*, Amsterdam, 1995, p. 133 ff; see also Piet de Rooy, 'Vetkuifje waarheen? Jongeren in Nederland in de jaren vijftig en zestig' in *Bijdragen en Mededelingen betreffende de Geschiedenis der Nederlanden (BMGN)* 101 (1986), number 1, p. 76 ff.

10. Hein Klemann, *Nederland 1938–1948. Economie en samenleving in de jaren van oorlog en bezetting*, Amsterdam, 2002, pp. 299–302, 565 ff.

11. Kees Schuyt and Ed Taverne, *1950*, The Hague, 2000, p. 69 ff.

Notes

12. Schuyt and Taverne, *1950*, p. 75.

13. For greater detail, see J. C. C. Rupp, *Van oude en nieuwe universiteiten. De verdringing van Duitse door Amerikaanse invloeden op de wetenschapsbeoefening en het hoger onderwijs in Nederland, 1945–1975*, The Hague, 1997.

14. Schuyt and Taverne, *1950*, pp. 53–4.

15. Ido de Haan, 'De maakbaarheid van de samenleving en het einde van de ideologie, 1945–1965' in Jan Willem Duyvendak and Ido de Haan (eds), *Maakbaarheid. Liberale wortels en hedendaagse kritiek van de maakbare samenleving*, Amsterdam, 1997, p. 91.

16. Hans Righart and Piet de Rooy, 'In Holland staat een huis. Weerzin en vertedering over de jaren vijftig' in Paul Luykx and Pim Slot (eds), *Een stille revolutie? Cultuur en mentaliteit in de lange jaren vijftig*, Hilversum, 1997, p. 11 ff.

17. Van Zanden, *Een klein land*, pp. 182–3.

18. Friso Wielenga, *West-Duitsland: Partner uit noodzaak. Nederland en de Bondsrepubliek 1949–1955*, Utrecht, 1989, p. 34 ff.

19. Albert E. Kersten, *Maken drie kleinen een grote? De politieke invloed van de Benelux 1945–1955*, Bussum, 1982.

20. For Dutch security policy at this time, see Cees Wiebes and Bert Zeeman, *Belgium, the Netherlands and Alliances 1940–1949*, Amsterdam, 1993; see also Alfred van Staden, *Een trouwe bondgenoot. Nederland en het Atlantisch Bondgenootschap (1960–1971)*, Baarn, 1974; Hellema, *Nederland in de wereld*, p. 148 ff. For the Netherlands and European integration, see A. G. Harryvan and J. van der Harst (eds), *Verloren consensus, Europa in het Nederlandse parlementaire politieke debat 1945–2013*, Amsterdam, 2013.

21. For greater detail, see Friso Wielenga, *Van vijand tot bondgenoot. Nederland en Duitsland na 1945*, Amsterdam, 1999, p. 41 ff.

22. Wielenga, *West-Duitsland*, pp. 79–225.

23. A. G. Harryvan, J. van der Harst and S. van Voorst (eds), *Voor Nederland en Europa. Politici en ambtenaren over het Nederlandse Europabeleid en de Europese integratie, 1945–1975*, Amsterdam, 2001, p. 17 ff.

24. For Beyen, see W. H. Weenink, *Bankier van de wereld. Bouwer van Europa. Johan Willem Beyen 1897–1976*, Amsterdam/Rotterdam, 2005.

25. Wielenga, *Van vijand tot bondgenoot*, p. 93 ff.

26. Wim van den Doel, 'Das kleine Land mit dem großen Imperium. Die moderne niederländische Kolonialgeschichte' in Friso Wielenga and Ilona Taute (eds), *Länderbericht Niederlande. Geschichte – Wirtschaft – Gesellschaft*, Bonn, 2004, p. 265.

27. For an extensive discussion of the New Guinea question, see Duco Hellema, *De Karel Doorman naar Nieuw-Guinea. Nederlands machtsvertoon in de Oost*, Amsterdam, 2005; P. J. Drooglever, *Een daad van vrije keuze. De Papoea's van westelijk Nieuw-Guinea en de grenzen van het zelfbeschikkingsrecht*, Amsterdam, 2005.

28. Wim van den Doel, *Afscheid van Indië. De val van het Nederlandse imperium in Azië*, Amsterdam, 2001, p. 338.

29. Quoted in Van den Doel, *Afscheid van Indië*, p. 341 ff.

30. Joop de Jong, *De waaier van het fortuin. Van handelscompagnie tot koloniaal imperium. De Nederlanders in Azië en de Indonesische archipel 1595–1950*, The Hague, 2000, p. 600.

31. Gert Oostindie, *Soldaat in Indonesië 1945–1950. Getuigenissen van een oorlog aan de verkeerde kant van de geschiedenis*, Amsterdam, 2016, p. 26.

32. For more detail see Stef Scagliola, *Last van de Oorlog. De Nederlandse oorlogsmisdaden in Indonesië en hun verwerking*, Amsterdam, 2002, p. 108 ff.

33. For the text of this report see Jan Bank (ed.), *De excessennota. Nota betreffende het archiefonderzoek naar de gegevens omtrent excessen in Indonesië begaan door Nederlandse militairen in de periode 1945-1950*, The Hague, 1995.

34. L. de Jong, *Het Koninkrijk*, volume 14, p. 900 ff.

35. Besides Stef Scagliola, *Last van de oorlog*, see also Helma Lutz and Katrin Gawarecki (eds), *Kolonialismus und Erinnerungskultur. Die Kolonialvergangenheit im kollektiven Gedächtnis der deutschen und niederländischen Einwanderungsgesellschaft*, Münster, 2005.

36. For a Dutch version of the complete speech see *de Volkskrant*, 22 August 1995.

37. Rémy Limpach, *De brandende kampongs van Generaal Spoor*, 4th edition, Amsterdam, 2018.

38. W. Willems, *De uittocht uit Indië 1945-1995*, Amsterdam, 2001; Hans Meijer, *In Indië geworteld. De twintigste eeuw*, Amsterdam, 2004.

39. 'Zwischen Königin und Rasputin. Geheimnisse im Haus Oranien' in *Der Spiegel*, 13 June 1956, p. 31 ff. For the background to this article in *Der Spiegel* see interviews with Prince Bernhard published after his death in Pieter Broertjes and Jan Tromp, *De prins spreekt*, Amsterdam, 2004, pp. 46–47. For a comprehensive overview of the affair see Hans Daalder, *Drees en Soestdijk. Over de zaak-Hofmans en andere crises 1948-1958*, Amsterdam, 2006; Lambert Giebels, *De Greet Hofmans-affaire. Hoe de Nederlandse monarchie bijna ten onder ging*, Amsterdam, 2007; Cees Fasseur, *Juliana & Bernhard. Het verhaal van een huwelijk. De jaren 1936-1956*, Amsterdam, 2008. See also Jolande Withuis *Juliana. Vorstin in een mannenwereld*, Amsterdam, 2016.

40. H. J. H. Hofland, *Tegels lichten of ware verhalen over de autoriteiten in het land van voldongen feiten*, Amsterdam, 1972, p. 118.

41. Fasseur, *Juliana en Bernhard*, p. 416.

42. James Kennedy, *Nieuw Babylon in aanbouw. Nederland in de jaren zestig*, 2nd edition, Amsterdam, 2016, p. 86.

43. Hans Righart, *De eindeloze jaren zestig. Geschiedenis van een generatieconflict*, Amsterdam, 1995, p. 59 ff.

44. Jos Becker and Joep de Hart, *Godsdienstige veranderingen in Nederland. Verschuivingen in de binding met de kerken en de christelijke traditie*, The Hague 2006, p. 37 ff.

45. James Kennedy, *Nieuw Babylon*, p. 186.

46. J. A. Bornewasser, *Katholieke Volkspartij 1945-1980*, Volume 2: *Heroriëntatie en integratie (1963-1980)*, p. 3 ff.; H.-M. T. D. ten Napel, *'Een eigen weg'. De totstandkoming van het CDA (1952-1980)*, Kampen, 1992 and D. Verkuil, *Een positieve grondhouding. De geschiedenis van het CDA*, The Hague, 1992.

47. Quoted by James Kennedy, *Nieuw Babylon*, p. 97; for the ARP at this time see Jan-Jaap van den Berg, *Deining. Koers en karakter van de ARP ter discussie, 1956-1973*, Kampen, 1999; for the party's history see also George Harinck, Roel Kuiper and Peter Baks (eds), *De Antirevolutionaire Partij 1826-1980*, Utrecht, 2001.

48. Niek Pas, *Imaazje! De verbeelding van Provo (1965-1967)*, Amsterdam, 2003.

49. Righart, *De eindeloze jaren zestig*, p. 233.

50. Friso Wielenga, 'Ausgrenzung und Integration. "1968" und die Folgen in Deutschland und den Niederlanden' in Friso Wielenga and Loek Geeraedts (eds), *Jahrbuch Zentrum für Niederlande-Studien* 12 (2001), pp. 137–62.

Notes

51. For the history of MVM, see Anneke Ribberink, *Leidsvrouwen en zaakwaarneemsters. Een geschiedenis van de actiegroep Man Vrouw Maatschappij*, Hilversum, 1998; for feminism at this time, see also Henriët van Rossum, 'De gesubsidieerde revolutie? Geschiedenis van de Nederlandse vrouwenbeweging 1968–1989' in Jan Willem Duyvendak, Hein-Anton van der Heijden, Ruud Koopmans and Luuk Wijmans (eds), *Tussen verbeelding en macht. 25 jaar nieuwe sociale bewegingen in Nederland*, Amsterdam, 1992, pp. 161–80.

52. See for example the biographies of Joop den Uyl and Dries van Agt: Anet Bleich, *Joop den Uyl 1919–1987, Dromer en doordouwer*, Amsterdam, 2008; Johan van Merriënboer et al. *Van Agt. Tour de Force. Biografie*, Amsterdam, 2008. See also Peter Bootsma and Willem Breedveld, *De verbeelding aan de macht. Het kabinet-Den Uyl 1973–1977*, The Hague, 1999.

53. Herman de Liagre van Böhl, 'Consensus en polarisatie. Spanningen in de verzorgingsstaat, 1945–1990' in Aerts, Liagre Böhl, de Rooy and te Velde, *Land van kleine gebaren*, p. 312.

54. Kees van Paridon, 'Wiederaufbau – Krise – Erholung' in Friso Wielenga and Ilona Taute (eds), *Länderbericht Niederlande*, Bonn, 2004, p. 383ff.

55. Kees Schuyt and Ed Taverne, *1950*, p. 277 ff.

56. Jan Luiten van Zanden, *Een klein land*, Utrecht, 1997, p. 221.

57. Quoted in Anet Bleich, *Joop den Uyl*, p. 338 ff.

58. For a more detailed description see Anet Bleich, *Joop den Uyl*, p. 334 ff. and Johan van Merriënboer et al. *Van Agt*, p. 165 ff.

59. Anet Bleich, *Joop den Uyl*, p. 342 ff.

60. Johan van Merriënboer et al. *Van Agt*, p. 179 ff.

61. Gert Oostindie and Inge Klinkers, *Knellende Koninkrijksbanden. Het Nederlandse dekolonisatiebeleid in de Caraïben, 1940–2000*, volume 2: 1954–1975, Amsterdam 2001, p. 167.

62. Oostindie and Klinkers, *Knellende Koninkrijksbanden*, volume 2: p. 87.

63. Oostindie and Klinkers, *Knellende Koninkrijksbanden*, volume 2: p. 125.

64. Oostindie and Klinkers, *Knellende Koninkrijksbanden*, volume 3: 1975–2000, p. 410.

65. Bleich, *Joop den Uyl*, p. 321.

66. For a clear overview see Peter Bootsma, *De Molukse acties. Treinkapingen en gijzelingen 1970–1978*, 2nd edition, Amsterdam, 2015. For a journalistic report of the 1977 hostage taking see Ralph Barker, *Not here, but in another place, a true story of captors and hostages*, New York, 1980.

67. Doeko Bosscher and Berteke Waaldijk, *Ambon. Eer & schuld. Politiek en pressie rond de republiek Zuid-Molukken*, Weesp, 1985.

68. Van Paridon, 'Wiederaufbau – Krise – Erholung' in Wielenga and Taute (eds), *Länderbericht*, p. 397; Van Zanden, *Een klein land*, p. 227 ff.

69. Maarten van Bottenburg, *Aan den Arbeid! In de wandelgangen van de Stichting van de Arbeid 1945–1995*, Amsterdam, 1995, p. 200.

70. J. A. A. van Doorn, 'De onvermijdelijke presentie van de confessionelen' in Jos de Beus, Jacques van Doorn and Piet de Rooy, *De ideologische driehoek. Nederlandse politiek in historisch perspectief*, Amsterdam, 1996, p. 133.

71. René Cuperus, 'Paars in internationaal perspectief. Over afnemende vrijheidsgraden van de politiek' in Frans Becker et al. (eds), *Zeven jaar paars. Tweeëntwintigste jaarboek voor het democratisch socialisme*, Amsterdam, 2001, p. 197.

72. Jelle Visser and Anton Hemerijck, '*A Dutch miracle'. Job growth, welfare reform and corporatism in the Netherlands*, Amsterdam, 1997, p. 185.

73. Wim Kok, 'We laten niemand los' in Stichting Dr. J.M. den Uyl-lezing (ed), *We laten niemand los. Den Uyl-lezingen 1993–1999*, Amsterdam, 2000, p. 78.

74. Gabriël van den Brink, *Mondiger of moeilijker? Een studie naar de politieke habitus van hedendaagse burgers*, The Hague, 2002, p. 30.

75. Max van Weezel and Michiel Zonneveld, *De onttovering van Paars. Een geschiedenis van de kabinetten-Kok*, Amsterdam, 2002, p. 95 ff; see also Addie Schulte and Bas Soetenhorst, *De achterkamer. Het drama van de PvdA 1998–220*, Amsterdam, 2002; Piet de Rooy and Henk te Velde, *Met Kok over veranderend Nederland*, Amsterdam, 2005, p. 189.

76. Nederlands Instituut voor Oorlogsdocumentatie (ed.), *Srebrenica. Een 'veilig' gebied. Reconstructie,achtergronden, gevolgen en analyses van de val van een safe area*, Amsterdam, 2002.

77. Remco van Diepen, *Hollanditis. Nederland en het Kernwapendebat 1977–1987*, Amsterdam, 2004; see also Hellema, *Nederland in de wereld*, p. 306 ff.

78. Jan van der Harst, 'Von der Vorhersehbarkeit zur Unsicherheit. Über die Veränderungen der niederländischen Europapolitik der Nachkriegszeit' in Friso Wielenga and Loek Geeraedts (eds), *Jahrbuch Zentrum für Niederlande-Studien* 15 (2004), p. 29; Duco Hellema, *Nederland in de wereld*, p. 394 ff.

79. Jan Rood, 'Nederland zoekende in een veranderend Europa' in Alfred van Staden (ed.), *De herontdekking van de wereld. Nederlands buitenlands beleid in revisie*, The Hague, 2004, p. 49 ff; see also Anjo G. Harryvan and Jan van der Harst (eds), *Verloren consensus. Europa in het Nederlandse parlementaire debat 1945–2013*, Amsterdam, 2013.

80. For the European policy of the Netherlands, see Mathieu Segers, *Reis naar het continent. Nederland en de Europese integratie, 1950 tot heden*, Amsterdam, 2013.

81. For Fortuyn see for example Paul Lucardie and Gerrit Voerman, *Populisten in de polder*, Amsterdam, 2012, p. 71 ff.

82. For Wilders see for example Koen Vossen, *The Power of Populism. Geert Wilders and the Party for Freedom in the Netherlands*, Abingdon, 2016.

83. For these conclusions see *Rapport Commissie van onderzoek besluitvorming Irak*, Amsterdam, 2010, p. 423 ff.

84. Jean Tillie, Joop van Holsteyn et al. *Rumoer. Nederlandse kiezers en politiek 1998–2012*, Amsterdam, 2016, p. 121 ff.

85. For the history of government formation see Carla van Baalen and Alexander van Kessel (eds), *Kabinetsformaties 1977–2012*, Amsterdam, 2016; see also Peter Bootsma, *Coalitievorming. Een vergelijking tussen Nederland en Duitsland*, Amsterdam, 2017, pp. 231 ff.

86. Peter Mair, 'Electoral Volatility and the Dutch Party System' in *Acta Politica* 43 (2008), volume 2–3, p. 239.

87. See also Friso Wielenga, Carla van Baalen and Markus Wilp (eds), *Eine zersplitterte Landschaft. Beiträge zur Geschichte und Gegenwart niederländischer politischer Parteien*, Amsterdam, 2018.

88. For an analysis of the 2005 referendum result see Kees Aarts and Henk van der Kolk, *Nederland en Europa. Het referendum over de Europese grondwet*, Amsterdam, 2005.

Chapter Eight

1. J. C. H. Blom, 'Leiden als Warnung. Konstanten und Variablen im niederländischen Umgang mit der Besatzungszeit' in Norbert Fasse, Johannes Houwink ten Cate and Horst Lademacher (eds), *Nationalsozialistische Herrschaft und Besatzungszeit. Historische Erfahrung und Verarbeitung aus niederländischer und deutscher Sicht*, Münster, 2000, p. 324.

2. See also van Sas, *Metamorfose*, p. 41 ff.

3. Kees Schuyt, 'Tolerantie en democratie' in Douwe Fokkema and Frans Grijzenhout (eds), *Rekenschap. 1650-2000*, The Hague, 2001, pp. 115-43. This compilation also contains contributions about the issue of continuity and discontinuity since the seventeenth century.

4. Schutte, *Het Calvinistisch Nederland*, p. 1; see also Schutte, 'Eine calvinistische Nation? Mythos und Wirklichkeit' in Wielenga and Taute (eds), *Länderbericht*, p. 131 ff; Mirjam van Veen, *Een nieuwe tijd, een nieuwe kerk. De opkomst van het 'calvinisme' in de Lage Landen*, Zoetermeer, 2009, p. 10 ff.

5. Paul Brusse and Wijnand Mijnhardt, *Towards a New Template for Dutch History*, pp. 75, 80.

6. Maarten Prak, 'The Dutch Republic as a Bourgeois Society' in *BMGN The Low Countries Historical Review* 125 (2010), numbers 2 and 3, pp. 135-6; for the influence of the nobility, see Brusse and Mijnhardt, *Towards a New Template for Dutch History*, p. 87 ff.

7. Remieg Aerts, 'Civil Society or Democracy? A Dutch Paradox' in *BMGN The Low Countries Historical Review*, 125 (2010), numbers 2 and 3, p. 217.

8. Remieg Aerts, 'Alles in verhouding. De burgerlijkheid van Nederland' in Remieg Aerts and Henk te Velde (eds), *De stijl van de burger. Over Nederlandse burgerlijke cultuur vanaf de middeleeuwen*, Kampen, 1998, pp. 276 ff, 291-2.

9. Kennedy, *Een weloverwogen daad*, p. 16 ff.

10. Van Sas, *Metamorfose*, p. 57.

11. Van Sas, *Metamorfose*, p. 45.

TIMELINE

1524–43	Charles V adds Friesland, Utrecht, Overijssel, Drenthe and Guelders to his Dutch territories.
1544	William of Nassau, born in 1533, inherits the French Principality of Orange and, as Prince of Orange, receives a Catholic education at the court of Charles V in Brussels.
1548	At the request of Charles V, the Holy Roman Empire groups the seventeen Dutch provinces in an imperial circle, *kreits*. Shortly afterwards, Charles V decides that this area will be unified and indivisible 'in perpetuity'.
1555	In Brussels, Charles V transfers government of the Netherlands to his son, Philip II.
1559	Philip II leaves the Netherlands for good and goes to Spain. His half-sister Margaret, Duchess of Parma, becomes governess and William of Orange becomes stadholder of Holland, Zeeland and Utrecht.
1566	Petition of the Nobles and iconoclasm.
1567	Violence and conflicts worsen with the arrival of the Duke of Alba. William of Orange flees to Germany.
1568	Failed attempt by William of Orange to regain his position in the Netherlands through a military attack.
1572	The Sea Beggars conquer Den Briel. A number of other towns and cities in Holland and Zeeland side with William of Orange.
1576	Pacification of Ghent: the States General and the rebellious provinces of Holland and Zeeland form an alliance with the aim of driving Spanish troops out of all provinces.
1579	Union of Arras and Union of Utrecht: the return of two Catholic provinces to the Spanish side (Union of Arras) is followed by the formation of the Union of Utrecht by northern provinces. This is the start of the division between the Northern and Southern Netherlands.
1580	Philip II outlaws William of Orange.
1581	The States General declares independence from Spain through the Act of Abjuration.

Timeline

1584 William of Orange is murdered.

1585 Antwerp is conquered by Spanish troops. Prince Maurice becomes stadholder of Holland and Zeeland.

1588 The states of the northern provinces assume sovereignty after the failed experiments with Anjou and Leicester as rulers. This results in the creation of the Republic. Advocate of Holland Oldenbarnevelt and Stadholder Maurice give successful leadership. The Republic and the English defeat the Spanish fleet – an important military turning point.

1590–8 The Republic regains territory in the southern, eastern and northern provinces. In 1596, England, France and the Republic form a Triple Alliance against Spain, which implies recognition of the Republic's sovereignty by the great powers of England and France.

1602 Establishment of the Dutch East India Company (VOC).

1609–21 Twelve Years' Truce. Increasing tensions between Oldenbarnevelt and Maurice. Theological conflict between Remonstrants and Counter-Remonstrants.

1618 Maurice seizes power. Oldenbarnevelt and Hugo Grotius are arrested.

1619 Oldenbarnevelt is beheaded. The Synod of Dordrecht (1618–19) confirms the victory of the Counter-Remonstrants.

1621 War with Spain resumes. Because of the Thirty Years' War (1618–48), the struggle against Spain is now more a part of a greater European conflict than it was before 1609. Establishment of the Dutch West India Company (WIC).

1625 Stadholder Maurice dies. He is succeeded by his half-brother Frederick Henry, who leads the conquest of Brabant and Limburg. Under Stadholder Frederick Henry, the Republic's territory takes on the contours of today's Netherlands.

1625 Hugo Grotius publishes *De jure belli ac pacis*.

1642 Rembrandt completes *The Night Watch*, which will later be considered as the peak of seventeenth-century Dutch painting.

1647 Stadholder Frederick Henry dies. His son William II succeeds him.

1648 Peace between Spain and the Netherlands (Peace of Münster) as part of the Peace of Westphalia. End of the Eighty Years' War.

1650 Stadholder William II dies. Beginning of the First Stadholderless Period (until 1672).

1652–4 First Anglo–Dutch War.

1653–72   Johan de Witt is grand pensionary of Holland.

1655   Amsterdam's new town hall, currently the Royal Palace Amsterdam in Dam Square, opens. It is the largest public building of the seventeenth century and is a symbol of the Republic's great self-confidence.

1665–7   Second Anglo–Dutch War.

1672   'Disaster Year' (*Rampjaar*). The Republic is attacked by France, England and the bishoprics of Münster and Cologne. William III becomes stadholder. Johan and Cornelis de Witt are lynched in The Hague by furious citizens.

1674   End of the Third Anglo–Dutch War, which started during the Disaster Year. Peace is also made with the bishoprics of Münster and Cologne.

1677   Spinoza's *Ethics* is published a few months after his death. A year later all Spinoza's works are banned in the Republic.

1678   Peace of Nijmegen: end of the war with France.

1685   Louis XIV revokes the Edict of Nantes (1598). Tens of thousands of Huguenots flee to the Republic. Tensions with France mount, due in part to trade disputes.

1688   Glorious Revolution: Stadholder William III drives his Catholic father-in-law James II from the English throne at the request of English Protestants. A year later, William III and his wife Mary Stuart become king and queen of England.

1688–97   Nine Years' War with France, which ends with the Treaty of Rijswijk.

1702   Stadholder-King William III dies. Start of the Second Stadholderless Period (until 1747 in Holland, Zeeland, Utrecht and Overijssel).

1702–13   War of the Spanish Succession, which ends with the Peace of Utrecht. The Republic is substantially weakened by the war. Domestic unrest (Old Crew/New Crew).

1740–8   War of the Austrian Succession. In 1747, France occupies a small part of Zeeland. People recall the Disaster Year and there is panic in some parts of the Republic. There are calls in the provinces without a stadholder for the return of Orange.

1747   William IV, stadholder of Friesland, becomes stadholder of all provinces.

1748   The Targeters Movement attempts in vain to bring political reforms and receives no support from William IV.

1751   Stadholder William IV dies. His son William V, aged three, becomes his successor as hereditary stadholder. His mother Anne, Princess Royal, is his guardian until 1759, and is followed from then until 1766 by Louis Ernest, Duke of Brunswick-Wolfenbüttel.

1756–63 Seven Years' War between France and Austria (until 1762, also Russia) on one side, and England and Prussia on the other. Despite its neutrality, the Republic declines further because of the war.

1780–4 Fourth Anglo–Dutch War. Dramatic weakening of the Republic.

1780–7 The Patriot Movement seeks to introduce political reforms and a greater role for the citizenry. In 1781, the pamphlet *To the People of the Netherlands* is published.

1784 Establishment of the Public Welfare Association (which exists to this day) that, under the influence of the Enlightenment, has the goal of disseminating culture, knowledge and education among citizens and instructing the lower classes.

1785 Stadholder William V and his wife Wilhelmina of Prussia move to Nijmegen because of domestic disturbances.

1787 On her journey from Nijmegen to The Hague, Princess Wilhelmina is prevented from proceeding by Patriots at Goejanverwellesluis. King Frederick William II of Prussia, Princess Wilhelmina's brother, terminates the Patriot era using military force. William V returns to The Hague as stadholder. Thousands of Patriots flee to France.

1795 Advance by French troops and former Patriots into the Republic. Stadholder William V flees to England. Beginning of the Batavian Republic.

1798 First Dutch constitution. The Netherlands becomes a unitary state. There are several regime changes and constitutional amendments in the years thereafter.

1806 Beginning of the Kingdom of Holland under King Louis Bonaparte, a brother of Napoleon.

1810 End of the Kingdom of Holland. Annexation by the French Empire.

1813 William Frederick of Orange, son of the former Stadholder William V, returns to the Netherlands.

1814–15 Congress of Vienna: the Northern and Southern Netherlands are combined to form the United Kingdom of the Netherlands under King William I, who also becomes Grand Duke of Luxembourg.

1815–30 Era of the United Kingdom of the Netherlands.

1824 Establishment of the Netherlands Trading Society (NHM).

1830 Introduction of the Cultivation System in the Dutch East Indies – obligatory contributions of specified crops. Big profits from the colony.

1830	Revolt in the south of the kingdom leading to the independence of Belgium.
1839	The Netherlands recognizes the 1831 Belgian secession settlement.
1840	King William I abdicates. Start of William II's reign.
1848	Fearful of revolution among other things, King William II instructs Thorbecke to write a liberal constitution. It comes into force the same year.
1849	King William II dies. Start of William III's reign.
1853	Restoration of the Catholic bishoprics in the Netherlands. Many Dutch Protestants are opposed to this and demonstrate their abhorrence of Catholicism through the April Movement.
1860	Publication of Multatuli's *Max Havelaar*.
1867	End of the institutional tie between Germany on the one side and the grand duchy of Luxembourg (under a Dutch king) and the Dutch province of Limburg on the other. Luxembourg and Limburg were part of the German Confederation until 1866.
1871	Establishment of the General Dutch Workers' Association (ANWV), the first trade union in the Netherlands.
1874	The very first social legislation – Van Houten's Child Labour Act – comes into force.
1878	The new Primary Education Act sets tougher requirements for education and confirms that only non-denominational schools open to the public will be financed by the state. Denominational Christian schools have to fund themselves. Escalation of the schools conflict.
1879	Abraham Kuyper establishes the orthodox Protestant ARP, the first political party in the Netherlands.
1887	Amended constitution extending suffrage; state financing of private primary education is also made possible.
1890	King William III dies. His ten-year-old daughter Wilhelmina formally becomes queen. Her mother, Emma of Waldeck and Pyrmont, is queen regent until 1898.
1901	Beginning of the 'ethical policy' in the Dutch East Indies. The aim to improve the prosperity of the indigenous population by no means excludes violent oppression. Further expansion of colonial territory at this time.
1914	Outbreak of the First World War. The Netherlands remains neutral.
1917	Pacification of 1917: amended constitution introduces universal and secret male suffrage and the proportional representation system. Equal financial

status of state and private primary education, and thus the end of the schools conflict.

1918	The social democrat leader Pieter Jelles Troelstra makes a half-hearted and unsuccessful attempt to start a revolution.
1919	Introduction of universal and secret female suffrage.
1920	The Netherlands joins the League of Nations. End of the policy of strict neutrality.
1922	First Lower House elections with universal male and female suffrage. Confirmation of the religious parties' dominant position, which started in 1918 and is to continue throughout the period between the wars.
1929	Start of the international economic crisis, which hits the Netherlands hard, starting in 1931. The nadir is reached during the winter of 1935–6 with some 590,000 unemployed (about 20 per cent of the workforce).
1932	The Zuiderzee is sealed off by the Lake IJssel Dam. The Zuiderzee becomes Lake IJssel.
1935	The National Socialist Movement (NSB) gets almost 8 per cent of the votes in provincial elections, the best result in its history.
1936–8	The Netherlands gradually returns to a policy of strict neutrality because of growing international tension.
1939	De Geer government: the first cabinet with social democrat ministers.
1940	10 May: Germany attacks the Netherlands (as well as Belgium, Luxembourg and France). Rapid advance, followed by the bombing of Rotterdam and capitulation on 14 May.
1941	End of February: strikes protesting against more severe persecution of Jews.
1942	9 March: Dutch troops in the Dutch East Indies capitulate. Start of the Japanese occupation.
1942	Deportation of Jews from the Netherlands starts.
1943	Increasing hardening of German occupation policy, increase in the number of Dutch forced labourers in Germany, growing resistance.
1944	Allies liberate parts of the southern provinces in the late summer and early autumn. Dutch famine or 'hunger winter' of 1944–5 in the occupied western part of the country with tens of thousands of deaths.
1945	5 May: German capitulation signed in Wageningen. Japan capitulates on 15 August. Sukarno and Mohammed Hatta proclaim the Republic of Indonesia two days later.

1945–6   Return of the pre-war political parties. Attempt to break through the old relationships fails despite the establishment of the Labour Party (PvdA).

1947–8   Escalation of the colonial war in Indonesia (euphemistically called 'police actions').

1948   Queen Wilhelmina abdicates and her daughter Juliana succeeds her.

1948–9   The Netherlands is co-founder of the Western European Union (Treaty of Brussels, 1948) and the North Atlantic Treaty Organization (NATO, 1949). Definitive end of the traditional neutrality policy.

1949   Transfer of sovereignty to the Republic of Indonesia.

1951   The Netherlands is co-founder of the ECSC.

1957   The Netherlands is co-founder of the EEC.

1965–9   Rise and fall of the Provo movement, establishment of new political parties, emergence of students' and women's movements, start of the depillarization of politics and society.

1973–7   Government led by Joop den Uyl (PvdA).

1975   Transfer of sovereignty to Suriname.

1975–8   Terrorist actions by young South Moluccans (including train hijackings and hostage taking in a primary school).

1979   NATO double-track decision as the Western response to the deployment of SS-20 missiles by the Soviet Union. In the early 1980s, many people join the peace movement against nuclear weapons.

1980   Establishment of the CDA by the ARP, CHU and KVP, after these parties had already taken part in the 1977 Lower House elections as the CDA.

1980   Queen Juliana abdicates and is succeeded by her daughter Beatrix.

1982   Wassenaar Agreement: employers and employees sign a declaration of intent about employment and wage restraint.

1994   Formation of the first government since 1918 without Christian democrats, headed by PvdA leader Wim Kok (purple coalition).

1995   Some 8,000 Bosnian Muslim men and boys from the Srebrenica safe area are massacred by Bosnian Serbs. Dutch soldiers stationed there and the UN do not prevent the tragedy.

2002   End of the second Kok government. Murder of the right-wing populist politician Pim Fortuyn. In the Lower House elections shortly afterwards, the Pim Fortuyn List (LPF) is the second strongest faction in the Lower House after the CDA. The LPF becomes a coalition partner in the first Balkenende government.

2003   New elections after cabinet crisis. End of the LPF's political significance.

2004   Murder of the film director and writer Theo van Gogh. Intensified polarization and growing tensions about integration policy.

2005   The Dutch (like the French) reject the European Union constitution in a referendum. Crisis in the European Union.

2006–7   There are early Lower House elections after a number of political crises. Formation of a government by the CDA, PvdA and Christian Union.

2010   Once again there is a government crisis followed by early elections. Geert Wilders's Party for Freedom (PVV) becomes the second biggest force in the Lower House and 'tolerance partner' of the VVD/CDA government led by Mark Rutte.

2012   The PVV withdraws its tolerance support; early elections. Formation of a VVD/PvdA government.

2013   Queen Beatrix abdicates and is succeeded by her son William-Alexander.

2017   Lower House election with a historically large loss for the PvdA (from 24.7 per cent in 2012 to 4.7 per cent). Medium-sized (between 9 and 13 per cent) and small parties dominate the political landscape. The advent of a government comprising VVD, CDA, D66 and CU after the longest cabinet formation period ever in Dutch history (225 days).

BIBLIOGRAPHY

Aarts, Kees and Henk van der Kolk, *Nederland en Europa. Het referendum over de Europese grondwet*, Amsterdam, 2005.

Abbenhuis, Maartje, *The Art of Staying Neutral. The Netherlands in the First World War*, Amsterdam, 2006.

Aerts, Remieg, *Thorbecke wil het: biografie van een staatsman*, Amsterdam, 2018.

Aerts, Remieg and Henk te Velde, *De stijl van de burger. Over Nederlandse burgerlijke cultuur vanaf de middeleeuwen*, Kampen, 1998.

Aerts, Remieg, Herman de Liagre Böhl, Piet de Rooy and Henk te Velde, *Land van kleine gebaren. Een politieke geschiedenis van Nederland 1780-1990*, 5th edition, Nijmegen, 2007.

Algemene Geschiedenis der Nederlanden in fifteen volumes, Bussum, 1982.

Amersfoort, Herman and Piet Kamphuis (eds), *Mei 1940. De strijd op Nederlands grondgebied*, Amsterdam, 2005.

Andeweg, Rudy B. and Galen A. Irwin, *Governance and Politics in the Netherlands*, 3rd edition, Basingstoke, 2009.

Arblaster, Paul, *A History of the Low Countries*, Basingstoke, 2006.

Baalen, Carla van and Alexander van Kessel (eds), *Kabinetsformaties 1977-2012*, Amsterdam, 2016.

Bank, Jan, *Opkomst en ondergang van de Nederlandse Volksbeweging (NVB)*, Deventer, 1978.

Bank, Jan and Maarten van Buuren, *1900: The Age of Bourgeois Culture*, Basingstoke, 2004.

Bank, Jan, Gijsbert van Es and Piet de Rooy, *In Short, the Netherlands. Everything You Always Wanted to Know about Dutch History*, Wormer, 2005.

Bank, Jan, J. J. Huizinga and J. T. Minderaa, *Nederlandse verleden in vogelvlucht. De nieuwste tijd: 1813 tot heden*, Groningen, 1993.

Barker, Ralph, *Not Here, But in Another Place: A True Story of Captors and Hostages*, New York, 1980.

Barnouw, David, *De bezetting in een notendop. Alles wat je altijd wilde weten over Nederland in de Tweede Wereldoorlog*, Amsterdam, 2005.

Becker, Jos and Joep de Hart, *Godsdienstige veranderingen in Nederland. Verschuivingen in de binding met de kerken en de christelijke traditie*, The Hague, 2006.

Becker, Uwe (ed), *Nederlandse politiek in historisch en vergelijkend perspectief*, Amsterdam, 1993.

Beening, André, *Onder de vleugels van de adelaar. De Duitse buitenlandse politiek ten aanzien van Nederland in de periode 1890-1914*, Thesis University of Amsterdam, 1994.

Bejczy, István, *Een kennismaking met de Nederlandse geschiedenis*, Bussum, 2010.

Berg, J. T. J van den and J. J. Vis, *De eerste honderdvijftig jaar parlementaire geschiedenis van Nederland, 1797-1946*, Amsterdam, 2013.

Berkel, Klaas van and Leonie de Goei, *The International Relevance of Dutch History* (special edition of *Bijdragen en Mededelingen betreffende de Geschiedenis der Nederlanden (BMGN)/ Low Countries Historical Review (LCHR)* 125 (2010), numbers 2-3.

Beus, Jos de, Jacques van Doorn and Piet de Rooy, *De ideologische driehoek. Nederlandse politiek in historisch perspectief*, Amsterdam, 1996.

Binneveld, Hans, Martin Kraayestein, Marja Roholl and Paul Schulten (eds), *Leven naast de catastrofe. Nederland tijdens de Eerste Wereldoorlog*, Hilversum, 2001.

Bleich, Anet, *Joop den Uyl 1919-1987. Dromer en doordouwer*, 3rd edition, Amsterdam, 2008.

Bibliography

Blockmans, W. P., *Metropolen aan de Noordzee. De geschiedenis van Nederland, 1100–1560*, Amsterdam, 2010.

Blokker, B., Gijsbert van Es and Hendrik Spiering, *Nederland in een handomdraai. De vaderlandse geschiedenis in jaartallen*, Amsterdam, 2005.

Blom, J. C. H., *Crisis, bezetting en herstel. Tien studies over Nederland 1930–1950*, The Hague, 1989.

Blom, J. C. H., *De muiterij op de Zeven Provinciën. Reacties en gevolgen in Nederland*, Utrecht, 1983.

Blom, J. C. H., *In de ban van goed en fout. Geschiedschrijving over de bezettingstijd in Nederland*, Amsterdam, 2007.

Blom, J. C. H. and E. Lamberts (eds), *Geschiedenis van de Nederlanden*, 4th edition, Baarn, 2006; also published in English: *History of the Low Countries*, New York/Oxford, 2006.

Blom, J. C. H., R. G. Fuks-Mansfeld and I. Schöffer (eds), *Geschiedenis van de Joden in Nederland*, 2nd edition, Amsterdam, 2004.

Boogman, J. C. et al., *Geschiedenis van het moderne Nederland. Politieke, economische en sociale ontwikkelingen*, Houten, 1988.

Bootsma, Peter, *De Molukse acties. Treinkapingen en gijzelingen 1970–1978*, 2nd edition, Amsterdam, 2015.

Bootsma, Peter, *Coalitievorming. Een vergelijking tussen Nederland en Duitsland*, Amsterdam, 2017.

Bornewasser, J. A., *Katholieke Volkspartij 1945–1980*. Volume I: *Herkomst en groei (tot 1963)* and Volume 2: *Heroriëntatie en integratie (1963–1980)*, Nijmegen, 1995–2000.

Bosmans, Jac (ed), *Europagedanke, Europabewegung und Europapolitik in den Niederlanden und Deutschland seit dem Ersten Weltkrieg*, Münster, 1996.

Bosmans, Jac, *Romme. Biografie 1896–1946*, Utrecht, 1991.

Bosmans, Jac and Alexander van Kessel, *Parlementaire geschiedenis van Nederland*, Amsterdam, 2011.

Boterman, Frits and Piet de Rooy, *Op de grens van twee culturen. Nederland en Duitsland in het Fin de Siècle*, Amsterdam, 1999.

Brandon, Pepjin, *War, Capital and the Dutch State 1588–1795*, Chicago, 2017.

Broek, Ilja van den, *Heimwee naar de politiek. De herinnering aan het kabinet-Den Uyl*, Amsterdam, 2002.

Broertjes, Pieter and Jan Tromp, *De prins spreekt*, Amsterdam, 2004.

Bruijn, Jaap R., *Varend verleden. De Nederlandse oorlogsvloot in de zeventiende en achttiende eeuw*, Amsterdam, 1998.

Bruin, Guido de, *Geheimhouding en verraad. De geheimhouding van staatszaken ten tijde van de Republiek (1600–1750)*, The Hague, 1991.

Brunn, Gerhard and Cornelius Neutsch (eds), *Sein Feld war die Welt. Johann Moritz von Nassau-Siegen (1604–1679). Von Siegen über die Niederlande nach Brasilien und Brandenburg*, Münster, 2008.

Brusse, Paul and Wijnand W. Mijnhardt, *Towards a New Template for Dutch History. De-urbanization and the Balance between City and Countryside*, Zwolle, 2011.

Burg, Martijn van der, *Nederland onder Franse invloed. Culturele overdracht en staatsvorming in de napoleontische tijd, 1799–1813*, Amsterdam, 2009.

Coninck, Pieter de, *Een les uit Pruisen. Nederland en de Kulturkampf, 1870–1880*, Hilversum, 2005.

Daalder, Hans, *Drees en Soestdijk. Over de zaak-Hofmans en andere crises 1948–1958*, Amsterdam, 2006.

Dam, Peter van, *Staat van verzuiling. Over een Nederlandse mythe*, Amsterdam, 2011.

Davids, Karel and Leo Noordegraaf (eds), *The Dutch Economy in the Golden Age. Nine Studies*, Amsterdam, 1993.

Dethlefs, Gerd (ed), *Der Frieden von Münster – De vrede van Munster 1648*, Münster, 1998.

Deursen, Arie T. van, *Bavianen en Slijkgeuzen. Kerk en kerkvolk ten tijde van Maurits en Oldenbarnevelt*, Assen, 1974.

Deursen, Arie T. van, *De last van veel geluk. De geschiedenis van Nederland, 1555–1702*, Amsterdam, 2004.

Deursen, Arie T. van, *Maurits van Nassau, 1567–1625. De winnaar die faalde*, Amsterdam, 2000.

Deursen, Arie T. van, *Mensen van klein vermogen. Het 'kopergeld' van de Gouden Eeuw*, 4th edition, Amsterdam, 1999.

Deursen, Arie T. van, *Willem van Oranje. Een biografisch portret*, Amsterdam, 1995.

Deursen, Arie T. van, Jaap R. Bruijn and Johanna Elisabeth Korteweg, *De Admiraal. De wereld van Michiel Adriaenszoon de Ruyter*, Franeker, 2007.

Diepen, Remco van, *Hollanditis. Nederland en het Kernwapendebat 1977–1987*, Amsterdam, 2004.

Diepen, Remco van, *Voor Volkenbond en vrede. Nederland en het streven naar een nieuwe wereldorde 1919–1946*, Amsterdam, 1999.

Ditzhuyzen, R. E. van, A. E. Kersten, A. L. M. van Zeeland and A. C. van der Zwan (eds), *The Foreign Ministry: 200 Years*, The Hague, 1998.

Doel, H. W. van den, *Afscheid van Indië. De val van het Nederlandse imperium in Azië*, Amsterdam, 2001.

Doel, H. W. van den, *Zo ver de wereld strekt. De geschiedenis van Nederland overzee vanaf 1800*, Amsterdam, 2011.

Dongen, Bas van, *Revolutie of integratie. De Sociaal-Democratische Arbeiderspartij in Nederland (SDAP) tijdens de Eerste Wereldoorlog*, Amsterdam, 1992.

Drentje, Jan, *Thorbecke. Een filosoof in de politiek*, Amsterdam, 2004.

Duyvendak, Jan Willem and Ido de Haan (eds), *Maakbaarheid. Liberale wortels en hedendaagse kritiek van de maakbare samenleving*, Amsterdam, 1997.

Duyvendak, Jan Willem, Hein-Anton van der Heijden, Ruud Koopmans and Luuk Wijmans (eds), *Tussen verbeelding en macht. 25 jaar nieuwe sociale bewegingen in Nederland*, Amsterdam, 1992.

Eijnatten, Joris van and Fred van Lieburg, *Nederlandse religiegeschiedenis*, Hilversum, 2006.

Emmer, P. C., *De Nederlandse slavenhandel 1500–1850*, 3rd edition, Amsterdam, 2007.

Erbe, Michael, *Belgien, Niederlande, Luxemburg. Geschichte des niederländischen Raumes*, Stuttgart, 1993.

Fasse, Norbert, Johannes Houwink ten Cate and Horst Lademacher (eds), *Nationalsozialistische Herrschaft und Besatzungszeit. Historische Erfahrung und Verarbeitung aus niederländischer und deutscher Sicht*, Münster, 2000.

Fasseur, Cees, *Wilhelmina. De jonge koningin*, Amsterdam, 1998.

Fasseur, Cees, *Wilhelmina. Krijgshaftig in een vormeloze jas*, Amsterdam, 2001.

Fasseur, Cees, *Juliana & Bernhard. Het verhaal van een huwelijk. De jaren 1936–1956*, Amsterdam, 2008.

Fokkema, Douwe and Frans Grijzenhout (eds), *Rekenschap 1650–2000*, The Hague, 2001.

Frey, Marc, *Der Erste Weltkrieg und die Niederlande. Ein neutrales Land im politischen Kalkül der Kriegsgegner*, Cologne, 1996.

Frijhoff, Willem and Marijke Spies, *Nederlandse cultuur in Europese context. 1650 Bevochten eendracht*, 2nd edition, The Hague, 2000.

Fritschy, Wantje, *De patriotten en de financiën van de Bataafse Republiek. Hollands krediet en de smalle marges voor een nieuw beleid (1795–1801)*, Leiden, 1988.

Fritschy, Wantje and Joop Toebes (eds), *Het ontstaan van het moderne Nederland. Staats- en natievorming tussen 1780 en 1830*, Nijmegen s.a. (1996).

Führer, Harald, *Nachspiel. Die niederländische Politik und die Verfolgung von Kollaborateuren und NS-Verbrechern, 1945–1989*, Münster, 2005.

Gaastra, Femme S., *Geschiedenis van de VOC. Opkomst, bloei en ondergang*, Zutphen, 2009.

Bibliography

Gabel, Helmut and Volker Jarren, *Kaufleute und Fürsten. Außenpolitik und politisch-kulturelle Perzeption im Spiegel niederländisch-deutscher Beziehungen 1648–1748*, Münster, 1998.

Gabriëls, A. J. C. M., *De heren als dienaren en de dienaar als heer. Het stadhouderlijk stelsel in de tweede helft van de achttiende eeuw*, The Hague, 1990.

Gelderen, Martin van, *Op zoek naar de Republiek. Politiek denken tijdens de Nederlandse Opstand (1555–1990)*, Hilversum, 1991.

Giebels, Lambert, *De Greet Hofmans-affaire. Hoe de Nederlandse monarchie bijna ten onder ging*, Amsterdam, 2007.

Griffioen, Pim and Ron Zeller, *Jodenvervolging in Nederland, Frankrijk en België, 1940–1945. Overeenkomsten, verschillen, oorzaken*, Amsterdam, 2011.

Grijzenhout, F., W. W. Mijnhardt and N. C. F. van Sas (eds), *Voor Vaderland en Vrijheid. De revolutie van de patriotten*, Amsterdam, 1987.

Groen, Petra (ed.), *De Tachtigjarige Oorlog. Van Opstand naar geregelde oorlog, 1568–1648*, Amsterdam, 2013.

Groenveld, Simon, *Unie – Bestand – Vrede. Drie fundamentele wetten van de Republiek der Verenigde Nederlanden*, Hilversum, 2009.

Groenveld, Simon and Huib L. Ph. Leeuwenberg, *De Tachtigjarige Oorlog, Opstand en consolidatie in de Nederlanden (ca. 1560–1650)*, Zutphen, 2008.

Groenveld, Simon and Gerrit Schutte, *Nederlands verleden in vogelvlucht. De Niewe tijd: 1500 tot 1813*, Leiden/Antwerp, 1992.

Haan, Ido de, *Het beginsel van leven en wasdom. De constitutie van de Nederlandse politiek in de negentiende eeuw*, Amsterdam, 2003.

Hagen, Piet, *Politicus uit hartstocht. Biografie van Pieter Jelles Troelstra*, Amsterdam, 2010.

Haks, Donald, *Vaderland en vrede 1672–1713. Publiciteit over de Nederlandse Republiek in oorlog*, Hilversum, 2013.

Ham, Gijs van der, *Geschiedenis van Nederland*, 2nd edition, Amsterdam, 2009.

Happe, Katja, *Viele falsche Hoffnungen. Judenverfolgung in den Niederlanden 1940–1945*, Paderborn, 2017.

Harinck, Roel, Roel Kuiper and Peter Baks (eds), *De Antirevolutionaire Partij 1826–1980*, Utrecht, 2001.

Harryvan, Anjo G. and Jan van der Harst (eds), *Verloren consensus. Europa in het Nederlandse parlementair debat 1945–2013*, Amsterdam, 2013.

Harryvan, Anjo G., Jan van der Harst and S. van der Voorst (eds), *Voor Nederland en Europa. Politici en ambtenaren over het Nederlandse Europabeleid en de Europese integratie, 1945–1975*, Amsterdam, 2001.

Hart, Marjolein 't, Joost Jonker and Jan Luiten van Zanden, *A Financial History of the Netherlands*, Cambridge, 1997.

Have, Wichert ten, *De Nederlandse Unie. Aanpassing, vernieuwing en confrontatie in bezettingstijd 1940–1941*, Amsterdam, 1999.

Heijden, Chris van der, *Grijs verleden. Nederland en de Tweede Wereldoorlog*, Amsterdam, 2001.

Heijer, Henk den, *De geschiedenis van de WIC*, 3rd edition, Zutphen, 2012.

Hellema, Duco, *Nederland in de wereld. De buitenlandse politiek van Nederland*, 4th edition, Utrecht, 2010; also published in English: *Dutch Foreign Policy. The Role of the Netherlands in World Politics*, Dordrecht, 2009.

Hellema, Duco, Friso Wielenga and Markus Wilp (eds), *Radikalismus und politische Reformen. Beiträge zur deutschen und niederländischen Geschichte in den 1970er Jahren*, Münster, 2012.

Helmers, Helmer J. and Geert H. Jansen, *The Cambridge Companion to the Dutch Golden Age*, Cambridge, 2018.

Hertog, Johan den, *Cort van der Linden (1846–1935). Minister-president in oorlogstijd. Een politieke biografie*, Amsterdam, 2007.

Hirschfeld, Gerhard, *Bezetting en collaboratie. Nederland tijdens de Oorlogsjaren 1940–1945*, Haarlem, 1991.

Hoekstra, Hanneke, *Het hart van de natie. Morele verontwaardiging en politieke verandering in Nederland 1870–1919*, Amsterdam, 2005.

Hondius, Dienke, *Terugkeer. Antisemitisme in Nederland rond de bevrijding*, The Hague, 1998.

Hooff, Anton van, *Het Plakkaat van Verlatinge. De eerste onafhankelijkheidsverklaring*, Utrecht, 2018.

Hooven, Marcel ten and Ron de Jong, *Geschiedenis van de Christelijk-Historische Unie 1908–1980*, Amsterdam, 2008.

Horst, Han van der, *Nederland. De vaderlandse geschiedenis van de prehistorie tot nu*, 10th edition, Amsterdam, 2011.

Houkes, Annemarie, *Christelijke vaderlanders. Godsdienst, burgerschap en de Nederlandse natie (1850–1900)*, Amsterdam, 2009.

Ilsemann, Sigurd von, *Wilhelm II in Nederland 1918–1941. Dagboekfragmenten bezorgd door Jacco Pekelder en Wendy Landewé*, Soesterberg, 2015.

Israel, Jonathan I., *The Dutch Republic: Its Rise, Greatness and Fall, 1477–1806*, Oxford, 1995.

Jacob, Margaret C. and Wijnand Mijnhardt (eds), *The Dutch Republic in the Eighteenth Century: Decline, Enlightenment and Revolution*, Ithaca, 1992.

Jagtenberg, Fred, *Willem IV. Stadhouder in roerige tijden 1711–1751*, Nijmegen, 2018.

Janse, Maartje, *De afschaffers. Publieke opinie, organisatie en politiek in Nederland 1840–1880*, Amsterdam, 2007.

Jong, Joop de, *De waaier van het fortuin. De Nederlanders in Azië en de Indonesische archipel 1595–1950*, The Hague, 2000.

Jong, Joop de, *Een deftig bestaan. Het dagelijks leven van regenten in de 17de en 18de eeuw*, Utrecht, 1987.

Jong, Jos de, *Democratie in Kinderschoenen. Twee referenda over de eerste Nederlandse grondwet 1797–1798*, Nijmegen, 2018.

Jong, L. de, *Het Koninkrijk der Nederlanden in de Tweede Wereldoorlog*, volumes 1–14, The Hague/Amsterdam, 1969–1991.

Jong, Michiel de, Gerrit Knaap and Henk den Heyer, *Militaire geschiedenis van Nederland – oorlogen overzee. Militair optreden door compagnie en staat buiten Europa 1595–1814*, Amsterdam, 2015.

Jong, Ron de, *Van standspolitiek naar partijloyaliteit. Verkiezingen voor de Tweede Kamer 1848–1887*, Hilversum, 1999.

Jonge, A. A. de, *Crisis en critiek der democratie. Anti-democratische stromingen en de daarin levende denkbeelden over de staat in Nederland tussen de wereldoorlogen*, Utrecht, 1982 (1st edition Assen, 1968).

Keizer, Madelon de, *De gijzelaars van Sint Michielsgestel. Een eliteberaad in oorlogstijd*, Alphen aan den Rijn, 1979.

Keizer, Madelon de, *Putten. De razzia en de herinnering*, Amsterdam, 1998.

Keizer, Madelon de, Jos Perry, Maarten van Rossem, Louis Zweers and Maarten Brinkman (eds), *Honderd jaar sociaal-democratie in Nederland 1894–1994*, Amsterdam, 1994.

Kennedy, James C., *Een weloverwogen dood. Euthanasie in Nederland*, Amsterdam, 2002.

Kennedy, James C., *Nieuw Babylon in aanbouw. Nederland in de jaren zestig*, 2nd edition, Amsterdam, 2016.

Kennedy, James C., *A Concise History of the Netherlands*, Cambridge, 2017.

Kersten, Albert E., *Luns. Een politieke biografie*, Amsterdam, 2010.

Kersten, Albert E., *Maken drie kleinen een grote? De politieke invloed van de Benelux 1945–1955*, Bussum, 1982.

Klein, Stefan, *Patriots republikanisme. Politieke cultuur in Nederland (1766–1787)*, Utrecht, 1995.

Bibliography

Klemann, Hein, *Nederland 1938–1948. Economie en samenleving in de jaren van oorlog en bezetting*, Amsterdam, 2002.

Klemann, Hein, *Waarom bestaat Nederland eigenlijk nog? Nederland-Duitsland: Economische integratie en politieke consequenties 1860–2000*, Rotterdam, 2006.

Klemann, Hein A. M. and Friso Wielenga (eds), *Deutschland und die Niederlande. Wirtschaftsbeziehungen im 19. und 20. Jahrhundert*, Münster, 2009.

Klinken, Gert van, *Actieve burgers. Nederlanders en hun politieke partijen*, Amsterdam, 2003.

Klinkert, Wim, *Defending Neutrality. The Netherlands Prepares for War, 1900–1925*, Leiden, 2013.

Kloek, Joost J. and Wijnand Mijnhardt, *Nederlandse cultuur in Europese context. 1800 Blauwdrukken voor een samenleving*, The Hague, 2001; also published in English: *Dutch Culture in a European Perspective. Volume 2. Blueprints for a National Community*, Basingstoke/New York, 2004.

Knapen, Ben, *De man en zijn staat. Johan van Oldenbarnevelt. 1547–1619*, 2nd edition, Amsterdam, 2005.

Knippenberg, Hans, *De religieuze kaart van Nederland. Omvang en geografische spreiding van de godsdienstige gezindten vanaf de Reformatie tot heden*, Assen/Maastricht, 1992.

Knippenberg, Hans and Ben de Pater, *De eenwording van Nederland. Schaalvergroting en integratie sinds 1800*, Nijmegen, 1988.

Koch, Jeroen, *Abraham Kuyper. Een biografie*, Amsterdam, 2006.

Koch, Jeroen, *Koning Willem I, 1772–1843*, Amsterdam, 2013.

Koch, Jeroen, *Oranje in revolutie en oorlog. Een Europese geschiedenis 1772–1890*, Amsterdam, 2018.

Koll, Johannes, *Arthur Seyß-Inquart und die deutsche Besatzungspolitik in den Niederlanden 1940–1945*, Vienna, 2015.

Kossmann, Ernst H., *De Lage Landen 1780/1980. Twee eeuwen Nederland en België*, volume II 1914–1980, Amsterdam, 1986.

Kossmann, Ernst H., *Naoogst* (compiled and introduced by H. L. Wesseling), Amsterdam, 2007.

Kossmann, Ernst H., *The Low Countries: 1780–1940*, Oxford, 1978.

Kraaijestein, Martin and Paul Schulten (eds), *Wankel evenwicht. Neutraal Nederland en de Eerste Wereldoorlog*, Soesterberg, 2007.

Kuitenbrouwer, Maarten, *Nederland en de opkomst van het moderne imperialisme. Koloniën en buitenlandse politiek, 1870–1902*, Amsterdam, 1985.

Lademacher, Horst, *Die Niederlande. Politische Kultur zwischen Individualität und Anpassung*, Berlin, 1993.

Lademacher, Horst, *Geschiedenis van Nederland*, Utrecht, 1993.

Lademacher, Horst (ed), *Oranien-Nassau, die Niederlande und das Reich, Beiträge zur Geschichte einer Dynastie*, Münster, 1995.

Lademacher, Horst, *Phönix aus der Asche? Politik und Kultur der niederländischen Republik im Europa des 17. Jahrhunderts*, Münster, 2007.

Lademacher, Horst and Jac Bosmans (eds), *Tradition und Neugestaltung. Zu Fragen des Wiederaufbaus in Deutschland und den Niederlanden in der frühen Nachkriegszeit*, Münster, 1991.

Lademacher, Horst and Walter Mühlhausen (eds), *Freiheitsstreben – Demokratie – Emanzipation. Aufsätze zur politischen Kultur in Deutschland und den Niederlanden*, Münster, 1993.

Lademacher, Horst, Renate Loos and Simon Groenveld (eds), *Ablehnung – Duldung – Anerkennung. Toleranz in den Niederlanden und Deutschland. Ein historischer und aktueller Vergleich*, Münster, 2004.

Langeveld, Herman, *Dit leven van krachtig handelen. Hendrikus Colijn 1869–1944, Deel Een 1869–1933*, 2nd edition, Amsterdam, 1998, *and: Schipper naast God. Hendrikus Colijn 1869–1944*, volume 2, *1933–1944*, Amsterdam, 2004.

Lem, Anton van der, *De Opstand in de Nederlanden (1555–1609)*, Utrecht/Antwerp, 1995.

Lem, Anton van der, *De Opstand in de Nederlanden (1568–1648). De Tachtigjarige Oorlog in woord en beeld*, Nijmegen, 2014.

Lepszy, Norbert, *Regierung, Parteien und Gewerkschaften in den Niederlanden. Entwicklung und Strukturen*, Düsseldorf, 1979.

Liempt, Ad van, *De oorlog*, Amsterdam, 2009.

Liempt, Ad van and Jan Kompagnie, *Jodenjacht. De onthutsende rol van de Nederlandse politie in de Tweede Wereldoorlog*, Amsterdam, 2011.

Lijphart, Arend, *Verzuiling, pacificatie en kentering in de Nederlandse politiek*, 3rd edition, Amsterdam, 1979, (*The Politics of Accommodation. Pluralism and Democracy in the Netherlands*, 2th edition, Berkely, 1975).

Limpach, Rémy, *De brandende kampongs van Generaal Spoor*, Amderdam, 2016.

Loots, Jasper, *Voor het volk, van het volk. Van districtenstelsel naar evenredige vertegenwoordiging*, Amsterdam, 2004.

Lucardie, Paul and Gerrit Voerman, *Populisten in de polder*, Amsterdam, 2012.

Lucassen, Leo and Jan Lucassen, *Winnaars en verliezers. Een nuchtere balans van vijfhonderd jaar immigratie*, Amsterdam, 2011.

Lutz, Helma, and Kathrin Gawarecki (eds), *Kolonialismus und Erinnerungskultur. Die Kolonialvergangenheit im kollektiven Gedächtnis der deutschen und niederländischen Einwanderungsgesellschaft*, Münster, 2005.

Luykx, Paul and Hans Righart (eds), *Van de pastorie naar het torentje. Een eeuw confessionele politiek*, The Hague, 1991.

Luykx, Paul and Pim Slot (eds), *Een stille revolutie? Cultuur en mentaliteit in de lange jaren vijftig*, Hilversum, 1997.

Maczkiewitz, Dirk, *Der niederländische Aufstand gegen Spanien (1568–1609). Eine kommunikationswissenschaftliche Analyse*, Münster, 2007.

Mak, Geert, *Geschichte der Niederlande. Ein historisches Porträt*, München, 2013.

Mak, Geert, Jan Bank, Gijsbert van Es, Piet de Rooy and René van Stipriaan, *Verleden van Nederland*, Amsterdam, 2008.

Mallinson, William, *From Neutrality to Commitment. Dutch Foreign Policy, NATO and European Integration*, London, 2010.

Meerkerk, Edwin van, *Willem V en Wilhelmina van Pruisen. De laatste stadhouders*, Amsterdam, 2009.

Meulen, Dik van der, *Koning Willem III, 1817–1890*, Amsterdam, 2013.

Meyer, Christoph, *Anpassung und Kontinuität. Die Außen- und Sicherheitspolitik der Niederlande 1989 bis 1998*, Münster, 2007.

Meyers, Jan, *Mussert, een politiek leven*, Soesterberg, 2005.

Middelkoop, Teo van, *Een soldaat doet zijn plicht. Generaal H.G. Winkelman, zijn leven en betekenis als militair (1876–1952)*, The Hague, 2002.

Moeyes, Paul, *Buiten schot. Nederland tijdens de Eerste Wereldoorlog 1914–1918*, Amsterdam/Antwerp, 2001.

Moore, Bob, *Slachtoffers en overlevenden. De nazi-vervolging van de Joden in Nederland*, Amsterdam, 1998; also published in English: *Victims and Survivors: The Nazi Persecution of the Jews in the Netherlands 1940–1945*, London, 1997.

Mörke, Olaf, '*Stadtholder' of 'Staetholder'? Die Funktion des Hauses Oranien und seines Hofes in der politischen Kultur der Republik der Vereinigten Niederlande im 17. Jahrhundert*, Münster, 1997.

Mörke, Olaf, *Willem van Oranje (1533–1584). Vorst en 'vader' van de Republiek*, Amsterdam, 2010.

Napel, Hans-Martien ten, '*Een eigen weg'. De totstandkoming van het CDA (1952–1980)*, Kampen, 1992.

Nierstrasz, Chris, *In the Shadow of the Company. The Dutch East India Company and its Servants in the Period of its Decline (1740–1796)*, Leiden, 2012.

Bibliography

Nimwegen, Olaf van, *De Nederlandse Burgeroorlog (1748–1815)*, Amsterdam, 2017.

North, Michael, *Geschichte der Niederlande*, 3rd edition, Munich, 2008.

Oddens, Joris, *Pioniers in schaduwbeeld. Het eerste parlement van Nederland 1796–1798*, Nijmegen, 2012.

Oostindie, Gert J. (ed), *Fifty Years Later. Antislavery, Capitalism and Modernity in the Dutch Orbit*, Pittsburgh, 1996.

Oostindie, Gert J., *Paradise Overseas. The Dutch Caribbean: Colonialism and its Transatlantic Legacies*, London, 2005.

Oostindie, Gert J., *De parels en de kroon. Het koningshuis en de koloniën*, Amsterdam, 2006.

Oostindie, Gert J. (ed), *Dutch Colonialism, Migration and Cultural Heritage*, Leiden, 2008.

Oostindie, Gert J., *Postcolonial Netherlands. Sixty-five Years of Forgetting, Commemorating, Silencing*, Amsterdam, 2011.

Oostindie, Gert J., *Soldaat in Indonesië 1945–1950. Getuigenissen van een oorlog aan de verkeerde kant van de geschiedenis*, Amsterdam, 2016.

Oostindie, Gert J. and Inge Klinkers, *Decolonising the Caribbean. Dutch Policies in a Comparative Perspective*, Amsterdam, 2003.

Oostindie, Gert J. and Inge Klinkers, *Knellende Koninkrijksbanden. Het Nederlandse dekolonisatiebeleid in de Caraïben, 1940–2000*, volumes I, II, III, Amsterdam, 2001.

Oostindie, Gert J. and Inge Klinkers, *Gedeeld Koninkrijk. De ontmanteling van de Nederlandse Antillen en de herstructurering van het Koninkrijk der Nederlanden*, Amsterdam, 2012.

Oostrom, Frits P. van (ed), *The Netherlands in a Nutshell. Highlights from Dutch History and Culture*, Amsterdam, 2008.

Oostrom, Frits P. van and Hubert Slings (eds), *A Key to Dutch History. The Cultural Canon of the Netherlands*, Amsterdam, 2007.

Ormrod, David, *The Rise of Commercial Empires. England and the Netherlands in the Age of Mercantilism, 1650–1770*, Cambridge, 2003.

Palm, Jos, *De vergeten geschiedenis van Nederland. Waarom Nederlanders hun verleden zouden moeten kennen*, Amsterdam, 2005.

Panhuysen, Luc, *De Ware Vrijheid. De levens van Johan en Cornelis de Witt*, 2nd edition, Amsterdam/Antwerp, 2005.

Panhuysen, Luc, *Rampjaar 1672. Hoe de Republiek aan de ondergang ontsnapte*, Amsterdam/Antwerp, 2009.

Parker, Geoffrey, *The Dutch Revolt*, London, 1977.

Pas, Niek, *Imaazje! De verbeelding van Provo (1965–1967)*, Amsterdam, 2003.

Pastoors, Sven, *Anpassung um jeden Preis? Die europapolitischen Strategien der Niederlande in den Neunziger Jahren*, Münster, 2005.

Pekelder, Jacco, *Nederland en de DDR. Beeldvorming en betrekkingen 1949–1989*, Amsterdam, 1998.

Pekelder, Jacco, *Neue Nachbarschaft. Deutschland und die Niederlande. Bildformung und Beziehungen seit 1990*, Münster, 2013.

Poelhekke, J. J., *Frederik Hendrik. Prins van Oranje. Een biografisch drieluik*, Zutphen, 1978.

Pollmann, Tessel, *Mussert & Co. De NSB-Leider en zijn vertrouwelingen*, Amsterdam, 2012.

Postma, Jan, *Alexander Gogel (1765–1821). Grondlegger van de Nederlandse staat*, Hilversum, 2017.

Prak, Maarten, *Gouden Eeuw. Het raadsel van de Republiek*, Nijmegen, 2002; also published in English: *The Dutch Republic in the Seventeenth Century*, Cambridge, 2005.

Prak, Maarten, *Republikeinse veelheid, democratisch enkelvoud. Sociale verandering in het Revolutietijdvak, 's-Hertogenbosch 1770–1820*, Nijmegen, 1999.

Prak, Maarten and Jan Luiten van Zanden, *Nederand en het poldermodel. Sociaal-economische geschiedenis van Nederland, 1000–2000*, Amsterdam, 2013.

Price, John L., *Dutch Culture in the Golden Age*, London, 2011.

Price, John L., *Dutch Society 1588–1713*, Harlow etc., 2000.

Prud'homme van Reine, Ronald, *Moordenaars van Jan de Witt. De zwartste bladzijde van de Gouden Eeuw*, Amsterdam, 2013.

Raak, Ronald van, *In naam van het volmaakte. Conservatisme in Nederland in de negentiende eeuw*, Amsterdam, 2001.

Reef, Johannes, *Die Niederlande im internationalen System. Fallstudien zum Einfluß eines Kleinstaates*, Münster, 1995.

Reinders, Michel, *Gedrukte chaos. Populisme en moord in het Rampjaar 1672*, Amsterdam, 2010.

Ribberink, Anneke, *Leidsvrouwen en zaakwaarneemsters. Een geschiedenis van de actiegroep Man Vrouw Maatschappij*, Hilversum, 1998.

Riemens, Michael, *De passie voor vrede. De evolutie van de internationale politieke cultuur in de jaren 1880–1940 en het recipiëren door Nederland*, Amsterdam, 2005.

Rietbergen, P. J., *A Short History of the Netherlands*, 6th edition, Amersfoort, 2007.

Righart, Hans, *De katholieke zuil in Europa. Een vergelijkend onderzoek naar het ontstaan van verzuiling onder katholieken in Oostenrijk, Zwitserland, België en Nederland*, Amsterdam, 1986.

Righart, Hans, *De eindeloze jaren zestig. Geschiedenis van een generatieconflict*, Amsterdam, 1995.

Romijn, Peter, *Snel, streng en rechtvaardig. Politiek beleid inzake de bestraffing en reclassering van 'foute' Nederlanders*, Groningen, 1989.

Romijn, Peter, *Burgemeesters in oorlogstijd. Besturen onder Duitse bezetting*, Amsterdam, 2006.

Romijn, Peter, *Der lange Krieg der Niederlande. Gewalt und Neuorientierung in den vierziger Jahren*, Göttingen, 2017.

Rooden, Peter van, *Religieuze regimes. Over godsdienst en maatschappij in Nederland, 1570–1990*, Amsterdam, 1996.

Roon, Ger van, *Kleine Landen in crisistijd. Van Oslostaten tot Benelux 1930–1940*, Amsterdam, 1985.

Roowaan, Ries, *Im Schatten der Großen Politik. Deutsch-niederländische Beziehungen zur Zeit der Weimarer Republik 1918–1933*, Münster, 2006.

Rooy, Piet de, *De rode droom. Een eeuw sociaal-democratie in Nederland*, Nijmegen, 1995.

Rooy, Piet de, *Republiek van Rivaliteiten. Nederland sinds 1813*, 4th edition, Amsterdam, 2010.

Rooy, Piet de, *Ons stipje op de waereldkaart. De politieke cultuur van Nederland in de negentiende en twintigste eeuw*, Amsterdam, 2014.

Rosendaal, Joost, *De Nederlandse Revolutie. Vrijheid, volk en vaderland 1783–1799*, Nijmegen, 2005.

Rowen, H., *John de Witt, Statesman of the 'True Freedom'*, Cambridge, 1986.

Rupp, J. C. C., *Van oude en nieuwe universiteiten. De verdringing van Duitse door Amerikaanse invloeden op de wetenschapsbeoefening en het hoger onderwijs in Nederland, 1945–1975*, The Hague, 1997.

Sas, N. C. F. van, *De metamorfose van Nederland. Van oude orde naar moderniteit, 1750–1900*, Amsterdam, 2004.

Sas, N. C. F. van, *Onze Natuurlijkste Bondgenoot. Nederland, Engeland en Europa, 1813–1831*, Groningen, 1985.

Sas, N. C. F. van and H. te Velde (eds), *De eeuw van de grondwet. Grondwet en politiek in Nederland, 1798–1917*, Deventer, 1998.

Scagliola, Stef, *Last van de Oorlog. De Nederlandse oorlogsmisdaden in Indonesië en hun verwerking*, Amsterdam, 2002.

Schama, Simon, *Patriots and Liberators: Revolution in the Netherlands, 1780–1813*, London, 1977.

Schama, Simon, *The Embarrassment of Riches: An Interpretation of Dutch Culture in the Golden Age*, London, 1987.

Schie, Patrick van, *Vrijheidsstreven in verdrukking. Liberale partijpolitiek in Nederland 1901–1940*, Amsterdam, 2005.

Bibliography

Schutte, Gerrit J., *De Nederlandse Patriotten en de koloniën. Een onderzoek naar hun denkbeelden en optreden 1770–1800*, Groningen, 1974.

Schutte, Gerrit J., *Het Calvinistisch Nederland*, Utrecht, 1988.

Schutte, Gerrit J., *Oranje in de achttiende eeuw*, Amsterdam, 1999.

Schuursma, Rolf, *Jaren van opgang. Nederland 1900–1930*, Amsterdam, 2000.

Schuursma, Rolf, *Vergeefs onzijdig. Nederlands neutraliteit 1919–1940*, Utrecht, 2005.

Schuyt, Kees and Ed Taverne, *1950. Welvaart in zwart-wit*, The Hague, 2000.

Slaa, Robin te and Edwin Klijn, *De NSB. Ontstaan en opkomst van de Nationaal-Socialistische Beweging, 1931–1935*, Amsterdam, 2009.

Soltow, Lee and Jan Luiten van Zanden, *Income and Wealth Inequality in the Netherlands 16th–20th Century*, Amsterdam, 1998.

Staden, Alfred van, *Een trouwe bondgenoot. Nederland en het Atlantisch Bondgenootschap (1960–1971)*, Baarn, 1974.

State, Paul F., *A Brief History of the Netherlands*, New York, 2008.

Stutje, Jan Willem, *Ferdinand Domela Nieuwenhuis. Een romantische revolutionair*, Amsterdam, 2012.

Stuurman, Siep, *Wacht op onze daden. Het liberalisme en de vernieuwing van de Nederlandse staat*, Amsterdam, 1992.

Tames, Ismee, *Oorlog voor onze gedachten. Oorlog, neutraliteit en identiteit in het Nederlandse publieke debat 1914–1918*, Hilversum, 2006.

Tamse, C. A. and E. Witte (eds), *Staats- en Natievorming in Willem I's Koninkrijk (1815–1830)*, Brussels, 1992.

Tanja, Erie, *Goede politiek. De parlementaire cultuur van de Tweede Kamer, 1866–1940*, Amsterdam, 2010.

Tracy, James D., *The Founding of the Dutch Republic. War, Finance and Politics in Holland, 1572–1588*, Oxford, 2008.

Tromp, Bart, *Het sociaal-democratisch programma. De beginselprogramma's van SDB, SDAP en PvdA 1878–1977*, Amsterdam, 2002.

Troost, Wout, *Stadhouder-koning Willem III. Een politieke biografie*, Hilversum, 2001.

Turpijn, Jouke, *Mannen van gezag. De uitvinding van de Tweede Kamer 1848–1888*, Amsterdam, 2008.

Tuyll van Serooskerken, Hubertus P. van, *The Netherlands and World War I. Espionage, Diplomacy and Survival*, Leiden, 2001.

Veen, Mirjam van, *Een nieuwe tijd, een nieuwe kerk. De opkomst van het 'calvinisme' in de Lage Landen*, Zoetermeer, 2009.

Velde, Henk te, *Gemeenschapszin en plichtsbesef. Liberalisme en nationalisme in Nederland, 1870–1918*, The Hague, 1992.

Velde, Henk te, *Stijlen van leiderschap. Persoon en politiek van Thorbecke tot Den Uyl*, Amsterdam, 2002.

Velde, Henk te, *Van regentenmentaliteit tot populisme. Politieke tradities in Nederland*, Amsterdam, 2010.

Voerman, Gerrit (ed), *De conjunctuur van de macht. Het Christen-Democratisch Appèl 1980–2010*, Amsterdam, 2011.

Voerman, Gerrit and Paul Lucardie, *Populisten in de polder*, Amsterdam, 2012.

Voerman, Gerrit and Paul Lucardie (eds), *Van de straat naar de staat? GroenLinks, 1990–2010*, Amsterdam, 2010.

Voogd, Christoph de, *Geschiedenis van Nederland. Vanaf de prehistorie tot heden*, 2nd edition, Amsterdam, 2000.

Voorhoeve, Joris J. C., *Peace, Profits and Principles. A Study of Dutch Foreign Policy*, Leiden, 1985.

Vossen, Koen, *Vrij vissen in het Vondelpark. Kleine politieke partijen in Nederland 1918–1940*, Amsterdam, 2003.

Vossen, Koen, *The Power of Populism. Geert Wilders and the Party for Freedom in the Netherlands*, Abingdon, 2016.

Vries, Jan de and Ad van der Woude, *Nederland 1500–1815. De eerste ronde van moderne economische groei*, 3rd edition, Amsterdam, 2005.

Wansink, Hans, *De erfenis van Fortuyn. De Nederlandse democratie na de opstand van de kiezers*, Amsterdam, 2004.

Wartena, Bert H., *Goeman Borgesius (1847–1917). Vader van de verzorgingsstaat. Een halve eeuw economische en sociale politiek in Nederland*, Amsterdam, 2003.

Weenink, W. H., *Bankier van de wereld. Bouwer van Europa. Johan Willem Beyen 1897–1976*, Amsterdam/Rotterdam, 2005.

Wiebes, Cees and Bert Zeeman, *Belgium, the Netherlands and Alliances 1940–1949*, Amsterdam, 1993.

Wielenga, Friso, *West-Duitsland: partner uit noodzaak. Nederland en de Bondsrepubliek 1949–1955*, Utrecht, 1989.

Wielenga, Friso, *Van vijand tot bondgenoot. Nederland en Duitsland na 1945*, Amsterdam, 1999.

Wielenga, Friso, *Nederland in de twintigste eeuw*, 3rd edition, Amsterdam, 2013.

Wielenga, Friso (ed), *Politische Kulturen im Vergleich. Beiträge über die Niederlande und Deutschland seit 1945*, Bonn, 2002.

Wielenga, Friso and Florian Hartleb (eds), *Populismus in der modernen Demokratie. Die Niederlande und Deutschland im Vergleich*, Münster, 2011.

Wielenga, Friso and Ilona Taute (eds), *Länderbericht Niederlande. Geschichte – Wirtschaft – Gesellschaft*, Bonn, 2004.

Wielenga, Friso and Markus Wilp (eds), *Landeskunde Niederlande. Eine Einführung*, Münster, 2007.

Wielenga, Friso and Markus Wilp (eds), *Die Niederlande. Ein Länderbericht*, Bonn, 2015.

Wielenga, Friso, Carla van Baalen and Markus Wilp (eds), *Eine zersplitterte Landschaft. Beiträge zur Geschichte und Gegenwart niederländischer politischer Parteien*, Amsterdam, 2018.

Wielenga, Friso, Loek Geeraedts and Markus Wilp (eds), *Jahrbücher des Zentrums für Niederlande-Studien, Münster, sinds 2000* (editing during the 1990–1998 period by Horst Lademacher and Loek Geeraedts).

Wilp, Markus, *Das politische System der Niederlande. Eine Einführung*, Wiesbaden, 2012.

Withuis, Jolande, *Juliana. Vorstin in een mannenwereld*, Amsterdam, 2016.

Wolf, Susanne, *Guarded Neutrality. Diplomacy and Internment in the Netherlands during the First World War*, Leiden, 2013.

Wolffram, Dirk Jan, *Vrij van wat neerdrukt en beklemt. Staat, gemeenschap en sociale politiek, 1870–1919*, Amsterdam, 2003.

Woltjer, J. J., *Op weg naar tachtig jaar oorlog. Het verhaal over de eeuw waarin ons land ontstond*, Amsterdam, 2011.

Woltjer, J. J., *Recent verleden. De geschiedenis van Nederland in de twintigste eeuw*, 3rd edition, Amsterdam, 2005.

Wood, John Halsey, *Going Dutch in the Modern Age. Abraham Kuyoer's Struggle for a Free Church in the Nineteenth Century Netherlands*, Oxford, 2013.

Woud, Auke van der, *Een nieuwe wereld. Het ontstaan van het moderne Nederland*, Amsterdam, 2006.

Woud, Auke van der, *Koninkrijk vol sloppen. Achterbuurten en vuil in de negentiende eeuw*, Amsterdam, 2010.

Zahn, Ernest, *Das unbekannte Holland. Regenten, Rebellen und Reformatoren*, Munich, 1993.

Zanden, Jan Luiten van, *De dans om de gouden standaard. Economisch beleid in de depressie van de jaren dertig*, Amsterdam, 1988.

Zanden, Jan Luiten van, 'De economie van Holland in de periode 1650–1805: groei of achteruitgang? Een overzicht van bronnen, problemen en resultaten' in *Bijdragen en Mededelingen betreffende de Geschiedenis der Nederlanden* 102 (1987), number 4, pp. 562–609.

Bibliography

Zanden, Jan Luiten van, *Een klein land in de twintigste eeuw. Economische geschiedenis van Nederland 1914–1995*, Utrecht, 1997.

Zanden, Jan Luiten van, *The Rise and Decline of Hollands Economy. Merchant Capitalism and the Labour Market*, Manchester, 1993.

Zanden, Jan Luiten van and Arthur van Riel, *Nederland 1780–1914. Staat, instituties en economische ontwikkeling*, Amsterdam, 2000.

Zanten, Jeroen van, *Koning Willem II, 1792–1849*, Amsterdam, 2013.

Zanten, Jeroen van, *Schielijk, Winzucht, Zwaarhoofd en Bedaard. Politieke discussie en oppositievorming 1813–1840*, Amsterdam, 2004.

INDEX OF NAMES

Index of Names

Index of Names

GENERAL INDEX

General Index

First Boer War (1880–1) 169
Free-thinking Democratic League (VDB) 164, 202

General Assembly
  – First (1651) 56, 57, 64, 66, 67
  – Second (1716–7) 107
General Dutch Workers' Association (ANWV) 162, 317
Glorious Revolution (1688) 43, 79, 80, 94, 315
Greet Hofmans affair 239–41, 252

Het Parool 216
Hollandsche Spectator 112
Huguenots 21, 60, 315

Iconoclasm (1566) 3, 18, 19, 313

Kellogg-Briand Pact (1928) 206
Kingdom of Holland (1806 – 10) 129, 130, 316

Labour Foundation (STAR) 223, 224
Labour Party (PvdA) 220, 222–4, 226, 234, 247–9, 258, 260–3, 266, 268, 269, 271–7, 285, 319, 320
League of Armed Neutrality 105
League of Nations 206–8, 318
Locarno Treaties (1925) 206
Lockheed affair 252, 253

Maatschappij tot Nut van 't Algemeen (Society for the Public Good) 112, 174
Man Woman Society (MVM) 246, 247
Marshall Plan 227, 229–31, 235

National Federation of Christian Trade Unions in the Netherlands (CNV) 228, 250
National Socialist Movement (NSB) 203–5, 211–3, 318
National Synod Dordrecht (1618–9) 21, 47, 50, 96, 148, 157, 314
Navigation Act (1651, 1660) 69, 71, 81
Netherlands Bureau for Economic Policy Analysis (CPB) 227
Netherlands Trading Society (NHM) 142, 143, 151, 316
New crew (*nieuwe plooi*) 106, 109, 118, 280, 315
New Guinea conflict 235, 236
Nieuwe Rotterdamsche Courant 150, 203
Nine Men's Proposal (1844) 149, 152
Nine Years' War (1688–97) 80, 82, 315
NIOD Institute for War, Holocaust and Genocide Studies 209, 213, 265, 266
North Atlantic Treaty Organization (NATO) 220, 229–31, 266, 267, 278, 319

Old crew (*oude plooi*) 106, 109, 118, 280, 315
Organization for European Economic Co-operation (OEEC) 231

Pacification of Ghent (1576) 23–5, 27, 35, 313
Papal encyclical Quanta Cura 158
Papal encyclical Rerum Novarum 160, 161
Partai Kommunis Indonesia (PKI) 232
Party for Freedom (PVV) 221, 271–4, 277, 320
Peace of Aachen (1748) 104
Peace of Nijmegen (1678) 78–80, 315
Peace of Utrecht (1713) 103, 104, 315
Peace of Westphalia/Münster (1648) 1, 8, 15, 43, 44, 53, 54, 56, 57, 67–69, 82, 176, 314
Peace Palace (1913) 170, 206
People's Party for Freedom and Democracy (VVD) 220, 223, 249, 250, 258, 260–3, 266, 268, 269, 271, 273–5, 277, 285, 320
Permanent Court
  – of Arbitration 170
  – of International Justice 206
Perpetual Edict (1667, 1670) 74, 75
Perserikatan Nasional Indonesia 232
Petition of Nobles (1566) 18, 313
Pim Fortuyn List (LPF) 261, 269, 319, 320
Plan for Labour (1935) 201, 227
Polder model 221, 224, 258, 262, 263, 268, 279
Political Party of Radicals (PPR) 247, 248
Pragmatic sanction (1548) 8
Provo 243–5, 319

Referendum European Constitution (2005) 271, 277, 320
Remonstrants (Arminians) 46–8, 50, 67, 282, 314
Republic of South Maluku (RMS) 256–8
Right-wing populism 6, 221, 276, 279
Roman Catholic State Party (RKSP) 161, 183, 193, 202, 203
Royal Netherlands East Indies Army (KNIL) 237, 256, 257

Sarekat Islam 232
Second Boer War (1899–1902) 169, 177
Seven Years' War (1756–63) 104, 105, 316
Social and Economic Council (SER) 223, 224, 246
Social Democratic League (SDB) 162
Social Democratic Workers Association of Radio Amateurs (VARA) 195, 226, 238
Social Democratic Workers' Party (SDAP) 162, 176, 189, 193, 195, 196, 201, 202, 204, 222
Social democrats (see also SDAP and Labour Party) 160, 176, 177, 181–4, 186, 188, 189, 193, 195–7, 202, 204, 220, 222–4, 228, 260, 262, 264, 271, 274, 276
Socialist Party (SP) 271, 272, 274, 277, 285

St Bartholomew's Day 21
Stadholderless Period
- First (1650–72) 43, 48, 57, 61, 64, 69, 73, 75,
    94, 98, 280, 314
- Second (1702–47) 82, 101, 104, 315

Thirty Years War (1618–1648) 50–2, 60, 83,
    314
Treaty of Breda (1676) 71, 74
Treaty of Brussels (1948) 229, 319
Treaty of Rijswijk (1697) 80, 315
Treaty of The Hague (1795) 123
Treaty of Versailles (1919) 205–7

Triple Alliance (1668) 31, 72, 73, 314
Trouw 216, 217

Union of Arras (1579) 24, 313
Union of Utrecht (1579) 24, 25, 50, 56, 63, 105, 135,
    313
University Administration Reform Act (1970) 244

Vrij Nederland 216

War of Austrian Succession (1740 – 48) 104, 315
War of Spanish Succession (1702 – 13) 81, 82,
    101–3, 118, 315

ABOUT THE AUTHOR

Friso Wielenga (born 1956) read history at VU Amsterdam and the University of Bonn. He received his doctorate in 1989 at the VU Amsterdam and from 1990 to 1999 was a senior lecturer at Utrecht University. During the 1992–1997 period he combined this post with a special chair of Germany studies at the University of Groningen and from 1997 to 1999 with a special chair of modern German history at Utrecht University. Since 1999 he has been Director of the Centre for Dutch Studies at the University of Münster. His research field is Dutch and German contemporary history and Dutch–German relations in the twentieth century. He is currently working on a monograph about the Netherlands in the early twenty-first century.